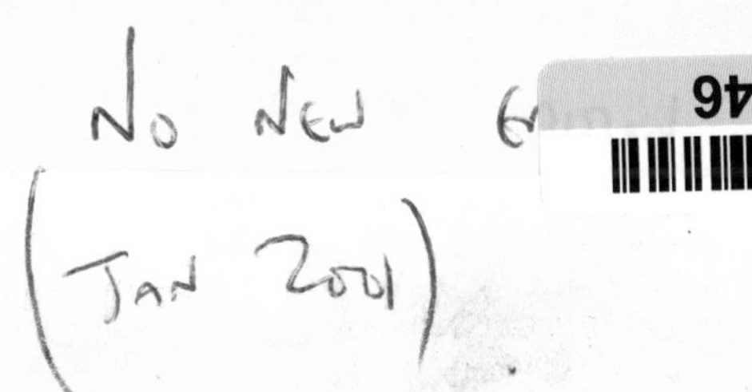

McGraw-Hill Dictionary of Business Acronyms, Initials, and Abbreviations

Other McGraw-Hill Books by Jerry M. Rosenberg

McGraw-Hill Dictionary of Wall Street Acronyms, Initials, and Abbreviations

McGraw-Hill Dictionary of Information Technology and Computer Acronyms, Initials, and Abbreviations

McGraw-Hill Dictionary of Business Acronyms, Initials, and Abbreviations

Jerry M. Rosenberg, Ph.D.
Professor
Graduate School of Management
Department of Business Administration
Faculty of Arts and Sciences
Rutgers University

McGraw-Hill, Inc.
New York St. Louis San Francisco Auckland Bogotá
Caracas Lisbon London Madrid Mexico Milan
Montreal New Delhi Paris San Juan São Paulo
Singapore Sydney Tokyo Toronto

Library of Congress Cataloging-in-Publication Data

Rosenberg, Jerry Martin.
McGraw-Hill dictionary of business acronyms, initials, and abbreviations / Jerry M. Rosenberg.
p. cm.
ISBN 0-07-053734-8 : —ISBN 0-07-053935-9 (pbk.) :
1. Business—Acronyms—Dictionaries. 2. Business—Abbreviations—Dictionaries. I. Title. II. Title: Dictionary of business acronyms, initials, and abbreviations.
HF1002.5.R67 1991 91-23464
650′.03—dc20 CIP

1 2 3 4 5 6 7 8 9 0 DOC/DOC 9 7 6 5 4 3 2 1

ISBN 0-07-053734-8 {HC}
ISBN 0-07-053935-9 {PBK}

The sponsoring editor for this book was Betsy Brown, the editing supervisor was Alfred Bernardi, and the production supervisor was Suzanne W. Babeuf. It was set in Century Schoolbook by McGraw-Hill's Professional Book Group composition unit.

Printed and bound by R. R. Donnelley & Sons Company.

For Ben and Bernice—
You offered love and guidance.
I, in turn, offer love and appreciation.

Preface

Fifteen years after I had published the first in a series of five business-oriented dictionaries, I began to see the need for yet another type of dictionary. This time, the proposed book would be a lexicon containing business acronyms, initials, and abbreviations. What had I noticed in my day-to-day life as a business consultant and educator to convince me of the compelling need for such a book?

First of all, everyone knows that in today's business world we are all confronted daily with a variety of common (and not so common) abbreviated terms. Whether these terms are communicated in written or verbal form, confusion can arise, since most of them frequently convey several different meanings. For example, IBM is a three-letter word that is quickly identified throughout the world as initials for International Business Machines. However, these same three letters also stand for the Institute for Burn Medicine, Industrias Biologicas Mexicana (Mexican Biological Industries), intercontinental ballistic missile, and the International Brotherhood of Magicians. And the two-letter words, IB or IM, have a list of several dozen possible spelled-out forms.

An anecdote taken from my own professional life might serve to further highlight the potential trouble that can come about when one of these terms is misinterpreted. As a young college professor, I once had occasion to take a plane trip to Boston in order to attend a professional conference. Seated next to me on the plane was a relentless name-dropper who, during the course of his career as a reporter, claimed to have interviewed JFK (President John F. Kennedy), LBJ (President Lyndon B. Johnson), and so on and so forth! After he had exhausted this line of conversation, the reporter turned to me and asked if I did consulting work. Seeing that my opportunity to speak (and to shine) had at last arrived, I answered by saying that yes, indeed, I did consulting in Boston for ADL. The reporter was quite impressed to hear that I worked for Arthur D. Little, a first-rate consulting firm. His enthusiasm waned, however, when I corrected his error and informed him that I was a consultant to the Anti-Defamation League!

The story is amusing, but it nicely summarizes the reason I have written this book. Clarity and precision are necessary components of business communications. They will be improved only when we are aware of the many different meanings that have been applied to each acronym, initial, abbreviation, or symbol by the general business community at large. Thus, I have tried to include in this volume as many of the commonly used designations from both the national and international worlds of business and commerce as is possible. When this book is used in conjunction with a business dictionary, the user should be amply equipped to comprehend clearly and communicate effectively.

Lastly, there are a few decisions made in the preparation of this book that the reader should be aware of as he or she begins to use it:

1. Conventional symbols have been used without specific identification, for instance: - (hyphen); / (diagonal); & (ampersand); = (equal sign); * (asterisk).
2. The use of capital, lowercase, or a combination of both capital and lowercase letters for the spelled-out versions of abbreviations or acronyms has never been universally agreed upon. In most cases in this book, I have used the preferred or most commonly used form. When an abbreviation involves the use of proper names, then capital letters are the correct choice. Otherwise, the form of capitalization that is adopted is more a matter of style than of correctness.

Acknowledgments

My library contains hundreds of sources of information that were used to prepare my five earlier dictionaries. These volumes have also been put to use in creating this book. In addition, both American and foreign agencies have been helpful in providing relevant information. I also received a good deal of assistance from trade associations (who, along with government departments, appear to be in the habit of creating new terms on a daily basis).

To the best of my knowledge, I have not quoted from any other copyrighted source. However, I have acquired much indirect assistance from the authors of numerous books, journal articles, and reference materials. Any attempt to list them here would be impossible.

Betsy Brown and Bill Sabin, my editors at McGraw-Hill, have been enlightened professional supporters of this dictionary. My wife, Ellen, my daughters, Elizabeth and Lauren, and my son-in-law, Robert, continue to be my inspiration. Time away from them, whether it is spent researching an article or struggling with a complex set of acronyms, initials, and abbreviations, is more than compensated for by their affection.

Finally, I acknowledge my reader—the ultimate judge. I continue to seek your critical comments and urge you to bring any errors or suggestions to my attention.

Jerry M. Rosenberg

About the Author

JERRY M. ROSENBERG, Ph.D., is professor at the Graduate School of Management and Department of Business Administration at Rutgers University. He is the author of the *McGraw-Hill Dictionary of Wall Street Acronyms, Initials, and Abbreviations* and the *McGraw-Hill Dictionary of Information Technology and Computer Acronyms, Initials, and Abbreviations*—both just published by McGraw-Hill. Dr. Rosenberg's previous reference works include the *Dictionary of Business and Management*, the *Dictionary of Banking and Financial Services*, the *Dictionary of Computers and Information Processing*, and the *Dictionary of Artificial Intelligence and Robotics*. In addition, Dr. Rosenberg serves as a consultant to the *Oxford English Dictionary* and the *Random House Dictionary*. He is acclaimed "America's foremost business and technical lexicographer."

McGraw-Hill Dictionary of Business Acronyms, Initials, and Abbreviations

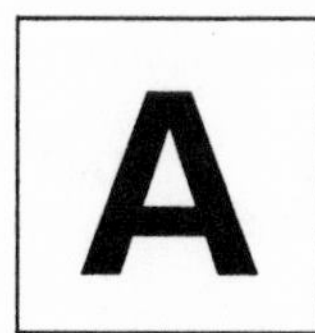

a: absent
absolute
account
adder
ampere
analog
angstrom
argent
asynchronous
attribute
audit
auditor
automatic

A: America
American
American Medical Buildings Inc. (ASE)
American Oil Company
Anchor Line
Class "A" or Series "A" (securities)
Total Average dollar inventory

A-1: First Class
First Rate
Highest class rating
Lloyd's Register indicating a ship's equipment is first rate

A&A: Arcade and Attica (railroad)

AA: Achievement Age
Acting Appointment
Active Account
Active Assets
Administrative Assistant
Aerolineas Argentinas (Argentine Airlines)
Aluminum Association
Aluminum Company of America (NYSE)
Always Afloat
American Airlines
Ann Arbor (railroad)
Ansett Airways
Arithmetic Average
Associate in Accounting
Automobile Association

AAA: Agricultural Adjustment Administration
American Academy of Advertising
American Accounting Association
American Arbitration Association
American S&L Association of Florida (NYSE)
Automobile Association of America
Standard & Poor's highest quality bond rating

AAAA: American Association of Advertising Agencies

AAAE: American Association of Airport Executives

AAAI: Affiliated Advertising Agencies International
American Association for Artificial Intelligence

AAAM: American Association of Aircraft Manufacturers

AAAS: American Association for the Advancement of Science

AAASM: Associated African States and Madagascar

AABM: Association of American Battery Manufacturers

AABPDF: Allied Association of Bleachers, Printers, Dyers, and Finishers

AABTM: American Association of Baggage Traffic Managers
AAC: Anacomp Inc. (NYSE)
Automatic Aperture Control
Automotive Advertisers Council
Average Annual Cost
AACCLA: Association of American Chambers of Commerce in Latin America
AACE: American Association of Cost Engineers
AACO: Arab Air Carriers Organization
AACP: American Association of Commercial Publications
AACS: Advanced Automatic Compilation System
AACSB: American Assembly (Association) of Collegiate Schools of Business
AACT: American Association of Commodity Traders
AAD: At A Discount
AADC: All-Application Digital Computer
AADFI: Association of African Development Finance Institutions
AAE: American Association of Engineers
AAEE: American Association of Electrical Engineers
AAF: American Advertising Federation
American Air Filter Company
AAFE: American Association of Feed Exporters
AAFRA: Association of African Airlines
AAHA: Awaiting Action of Higher Authority
AAICD: American Association of Imported Car Dealers
AAIE: American Association of Industrial Editors
American Association of Industrial Engineers
AAII: American Association of Individual Investors
Association for the Advancement of Invention and Innovation
AAIM: American Association of Industrial Management
AAIMS: An Analytical Information Management System
AAIN: American Association of Industrial Nurses
AAJ: Arab Airways
AAL: Absolute Assembly Language
Alexander & Alexander Services Inc. (NYSE)
American Airlines
AALA: American Automotive Leasing Association
AAlska: Arctic Alaska Fisheries Corp. (newspaper)
AALU: Association of Advanced Life Underwriting
AAMA: American Apparel Manufacturers Association
Architectural Aluminum Manufacturers Association
Automotive Accessories Manufacturers of America
AAMGA: American Association of Managing General Agents
AAMI: American Association of Machinery Importers
AAO: Authorized Acquisition Objective
AAP: Analyst Assistance Program
Apollo Applications Program
Association of American Publishers
AAPA: Advertising Agency Production Association

American Association of Port Authorities
AAPC: Afro-American Purchasing Center
AAR: AAR Corp. (newspaper)
Against All Risks
Association of American Railroads
AARC: Ann Arbor Railroad Company
AARR: Ann Arbor Railroad
AAS: Advanced Administrative System
Associate in Applied Science
Automatic Addressing System
AASB: American Association of Small Business
AASM: Association of American Steel Manufacturers
AASO: Association of American Ship Owners
AASRC: American Association of Small Research Companies
AAT: Association of Accounting Technicians
AATCC: American Association of Textile Chemists and Colorists
AATMS: Advanced Air Traffic Management Systems
AATT: American Association for Textile Technology
AAWPI: Association of American Wood Pulp Importers
AAXICO: American Air Export and Import Company
A&B: Antofagasta and Bolivia (railroad)
A/B: Aktiebolaget (joint stock company) (Swedish)
AB: ABI American Businessphones Inc. (ASE)
Assembly Bill
Keystone Commuter (airline)
ABA: American Bakers Association
American Bankers Association
American Bankers Association Number
American Bar Association
Annual Budget Authorization
Associate in Business Administration
ABAC: Association of Business and Administrative Computing
ABAJ: American Bar Association Journal
abandt: abandonment
ABB: Akron & Barberton Belt (railroad)
ABBB: Association of Better Business Bureaus
ABBMM: Association of British Brush Machinery Manufacturers
AB&C: Atlanta, Birmingham and Coast (railroad)
ABC: Abridged Building Classification (for Architects, Builders and Civil Engineers)
America, Britain, Canada
American Broadcasting Company
Approach By Concept
Associated Builders and Contractors
Audit Bureau of Circulation
ABCA: American, British, Canadian, Australian
American Business Communication Association
ABCA/UES: American Business Communication Association Unification of Engineering Standards
ABCC: Association of British Chambers of Commerce
ABCM: Association of Building Component Manufacturers
ABCS: Automatic Base Communication Systems

Automatic Broadcast Control System
ABCW: American Bakery and Confectionery Workers
ABD: ABIOMED Inc. (ASE)
ABDL: Automatic Binary Data Link
ABE: Association of Business Executives
ABED: Acid/Base Electrolyte Disorders
ABEND: Abnormal End of Task
ABES: Air Breathing Engine System
Association for Broadcast Engineering Standards
ABET: Accreditation Board for Engineering and Technology
ABEX: American Brake Shoe Company
ABF: Airborne Freight Corp. (NYSE)
ABFM: Association of Business Forms Manufacturers
ABG: American Ship Building Co., The (NYSE)
ABGSM: Association of British Generating Set Manufacturers
ABHM: Association of British Hardware Manufacturers
ABI: ABI American Businessphones Inc. (newspaper)
AmBrit Inc. (ASE)
Abimd: ABIOMED Inc. (newspaper)
Abitibi: Abitibi-Price Inc. (newspaper)
ABK: Alliance Bancorporation (ASE)
ABktCT: American Bank of Connecticut (newspaper)
ABL: Accepted Batch Listing
Alameda Belt Line (railroad)
American Biltrite Inc. (ASE)
ABldM: American Building Maintenance Industries (newspaper)
ABLP: Air Bearing Lift Pad
ABM: Advanced Bill of Materials
American Building Maintenance Industries (NYSE)
Associate in Business Management
Automated Batch Mixing
ABMA: American Boiler Manufacturers Association
American Brush Manufacturers Association
ABMEX: Association of British Mining Equipment Exporters
ABM G: ABM Gold Corp. (newspaper)
ABMPS: Automated Business Mail Processing System
ABMS: Automated Batch Manufacturing System
ABNCO: American Bank Note Company
ABNI: Available But Not Installed
ABP: Accounting Principles Board
American Business Press
American Business Products Inc. (NYSE)
ABPC: American Book Publishers' Council
ABPI: Association of the British Pharmaceutical Industry
ABR: Real Aerovias Brasil (Brazilian airline symbol)
A&BRC: Antofagasta and Bolivia Railway Company
ABrck: American Barrick Resources Corp. (newspaper)
ABRL: Army Ballistic Research Laboratories
ABRT: A/B Rederi Transatlantic (Pacific Australia Direct Line)
ABS: Albertson's Inc. (NYSE)
American Boxwood Society

American Brake Shoe
American Bureau of Shipping
Automated Bond System

ABSLDR: Absolute Loader

ABSTECH: American Bureau of Shipping Worldwide Technical Services

ABT: Abbott Laboratories (NYSE)
American Board of Trade

AbtLab: Abbott Laboratories (newspaper)

ABU: Asia-Pacific Broadcasting Union (Japan)

ABusPr: American Business Products Inc. (newspaper)

ABW: Advise By Wire
Armada Corp. (NYSE)

ABWA: American Business Women's Association

ABX: American Barrick Resources Corp. (NYSE)

ABY: Abitibi-Price Inc. (NYSE)

ABZ: Arkansas Best Corp. (NYSE)

a/c: account

AC: Account Current
Acoustic Coupler
Actual Count
Active Capital
Adaptive Control
African Coasters (steamship)
Air Canada (airline)
Algoma Central (railroad)
Alliance Capital Management LP (NYSE)
Alternating Current
Ante Christum (before Christ)
Area Code
Assistant Cashier
Associate in Commerce
Automatic Control

ACA: Aircraft Castings Association
American Capital Management & Research Inc. (NYSE)
Association of Chartered Accountants

ACAA: Agricultural Conservation and Adjustment Administration

ACAM: Augmented Content-Addressed Memory

ACAMPS: Automated Communications And Message Processing System

AcapBd: American Capital Bond Fund Inc. (newspaper)

ACapCv: American Capital Convertible Securities Inc. (newspaper)

ACapIn: American Capital Income Trust (newspaper)

ACAPS: Automated Cost And Planning System

ACARD: Advisory Committee on Advanced Research and Development

ACAS: Advisory, Conciliation and Arbitration Service
Association of Casualty Accounts and Statisticians

ACB: Advertising Checking Bureau
American Capital Bond Fund Inc. (NYSE)
Associated Credit Bureaus of America
Association of Customers' Brokers

ACB of A: Associated Credit Bureaus of America

ACBs: Associated Credit Bureaus

ACBS: Accrediting Commission for Business Schools

acc: accept
accepted
account
accumulate
accumulator

ACC: Active Clearance Control
American Capital Corp. (ASE)
Annual Capital Charge

Average Correlation Coefficients
ACCA: Air Charter Carriers Association
Association of Certified and Corporate Accountants
ACCAP: Autocoder to COBOL Conversion-Aid Program
ACCCI: American Coke and Coal Chemicals Institute
acce: acceptance
ACCEL: Automated Circuit Card Etching Layout
ACCESS: Access Characteristics Estimation System
Architects, Construction and Consulting Engineers, Specialist Service
Argonne Code Center Exchange and Storage System
Automatic Computer-Controlled Electronic Scanning System
ACCLAIM: Automated Circuit Card Layout and Implementation
ACCM: Association of Competition Car Manufacturers
ACCR: Annual Cost of Capital Recovery
Accrd Int: Accrued Interest
accred: accredited
acct: account
accountant
accounting
accum: accumulator
ACD: American Capital Income Trust (NYSE)
Automatic Call Distribution
Automatic Call Distributor
ACE: Acme Electric Corp. (NYSE)
Active Corps of Executives (of the Small Business Administration)
Air Cushion Equipment
Amex Commodities Exchange
Association for Cooperation in Engineering
Association of Consulting Engineers
Asynchronous Communication Element
Audit, Control and Evaluation
Automated Computing Engine
Automated Cost Estimates
Automatic Checkout Equipment
Average Cumulative Error
One-Dollar Bill (slang)
ACEA: Association of Computing in Engineering and Architecture
ACEC: American Consulting Engineers Council
ACEF: Association of Commodity Exchange Firms
ACentC: American Century Corp. (newspaper)
ACF: American Car and Foundry Company
ACG: ACM Government Income Fund Inc. (NYSE)
Air Cargo Express (symbol)
ACH: Attempts per Circuit per Hour
Automated Clearing House
AC&HBR: Algoma Central and Hudson Bay Railroad
ACI: Adjacent Channel Interference
Air Cargo Incorporated
Alloy Casting Institute
American Concrete Institute
Ashland Coal Inc. (NYSE)
ACIA: Asynchronous Communications Interface Adapter
ACICAFE: Association of the Coffee Trade and Industry in the European Community (EC)

ACID: Acceleration, Cruising, Idling, Deceleration
Ack: acknowledge
acknowledgment
ACK: Armstrong World Industries Inc. (NYSE)
ackt: acknowledgment
ACL: Action-Centered Leadership
Allowable Cargo Load
Atlantic Coast Line (railroad)
Atlantic Container Line (steamship)
Audit Command Language
ACLS: Automatic Carrier Landing System
ACLUM: Advisory Committee on Legal Units of Measurement
AcLv: Accrued Leave
ACM: ACM Government Opportunity Fund (newspaper)
Advanced Composite Materials
Association for Computing Machinery
Associative Communications Multiplexer
Atlas Consolidated Mining & Development Corp. (ASE)
Authorized Controlled Material
ACME: Association of Consulting Management Engineers
AcmeC: Acme-Cleveland Corp. (newspaper)
AcmeE: Acme Electric Corp. (newspaper)
AcmeU: Acme United Corp. (newspaper)
ACMIn: ACM Government Income Fund Inc. (newspaper)
ACMR: American Capital Management & Research Inc. (newspaper)
ACMS: Advance Configuration Management System
Application Control and Management System
ACMSc: ACM Government Securities Fund Inc. (newspaper)
ACMSp: ACM Government Spectrum Fund (newspaper)
ACOPS: Advisory Committee on Oil Pollution of the Sea
ACORD: Advisory Council on Research and Development for Fuel and Power (Dept. of Energy)
ACORN: Associative Content Retrieval Network
ACOUSTINT: Acoustical Intelligence
ACP: Accomplishment/Cost Procedure
Africa, Caribbean and Pacific states (EC)
American Real Estate Partners LP (NYSE)
ACPA: Association of Computer Programmers and Analysts
A/C Pay: Accounts Payable
ACPM: Advisory Committee on Program Management
acpt: accept
acceptance
Acq: Exchange Acquisition
ACQM: Automatic Circuit Quality Monitoring
ACQS: Association of Consultant Quantity Surveyors
acquis: acquisition(s)
AC&R: American Cable and Radio Corporation
ACR: Alternate Recovery
Angell Real Estate Company Inc. (NYSE)
ACRA: Association of Company Registration Agents
acrd: accrued
ACRE: Automatic Call Recording Equipment

A/C Rec: Accounts Receivable
ACRI: Air-Conditioning and Refrigeration Institute
ACRL: American Cruise Line Inc. (NYSE)
ACRODABA: Acronym Data Base
ACRS: Accelerated Cost Recovery System
AC&S: Atlantic City and Shore (railroad)
ACS: Advanced Communications Service
American Capital Convertible Securities Inc. (NYSE)
American Ceramic Society
American Chemical Society
American Coal Shipping (steamship)
American Crystal Sugar Company
Associate in Commercial Science
Association of Consultant Surveyors
Association of Consulting Scientists
Automatic Checkout System
Automatic Control System
Auxiliary Core Storage
ACSC: Australian Coastal Shipping Commission
ACSI: American Ceramic Society Inc.
ACSL: Advanced Continuous Simulation Language
ACSM: Assemblies, Components, Spare Parts and Materials
ACSMA: American Cloak and Suit Manufacturers Association
A/CS Pay: Accounts Payable
A/CS Rec: Accounts Receivable
ACSTI: Advisory Committee for Scientific and Technical Information
ACT: Active Control Technology
Actuarial Programming Language
Advance Corporation Tax
Advisory Council on Technology
American Century Corp. (NYSE)
Analogical Circuit Technique
ACTD: Automatic Telephone Call Distribution
Action: Action Industries Inc. (newspaper)
actnt: accountant
Acton: Acton Corp. (newspaper)
ACTRAN: Audocoder-to-COBOL Translation
ACTS: Advanced Communications Technology Satellite
ACTSU: Association of Computer Time-Sharing Users
Act Val: Actual Value
ACU: Acme United Corp. (ASE)
Address Control Unit
Automatic Calling Unit
ACUG: Association of Computer User Groups
ACUs: Asian Currency Units
ACUTE: Accountants Commuter Users Technical Exchange
ACV: Actual Cash Value
Alberto-Culver Co. (NYSE)
Analysis of Covariance
ACWA: Amalgamated Clothing Workers of America (union)
ACX: Action Industries Inc. (ASE)
AC&Y: Akron, Canton & Youngstown (railroad)
ACY: American Cyanamid Co. (NYSE)
ACyan: American Cyanamid Co. (newspaper)
ad: advertisement
advertising

A&D: Accounting and Disbursing
A/D: Analog/Digital
AD: Accrued Dividend
Aden Airways
After Date
Analog-to-Digital
Anno Domini (in the year of our Lord)
Ante Diem (before the day)
Antilles Air Boats (airline)
Armement Dieppe (steamship)
Assistant Director
Associate Director
Atlantic & Danville (railroad)
Availability Date
A-D: Advance-Decline ratio
ADA: Ada (Augusta Byron) (computer language)
Agricultural Development Association
Airlines Deregulation Act
Atomic Development Authority
Automatic Data Acquisition
ADABAS: Adaptable Data Base System
ADAC: Automatic Direct Analog Computer
ADACS: Automated Data Acquisition and Control System
AdaEx: Adams Express Co., The (newspaper)
ADAEX: Automatic Data Acquisition and Computer Complex
ADAL: Action Data Automation Language
ADAM: Adaptive Dynamic Analysis and Maintenance
Advanced Data Access Method
Advanced Data Management
AdamMl: Adams-Millis Corp. (newspaper)
ADANDAC: Administrative and Accounting Purposes
ADAPS: Automated Design and Packaging Service
ADAPSO: Association of Data-Processing Service Organizations
ADAPT: Automatic Density Analysis Profile Technique
ADAPTICOM: Adaptive Communication
ADAPTS: Analog/Digital/Analog Process and Test System
ADAT: Automatic Data Accumulation and Transfer
ADATE: Automatic Digital Assembly Test Equipment
ADAU: Auxiliary Data Acquisition Unit
ADB: Adjusted Debit Balance
Adobe Resources Corp. (NYSE)
African Development Bank
Asian Development Bank
ADC: Analog-to-Digital Converter
American Dock Company
Area Distribution Center
ADCAD: Airways Data Collection And Distribution
ADCCP: Advanced Data Communications Control Procedures
ADCIS: Association for the Development of Computer-based Instruction Systems
ADCO: Abu Dhabi Oil Company
American Dredging Company
ADCP: Advanced Data Communication Protocol
ADCU: Association of Data Communications
AD&D: Accidental Death and Dismemberment (insurance)
ADD: Ames Department Stores Inc. (NYSE)

Automatic Document Distribution

ADDAM: Adaptive Dynamic Decision Aiding Methodology

ADDAR: Automatic Digital Data Acquisition and Recording

ADDAS: Automatic Digital Data Assembly System

ADDDS: Automatic Direct Distance Dialing System

ADDM: Automated Drafting and Digitizing Machine

addr: adder
address
addressing

ADDR: Address Register

ADDS: Advanced Data Display System

ADDSRTS: Automated Digitized Document Storage, Retrieval and Transmission System

ADE: Automated Design Equipment
Automatic Data Entry

ADELA: Atlantic Community Development Group for Latin America

ADEM: Automatic Data Equalized Modem

ADEPT: Advanced Development Prototype

ADES: Automated Data Entry System

ADFAED: Abu Dhabi Fund for Arab Economic Development

ADGLC: Abu Dhabi Gas Liquefaction Company

ADI: Alternating Direction Implicit
Alternating Direction Iterative
American Documentation Institute
Analog Devices Inc. (NYSE)
Automatic Direction Indicator

ADIBOR: Abu Dhabi Interbank Offered Rate

ADIOS: Analog Digital Input Output System

ADIP: Automated Data Interchange Systems Panel

ADIS: Automatic Data Interchange System

ADIT: Automatic Detection and Integrated Tracking

adj: adjustment

ADL: Andal Corp. (ASE)
Automatic Data Link
Automatic Data Logger

ADLIPS: Automatic Data Link Plotting System

ADM: Activity Data Method
Advanced Development Models
Archer-Daniels-Midland Co. (NYSE)

ADMA: Aircraft Distributors and Manufacturers Association

admin: administration
administrative
administrator

admn: administration

admr: administrator

AdmRs: Adams Resources & Energy Inc. (newspaper)

ADMS: Automatic Digital Message Switching

ADMSC: Automatic Digital Message Switching Centers

AD&N: Ashley, Drew and Northern (railroad)

ADNOC: Abu Dhabi National Oil Company

ADO: Advanced Development Objectives
Audiotronics Corp. (ASE)

Adobe: Adobe Resources Corp. (newspaper)

ADONIS: Automatic Digital On-Line Instrumentation System
ADOPT: Approach to Distributed Processing Transaction
ADP: Acoustic Data Processor
Allied Products Corp. (NYSE)
Association of Database Producers
Automatic Data Processing
ADPACS: Automated Data Processing and Communications Service
ADPC: Abu Dhabi Petroleum Company
Automatic Data Processing Center
ADPCM: Adaptive Differential Pulse Code Modulation
ADPE: Automatic Data Processing Equipment
ADPE/S: Automatic Data Interchange System
Automatic Data Processing Equipment and Software
AdPlan: Advancement Planning
Advertising Planning
ADPREP: Automatic Data Processing Resource Estimating Procedures
ADPS: Automatic Data Processing System
adr: address
ADR: Agreement on the International Carriage of Dangerous Goods by Road (EC)
American Depository Receipts
Asset Depreciation Range
Automatical Digital Relay
ADRA: Automatic Dynamic Response Analyzer
ADRAC: Automatic Digital Recording And Control
ADRS: Analog-to-Digital Data Recording System
ADRT: Analog Data Recording Transcriber
ADS: Accurately Defined Systems
Activity Data Sheet
Advanced Debugging System
Autographed Document Signed
ADSCOM: Advanced Ships Communications
ADSE: Alternative Delivery Schedule Evaluator
ADSEL: Address Selective
ADSG: Alternative Delivery Schedule Generator
ADSHPDAT: Advise Shipping Data
ADSOL: Analysis of Dynamical Systems On-Line
ADSP: Advanced Digital Signal Processor
ADSTAR: Automatic Document Storage And Retrieval
ADSTKOH: Advise Stock On Hand
ADT: Automatic Detection and Tracking
Autonomous Data Transfer
ADTS: Automated Data and Telecommunications Service
Automatic Data Test System
ADU: Automatic Dialing Unit
adv: advice
advise
ADV: Ad Valorem (in proportion to the value)
Advest Group Inc., The (NYSE)
Ad Val: Ad Valorem
Adv Chgs: Advance Charges
advert: advertising
Advest: Advest Group Inc., The (newspaper)
Adv Frt: Advance Freight
Adv Pmt: Advance Payment
advt: advertise
advertisement

advertiser
advertising

ADX: Adams Express Co., The (NYSE)
Automatic Data Exchange
Automatic Digital Exchange

AE: Accommodation Endorsement
Account Executive
Adams Resources & Energy Inc. (ASE)
Aeronautical Engineer
African Enterprises (steamship)
Agricultural Engineer
Air Ceylon (airline)
Associate in Engineering

AEA: American Economic Association
American Electronics Association
American Engineering Association
American Export Airlines
Association of European Airlines
Atomic Energy Authority

A&EC: Atlantic and East Carolina (railroad)

AEC: Alaska Engineering Commission
Atlantic & East Carolina (railroad)
Atomic Energy Commission

AECT: Association for Educational Communications and Technology

AED: Association of Equipment Distributors
Automated Engineering Design

AEDCAP: Automated Engineering Design Circuit Analysis Program

AEDPS: Automated Engineering Documentation Preparation System

AEDS: Advanced Electric Distribution System

AEE: Aileen Inc. (NYSE)
Association of Energy Engineers

AEEC: Airline Electronic Engineering Committee

AEFR: Aurora, Elgin & Fox River (railroad)

AEIL: American Export-Isbrandtsen Lines

AEIMS: Administrative Engineering Information Management System

AEL: Anglo Energy Inc. (ASE)
Audit Error List

AELE: Association Européene de Libre-Echange (European Free Trade Association) (French)

AEIPw: American Electric Power Company Inc. (newspaper)

AEMS: American Engineering Model Society

AEN: Advance Evaluation Note
AMC Entertainment Inc. (ASE)

AEOP: Amend Existing Orders Pertaining to

AEP: Accrued Expenditure Paid
American Electric Power Company Inc. (NYSE)

AEPC: Appalachian Electric Power Company

AERC: Association of Executive Recruiting Consultants

AERIS: Automatic Electronic Ranging Information System

AERODESA: Aeronaves del Ecuador (airline)

AERONAVES: Aeronaves de Mexico (airline)

AERONORTE: Emprêsa de Transportes Aéreos Norte do Brasil

(North Brazil Airways)

AES: Apollo Extension System
Artificial Earth Satellite
Automatic Extraction System

AESA: Aerolineas el Salvador (Panama Airlines)

AESC: Automatic Electronic Switching Center

AESOP: Automated Engineering and Scientific Optimization Programing

AESS: Aerospace and Electronics Systems Society

AET: Acoustic Emission Testing
Aerlinte Eireann Teoranta (Irish Airlines)
Aetna Life & Casualty Co. (NYSE)
Associate in Electrical Technology
Automatic Exchange Tester

AetnLf: Aetna Life & Casualty Co. (newspaper)

AEU: Accrued Expenditure Unpaid

AEVS: Automatic Electronic Voice Switch

AEWM: Acoustic Emission Weld Monitor (monitoring)

AEX: Air Express International Corp. (ASE)

AExp: American Express Co. (newspaper)

A&F: Accounting and Finance
August and February (securities)

AF: Air France (airline)
Aspect Factor
Audio Frequency

AFA: Advertising Federation of America
American Finance Association
American Foundrymen's Association
Association of Federal Appraisers
Auditor Freight Accounts

AF of A: Advertising Federation of America

AFAC: American Fisheries Advisory Committee

AFAM: Automatic Frequency Assignment Model

AFaml: American Family Corp. (newspaper)

AFASE: Association For Applied Solar Energy

AFBD: Association of Futures Brokers and Dealers

AFBF: American Farm Bureau Federation

AFBMA: Anti-Friction Bearing Manufacturers Association

AFC: American Fructose Corp. (ASE)
Auditor Freight Claims
Automatic Field Control
Automatic Frequency Control
Average Fixed Cost

AFCM: Automatic Fine Cull Machine

AFCMA: Aluminum Foil Container Manufacturers

AFD: Association of Food Distributors
Association of Footwear Distributors

AfDB: African Development Bank

AFE: Administración de Ferrocarriles del Estado (State Railway Administration of Uruguay)

AFEA: American Farm Economic Association

AFES: Automatic Feature Extraction System

AFESD: Arab Fund for Economic and Social Development

affd: affirmed

affil: affiliated
afft: affidavit
AFG: AFG Industries Inc. (NYSE) (newspaper)
AFH: Acceptance For Honor
AFIPS: American Federation of Information Processing Societies
afirm: affirmative
AFL: Administración de los Ferrocarriles del Estado (Venezuelan State Railways Administration)
Aeroflot (Soviet Air Lines)
American Family Corp. (NYSE)
American Federation of Labor
AFL-CIO: American Federation of Labor and Congress of Industrial Organizations (union)
AFMD: Accounting and Financial Management Division
AFMR: American Foundation for Management Research
AFMS: Association of Fleet Maintenance Supervisors
AFN: Alfin Inc. (ASE)
AFO: Advanced File Organization
AFOS: Advanced Field Operating System
Authority For Purchase
AFPA: Automatic Flow Process Analysis
AFP/SME: Association for Finishing Processes of the Society of Manufacturing Engineers
AFR: Auditor Freight Receipts
Automatic Field/Format Recognition
AFRA: Average Freight Rate Assessment
AFRAA: African Airlines Association
AFRC: Automatic Frequency Ratio Controller
AFruc: American Fructose Corp. (newspaper)
AFS: New American Shoe Corp. (NYSE)
AFSBO: American Federation of Small Business Organizations
AFSCME: American Federation of State, County and Municipal Employees (union)
AFT: Air Freight Terminal
Analog Facility Terminal
Auditor Freight Traffic
Automatic Fund Transfers
AFTMA: American Fishing Tackle Manufacturers' Association
AFTRA: American Federation of Television and Radio Artists
AFUDC: Allowance for Funds Used During Construction
AG: AAT Airlines
Advisory Group
Aktiengesellschaft (joint stock company) (Austrian)
Allegheny International Inc. (NYSE)
Attorney General
silver (from argentum)
AGA: Accelerated Growth Area
Airgas Inc. (NYSE)
American Gas Association
American Gold Association
AGB: Any Good Brand
AGC: Automatic Gain Control
agcy: agency
AGE: Aerospace Ground Equipment
A.G. Edwards Inc. (NYSE)
AGER: Agricultural Economics Research
AGF: American Government Income Fund (NYSE)

agg: aggregate
aggr: aggregate
AGH: Atlantis Group Inc. (ASE)
AGI: Adjusted Gross Income
Alpine Group Inc., The (ASE)
AGL: Angelica Corp. (NYSE)
AGMA: American Gear Manufacturers' Association
AGnCp: American General Corp. (newspaper)
AGO: ABM Gold Corp. (ASE)
Adjutant General's Office
AGRE: Atlantic Gas Research Exchange
AGREP: Inventory of current agricultural research projects (EC)
agrl: agricultural
AGS: AGS Computers Inc. (NYSE) (newspaper)
Alabama Great Southern (railroad)
agt: agent
agreement
agy: agency
A&H: Accident and Health
Arm & Hammer (trademark)
AH: Alfred Holt (Blue Funnel Line) (steamship)
Air Algerie (airline)
Allis-Chalmers Corp. (NYSE)
AHA: Alpha Industries Inc. (ASE)
American Hospital Association
American Hotel Association
AHAM: Association of Home Appliance Manufacturers
AHB: Great Eastern Line (steamship)
AHC: Amerada Hess Corp. (NYSE)
AHE: American Health Properties Inc. (NYSE)
AHEM: Association of Hydraulic Equipment Manufacturers
AHerit: American Heritage Life Investment Corp. (newspaper)
AHH: AmeriHealth Inc. (ASE)
AHI: American Healthcare Management Inc. (ASE)
AHL: American Heritage Life Investment Corp. (NYSE)
Associated Humber Lines (steamship)
AHlthM: American Healthcare Management Inc. (newspaper)
AHltSv: American Health Services Corp. (newspaper)
AHM: H.F. Ahmanson & Co. (NYSE)
AHMA: American Hotel and Motel Association
Ahmans: H.F. Ahmanson & Co. (newspaper)
AHO: American Hoist & Derrick Co. (NYSE)
AHoist: American Hoist & Derrick Co. (newspaper)
AHome: American Home Products Corp. (newspaper)
AHP: American Home Products Corp. (NYSE)
AHR: Acceptable Hazard Rate
American Hotels & Realty Corp. (NYSE)
AHSE: Assembly, Handling, and Shipping Equipment
AHT: AIRCOA Hotel Partners LP (ASE)
A&I: Abstracting and Indexing
Agricultural and Industrial
AI: Accrued Interest
Accumulated Interest
Air India (airline)
Arrow Automotive Industries Inc. (ASE)
Artificial Intelligence
Attitude Indicator
AIA: Abrasive Industries Association

Accident/Incident Analysis
Aerospace Industries Association
American Institute of Accountants
American Institute of Aeronautics
Association of International Accountants

AIAA: American Institute of Aeronautics and Astronautics

AIB: American Institute of Banking

AIBD: Association of International Bond Dealers

AIC: American Institute of Chemists
Automatic Intercept Center

AICD: Accelerated Individual and Company Development

AICE: American Institute of Chemical Engineers
American Institute of Consulting Engineers

AICPA: American Institute of Certified Public Accountants

AICRO: Association of Independent Contract Research Organizations

AICS: Advanced Interior Communication System
Association of Independent Computer Specialists
Automated Industrial Control System

AID: Agency for International Development
Analog Interface Device
Automated Industrial Drilling
Automatic Information Distribution
Automatic Interaction Detection

AIDA: Attention-Interest-Desire-Action (marketing)

AIDAPS: Automatic Inspection, Diagnostic And Prognostic Systems

AIDAS: Advanced Instrumentation and Data Analysis System

AIDE: Automated Integrated Design and Engineering

AIDES: Automated Image Data Extraction System

AIDE/TPS: Advanced Interactive Data Entry/Transaction Processing System

AIDS: Acoustic Intelligence Data System
Advanced Impact Drilling System
Advanced Interactive Display System
Advanced Interconnection Development System
Automatic Inventory Dispatching System

AIEC: Association of Iron Exporting Countries

AIEEE: American Institute of Electrical and Electronics Engineers

AIF: AIFS Inc. (ASE)

AIFS: AIFS Inc. (newspaper)

AIFTA: American Institute for Foreign Trade
Anglo-Irish Free Trade Agreement

AIG: American International Group Inc. (NYSE)

AII: Allocable Installment Indebtedness
Altex Industries Inc. (ASE)

AIIA: Association of International Insurance Agents

AIIE: American Institute of Industrial Engineers

AIIM: Association for Information and Image Management

AIL: AMCA International Ltd. (NYSE)

Aileen: Aileen Inc. (newspaper)

AIM: Advanced Informatics and Medicine (EC)
Advanced Information in Medicine (EC)
American Institute of Management
Association for the Integration of Management
Atlantic International Marketing Association
Automated Inventory Management

AIMA: As Interest May Appear

AIMBW: American Institute of Men's and Boys' Wear

AIMC: Association of Internal Management Consultants

AIME: American Institute of Mining Engineers
American Institute of Mechanical Engineers

AIMES: Automated Inventory Management Evaluation System

AIMIS: Advanced Integrated Modular Instrumentation System

AIMMPE: American Institute of Mining, Metallurgical and Petroleum Engineers

AIMS: American Institute of Merchant Shipping
Automated Industrial Management System

AIntGr: American International Group Inc. (newspaper)

AIO: Action Information Organization

AIP: Accident Insurance Policy
Aerovias Panama (Panamanian airline)
American Israeli Paper Mills Ltd. (ASE)
Automated Imagery Processing

AIPE: American Institute of Plant Engineers

AIPU: Associative Information Processing Unit

AIR: AAR Corp. (NYSE)
Acoustic Intercept Receiver

AirbFrt: Airborne Freight Corp. (newspaper)

AIRCAL: Air California

AIR CAN: Air Canada

AIRCEY: Air Ceylon

Aircoa: AIRCOA Hotel Partners LP (newspaper)

AIREA: American Institute of Real Estate Appraisers

AirExp: Air Express International Corp. (newspaper)

Airgas: Airgas Inc. (newspaper)

Air Jam: Air Jamaica

Airlease: Airlease Ltd. (newspaper)

Air Mad: Air Madagascar

AIRMIC: Association of Insurance and Risk Managers in Industry and Commerce

AIRS: Alliance of Information and Referral Services
Automatic Image Retrieval System

AIS: Advanced Information Systems
American Israeli Shipping (Zim Lines)
Ampal-American Israel Corp. (ASE)
Answer In Sentence
Automated Information System
Automatic Intercept System

AISB: Society for the Study of Artificial Intelligence and the Simulation of the Brain

AISC: American Institute of Steel Construction
Association of Independent Software Companies

AISE: Association of Iron and Steel Engineers

AISG: Accountants International Study Group
AISI: American Iron and Steel Institute
AIsrael: American Israeli Paper Mills Ltd. (newspaper)
AIST: Agency of Industrial Science and Technology (MITI) (Japan)
Automatic Informational Station
AIT: Advanced Individual Training
Advanced Information Technology
American Information Technologies Corp. (NYSE)
AIX: Amcast Industrial Corp. (NYSE)
Aj: adjustment
AJ: Air Jordan
Alma & Jonquieres (railroad)
AJG: Arthur J. Gallagher & Co. (NYSE)
AJOJ: April, July, October, January (securities)
AK: Alaska Coastal-Ellis (airline)
Altair (airline)
AKA: Akusuhrkredit GMBH
Also Known As
AKV: Auslandskassenverein
AL: Accrued Liabilities
Alamanor (railroad)
Alcan Aluminum Ltd. (NYSE)
Annual Lease
Assembler Language
Assembly Language
ALA: Alliance for Labor Action
ALABOL: Algorithmic And Business-Oriented Language
ALAC: Latin American Free Trade Area
ALACHA: Alabama Automated Clearing House Association
ALADIN: Algebraic Automated Digital Iterative Network
ALAF: Asociación Latinoamericana da Ferrocarriles (Latin-American Railways Association)
ALALC: Asociación Latinoamericana de Libre Comercio (Latin-America Free Trade Association)
ALAM: Association of Lightweight Agggregate Manufacturers
Alamco: Alamco Inc. (newspaper)
ALAP: Associative Linear Array Processor
ALARA: As Low As Reasonably Achievable
ALASKA: Alaska Airlines
ALB: Assembly Line Balancing
AlbaW: Alba-Waldensian Inc. (newspaper)
Alberto: Alberto-Culver Co. (newspaper)
ALBO: Automatic Line Build-Out
Albtsn: Albertson's Inc. (newspaper)
ALC: Adaptive Logic Circuit
ALCA: American Leather Chemists Association
Alcan: Alcan Aluminum Ltd. (newspaper)
ALCAN: Alaska-Canada Highway
ALCAPP: Automative List Classification And Profile Production
ALCATEL: Société Alsacienne de Constructions Atomiques, de Télécommunications et d'Electronique (France)
ALCOA: Alcoa Steamship Company
Aluminum Company of America (newspaper)
AlcoS: Alco Standard Corp. (newspaper)

ALD: Advanced Logic Design
Allied-Signal Inc. (NYSE)
At a Later Date
Automated Logic Diagram

ALDEP: Automated Layout Design Program

ALDP: Automatic Language-Data Processing

ALDS: Analysis of Large Data Sets

ALE: Automatic Line Equalization

ALEA: Airlines Employees Association

ALEC: Analysis of Linear Electronic Circuits

ALEM: Association of Loading Equipment Manufacturers

AlexAlx: Alexander & Alexander Services Inc. (newspaper)

Alexdr: Alexander's Inc. (newspaper)

ALFA: Automatic Line Fault Analysis

ALFC: Automatic Load-Frequency Control

Alfin: Alfin Inc. (newspaper)

ALG: Arkla Inc. (NYSE)

ALGEC: Algorithmic Language for Economic Problems

AlgInt: Allegheny International Inc. (newspaper)

AlgLud: Allegheny Ludlum Corp. (newspaper)

ALGOL: Algorithmic Language

ALI: American Law Institute
Annual Limit of Intake

ALIA: Royal Jordanian Airlines

ALIT: Automatic Line Insulation Test

ALITALIA: Aerolinee Italiane (Italian Airlines)

ALK: Alaska Air Group Inc. (NYSE)

ALL: Adams-Millis Corp. (NYSE)
Anchor Line Limited (steamship)

AL Lab: A.L. Laboratories Inc. (newspaper)

AlldPd: Allied Products Corp. (newspaper)

AllegCp: Allegheny Corp. (newspaper)

AllenG: Allen Group Inc. (newspaper)

AllgPw: Allegheny Power System Inc. (newspaper)

AlliBc: Alliance Bancorporation (newspaper)

AllisC: Allis-Chalmers Corp. (newspaper)

Allstr: Allstar Inns LP (newspaper)

ALLTL: ALLTEL Corp. (newspaper)

A&LM: Arkansas and Louisiana Missouri (railroad)

ALM: Allstate Municipal Income Trust (NYSE)
Antilliaanse Luchtvaart Maatschappij (Dutch Antillean Airlines)

ALMS: Automated Logic Mapping System

ALN: Albany and Northern (railroad)
Allen Group, The (NYSE)

AlnCap: Alliance Capital Management LP (newspaper)

AlnTre: Alliance Tire & Rubber Company Ltd. (newspaper)

aloc: allocation

ALOHA: Aloha Airlines

alot: allotment

ALP: Arithmetic and Logic Processor
Assembly Language Program
Automated Learning Process

ALPA: Air Lines Pilots' Association

AlphaIn: Alpha Industries Inc. (newspaper)

alphanum: alphanumeric

AlpinGr: Alpine Group Inc., The (newspaper)

ALPS: Assembly Line Planning System
ALQS: Aliquippa and Southern (railroad)
ALS: Advanced Logistics System
Allegheny Ludlum Corp. (NYSE)
Alton & Southern (railroad)
ALSC: Automatic Level and Slope Control
AlskAir: Alaska Air Group Inc. (newspaper)
AlsMI: Allstate Municipal Income Trust II (newspaper)
ALSPEC: Automated Laser Seeker Performance Evaluation System
AlstMu: Allstate Municipal Income Trust (newspaper)
ALT: Aer Lingus (Irish Air Lines)
Allstate Municipal Income Trust II (NYSE)
Average Logistic Time
ALTA: American Land Title Association
Association of Local Transport Airlines
ALTAPE: Automatic Line Tracing And Processing Equipment
Altex: Altex Industries Inc. (newspaper)
ALU: Advanced Logical Unit
Arithmetic and Logic Unit
Automatic Link Unit
ALX: Alexander's Inc. (NYSE)
Alza: ALZA Corp. (newspaper)
A&M: Agricultural and Mechanical
AM: Academy of Management
Active Market
Aeronaves de Mexico (Mexican Airlines)
After Market
Agricultural Marketing
Air Mail
AM International Inc. (NYSE)
Amplitude Modulation
Anno Mundi (in the year of the world)
Ante Meridiem (before noon)
A&MA: Advertising and Marketing Association
AMA: Acoustical Materials Association
Adhesives Manufacturers Association
Agricultural Marketing Administration
American Machinery Association
American Management Association
American Marketing Association
Amfact Inc. (NYSE)
Asset Management Account
Automatic Message Accounting
Automobile Manufacturers Association
amal: amalgamation
amalg: amalgamated
AMA/MTR: Automatic Message Accounting-Magnetic Tape Recording
AMAVU: Advanced Modular Audio Visual Unit
Amax: AMAX Inc. (newspaper)
AMB: Adjusted Monetary Base
Airways Modernization Board
American Brands (NYSE)
AMBAC: American Municipal Bond Assurance Corporation
AmBilt: American Biltrite Inc. (newspaper)
AMBld: American Medical Buildings Inc. (newspaper)
AmBrit: AmBrit Inc. (newspaper)
AmBrnd: American Brands Inc. (newspaper)

AMC: Amador Central (railroad)
AMC Entertainment Inc. (newspaper)
American Mining Congress
Association of Management Consultants
AMCA: AMCA International Ltd. (newspaper)
AmCap: American Capital Corp. (newspaper)
AMCAP: Advanced Microwave Circuit Analysis Program
Amcast: Amcast Industrial Corp. (newspaper)
AMC&BW: Amalgamated Meat Cutters and Butcher Workmen (union).
AMD: Advanced Micro Devices Inc. (NYSE) (newspaper)
Amdahl: Amdahl Corp. (newspaper)
AMDEA: Association of Manufacturers of Domestic Electrical Appliances
AMDF: Absolute Magnitude Difference Function
AME: AMETEK Inc. (NYSE)
Angle Measuring Equipment
Automatic Monitoring Equipment
AMEDA: Automatic Microscope Electronic Data Accumulator
AMEDS: Automated Measurement Evaluator and Director System
AMEME: Association of Mining, Electrical and Mechanical Engineers
AMERICAN: American Airlines
Ameron: Ameron Inc. (newspaper)
AMES: Automatic Message Entry System
AmesDp: Ames Department Stores Inc. (newspaper)
Ametk: AMETEK Inc. (newspaper)
AmevSc: AMEV Securities Inc. (newspaper)
AMEX: American Stock Exchange
Amexco: American Express Company
AMF: Airport Mail Facility
Amfac: Amfac Inc. (newspaper)
AmFGr: American First Guaranteed Income Fund (newspaper)
AMFIS: Automatic Microfilm Information System
AmGvI: American Government Income Fund (newspaper)
AMH: Amdahl Corp. (ASE)
Automated Materials Handling
AmHes: Amerada Hess Corp. (newspaper)
Amhlth: AmeriHealth Inc. (newspaper)
AmHotl: Americana Hotels & Realty Corp. (newspaper)
AMHS: American Material Handling Society
AMI: Alternative Mortgage Instrument
American Management Institute
American Meat Institute
Association of Multi-Image
Average Mutual Information
AM Intl: AM International Inc. (newspaper)
AmIPrp: American Income Properties LP (newspaper)
AMIS: Automated Management Information System
AMK: American Technical Ceramics Corp. (ASE)
AML: A Manufacturing Language
American Mail Line (steamship)
Amplitude Modulated Link
AmList: American List Corp. (newspaper)

AmLnd: American Land Cruisers Inc. (newspaper)
AMM: Advanced Manufacturing Methods
Alternative Method of Management
AMRE Inc. (NYSE)
AMME: Automated Multi-Media Exchange
AMMINET: Automated Mortgage Management Information Network
AMMO: Alliance of Manufacturing and Management Organizations
AMMS: Automated Multi-Media Switch
AMMSS: Automatic Message and Mail Sorting Systems
AMN: Ameron Inc. (NYSE)
AMNIP: Adaptive Man-Machine Non-Arithmetical Information Processing
AMO: Area Maintenance Office
AMOCO: American Oil Company
American Oil Company (steamship)
Amoco Corp. (newspaper)
AmOil: American Oil & Gas Corp. (newspaper)
AMOS: Adjustable Multi-Class Organizing System
Amex Options Switching System
AMOSS: Adaptive Mission-Oriented Software System
AMP: AMP Inc. (NYSE) (newspaper)
Ampal: Ampal-American Israel Corp. (newspaper)
Ampco: Ampco-Pittsburgh Corp. (newspaper)
AmPetf: American Petrofina Inc. (newspaper)
AMPP: Advanced Microprogrammable Processor
AMPS: Advanced Mobile Phone Service
Assembly Manufacturing Payroll System
Automatic Message Processing System
AMR: American Airlines Corporation
AMR Corp. (NYSE) (newspaper)
Arcata and Mad River (railroad)
Automatic Message Routing
Amre: AMRE Inc. (newspaper)
Amrep: AMREP Corp. (newspaper)
AMRF: Automated Manufacturing Research Facility
AmRlty: American Realty Trust (newspaper)
AMRPD: Applied Manufacturing Research and Process Development
Amrtc: American Information Technologies Corp. (newspaper)
AMS: Administration Management Society
Agricultural Marketing Service
American Management Society
American Shared Hospital Services (ASE)
Automated Maintenance System
AMSA: Aeronaves de Mexico (Mexico Airlines)
American Metal Stamping Association
AMSEC: Analytical Method for System Evaluation and Control
AmShrd: American Shared Hospital Services (newspaper)
AMSO: Association of Market-Survey Organizations

Automated Microform Storage and Retrieval

AmSth: AmSouth Bancorporation (newspaper)

AmStor: American Stores Co. (newspaper)

amt: amount

AMT: Acme-Cleveland Corp. (NYSE)
Advanced Manufacturing Technique
Advanced Manufacturing Technology
Alternative Minimum Tax
Associate in Mechanical Technology
Associate in Medical Technology
Automated Microfiche Terminal

AMTC: Advanced Manufacturing Technology Committee

AMTD: Automatic Magnetic Tape Dissemination

AMTDA: Agricultural Machinery and Tractor Dealers Association

AMTORG: American Trade Organization (USSR)

AMTRAK: American Railroad Tracks

AMTRAN: Automatic Mathematical Translator

AMV: AMEV Securities Inc. (NYSE)

AMW: Amwest Insurance Group Inc. (ASE)
Average Monthly Wage

Amwest: Amwest Insurance Group Inc. (newspaper)

AmWtr: American Water Works Company Inc. (newspaper)

AMX: AMAX Inc. (NYSE)

AmxG: Amax Gold Inc. (newspaper)

AMZ: American List Corp. (ASE)

AMze: American Maize-Products Co. (newspaper)

a/n: alphanumeric

A&N: Albany and Northern (railroad)

AN: Account Number
Amoco Corp. (NYSE)
Ansett Airlines of Australia
Apalachicola Northern (railroad)

ANA: All Nippon Airways
Association of National Advertisers
Australian National Airways
Automatic Number Analysis

Anacmp: Anacomp Inc. (newspaper)

AnaCom: Analog Computer

ANACONDA: Analytical Control and Data

Anadrk: Anadarko Petroleum Corp. (newspaper)

ANALIT: Analysis of Automatic Line Insulation Tests

Analog: Analog Devices Inc. (newspaper)

ANATRAN: Analog Translator

ANB&TC: American National Bank & Trust Company

ANC: All-Numbers Calling

ANCHOR: Alpha-Numeric Character Generator

ANCOVA: Analysis of Covariance

ANCS: American Numerical Control Society

AND: Alpha-Numeric Display
Andrea Radio Corp. (ASE)

Andal: Andal Corp. (newspaper)

ANDES: Aerolineas Nacionales del Ecuador (Ecuador Airlines)

ANDMS: Advanced Network Design and Management System

Andrea: Andrea Radio Corp. (newspaper)

ANDVT: Advanced Narrow-band Digital Voice Terminal
ANF: Angeles Finance Partners (ASE)
ANFM: August, November, February, May (securities)
ANG: American Newspaper Guild
Angeles Corp. (ASE)
AngE: Anglo Energy Inc. (newspaper)
Angeles: Angeles Corp. (newspaper)
Angelic: Angelica Corp. (newspaper)
AnglFn: Angeles Finance Partners (newspaper)
AnglRl: Angell Real Estate Company Inc. (newspaper)
AngMtg: Angeles Mortgage Partners Ltd. (newspaper)
Anheus: Anheuser-Busch Companies Inc. (newspaper)
ANI: Automatic Number Identification
ANIM: Association of Nuclear Instrument Manufacturers
ANIRC: Annual National Information Retrieval Colloquium
ANL: Above-Normal Loss
Australian National Line (steamship)
ANLP: Alpha-Numeric Logic Package
ANM: Angeles Mortgage Partners Ltd. (ASE)
ann: annual
annuity
ANN ARBOR: Detroit, Toledo and Ironton Railroad
ANN CAS: Annotated Cases
annot: annotated
ANN REPT: Annual Report
ANOM: Analysis Of Means
AnOVa: Analysis Of Variance
ANPA: American Newspaper Publishers' Association
ANR: Angelina and Neches River (railroad)
ANSETT: Ansett Airways
ANSETT-ANA: Ansett Australian National Airways
ANSI: American National Standards Institute
ANSIM: Analog Simulator
ANSR: Add-On Non-Stop Reliability
ANSWER: Algorithm for Non-Synchronized Waveform Error Reduction
ANT: Anthony Industries Inc. (NSYE)
Assessment of New Techniques
ANTEC: Annual Technical Conference
Anthm: Anthem Electronics Inc. (newspaper)
Anthony: Anthony Industries Inc. (newspaper)
A&O: April and October (securities)
AO: Account Of
Announcement of Opportunity
Area Office
Associate Office
Average out
Aviaco (airline)
AOA: Ascending Order Arrangement
At Or Above
AOB: At Or Below
AOC: Aon Corp. (NYSE)
Arabian Oil Company
Auditor Overcharge Claims
AOCR: Advanced Optical Character Reader
Advanced Optical Character Recognition
AOCS: American Oil Chemists Society
AOE: Auditing Order Error
AOF: ACM Government Opportunity Fund (NYSE)

AOG: American Oil & Gas Corp. (ASE)
Arrival of Goods
AOGA: Alaska Oil and Gas Association
AOI: Acousto-Optical Imaging
AOI Coal Co. (ASE) (newspaper)
AOM: Acoustic-Optic Modulator
AON: All Or None order
Aon Cp: Aon Corp. (newspaper)
AOPA: Airplane Owners and Pilots Association
AOQ: Average Outgoing Quality
AOQL: Average Outgoing Quality Limit
AORS: Abnormal Occurrence Reporting System
AOS: Advanced Operating System
AOSP: Automatic Operating and Scheduling Program
AOV: Analysis Of Variance
A&P: Great Atlantic & Pacific Tea Company
AP: Account Paid (or Payable)
Additional Premium
Air Paris (airline)
American Pioneer Lines (steamship)
Ampco-Pittsburgh Corp. (NYSE)
Apache Airlines
Application Program
Assessment Paid
Associated Press
Associative Processor
Atlantska Plovidba (Yugoslavian-Atlantic Line) (steamship)
Attached Processor
Audio Processing
Authority to Pay (or Purchase)
APA: Administrative Procedure Act
Aerovias Panama Airways
American Pulpwood Association
Apache Corp. (NYSE)
Apache Railway Company
Associate in Public Administration
APAA: Automotive Parts and Accessories Association
Apache: Apache Corp. (newspaper)
APACHE: Analog Programming And Checking
APACS: Adaptive Planning And Control Sequence (Marketing)
APAS: Adaptable-Programmable Assembly System
APB: Accounting Principles Board
All Points Bulletin
Asia Pacific Fund Inc., The (NYSE)
APBA: American Power Boat Association
APC: American Power Conference
Anadarko Petroleum Corp. (NYSE)
Area Positive Control
Auditing Practices Committee
Automatic Phase Control
Automatic Potential Control
APCC: Association of Professional Computer Consultants
APCHE: Automatic Programmed Checkout Equipment
APCM: Adaptive Pulse Code Modulator
Authorized Protective Connecting Module
APCS: Associative Processor Computer System
Attitude and Pointing Control System
APD: Air Products & Chemicals Inc. (NYSE)
Albany Port District (railroad)
Approach Progress Display
Automated Payment and Deposit

APDL: Algorithmic Processor Description Language
APDM: Associative Push Down Memory
APET: Application Program Evaluator Tool
APEX: Advance-Purchase Excursion Plan
Assembler and Process Executive
ApexM: Apex Municipal Fund (newspaper)
APF: Association of Paper Finishers
Authorized Program Facility
APFA: American Production Finishers Association
APG: Application Program Generator
APHA: American Public Health Association
API: American Paper Institute
American Petrofina Inc. (ASE)
American Petroleum Institute
APICS: American Production and Inventory Control Society
APL: American President Lines (steamship)
A Programming Language
APLL: Analog Phased-Locked Loop
Automatic Phased-Locked Loop
APM: Applied Magnetics Corp. (NYSE)
APME: Advisory Panel on Management Education
APMS: Automatic Performance Management System
APOLLO: Article Procurement with On-Line Local Ordering
APP: Advance Procurement Plan
Aggregate Production Planning
Associative Parallel Processor
APPI: Advanced Planning Procurement Information
ApplBk: Apple Bank for Savings (New York) (newspaper)
APPLE: Analog Phased Processing Loop Equipment
ApplM: Applied Magnetics Corp. (newspaper)
appln: application
approx: approximate
appx: appendix
apr: apprentice
APR: Alternate Path Retry
American Precision Industries Inc. (ASE)
Annual Percentage Rate
Annual Progress Reports
Association of Petroleum Re-Refiners
APRCG: Asia-Pacific Railway Cooperation Group
APrec: American Precision Industries Inc. (newspaper)
APresd: American President Companies Inc. (newspaper)
APRICOT: Automatic Printed Circuit Board Routing with Intermediate Control of the Tracking
APRIL. Automatically Programmed Remote Indication Logging
APROC: Adaptive Statistical Processor
APRS: Automatic Position Reference System
APRST: Averaged Probability Ratio Sequential Test
aprx: approximately
APS: American Physical Society
American Physics Society
American President Companies Ltd. (NYSE)
Assembly Programming System
Auxiliary Power System

APSA: Aerolineas Peruanas Sociedad Anónima (Peruvian Air Lines)
APSTRAT: Aptitude Strategies
APT: Automatically Programmed Tool
APTE: Automatic Production Test Equipment
APTI: Automatic Print Transfer Instrument
APU: Assessment of Performance Unit
Auxiliary Power Unit
APWA: American Public Works Association
APWU: American Postal Workers Union
apx: appendix
AQ: Achievement Quotient
Any Quantity
AQC: Air Quality Control
AQL: Acceptable (or Average) Quality Level
AQM: QMS Inc. (NYSE)
A&R: Aberdeen and Rockfish (railroad)
Account and Risk
AR: Account Receivable
Advisory Report
Aerolineas Argentinas (airline)
All Risks
Annual Report
Annual Return
Applied Research
ASARCO Inc. (NYSE)
Aspect Ratio
ARA: Agricultural Research Administration
American Railway Association
Arcade and Attica Railroad
Area Redevelopment Act (Administration)
Attitude Reference Assembly
Automatic Retailers of America
ARAC: Array Reduction Analysis Circuit
ARACHA: Arkansas Automated Clearing House Association
ARAL: Automatic Record Analysis Language
ARAMIS: Automation Robotics and Machine Intelligence System
arb: arbitrager
arbitrary
arbitration
ARB: American Realty Trust (NYSE)
Audience Research Bureau
ARBA: American Road Builders Association
Associated Retail Bakers of America
ARB&AW: Arbitration and Award
ARBL: Assets Repriced Before Liabilities
arbtrn: arbitration
arbtror: arbitrator
ARC: Alexander Railroad (Southern)
American Red Cross
ARC International Corp. (newspaper)
Atlantic Richfield Co. (NYSE)
Attached Resource Computer
Automatic Revenue Collection
ARCA: Asbestos Removal Contractors Association
ARCADE: Automatic Radar Control And Data Equipment
ARCAIC: Archives and Record Catologing And Indexing by Computer
ArchDn: Archer-Daniels-Midland Co. (newspaper)

ArcoCh: ARCO Chemical Co. (newspaper)
ARCS: Automated Revenue Collection System
Automated Ring Code System
ARD: Agricultural Research Service
Automatic Release Date
ARDI: Analysis, Requirements Determination, Design and Development, and Implementation and Evaluation
ARDS: Advance Remote Display System
AREA: Aerovias Ecuatorianas (Ecuadorian Airways)
American Railway Engineering Association
Association of Records Executives and Administrators
ARENTS: Advanced Research Environmental Test Satellite
ARES: Agricultural Research
AREst: American Real Estate Partners LP (newspaper)
ARestr: American Restaurant Partners LP (newspaper)
ARF: Apparel Research Foundation
arg: argument
ARG: Accident Response Group
Aerolineas Argentinas (Argentine Airlines)
Akron Rubber Group
ARGE: European Federation of Associations of Lock and Builders Hardware Manufacturers
ARGS: Advanced Raster-Graphics System
ARI: Air-Conditioning and Refrigeration Institute
Automated Readability Index
ARIANA: Ariana Afghan Airlines
ARIEL: Automated Real-time Investments Exchange
ARIES: Automated Reliability Interactive Estimation System
ARIMA: Autoregressive Integrated Moving Average
ARIS: Activity Reporting Information System
Automated Reactor Inspection System
Aristec: Aristech Chemical Corp. (newspaper)
ArizCm: Arizona Commerce Bank (newspaper)
ARK: Apple Bank for Savings (New York) (NYSE)
ArkBst: Arkansas Best Corp. (newspaper)
ARKIA: Israel Inland Airlines
Arkla: Arkla Inc. (newspaper)
ArkRst: Ark Restaurants Corp. (newspaper)
ARL: Average Run Length
ARM: Adjustable-Rate Mortgage
Armtek Corp. (NYSE)
ARMA: American Records Management Association
Association of Records Managers and Administrators
Autoregressive Moving Average
Armada: Armada Corp. (newspaper)
ARMAN: Artificial Methods Analyst
Armco: Armco Inc. (newspaper)
ARMI: American Research Merchandising Institute
ARMM: Automatic Reliability Mathematical Model
ARMMS: Automated Reliability and Maintainability Measurement System
Armtek: Armtek Corp. (newspaper)
Armtrn: Armatron International Inc. (newspaper)
ArmWI: Armstrong World Industries Inc. (newspaper)
ARO: After Receipt of Order

AROM: Alterable Read-Only Memory
ArowE: Arrow Electronics Inc. (newspaper)
ARP: Adjustable-Rate Preferred Stock
Analogous Random Process
ARPS: Advanced Real-Time Processing System
ARQ: Answer-Return Query
Automatic Request for Repetition
ARR: Alaska Railroad
ArrowA: Arrow Automotive Industries Inc. (newspaper)
ARS: Advanced Record System (of General Services Administration
Agricultural Research Service
Aristech Chemical Corp. (NYSE)
Automatic Route Setting
ARSTEC: Adaptive Random Search Technique
ART: American Refrigerator Transit (railroad)
Applied Research and Technology
Armatron International Inc. (ASE)
Automated Request Transmission
ARTEMIS: Administrative Real Time Express Mortgage and Investment System
Artra: ARTRA GROUP Inc. (newspaper)
ARTS: Audio Response Time-Shared System
ARU: American Railway Union
Audio Response Unit
Auxiliary Read-Out Unit
ARV: Arvin Industries Inc. (NYSE)
Arvin: Arvin Industries Inc. (newspaper)
ARW: Arkansas Western (railway)
Arrow Electronics Inc. (NYSE)
ARX: ARX Inc. (NYSE) (newspaper)
ArzLd: Arizona Land Income Corp. (ASE)
A&S: Alton & Southern (railroad)
A/S: Aktjeselskap (joint stock company) (Norwegian)
Aktieselskab (joint stock company) (Danish)
AS: Abilene & Southern (railroad)
Academy of Science
Accumulated Surplus
Active Securities
Artificial Satellite
Alaska Airlines
Armco Inc. (NYSE)
Assented Securities
Assessable Stock
Associate in Science
Auxiliary Storage
ASA: Acoustical Society of America
Advertising Standards Authority
Aerovias Sud Americana (South American Airways)
Aluminum Stockholders Association
American Society of Appraisers
American Standards Association
American Statistical Association
American Subcontractors Association
ASA Ltd. (NYSE) (newspaper)
Association of Southeast Asia
Automatic Separation System
Automatic Spectrum Analyzer
A&SAB: Atlanta and St. Andrews Bay (railroad)

ASAE: American Society of Association Executives
ASAP: Airlines of South Australia
As Soon As Possible
Automated Statistical Analysis Program
Automatic Spooling with Asynchronous Processing
Asarco: ASARCO Inc. (newspaper)
ASBC: American Standard Building Code
asbl: assemble
ASC: Accounting Standards Committee
Adaptive Speed Control
Adelaide Steamship Company
Alaska Steamship Company
American Society for Cybernetics
American Stores Co. (NYSE)
Associative Structure Computer
Automatic System Controller
ASCC: American Society of Concrete Constructors
Automatic Sequence Controller Calculator
ASCE: American Society of Civil Engineers
Association of Sound and Communication Engineers
AsciE: American Science & Engineering Inc. (newspaper)
ASCII: American Standard Code for Information Interchange
ASCOM: Association of Telecommunication Services
ASCON: Automated Switched Communications Network
ASCU: Association of Small Computer Users
ASD: assented (NYSE)
ASDA: Accelerate-Stop Distance Available
Asbestos and Danville (railroad)
AsDB: Asian Development Bank
ASDE: Asbestos and Danville (railroad)
ASDI: Automatic Selective Dissemination of Information
ASDIC: Association of Information and Dissemination Centers
ASDM: Association of Steel Drum Manufacturers
ASE: American Science & Engineering Inc. (ASE)
American Stock Exchange
Automatic Stabilization Equipment
ASEAN: Association of South East Asian Nations
ASEE: American Society for Engineering Education
ASEF: Association of Stock Exchange Firms
ASEM: American Society of Engineering Management
ASEP: American Society of Electroplated Plastics
ASFS: Alaska State Ferry System
asg: assignment
ASG: Advanced Study Group
ASH: Ashland Oil Inc. (NYSE)
AshCoal: Ashland Coal Inc. (newspaper)
AShip: American Ship Building Co., The (newspaper)
AshOil: Ashland Oil Inc. (newspaper)
ASHRACE: American Society of Heating, Refrigerating and Air-Conditioning Engineers
ASI: American Standards Institute
Astrex Inc. (ASE)
Asialease: Asian Leasing Association
AsiaPc: Asia, Pacific Fund Inc., The (newspaper)
ASIC: Application Specific Integrated Circuit

ASID: Address Space Identifier
ASIDP: American Society of Information and Data Processing
ASII: American Science Information Institute
ASIS: American Society for Industrial Security
American Society for Information Science
ASKS: Automatic Station Keeping System
ASLFla: American S&L Association of Florida (newspaper)
ASLO: Assembly Layout
ASLRA: American Short Line Railroad Association
asm: assembler
ASM: American Society for Metals
Asamera Inc. (ASE)
Association for Systems Management
Asynchronous Sequential Machine
asmblr: assembler
ASMC: Association of Stores and Materials Controllers
ASME: American Society of Mechanical Engineers
ASMMA: American Supply and Machinery Manufacturers Association
Asmr: Asamera Inc. (newspaper)
ASN: Alco Standard Corp. (NYSE)
Atlantic Steam Navigation (steamship)
Average Sample Number
ASO: AmSouth Bancorporation (NYSE)
ASOK: Angfartigas Svenska Ostasiatiske Kompaniet (Swedish East Asiatic Steamship Company)
ASP: Acoustic Signal Processor
American Selling Price
Association-Storing Processor
Attached Support Processor
ASPA: American Society for Personnel Administrators
ASPE: American Society of Plumbing Engineers
ASPEX: Automated Surface Perspectives
ASQC: American Society for Quality Control
ASR: American Southwest Mortgage Investments Corp. (ASE)
Analog Shift Register
Association of Southeastern Railroads
Automatic Send/Receive
Automatic Storage/Retrieval
Available Supply Rate
ASRL: Average Sample Run Length
ASRM: American Society of Range Management
ASRS: Automatic Storage and Retrieval System
ASRWPM: Association of Semi-Rotary Wing Pump Manufacturers
ASS: Associate in Secretarial Science (Studies)
ASSE: American Society of Safety Engineers
American Society of Sanitary Engineers
ASSET: Advanced Systems Synthesis and Evaluation Technique
Automated System for Security Entries and Transactions
assm: assembler
assmt: assessment
assn: association
ASSORT: Automatic System for Selection Of Receiver and Transmitter

ASSR: Automated Systems Service Request
Autonomous Soviet Socialist Republic
asst: assistant
Asst Cash: Assistant Cashier
ASSUC: Association des Organisation Professionnelles de Commerce des Sucres (Association of Sugar Trade Organizations for the European Community countries) (French) (EC)
AST: Advanced Simulation Technology
Automatic Scan Tracking
ASTA: American Seed Trade Association
American Society of Travel Agents
Association of Short-Circuit Testing Authorities
Automatic System Trouble Analysis
astd: assented
ASTD: American Society for Training and Development
ASTE: American Society of Tool Engineers
ASTI: Automated System for Transport Intelligence
ASTM: American Society for Testing Metals (or Materials)
ASTME: American Society of Tool and Manufacturing Engineers
ASTOVL: Advanced Short Take-Off and Vertical Landing
ASTRA: Advanced Structural Analyzer
Automatic Scheduling and Time-dependent Resource Allocation
Automatic Scheduling and Time-integrated Resource Allocation
ASTRAIL: Analog Schematic Translator to Algebraic Language
Assurance and Stabilization Trends for Reliability by Analysis of Lots
Astrex: Astrex Inc. (newspaper)
ASTS: Air to Surface Transport System
ASVIP: American Standard Vocabulary for Information Processing
ASW: Applications Software
Association of Scientific Workers
ASwM: American Southwest Mortgage Investment Corp. (newspaper)
asynch: asynchronous
A&T: Assemble and Test
AT: Absolute Title
Address Translator
ALLTEL Corp. (NYSE)
Anomalous Transmission
Appropriate Technology
Assay Ton
Automatic Transmission
Royal Air Maroc (airline)
ATA: Air Transport Association
American Trucking Association
ARTRA GROUP Inc. (NYSE)
Associate Technical Aide
ATAE: Associated Telephone Answering Exchanges
AtalSos: Atalanta/Sosnoff Capital Corp. (newspaper)
ATAP: Automated Time and Attendance Procedures
Atari: Atari Corp. (newspaper)
ATARS: Automated Travel Agents Reservation Systems

ATAS: Automated Telephone Answering System
ATB: Across The Board
ATBM: Average Time between Maintenance
ATC: Advanced Technology Components
Air Traffic Control
Arnold Transit Company
Atari Corp. (ASE)
Automated Technical Control
Automatic Tool Charger
Average Total Cost
ATCD: Automatic Telephone Call Distribution
ATDE: Advanced Technology Demonstrator Engine
ATDM: Asynchronous Time-Division Multiplexing
AT&E: A.T.& E. Corp. (newspaper)
ATE: Atlantic Energy Inc. (NYSE)
Automatic Test Equipment
ATEC: Automated Technical Control
Automated Test Equipment Complex
ATechC: American Technical Ceramics Corp. (newspaper)
ATEMIS: Automatic Traffic Engineering and Management Information System
ATEV: Approximate Theoretical Error Variance
ATF: AT&T Stock Fund (ASE)
ATFA: Association of Technicians in Financing and Accounting
ATFB: Alcohol, Tobacco, Firearms Bureau (U.S. Department of the Treasury)
ATFC: Automatic Traffic-Flow Control
ATG: Atlanta Gas Light Co. (NYSE)
Automatic Test Generation
ATH: Athlone Industries Inc. (NYSE)
Athlone: Athlone Industries Inc. (newspaper)
ATI: Aerotransporti Italiani (Italian Air Transport)
ATI Medical Inc. (ASE) (newspaper)
Average Total Inspection
ATIS: Automatic Terminal Information Service
Automatic Transmitter Identification System
ATL: Analog-Threshold Logic
Applications Terminal Language
Atalanta/Sosnoff Capital Corp. (NYSE)
ATLANTIC: Atlantic Refining Company
Atlants: Atlantis Group Inc. (newspaper)
ATLAS: Automatic Tabulating, Listing And Sorting System
AtlasCp: Atlas Corp. (newspaper)
ATLB: Air Transport Licensing Board
AtlEnrg: Atlantic Energy Inc. (newspaper)
AtlGas: Atlanta Gas Light Co. (newspaper)
AtlRich: Atlantic Richfield Co. (newspaper)
AtlsCM: Atlas Consolidated Mining & Development Corp. (newspaper)
ATM: Advanced Technology Mining
Air Traffic Management
Anthem Electronics Inc. (NYSE)
Association of Teachers of Management
Asynchronous Time Multiplexing
At The Market

Automated Teller Machine
Automatic Teller Machine

ATMA: American Textile Machinery Association
American Textile Manufacturers Association

ATMI: American Textile Manufacturers Institute

ATMS: Advanced Text Management System
Automatic Transmission Measuring System

ATMSS: Automatic Telegraph Message Switching System

AT&N: Alabama, Tennessee and Northern (railroad)

ATN: Acton Corp. (ASE)

ATO: At The Opening

ATOLS: Automatic Testing On-Line System

ATOMS: Automated Technical Order Maintenance Sequence(s)

ATP: Authority To Purchase

ATPC: Association of Tin Producing Countries

atr: attribute

ATR: Alliance Tire & Rubber Company Ltd. (ASE)

ATRAC: Angle Tracking Computer

ATS: Advanced Technology Satellite
Analytic Trouble Shooting
Automated Test System
Automatic Transfer Service

ATSF: Atchison, Topeka and Santa Fe (railroad)

ATSS: Automatic Test Support Systems

ATSU: Association of Time-Sharing Users

AT&T: American Telephone and Telegraph Co. (newspaper)

ATT Fd: AT&T Stock Fund (also known as Equity Income Fund) (newspaper)

attn: attention

atty: attorney

ATV: ARC International Corp. (ASE)
Automatic Ticket Vendor

ATW: A.T.& E. Corp. (ASE)
Atlantic and Western (railroad)

ATX: A.T. Cross Co. (ASE)

AU: Amax Gold Inc. (NYSE)
Arithmetic Unit
Austral (airline)
gold (from aurum)

AUA: Austrian Airlines

AUBTW: Amalgamated Union of Building Trade Workers

aud: audit
auditor

AUD: Asynchronous Unit Delay
Automatic Data Processing Inc. (NYSE)

AUDDIT: Automatic Dynamic Digital Test System

Audiotr: Audiotronics Corp. (newspaper)

AudVd: Audio/Video Affiliates Inc. (newspaper)

Audvx: Audiovox Corp. (newspaper)

AUG: Augat Inc. (NYSE)
Augusta (railroad)

Augat: Augat Inc. (newspaper)

AUL: Above Upper Limit

AUNTIE: Automatic Unit for National Taxation and Insurance

AUS: Augusta and Summerville (railroad)
Ausimont Compo N.V. (NYSE)

Ausimt: Ausimont Compo N.V. (newspaper)

AUT: Advanced User Terminal
American Union Transport (steamship)
Assembly Under Test
Automated Unit Test

auth: authority
AUTODIN: Automatic Digital Network (Western Union)
AUTODOC: Automated Documentation
AutoDt: Automatic Data Processing Inc. (newspaper)
AUTOMAST: Automatic Mathematical Analysis and Symbolic Translation
AUTOMAT: Automatic Methods And Times
AUTOMEX: Automatic Message Exchange
automtn: automation
AUTONET: Automatic Network Display Program
AUTOPROS: Automated Process Planning System
AUTOSATE: Automated Data Systems Analysis Technique
AUTOSEVOCOM: Automatic Secure Voice Communications (system)
AUTOSPOT: Automatic System for Positioning Tools
AUTOVON: Automatic Voice Network
AUTRAN: Automatic Translation
Automatic Utility Translator
AUW: All-Up-Weight
aux: auxiliary
AUXRC: Auxiliary Recording Control Circuit
av: average
AV: Actual Value
Ad Valorem (in proportion to the value)
Analysis of Variance
Avianca (airline)
AVA: Audio/Video Affiliates Inc. (NYSE)
Avalon: Avalon Corp. (newspaper)
AVC: Automatic Volume Control
Average Variable Cost
avdps: avoirdupois
AVE: AVEMCO Corp (NYSE)
AVEM: Association of Vacuum Equipment Manufacturers
AVENSA: Aerovias Venezolonas Sociedad Anónima (Venezuelan Airlines)
AVERE: European Electric Road Vehicle Association
Avery: Avery International Corp. (newspaper)
avg: average
AVI: Automatic Vehicle Identification
AVIANCA: Aerovias Nacionales de Colombia (Colombian National Airlines)
AVL: Aroostook Valley (railroad)
Avalon Corp. (NYSE)
AVMC: AVEMCO Corp. (newspaper)
Avnet: Avnet Inc. (newspaper)
AVOCON: Automated Vocabulary Control
Avon: Avon Products Inc. (newspaper)
AVOS: Acoustic Valve Operating System
AVP: Avon Products Inc. (NYSE)
AVR: Automatic Volume Recognition
AVT: Ad Valorem Taxes
Avnet Inc. (NYSE)
Value-Added Tax
AVX: AVX Corp. (NYSE) (newspaper)
AVY: Avery International Corp. (NYSE)
A&W: Ahnapee and Western (railroad)
Air Niger (airline)
Atlantic and Western (railroad)

AW: Actual Weight
Arkansas Western (railroad)
AWA: Aluminum Window Association
AWAR: Area Weighted Average Resolution
AWB: Air Way Bill
AWED: American Woman's Economic Development Corporation
AWES: Association of Western Europe Shipbuilders
AWF: Acceptable Work-Load Factor
AWI: American Watchmakers Institute
AWIU: Allied Workers International Union
AWK: American Water Works Company Inc. (NYSE)
AWL: Absent With Leave
AWOL: Absent Without Leave
A&WP: Atlanta and West Point (railroad)
AWPA: American Wood Preservers Association
AWPI: American Wood Preservers Institute
AWS: Alba-Waldensian Inc. (ASE)
American Welding Society
AWT: Actual Work Time
AWU: Aluminum Workers Union
AWW: Algers, Winslow and Western (railway)
AWWA: American Water Works Association
AWWU: American Watch Workers Union
awy: airway
AX: Air Togo (airline)
AXO: Alamco Inc. (ASE)
AXP: American Express Co. (NYSE)
AXR: AMREP Corp. (NYSE)
A&Y: Atlantic and Yadkin (railroad)
AY: Allegheny and Western (railway)
Annual Yield
Finnair (airline)
AYD: Aydin Corp. (NYSE)
Aydin: Aydin Corp. (newspaper)
AYP: Allegheny Power System Inc. (NYSE)
AYSS: Allegheny and South Side (railroad)
AZ: Alitalia (Linee Aeree Italiane)
Atlas Corp. (NYSE)
AZA: ALZA Corp. (ASE)
AZAS: Adjustable Zero Adjustable Span
AZB: Arizona Commerce Bank (ASE)
AZE: American Maize-Products Co. (ASE)
AZL: Arizona Land Income Corp. (ASE)

B

b: base
batch
bel
bid
binary
bit
block
boolean
bus
byte

B: Barnes Group Inc. (NYSE)
Base (money)

B&A: Baltimore and Annapolis (railroad)
Bangor and Aroostook (railroad)
Bid and Asked
Boston and Albany (railroad)

B/A: Billed At

BA: Bank Acceptance
Boeing Co., The (NYSE)
British Airways (airline)
Budget Authority
Business Agent (union)

BAA: British Association of Accountants and Auditors

BAB: British Airways Board (UK)
British Airways Plc. (NYSE)

BAC: BankAmerica Corp. (NYSE)
Bendix Aviation Company
Boeing Airplane Company

back: backwardation

BACM: British American Construction and Materials, Limited (UK)

BACS: Bankers Automated Clearing Services

BACT: Best Available Control Technology

Badger: Badger Meter Inc. (newspaper)

BAE: Bureau of Agricultural Economics

BA&F: Budget, Accounting, and Finance

BAF: Belgian African Line (steamship)

BAFA: British Accounting and Finance Association (UK)

BAI: Bank Administration Institute

Bairnco: Bairnco Corp. (newspaper)

BAK: backup

Baker: Michael Baker Corp. (newspaper)

BakrHu: Baker Hughes Inc. (newspaper)

bal: balance

BAL: Baldwin Securities Corp. (ASE)
Basic Assembly Language
Belgian African Line
Bonanza Airlines

Baldor: Baldor Electric Co. (newspaper)

BaldsS: Baldwin Securities Corp. (newspaper)

Baldwin: Baldwin Technology Company Inc. (newspaper)

Ball: Ball Corp. (newspaper)

BallyMf: Bally Manufacturing Corp. (newspaper)

BALM: Block And List Manipulator

BALPA: Balance of Payments

BaltBcp: Baltimore Bancorp (Maryland) (newspaper)

BaltGE: Baltimore Gas & Electric Co. (newspaper)

BALUN: Balanced to Unbalanced

BAM: Basic Access Method

BambP: Bamberger Polymers Inc. (newspaper)
BAMP: Basic Analysis and Mapping Program
BAN: Banister Continental Ltd. (ASE)
Bandag: Bandag Inc. (newspaper)
BanFd: Bancroft Convertible Fund Inc. (newspaper)
BANK: International Bank for Reconstruction and Development
Bank Clgs: Bank Clearings
BankTr: Bankers Trust New York Corp. (newspaper)
Banner: Banner Industries Inc. (newspaper)
BANs: Bond Anticipation Notes
Banstr: Banister Continental Ltd. (newspaper)
BANTSA: Bank of American National Trust and Savings Association
BanTx: BancTEXAS Group Inc. (newspaper)
BA&P: Butte, Anaconda & Pacific (railroad)
BAP: Basic Assembly Program
Biotechnology Action Program
BAPCO: Bahrain Petroleum Company
BAPTA: Bearing and Power Transfer Assembly
BAR: Bangor and Aroostook Railroad
Barry Wright Corp. (NYSE)
Base Address Register
Broadcast Advertisers Reports
BARC: Baltimore and Annapolis Railroad Company
Barclay: Barclays PLC (newspaper)
Bard: C.R. Bard Inc. (newspaper)
Barister: Barrister Information Systems Corp. (newspaper)
Barnet: Barnett Banks of Florida Inc. (newspaper)
BarnGP: Barnes Group Inc. (newspaper)
Barnwl: Barnwell Industries Inc. (newspaper)
BARON: Business/Accounts Reporting Operating Network
B&ARR: Boston and Albany Railroad
BarrLb: Barr Laboratories Inc. (newspaper)
BARS: Bell Audit Relate System (Telephone Laboratories)
BART: Bay Area Rapid Transit (San Francisco)
BARTD: Bay Area Rapid Transit District (San Francisco)
Baruch: Baruch-Foster Corp. (newspaper)
BaryWr: Barry Wright Corp. (newspaper)
BAS: BASIX Corp. (NYSE)
Bell Audit System (Telephone Laboratories)
Block Automation System
BASC: Booth American Shipping Corporation
BASE: BankAmericard Service Exchange
Brokerage Accounting System Elements
Business Assessment Study and Evaluation
BASIC: Banking And Securities Industry Committee
Beginner's All-Purpose Symbolic Instruction Code
BASIS: Bank Automated Service Information System
BASIX: BASIX Corp. (newspaper)
BASRM: Basic Analog Simulation System
BASYC: Benefit Assessment for System Change
bat: batch

BAT: B.A.T. Industries PLC (newspaper)
Best Available Technology
Bureau of Apprenticeship and Training

BATEA: Best Available Technology Economically Achievable

BatlMt: Battle Mountain Gold Co. (newspaper)

BAU: British Association Unit

Bausch: Bausch & Lomb Inc. (newspaper)

BAW: Blue Arrow PLC (NYSE)

BAX: Baxter International Inc. (NYSE)

Baxter: Baxter International Inc. (newspaper)

BAY: Bay Financial Corp. (NYSE)

BayFin: Bay Financial Corp. (newspaper)

Bayou: Bayou Steel Corporation of La Place (newspaper)

BayStG: Bay State Gas Co. (newspaper)

BB: Baby Bond
Bail Bond
Bank Building & Equipment Corporation of America (ASE)
Bearer Bond
Big Board
Birmingham Belt (railroad)
Break Bulk
Bureau of the Budget
Buy Back

BBA: Bachelor of Business Administration

BBAC: Bus-to-Bus Access Circuit

BBB: Baltimore Bancorp (Maryland) (NYSE)
Banker's Blanket Bond
Better Business Bureau
Quality rating for a municipal or corporate bond

BBC: Bergen Brunswig Corp. (ASE)
British Broadcasting Corporation (UK)

BBE: Belden & Blake Energy Co. (ASE)

BBF: Barnett Banks of Florida Inc. (NYSE)

bbl: barrel

BBN: Bolt Beranek & Newman Inc. (NYSE)

BBR: B-B Real Estate Investment Corp. (ASE)

BB REI: B-B Real Estate Investment Corp. (newspaper)

BBS: Bachelor of Business Science

BBY: Best Buy Company Inc. (NYSE)

B&C: Barre and Chelsea (railroad)
Bennettsville and Cheraw (railroad)

BC: Bachelor of Commerce
Bad Check
Before Christ
Bellefonte Central (railroad)
Bills for Collection
Binary Code
Blue Chip
Bogus Check
Brunswick Corp. (NYSE)

BCA: British Caledonian Airways
British Colonial Airlines

BCC: Block-Check Character
Boise Cascade Corp. (NYSE)

BCD: Binary-Coded Decimal
Business Cycle Development

BCE: BCE Inc. (NYSE) (newspaper)

BCDIC: Extended Binary Coded Decimal Interchange Code

BCE: Before Common Era

BCelts: Boston Celtics LP (newspaper)

BCF: British Columbia Ferries
Bureau of Commercial Fisheries
Burlington Coat Factory Warehouse Corp. (NYSE)

BCH: Bids per Circuit per Hour
Block Control Header

British Columbia Hydro and Power Authority
BCIA: Bounded Carry Inspection Adder
BCK: Bas-Congo au Katanga (French-Lower Congo-Katanga) (Railways of Zaire)
Buffalo Creek (railroad)
BCL: Base-Coupled Logic
Biocraft Laboratories Inc. (NYSE)
Bristol City Line (steamship)
BCM: Banco Central S.A. (NYSE)
Beyond Capability of Maintenance
Budget Correcting Mechanism
BCO: Binary Coded Octal
Blessings Corp. (ASE)
BCP: Borden Chemicals & Plastics LP (NYSE)
Budget Change Proposal
Byte Control Protocol
BCPA: British Commonwealth Pacific Airlines
BCR: Bureau Communautaire de Reference (EC)
C.R. Bard Inc. (NYSE)
BCRR: Boyne City Railroad
BCS: Bachelor Commercial Science
Barclays PLC (NYSE)
BCSC: British and Continental Steamship Company (UK)
BCU: Block Control Unit
BCUA: Business Computers Users Association
BCV: Bancroft Convertible Fund Inc. (ASE)
BCW: Bakery and Confectionery Workers (union)
BCYR: British Columbia Yukon Railway
bd: board
bond
B&D: Black & Decker
B/D: Broker-Dealer
BD: Bad Delivery
Bank Dividends
Bank Draft
Bills Discounted
Bloedel-Donovan (railroad)
British Midland Airways (airline)
BDAM: Basic Direct Access Method
BDC: Binary-Differential Computer
BDEAC: Bank for Development of Central African States
BDF: Backwards Differentiation Formulas
BD FT: Board Foot
BDG: Bandag Inc. (NYSE)
BDK: Black & Decker Corp., The (NYSE)
bdl: bundle
BDL: Building Description Language
BDM: BDM International Inc. (ASE) (newspaper)
BDO: Bottom Dropped Out
BDP: Business Data Processing
BDR: Bearer Depositary Receipt
Bd Rts: Bond Rights
bdry: boundary
BDS: Bergenske Dampskibsselskab (Norwegian-Bergen Steamship Line)
Building Design Systems
BDSC: Black Diamond Steamship Corporation
BDX: Becton Dickinson & Co. (NYSE)
BDZ: Bulgarian State Railways (Cyrillic transliteration)
B&E: Baltimore and Eastern (railroad)
B/E: Bill of Exchange
BE: Baltimore and Eastern (railroad)
Bank of England (UK)
Benguet Corp. (NYSE)
Bill of Entry
Bill of Exchange
British European Airways (airline)

B of E: Bank of England (UK)
BEA: British European Airways
Bureau of Economic Analysis
BEAC: Bank of Central African States
BEAIRA: British Electrical and Allied Industries Research Association (UK)
BEAM: Bidders Early Alert Message
BEAMS: Base Engineer Automated Management System
Beard: Beard Co., The (newspaper)
Bearing: Bearings Inc. (newspaper)
BearSt: The Bear Stearns Companies Inc. (newspaper)
BEAST: Brookings (Institute) Economics and Statistical Translator
BEB: British Export Board (UK)
BEC: Beard Co., The (ASE)
Board for Engineering Cooperation
Bureau of Employees' Compensation
Bureau Européen du Café (European Coffee Bureau) (French)
BECO: Boston Edison Company
BectDk: Becton, Dickinson & Co. (newspaper)
BEDT: Brooklyn Eastern District Terminal (railroad)
BEE: Business Efficiency Exhibition
BEEC: Binary Error-Erasure Channel
BEEF: Beef Energy and Economic Evaluator for Farms
BEEM: Beech Mountain (railroad)
BEEP: Bureau Européen de l'Education Populaire (European Bureau of Adult Education) (French)
BEI: Banque Européene d'Investissement (European Investment Bank) (French)
Beker: Beker Industries Corp. (newspaper)
BEL: Bell Atlantic Corp. (NYSE)
Bell Character
BeldBlk: Belden & Blake Energy Co. (newspaper)
BELF: Break-Even Load Factor
Bel Fcs: Belgian Francs
BelIn: Bell Industries Inc. (newspaper)
Bell: Bell System (American Telephone and Telegraph)
BellAtl: Bell Atlantic Corp. (newspaper)
BellSo: BellSouth Corp. (newspaper)
BeloAH: A.H. Belco Corp. (newspaper)
Belvdre: Belvedere Corp. (newspaper)
BEM: Beaufort and Morehead (railroad)
BEMA: Business Equipment Manufacturers' Association
BEMAC: British Export Marketing Advisory Committee (UK)
Bemis: Bemis Company Inc. (newspaper)
BEN: Franklin Resources Inc. (NYSE)
benef: beneficiary
BENELUX: Belgium, the Netherlands and Luxembourg
BenfCp: Beneficial Corp. (newspaper)
BengtB: Benguet Corp. (newspaper)
BEP: BET Public Limited Co. (NYSE)
Biomolecular Engineering Program
BER: Bearings Inc. (NYSE)
Bit Error Rate
BERD: European Bank for Reconstruction and Development

BergBr: Bergen Brunswig Corp. (newspaper)
Berkey: Berkey Inc. (newspaper)
BermSt: Bermuda Star Lines Inc. (newspaper)
BES: Best Products Company Inc. (NYSE)
Bureau of Employment Security
BEST: Basic Executive Scheduler and Timekeeper
Business EDP System Technique
BestBy: Best Buy Company Inc. (newspaper)
BestPd: Best Products Company Inc. (newspaper)
BET: Bethlehem Corp., The (ASE)
BET Public Limited Co. (newspaper)
BETA: Business Equipment Trade Association
BethCo: Bethlehem Corp., The (newspaper)
BethStl: Bethlehem Steel Corp. (newspaper)
BEUC: Bureau Européen des Union de Consommateurs (European Bureau of Consumer's Unions) (French)
BEV: Beverly Enterprises Inc. (NYSE)
BevIP: Beverly Investment Properties Inc. (newspaper)
Bevrly: Beverly Enterprises Inc. (newspaper)
BEX: Broadband Exchange
BEXEC: Budget Execution
BEZ: Baldor Electric Co. (NYSE)
BF: Bachelor of Finance
Backdoor Financing
Banque de France (Bank of France)
Belgian franc
Blocking Factor
Brought Forward
BFAP: Binary Fault Analysis Program
BFC: BankAtlantic Financial Corp. (ASE)
Bellefonte Central (railroad)
Bureau of Foreign Commerce
BFCE: Banque Française du Commerce Extérieure
BFCU: Bureau of Federal Credit Union
bfcy: beneficiary
BFD: Brown-Forman Corp. (ASE)
BFDC: Bureau of Foreign and Domestic Commerce
BFI: Browning-Ferris Industries Inc. (NYSE)
BFIC: Binary Fault Isolation Chart
BFL: Belgian Fruit Lines (steamship)
BFN: Beam-Forming Network
BFO: Baruch-Foster Corp. (ASE)
Beat Frequency Oscillator
BFOQ: Bona Fide Occupational Qualification
BFORM: Budget Formulation
BFP: Bona Fide Purchaser
BFPDDA: Binary Floating Point Digital Differential Analyzer
BFPR: Binary Floating Point Resistor
BFPV: Bona Fide Purchaser for Value
BFS: B.F. Saul Real Estate Investment Trust (NYSE)
BFT: Bachelor of Foreign Trade
Bulk Function Transfer
BFX: Buffton Corp. (ASE)
bg: background
BG: Brown Group Inc. (NYSE)
Guyana Airways (airline)
BGA: Business Graduates Association
BGC: Bay State Gas Co. (NYSE)
BG&E: Baltimore Gas and Electric

BGE: Baltimore Gas & Electric Co. (NYSE)
BGG: Briggs & Stratton Corp. (NYSE)
bgt: bought
B&H: B&H Ocean Carriers Ltd. (newspaper)
Bell & Howell Corporation
BH: Bahamas Airways (airline)
Bank Holiday
Bath and Hammondsport (railroad)
BHA: Biscayne Holdings Inc. (ASE)
BHC: Brock Hotel Corp. (NYSE)
BHI: Baker Hughes Inc. (NYSE)
BHL: Bunker Hill Income Securities Inc. (NYSE)
BHO: B&H Ocean Carriers Ltd. (ASE)
BHP: Broken Hill Proprietary, The (steamship)
Broken Hill Proprietary Company Ltd., The (NYSE) (newspaper)
B&HS: Bonhomie & Hattiesburg Southern (railroad)
BHY: Belding Heminway Company Inc. (NYSE)
B&I: Bankruptcy and Insolvency
Base and Increment
BI: Bell Industries Inc. (NYSE)
Bodily Injury (insurance)
Braniff International (airline)
BIA: Brazilian International Airlines
British Insurance Association (UK)
BIAC: Business and Industry Advisory Committee
B&IB: Billing and Instruction Book
BIB: Balanced Incomplete Block
BIBA: British Insurance Brokers Association (UK)
BIBO: Bounded-Input Bounded-Output
BIBOR: Bahrain Inter-Bank Offered Rate
BIC: BIC Corp. (ASE)
Bureau of International Commerce
BicCp: BIC Corp. (newspaper)
BICEPS: Basic Industrial Control Engineering Programming System
BICSI: Building Industry Consulting Service International
BID: Bid for (NYSE)
Sotheby's Holdings Inc. (ASE)
BIE: Boundary-Integral Equation
Britain In Europe (UK)
BIF: Bank Insurance Fund
BIFFEX: Baltic International Freight Futures Exchange
BIG: Bond International Gold Inc. (NYSE)
BILBO: Built-In Logic Block Observer
BIM: British Institute of Management (UK)
ICN Biomedicals Inc. (ASE)
BIMA: British Industrial Marketing Association
bin: binary
BIN: Bank Identification Number
Binks Manufacturing Co. (ASE)
BINGO: Business International Non-Governmental Organization
BinkMF: Binks Manufacturing Co. (newspaper)
BIO: Bio-Rad Laboratories Inc. (ASE)
Biocft: Biocraft Laboratories Inc. (newspaper)
Biophm: Biopharmaceuticals Inc. (newspaper)
BioR: Bio-Rad Laboratories Inc. (newspaper)
BIOR: Business Input-Output Rerun

BIOS: Basic Input-Output System
Biother: Biotherapeutics Inc. (newspaper)
BIP: Beverly Investment Properties Inc. (NYSE)
Binary Image Processor
BIR: Birmingham Steel Corp. (NYSE)
Bureau of Internal Revenue
BirmStl: Birmingham Steel Corp. (newspaper)
BIRS: Basic Indexing and Retrieval System
BIS: Bank for International Settlements
Barrister Information Systems Corp. (ASE)
Bureau of Information Science
Business Information System
BISAD: Business Information Systems Analysis and Design
BISAM: Basic Indexed Sequential Access Method
BiscH: Biscayne Holdings Inc. (newspaper)
BISNC: British India Steam Navigation Company
B&I SPC: British and Irish Steam Packet Company
BISYNC: Binary Synchronous Communication Protocol
BIT: Bachelor of Industrial Technology
Binary Digit
Built-In-Test
biz: business
BIZAD: Business Administration
BIZMAC: Business Machine Computer
BJ: Bakhtar Afghan Airlines
B of J: Bank of Japan
bk: bank
BK: Bank of New York Company Inc., The (NYSE)
BKS Air Transport (airline)
BkatlFn: BankAtlantic Financial Corp. (newspaper)
BKB: Bank of Boston Corp. (NYSE)
BkBost: Bank of Boston Corp. (newspaper)
BKC: American Bank of Connecticut (ASE)
bkcy: bankruptcy
bkg: banking
bookkeeping
bkgrd: background
BKH: Black Hills Corp. (NYSE)
BKI: Beker Industries Corp. (NYSE)
BKInv: Burger King Investors Master LP (newspaper)
BklyUG: Brooklyn Union Gas Co., The (newspaper)
BkNE: Bank of New England Corp. (newspaper)
BkNY: Bank of New York Company Inc., The (newspaper)
BKP: Burger King Investors Master LP (NYSE)
bkpg: bookkeeping
bkpr: bookkeeper
bkpt: bankrupt
bkr: broker
BKR: Michael Baker Corp. (ASE)
bks: books
BkSFr: Bank of San Francisco Holding Co. (newspaper)
BKT: Blackstone Income Trust Inc. (NYSE)
Bk Town: Banking Town
BKY: Berkey Inc. (NYSE)
B & L: Bausch & Lomb
Building and Loan (association or bank)
Burns and Laird Line (steamship)
B/L: Basic Letter
Bill of Lading
BL: Bank Larceny
Bergen Line (steamship)
Bibby Line (steamship)
Bill of Lading
Booth Line (steamship)
Brothers Air Service (airline)

BLA: Baltimore and Annapolis (railroad)
British Land of America Inc. (NYSE)

BlackD: Black & Decker Corp., The (newspaper)

B/L Atchd: Bill of Lading Attached

BLC: A.H. Belo Corp. (NYSE)

BLD: Baldwin Technology Company Inc. (ASE)

B&LE: Bessemer and Lake Erie (railroad)

BLE: Brotherhood of Locomotive Engineers (union)

Blessg: Blessings Corp. (newspaper)

BLEU: Belgo-Luxembourg Economic Union

BLF&E: Brotherhood of Locomotive Firemen and Enginemen (union)

BLI: Businessland Inc. (NYSE)

BLIC: Bureau de Liaison des Industries du Caoutchouc de la CE. (Rubber Industries Liaison Bureau of the European Community) (French) (EC)

BLISS: Basic List-Oriented Information Structures System

blk: block

BlkHC: Black Hills Corp. (newspaper)

BlkHR: H & R Block Inc. (newspaper)

Blkstn: Blackstone Income Trust Inc. (newspaper)

BLL: Ball Corp. (NYSE)
Below Lower Limit

BLM: Basic Language Machine
British Leland Motor
Bureau of Land Management

Blount: Blount Inc. (newspaper)

BLR: Bolar Pharmaceutical Company Inc. (ASE)

BlrPh: Bolar Pharmaceutical Company Inc. (newspaper)

bls: bales

BLS: BellSouth Corp. (NYSE)
Ben Line Steamers
Bureau of Labor Statistics

BLT: Blount Inc. (ASE)

BLU: Blue Chip Value Fund Inc. (NYSE)

BluChp: Blue Chip Value Fund Inc. (newspaper)

BLUE: Best Linear Unbiased Estimate

BlueAr: Blue Arrow PLC (newspaper)

BLV: Belvedere Corp. (ASE)

BLY: Bally Manufacturing Corp. (NYSE)

B&M: Boston and Maine (railroad)

BM: Aero Transporti Italiana (Italian Airline)
Banco de Mexico (Bank of Mexico)
Bear Market
Beaver, Meade and Englewood (railroad)
Bench Mark
Bill of Material
Board Measure
Boston and Maine (railroad)
British Methane Limited (steamship)
Bureau of Mines
Bureau of the Mint
Business Machine
Buyer's Market

B of M: Bank of Montreal
Bureau of Mines

BMC: BMC Industries Inc. (NYSE) (newspaper)
Bulk Mail Center

BMD: A. L. Laboratories Inc. (ASE)

BM&E: Beaver, Meade and Englewood (railroad)

BME: Bachelor of Mechanical Engineering
Bachelor of Mining Engineering

BMG: Battle Mountain Gold Co. (NYSE)

BMI: Badger Meter Inc. (ASE)
Book Manufacturers Institute
B&ML: Belfast & Moosehead Lake (railroad)
BML: Basic Machine Language
BMM: Belfast, Mersey and Manchester (steamship)
BMOM: Base Maintenance and Operational Model
BMP: Burnham American Properties Inc. (ASE)
BMPR: Bimonthly Progress Report
B&MRR: Beaufort and Morehead Railroad
BMRR: Beech Mountain Railroad
BMS: Bemis Company Inc. (NYSE)
BMT: Brooklyn-Manhattan Transit
BMW: Bayerische Motoren Werke (Bavarian Motor Works)
BMWE: Brother of Maintenance of Way Employees
BMY: Bristol-Myers Squibb Co. (NYSE)
B&N: Bauxite and Northern (railway)
BN: Bank Note
Borden Inc. (NYSE)
British United Airways
Brussels Nomenclature
Burlington Northern (railroad)
BNA: Bureau of National Affairs
BNC: Regional Financial Shares Investment Fund Inc. (NYSE)
BncCtr: Banco Central S.A. (newspaper)
BncOne: Banc One Corp. (newspaper)
BNDD: Bureau of Narcotics and Dangerous Drugs
BNE: Bowne & Company Inc. (ASE)
BNF: Backus Naur form
Backus Normal form
Braniff International Airways
BNI: Burlington Northern Inc. (NYSE)
BnkAm: BankAmerica Corp. (newspaper)
BnkBld: Bank Building & Equipment Corporation of America (newspaper)
BNL: Beneficial Corp. (NYSE)
BNO: Barrels of New Oil
BNP: Banque National de Paris (France)
Boddie-Noell Restaurant Properties Inc. (ASE)
BNR: Banner Industries Inc. (NYSE)
BNS: Brown & Sharpe Manufacturing Co. (NYSE)
BnSant: Banco Santander
BNT: Buffalo Niagara Transit
BNY: Bundy Corp. (NYSE)
BNZ: Bank of New Zealand
bo: bonding
B&O: Baltimore and Ohio (railroad)
BO: Back Order
Bad Order
Branch Office
Broker's Order
Buyer's Option
Buy Order
BOA: Basic Ordering Agreement
BOAC: British Overseas Airways Corporation (airline)
BOB: Bureau of the Budget
BOC: Back Office Crunch
Block-Oriented Computer
Breach of Contract
Burmah Oil Company
BOCI: Business Organization Climate Index
B&O - C&O: Baltimore and Ohio-Chesapeake and Ohio (railroad)
BOD: Board Of Directors
Boddie: Boddie-Noell Restaurant Properties Inc. (newspaper)
BOE: Bank Of England (UK)
Barrels of Oil Equivalent

Boeing: Boeing Co., The (newspaper)
BOF: Bank of San Francisco Holding Co. (ASE)
BOFADS: Business Office Forms Administration Data System
BOG: Board of Governors
BoiseC: Boise Cascade Corp. (newspaper)
BOL: Bausch & Lomb Inc. (NYSE)
BoltBr: Bolt Beranek & Newman Inc. (newspaper)
BOM: Beginning Of the Month
Bowmar Instrument Corp. (ASE)
Bureau Of Mines
Buying On Margin
BOMA: Building Owners and Managers Association
BOMP: Bill Of Material Processor
BOMS: Base Operations Maintenance Simulator
Bond: Bond International Gold Inc. (newspaper)
Bool: Boolean
boot: bootstrap
BOP: Balance Of Payments
Bit-Oriented Protocol
BOR: Bureau of Operating Rights
BordC: Borden Chemicals & Plastics LP (newspaper)
Borden: Borden Inc. (newspaper)
Bormns: Borman's Inc. (newspaper)
BOS: Boston Celtics LP (NYSE)
British Oil Shipping
BOSS: Business-Oriented Software System
BostEd: Boston Edison Co. (newspaper)
bot: bought
BOT: Beginning Of Tape
Board Of Trade
Board Of Trustees
BOTB: British Overseas Trade Board (UK)
BOW: Bowater Inc. (NYSE)
Bowatr: Bowater Inc. (newspaper)
BowlA: Bowl America Inc. (newspaper)
Bowmr: Bowmar Instrument Corp. (newspaper)
Bowne: Bowne & Company Inc. (newspaper)
BowVal: Bow Valley Industries Ltd. (newspaper)
BOYC: Boyne City (railroad)
BP: Batch Processing
Bills Payable
Book Profit
Botswana Airways (airline)
Breach of Promise
British Petroleum Company PLC, The (NYSE)
Burden of Proof
BPAM: Basic Partitioned Access Method
B Pay: Bills(s) Payable
BPBD: Bill Posters, Billers and Distributors (union)
BPC: British Phosphate Commissioners (UK)
BPCI: Bulk Packaging and Containerization Institute
BP&CO: Burns, Philip and Company (steamship)
BPD: Barrels per Day
BPDP: Brotherhood of Painters, Decorators, and Paperhangers (union)
BPH: Biopharmaceuticals Inc. (ASE)
BPI: Bamberger Polymers Inc. (ASE)
Bits Per Inch
Bytes Per Inch
BPL: Buckeye Partners LP (NYSE)
Business Planning Language
BPM: Batch Processing Monitor
BPP: Burnham Pacific Properties Inc. (ASE)

BPR: Bureau of Public Roads
By-Pass Ratio

BPS: Binary Program Space
Bits Per Second
Bureau of Product Safety
Bytes Per Second

BQ: Basic Quote

BQC: Qantel Corp. (NYSE)

BQR: Quick & Reilly Group Inc., The (NYSE)

br: branch
break

B/R: Bills Receivable

BR: Bank Rate
Base Register
Bills Receivable
Blue Ridge (railroad)
Bond Rating
British Rail (railways)
British United Airways (airline)
Builder's Risk
Burlington Resources Inc. (NYSE)
Burma Railways

BRA: Bankruptcy Reform Act

BRAC: Brotherhood of Railway and Airline Clerks

Brazil: Brazil Fund Inc. (newspaper)

BRB: British Railways Board (UK)

BRBMA: Ball and Roller Bearing Manufacturers Association

BRC: Belt Railway of Chicago
Business Reply Card

BRCA: Brotherhood of Railway Carmen of America

BRD: Basic Retirement Date
Brad Ragan Inc. (ASE)
Bureau of Research and Development

BRE: BRE Properties Inc. (NYSE) (newspaper)

BREC: Bills Receivable

BRF: Borman's Inc. (NYSE)

BRG: British Gas PLC (NYSE)

BRI: Burlington-Rock Island (railroad)

BRIDGE: Biotechnology Research for Innovation, Development and Growth in Europe (EC)

BrigSt: Briggs & Stratton Corp. (newspaper)

BristG: Bristol Gaming Corp. (newspaper)

BrisMyrSqb: Bristol-Myers Squibb Co. (newspaper)

BritAir: British Airways PLC (newspaper)

BRITE: Basic Research in Industrial Technologies for Europe (EC)

BritGas: British Gas PLC (newspaper)

BritLnd: British Land of America Inc. (newspaper)

BritPt: British Petroleum Company PLC, The (newspaper)

BritTel: British Telecommunications PLC (newspaper)

BRL: Barr Laboratories Inc. (ASE)

BrlNth: Burlington Northern Inc. (newspaper)

BrlRsc: Burlington Resources Inc. (newspaper)

BRM: Binary Rate Multiplier

BRMC: Business Research Management Center

BRN: Barnwell Industries Inc. (ASE)

BrnFA: Brown-Forman Corp. (newspaper)

Brnwk: Brunswick Corp. (newspaper)

Brock: Brock Hotel Corp. (newspaper)

brok: broker
brokerage

BROKERSGUIDE: Inventory of information brokers (EC)

BRS: Brascan Ltd. (ASE)
BR&SC: Brotherhood of Railway and Steamship Clerks (union)
Brscn: Brascan Ltd. (newspaper)
BrshWl: Brush Wellman Inc. (newspaper)
BR&T: Bowdon Railway and Transportation
BRT: Brotherhood of Railroad Trainmen (union)
BRT Realty Trust (NYSE) (newspaper)
Brt Fwd: Brought Forward
BRU: Basic Resolution Unit
BRUCE: Buffer Register Under Computer Edit
BR&W: Black River and Western (railroad)
BrwnF: Browning-Ferris Industries Inc. (newspaper)
BrwnGp: Brown Group Inc. (newspaper)
BRX: Biotherapeutics Inc. (ASE)
B&S: Bevier and Southern (railroad)
BS: Backspace Character
Back Spread
Balance Sheet
Bellweather Stock
Bethlehem Steel Corp. (NYSE)
Bill of Sale
Birmingham Southern (railroad)
Bits per Second
Block Sale
British Standard
Bureau of Ships
Bureau of Standards
Butterfly Spread
BSA: Bearing Specialists Association
Building Societies Association
BSAM: Basic Sequential Access Method
BSBA: Bachelor of Science in Business Administration
BSC: Bachelor of Science in Commerce
Baltic Steamship Company
Bear Stearns Companies Inc., The (NYSE)
Binary Synchronous Communication
BSCA: Binary Synchronous Communication Adapter
BSCP: Brotherhood of Sleeping Car Porters (union)
BSCS: Binary Synchronous Communication System
BSD: BSD Bancorp Inc. (ASE) (newspaper)
B&SE: Birmingham & Southeastern (railroad)
BSE: Boston Edison Co. (NYSE)
Boston Stock Exchange
BSEE: Bachelor of Science in Electrical Engineering
BSEM: Bachelor of Science in Engineering of Mines
BSEP: Bachelor of Science in Engineering Physics
BSES: Bachelor of Science in Engineering Sciences
BSH: Bush Industries Inc. (ASE)
BSI: British Standards Institution (UK)
BSIA: British Security Industry Association (UK)
BSIE: Bachelor of Science in Industrial Engineering
BSIR: Bachelor of Science in Industrial Relations
BSIT: Bachelor of Science in Industrial Technology
BS/L: Bills of Lading
BSL: Barber Steamship Lines
Bermuda Star Lines Inc. (ASE)
Bills of Lading
Black Star Line (steamship)

Blue Sea Line (steamship)
Blue Star Line (steamship)
Bull Steamship Lines

BS LAB REL: Bachelor of Science in Labor Relations

BSME: Bachelor of Science in Mechanical Engineering
Bachelor of Science in Mining Engineering

BSN: BSN Corp. (ASE) (newspaper)

BSNC: Bristol Steam Navigation Company (steamship)

BSO: Broad System of Ordering
Business Statistics Office

BSOIW: Bridge, Structural and Ornamental Iron Workers

BSPA: Bachelor of Science in Public Administration

BSQI: Basic Schedule of Quantified Items

BSS: Bachelor of Secretarial Science

BSSA: Bachelor of Science in Secretarial Administration

BSSS: Bachelor of Science in Secretarial Studies

BST: Bulk Supply Tariff

BST&IE: Bachelor of Science in Trade and Industrial Education

Bt: bought

BT: Bankers Trust New York Corp. (NYSE)

B of T: Board of Trade

BTA: Boston Transportation Authority

BTAM: Basic Telecommunications Access Method

BTC: Baltimore Transit Company
Bankers Trust Company
Bethlehem Transportation Corporation (steamship)

BTE: Business Terminal Equipment

BTG: Beating The Gun

BTI: B.A.T. Industries PLC (ASE)

BTL: Bell Telephone Laboratories

BTM: Bulling The Market

BTMA: Busy Tone Multiple-Access

BTN: Belton (railroad)
Brussels Tariff Nomenclature (EC)

BTR: Behind the Tape Reader

BTS: Batch Terminal Simulation

BTSS: Basic Time Sharing System

BTU: British Thermal Unit
Pyro Energy Corp. (NYSE)

BTX: BancTEXAS Group Inc. (NYSE)

BTY: British Telecommunications PLC (NYSE)

BU: Base Unit
Braathens Air Transport (airline)
Brooklyn Union Gas Co., The (NYSE)

BUA: British United Airways (airline)

BUC: Buffalo, Union-Carolina (railroad)

Buckeye: Buckeye Partners LP (newspaper)

BUD: Anheuser-Busch Companies Inc. (NYSE)

BUDS: Building Utility Design System

BUE: Buell Industries Inc. (ASE)
Built-Up-Edge

Buell: Buell Industries Inc. (newspaper)

buf: buffer

Buffton: Buffton Corp. (newspaper)

BUG: Basic Update Generator

BUIC: Back-Up Interceptor Control

bull: bulletin

BUMINES: Bureau of the Mines

Bundy: Bundy Corp. (newspaper)

BunkrH: Bunker Hill Income Securities Inc. (newspaper)

bur: bureau

BUREC: Bureau of Reclamation

BurnAM: Burnham American Properties Inc. (newspaper)

BurnPP: Burnham Pacific Properties Inc. (newspaper)

bus: business
Bush: Bush Industries Inc. (newspaper)
BUSH: Bush Terminal (railroad)
Businld: Businessland Inc. (newspaper)
BV: BEA Helicopters (airline)
Book Value
BVG: Berliner Verkehr Betriebe (German-Berlin Traffic Management)
BVI: Bow Valley Industries Ltd. (ASE)
BVS: Bevier & Southern (railroad)
B&W: Babcock and Wilcox
Brocklebank and Well Lines (steamship)
BW: Bendix-Westinghouse
Bid Wanted
Borg-Warner
British West Indian (airlines)
Brush Wellman Inc. (NYSE)
BWC: Pennsylvania New York Central Transportation Company
BWD: Basic Work Data
BWIA: British West Indies Airways
BWL: Bowl America Inc. (ASE)
BWM: Broom and Whisk Makers (union)
BwnSh: Brown & Sharpe Manufacturing Co. (newspaper)
BX: Base Exchange
Bellingham-Seattle (airline)
bypro(s): by-product(s)
BYR: British Yukon Railway
BZ: Air Congo (Brazzaville, Congo Republic) (airline)
Bairnco Corp. (NYSE)
BZF: Brazil Fund Inc. (NYSE)

c: capacitor
carat
carry
cash
cent
centi
chairman
clear
clock
computer
constant
control
controller
counter

C: Chrysler Corp. (NYSE)
Currency component of money
A liquidating dividend in stock listings of newspapers
The lowest quality rating for a municipal or corporate bond
A low-level general purpose programming language associated with the UNIX operating system

ca: callable (in bond tables and offering sheets)

C&A: Classification and Audit

CA: Capital Account
Capital Appreciation
Capital Assets
Carregadores Acoreanos (Portuguese-Azorean Cargo Carriers)
Cash Account
Cause of Action
Chartered Accountant (UK)
Chief Accountant
Claim Agent
Commercial Agent
Computer Associates International Inc. (NYSE)
Connecting Arrangement
Consumers Association
Control Area
Credit Account
Current Account
Current Assets
Custodian Account

CAA: Central African Airways Corporation
Civil Aeronautics Administration

CAAA: Commuter Airline Association of America

CAAD: Computer-Aided Architectural Design

CAAIS: Computer-Assisted Action Information System

CAAS: Computer-Aided Approach Sequencing

CAB: CasaBlanca Industries Inc. (ASE)
Citizens Advice Bureau
Civil Aeronautics Board
Consumers' Advisory Board

CABA: Charge Account Bankers Association

CABD: Computer-Aided Building Design

CABEI: Central American Bank for Economic Integration

Cablvsn: Cablevision Systems Corp. (newspaper)

CABMA: Canadian Association of British Manufacturers and Agencies

CABO: Council of American Building Officials

CABS: Computer-Aided Batch Scheduling
Computer-Augmented Block System

CAC: CoastAmerica Corp. (NYSE)
Computer Acceleration Control
Consumer Advisory Council

CACA: Computer-Aided Circuit Analysis

CACD: Computer-Aided Circuit Design

CACHA: Calwestern Automated Clearing House Association

CACI: Chicago Association of Commerce and Industry

CACM: Central American Common Market

CACSD: Computer-Aided Control System Design

CAD: Cadiz Railroad
Cash Against Disbursements
Cash Against Documents
Computer-Aided Design
Computer-Aided Detection
Computer-Aided Dispatching

CADA: Computer-Assisted Distribution and Assignment

CADAM: Computer-Graphics Augmented Design and Manufacturing

CADAR: Computer-Aided Design, Analysis and Reliability

CADAS: Computerized Automatic Data Acquisition System

CADAVRS: Computer-Assisted Dial Access Video Retrieval System

CAD/CAM: Computer-Aided Design/Computer-Aided Manufacturing

CADCOM: Computer-Aided Design for Communications

CADDIA: Cooperation in the Automation of Data Documentation for Import/Export and Agriculture (EC)

CADE: Computer-Aided Design and Engineering
Computer-Aided Design Evaluation
Computer-Assisted Data Evaluation

CADIC: Computer-Aided Design of Integrated Circuits

CADICS: Computer-Aided Design of Industrial Cabling Systems

CADLIC: Computer-Aided Design of Linear Integrated Circuits

CADMAT: Computer-Aided Design Manufacture and Testing

CADOCR: Computer-Aided Design of Optical Character Recognition

CADPIN: Customs Automated Data Processing Intelligence Network

CADS: Computer-Aided Design System
Content Addressable File Store

CADSYS: Computer-Aided Design System

CADTES: Computer-Aided Design and Test

CAE: Computer-Aided Engineering
Cost Analysis Cost Estimating

Caesar: Caesars World Inc. (newspaper)

CaesNJ: Caesars New Jersey Inc. (newspaper)

CAET: Corrective Action Evaluation Team

CAF: Clerical, Administrative, and Fiscal
Cost and Freight

Cost, Assurance, and Freight
Furr's/Bishop's Cafeterias LP (NYSE)

CAFC: Computer-Automated Frequency Control

CAFM: Commercial Air Freight Movement

CAFS: Content-Addressable File Store

CAG: ConAgra Inc. (NYSE)
Cooperative Automation Group

CAGD: Computer-Aided Geometric Design

CAGE: California Almond Growers Exchange

CagleA: Cagle's Inc. (newspaper)

CAI: Computer-Administered Instruction
Computer-Aided Instruction
Computer-Assisted Instruction

CAIC: Computer-Assisted Indexing and Classification

CAINS: Computer-Aided Instruction System

CAIOP: Computer Analog Input-Output

CAIRS: Computer-Assisted Information Retrieval System

CAIS: Computer-Aided Insurance System

CAL: CalFed Inc. (NYSE)
China Air Lines
Continental Air Lines
Conversational Algebraic Language

CALA: Computer-Aided Loads Analysis

CALB: Computer-Aided Line Balancing

CALD: Computer-Assisted Logic Design

CalEgy: California Energy Co. (newspaper)

CalFed: CalFed Inc. (newspaper)

CalFIP: Cal Fed Income Partners LP (newspaper)

CalJky: California Jockey Club (newspaper)

Callhn: Callahan Mining Corp. (newspaper)

Calmat: CalMat Co. (newspaper)

CALMS: Credit and Loan Management System

CALPA: Canadian Air Line Pilots Association

Calprop: Calprop Cor. (newspaper)

CalRE: California Real Estate Investment Trust (newspaper)

Calton: Calton Inc. (newspaper)

CAM: Calculated Access Method
Classified Advertising Manager
Communications Access Manager
Computer-Aided Manufacturing
Content Addressed Memory
Contract Audit Manual

CAMA: Centralized Automatic Message Accounting
Control and Automation Manufacturers Association

CAMAC: Computer-Aided Measurement and Control
Computer-Automated Measurement and Control

CAMA-ONI: Centralized Automatic Message Accounting-Operator Number Identification Operator

CAMC: Canadian Association of Management Consultants

CAMECEC: Computer-Aided Machine Loading

CAMELOT: Computerization and Mechanization of Local Office Tasks

CAMP: Companies, Agencies, Markets, Positions
Compiler for Automatic Machine Programming
Controls and Monitoring Processor
CAMPRAD: Computer-Assisted Message Preparation Relay and Distribution
CAMPS: Computer-Assisted Message Processing System
CamSp: Campbell Soup Co. (newspaper)
can: cancel
cancellation
CAN: Cancel (character)
Cannon Group Inc., The (NYSE)
canc: cancel
cancellation
CANDE: Culvert Analysis and Design
CANDO: Computer Analysis of Networks with Design Orientation
CanonG: Cannon Group Inc., The (newspaper)
CanTran: Cancel Transmission
CAO: Carolina Freight Corp. (NYSE)
Chief Administrative Officer
CAOS: Computer-Augmented Oscilloscope System
cap: capacity
capital
capitalization
CAP: Camas Prairie (railroad)
Capital Housing & Mortgage Partners (ASE)
Common Agricultural Policy (EC)
Computer-Aided Planning
Computer-Aided Programming
Convertible Adjustable Rate Preferred Stock
CAPABLE: Controls And Panel Arrangement By Logical Evaluation
CAPARS: Computer-Aided Placement and Routing System
CAPC: Computer-Aided Production Control
CapCits: Capital Cities/ABC Inc. (newspaper)
CAPE: Computer-Aided Planning and Estimating
CAPER: Computer-Aided Pattern Evaluation and Recognition
Cost of Attaining Personnel Requirements
CAPERTSIM: Computer-Assisted Program Evaluation Review Technique Simulation
CapHld: Capital Holding Corp. (newspaper)
CapHo: Capital Housing & Mortgage Partners (newspaper)
CAPM: Capital Asset Pricing Model
Computer-Aided Production Management
CAPP: Computer-Aided Part Planning
Computer-Aided Process Planning
CAPRI: Computerized Analysis for Programming Investments
CAPS: Computer-Aided Planning System
Computer-Aided Problem Solving
CAPSR: Cost Account Performance Status Report
CAPTAINS: Character and Pattern Telephone Access Information Network System

CAQA: Computer-Aided Quality Assurance
CAR: Carter-Wallace Inc. (NYSE)
Central Australia Railway
Civil Aeronautical Regulations
Computer-Aided Retrieval
CARAD: Computer-Aided Reliability and Design
CARDA: Computer-Aided Reliability Data Analysis
Cardis: Cardis Corp. (newspaper)
CARDIS: Cargo Data Interchange System
CARDS: Computer-Aided Reliability Data System
CareE: Care Enterprises Inc. (ASE)
CareerC: CareerCom Corp. (newspaper)
CargInd: Carriage Industries Inc. (newspaper)
Cargotainer: Cargo Container
CARICOM: Caribbean Community (Common Market)
CARIFTA: Caribbean Free Trade Association
CARIRI: Caribbean Industrial Research Institute
Carlisle: Carlisle Companies Inc. (newspaper)
Carmel: Carmel Container Systems Ltd. (newspaper)
C-ARMS: Commercial-Accounts Receivable Management System
CarnCr: Carnival Cruise Lines Inc. (newspaper)
CaroFt: Carolina Freight Corp. (newspaper)
CarolP: Carolco Pictures Inc. (newspaper)
CarPw: Carolina Power & Light Co. (newspaper)
carr: carrier
CARR: Carrollton Railroad
CARS: Computer-Aided Routing System
Computer-Audit Retrieval System
cart: cartridge
CartBc: Carteret Bancorp Inc. (newspaper)
CarTec: Carpenter Technology Corp. (newspaper)
CartH: Carter Hawley Hale Stores Inc. (newspaper)
CartWl: Carter-Wallace Inc. (newspaper)
CARW: Carolina Western (railroad)
CAs: Consumers Associations
Cooperative Associations
CAS: A.M. Castle & Co. (ASE)
Circuits And Systems
CASA: Computer and Automated Systems Association
CASB: Cost Accounting Standards Board
Casblan: CasaBlanca Industries (newspaper)
CASCADE: Centralized Administrative Systems Control and Design
CascNG: Cascade Natural Gas Corp. (newspaper)
CAS/CPA: Computer Accounting System/Computer Performance Analysis
CASD: Computer-Aided System Design
CASE: Computer-Aided Systems Engineering
Computer-Aided Systems Evaluation
CasFd: Castle Convertible Fund Inc. (newspaper)
cash: cashier
CASH: Cash Trade (NYSE)
Computer-Aided Stock Holdings
Computer-Aided System Hardware

CASL: Committee of American Steamship Lines
CASNET: Casual-Associative Network
CASO: Canada Southern (railway)
Computer-Assisted System Operation
CASOE: Computer Accounting System for Office Expenditure
Caspn: Caspen Oil Inc. (newspaper)
Cas Reps: Casualty Reports
CASS: Computer Automatic Scheduling System
CAST: Computer Applications and Systems Technology
Computer-Assisted Scanning Techniques
CastlA: A.M. Castle & Co. (newspaper)
CastlCk: Castle & Cooke Inc. (newspaper)
CAT: Caterpillar Inc. (NYSE)
Computer-Aided Testing
Computer-Aided Translation
Computer-Aided Typesetting
Computer-Assisted Teleconferencing
Credit Authorization Telephones
Credit Authorization Terminal
CATA: Canadian Air Transportation Administration
CataLt: Catalina Lighting Inc. (newspaper)
CATC: Computer-Assisted Test Construction
CATE: Computer-Automated Translation and Editing
Caterp: Caterpillar Inc. (newspaper)
catl: catalog
CATRALA: Car and Truck Renting and Leasing Association
CATS: Centralized Automatic Test System
Certificate of Accrual on Treasury Securities
Computer-Aided Trouble-Shooting
CATV: Cable Antenna Television
Cable Telecommunications and Video
Cable Television
Community Antenna Television
CATVA: Computer-Assisted Total Value Assessment
Catylst: Catalyst Energy Corp. (newspaper)
CavalH: Cavalier Homes Inc. (newspaper)
CAVN: Compañia Anónima Venezolana de Navegación (Venezuelan Navigation Company) (steamship)
CAW: Caesars World Inc. (NYSE)
Channel Address Word
CAWU: Clerical and Administrative Workers' Union
CAX: Community Automatic Exchange
CB: Callable Bond
Caribair (airline)
Carte Blanche
Cash Book
Census Bureau
Chubb Corp., The (NYSE)
Citizen's Band
Confidential Bulletin
Corporate Bonds
Coupon Bond
Currency Bond
C of B: Confirmation of Balance
CBA: Computer-Based Automation
Concrete Block Association
Cost-Benefit Analysis
CBBS: Computerized Bulletin Board Service
CBC: Canadian Broadcasting Corporation
Carbon County (railway)

Carteret Bancorp Inc. (NYSE)
Computer-Based Conferencing
Coordinated Building Commission

CBCT: Customer-Bank Communication Terminal

CBD: Cash Before Delivery
Central Business District
Commerce Business Daily

CBE: Cooper Industries Inc. (NYSE)

CBEMA: Canadian Business Equipment Manufacturers Association
Computer and Business Equipment Manufacturers Association

CBFM: Constant Bandwidth Frequency Modulation

CBH: CBI Industries Inc. (NYSE)

CBI: Caribbean Basin Initiative
Computer-Based Instruction
Curtice-Burns Foods Inc. (ASE)

CBI In: CBI Industries Inc. (newspaper)

CBIS: Computer-Based Information System

cbk: checkbook

CB/L: Commercial Bill of Lading

CBL: Conemaugh and Black Lick (railroad)
Corroon & Black Corp. (NYSE)

CBM: Confidence Building Measure

CBMA: Canadian Business Manufacturers Association

CBMIS: Computer-Based Management Information System

CBMS: Computer-Based Message Service

CBNM: Central Bureau of Nuclear Measurements (Euratom)

CBO: Compensation by Objectives
Congressional Budget Office

CBOE: Chicago Board Options Exchange

CBOSS: Count, Back Order, and Sample Select

CBQ: Chicago, Burlington & Quincy (railroad)

CBR: Common Bureau of References (EC)
Community Bureau of Reference (EC)
Crystal Brands Inc. (NYSE)

CBS: CBS Inc. (NYSE) (newspaper)
Columbia Broadcasting System

CBT: Cabot Corp. (NYSE)
Chicago Board of Trade
Computer-Based Training
Connecticut Bank and Trust Company

CBU: Chicago Board of Underwriters
Commodore International Ltd. (NYSE)

C&C: Canton & Carthage (railroad)
Cash and Carry
Command and Control

CC: Aerocosta (airline)
Cancellation Clause
Cancelled Check
Cash Commodity
Cashier's Check
Chamber of Commerce
Charge-Coupled
Chief Clerk
Circuit City Stores Inc. (NYSE)
Cluster Controller
Cold Canvassing
Command Chain
Communications Controller
Computerized Conferencing
Contra Credit
Control Computer
Control Counter
Corporation Commission
Cumberland Railway and Coal

CCA: Common Communication Adapter
Comprehensive Cooperative Agreement

Cosmopolitan Care Corp. (ASE)
Credit Control Act
Current Cost Accounting
Customer Cost Analysis

CCAB: Consultative Committee of Accountancy Bodies

CCAID: Charge-Coupled Area Imaging Device

CCAL: Christensen Canadian African Line (steamship)

CCB: Capital Cities/ABC Inc. (NYSE)
Configuration Control Board

CC&C: Cowlitz, Chehalis & Cascade (railroad)

CCC: Commercial Credit Corporation (NYSE)
Commodity Credit Corporation
Consumer Consultative Committee
Customs Cooperation Council
A quality rating for a municipal or corporate bond

CCCN: Customs Cooperation Council Nomenclature

CC CO: Commercial Cable Company

CCCS: Consumer Credit Counseling Services

CCCSL: Cleveland, Cincinnati, Chicago & St. Louis (railway)

CCD: Charge Couple Device

CCDA: Commercial Chemical Development Association

CCE: Coca-Cola Enterprises Inc. (NYSE)
Commercial Construction Equipment
Conseil des Communes d'Europe (Council of European Municipalities) (French)
Council of Construction Employers

CCEB: Combined Communications Electronics Boards

CCEI: Composite Cost Effectiveness Index

CCF: Complex Coherence Function
Compressed Citation File

CCFPCS: Cie des Chemins de Fer de la Plaine du Cul-de-Sac (French Cul-de-Sac Plaine Railroad Company) (Tahiti)

CCG: Crisis Coordination Group

CCH: Campbell Resources Inc. (NYSE)
Commercial Clearinghouse
Connections per Circuit per Hour

CCHS: Cylinder-Cylinder-Head Sector

CCI: Chambre de Commerce Internationale (International Chamber of Commerce)
Citicorp (NYSE)

CCIA: Computer and Communications Industry Association
Consumer Credit Insurance Association

CCIR: Comité Consultatif International de Radiocommunication

CCIS: Common Channel Interoffice Signaling
Computer-Controlled Interconnect System

CCITT: Comité Consultatif International Télégraphique et Téléphonique (International Telegraph and Telephone Consultation Committee) (French)

CCL: Carnival Cruise Lines Inc. (ASE)
Carolina, Clinchfield and Ohio (railway)
Common Command Language

CCM: Claremont Capital Corp. (ASE)
Counter-Countermeasures
CCMA: Canadian Council of Management Association
CCMD: Continuous Current Monitoring Device
CCMS: Computer Center Management System
CCMT: Computer-Controlled Machine Tool
CCN: Chris-Craft Industries Inc. (NYSE)
Common-Carrier Network
Companhia Colonial de Navegacão (Portuguese-Colonial Navigation Company) (steamship)
Contract Change Notice
CCNR: Consultative Committee for Nuclear Research of the Council of Europe
CC&O: Carolina, Clinchfield and Ohio (railway)
CCO: Current Controlled Oscillator
CC&ORSC: Carolina, Clinchfield and Ohio Railroad of South Carolina
CCP: Certificate in Computer Programming
Communication Control Program
Conditional Command Processor
Corcap Inc. (ASE)
Credit Card Purchase
CCPA: Consumer Credit Protection Act
Court of Customs and Patent Appeals
CCPF: Comité Central de la Propriété Forestière de la CE (Central Committee on Forest Property for the European Community) (French) (EC)
CCPMO: Consultative Council of Professional Management Organizations
CCR: Computer Character Recognition
Computer-Controlled Retrieval
Corinth and Counce Railroad
CCROS: Card Capacity Read-Only Storage
CCR&R: Covenants, Conditions, Restrictions, and Reservations
CC&S: Central Computer and Sequencer
CCS: Central Certificate Service
Common Channel Signaling
Computer Consoles Inc. (ASE)
Hundred Call Seconds
CCSA: Common-Control Switching Arrangement
Customer-Controlled Switching Arrangement
CCSB: Credit Card Service Bureau
CCST: Center for Computer Sciences and Technology
CCT: Central California Traction (railroad)
Common Customs Tariff
Computer-Compatible Tape
CCTV: Closed Circuit Television
Closed Circuit Cable Television
CCTV/LSD: Closed Circuit Television/Large Screen Display
CCU: Central Control Unit
Clear Channel Communications Inc. (ASE)
CCV: Control Configured Vehicle
CCW: Channel Command Word
Counter Clockwise
CCX: CCX Inc. (NYSE) (newspaper)
cd: card
C&D: Collection and Delivery

CD: Cardinal Airlines
Carried Down
Cash Discount
Certificate of Deposit
Compact Disc
Contracting Definition
Cum Dividend

CDA: Command and Data Acquisition
Computer Dealers Association
Control Data Corp. (NYSE)
Copper Development Association

CDB: Central Data Bank
Current Data Bit

CDC: Call Directing Code
Career Development Course
CompuDyne Corp. (ASE)
Computer Display Channel
Control Data Corporation

CDE: Coeur d'Alene Mines Corp. (ASE)

CDEC: Central Data Conversion Equipment

CDF: Combined Distribution Frame
Contiguous-Disk File
Cumulative Distributed Function

CDG: Canandaigua Wine Company Inc. (ASE)

CDHS: Comprehensive Data Handling System

CDI: CDI Corp. (ASE) (newspaper)

CDICS: Centralized Dealer Inventory Control System

CDL: Citadel Holding Corp. (ASE)
Computer Description Language
Computer Design Language

CDM: Cash Dispensing Machine
Code-Division Multiplexing

CDMA: Code-Division Multiple Access

CDMS: Commercial Data Management System

CdnOc: Canadian Occidental Petroleum Ltd. (newspaper)

CdnPac: Canadian Pacific Ltd. (newspaper)

CDO: Comdisco Inc. (NYSE)
Community Dial Office

CDP: Centralized Data Processing
Certificate in Data Processing
Communications Data Processor

CDPS: Computing and Data Processing Society

CDR: Card Reader
Continental Depositary Receipt

CDROM: Computer Disc Read-Only Memory

CDS: Cardis Corp. (ASE)
Case Data System
Central Dynamic System
Comprehensive Display System
Control Display System

CDSS: Customer Digital Switching System

CDT: Central Daylight Time

CDU: Control and Display Unit

CDV: Chambers Development Company Inc. (ASE)

C&E: Commission and Exchange

CE: Capital Expenditure
Cash Earnings
Catalyst Energy Corp. (NYSE)
Caveat Emptor
Commodity Exchange
Common Era
Concurrent Engineering
Consumption Entry
Critical Examination
Customer Engineer

CEA: Central Electricity Authority
Comité Européen des Assurance (European Insurance Committee) (French)
Commodity Exchange Authority

Communications-Electronics Agency
Confédération Européenne de l'Agriculture (European Confederation of Agriculture) (French)
Cost Effectiveness Analysis
Council of Economic Advisors

CEAC: Commission Européenne de l'Aviation Civile (European Civil Aviation Commission) (French)

CEC: Cetec Corp. (ASE)
Commission of the European Communities (EC)
Commodities Exchange Center
Commodity Exchange Commission
Commonwealth Edison Company
Consolidated Edison Company

CECA: Communauté Européenne du Charbon et de l'Acier (European Coal and Steel Community) (French)

CECUA: Confederation of European Computer User Association

CED: Committee for Economic Development
Computer Entry Device

CEDA: Communications Equipment Distributors Association

CEDAC: Computer Energy Distribution and Automated Control

CEDAR: Computer-Aided Environmental Design Analysis and Realization

CEDEFOP: European Center for the Development of Vocational Training (EC)

CEDEL: Centrale de Livraison de Valeurs Mobilières (EC)

CEDI: Centre Européen de Documentation et d'Information (European Documentation and Information Center) (French) (EC)

CedrF: Cedar Fair LP (newspaper)

CEE: Commission Économique pour l'Europe (Economic Commission for Europe) (French)
Communauté Économique Européenne (European Economic Community) (French) (EC)
Comunidade Económica Europeia (European Economic Community) (Portuguese) (EC)
C3 Inc. (NYSE)

CEEA: Communauté Européenne de l'Énergie Atomique (European Atomic Energy Community) (French) (EC)

CEEC: Council for European Economic Cooperation (EC)

CEEP: Centre Européene de l'Enterprise Publique (European Center for Public Enterprises) (French) (EC)

CEF: Central Fund of Canada Ltd. (ASE)
Closed-End Fund

CEFCO: Cooperative Export Financing Corporation

CEFIC: Conseil Européen des Fédérations de l'Industrie Chimique (European Council of Chemical Industry Federations) (French)

CEFS: Comité Européen des Fabricants de Sucre (European Committee of Sugar Manufacturers) (French)

C&EI: Chicago and Eastern Illinois (railroad)
CEI: Centre d'Études Industrielles (Center for Industrial Studies) (French)
Chicago & Eastern Illinois (railroad)
Contract End Item
Cost Effectiveness Index
CEIC: Closed-End Investment Company
CEIF: Council of European Industrial Federations
CEIR: Corporation for Economic and Industrial Research
CELEX: European Community legal database (EC)
CEM: Comprehensive Emergency Management
Cost and Effectiveness Method
CEMA: Canadian Electrical Manufacturers Association
Council of Economic Mutual Assistance
CEMAST: Control of Engineering Material, Acquisition, Storage and Transport
CEMIS: Client-Employee Management Information System
CeMPw: Central Maine Power Co. (newspaper)
CEMT: Conférence Européenne des Ministrès des Transport (European Conference of Ministers of Transport) (French)
CEN: Centronics Data Computer Corp. (NYSE)
Comité Européen de Normalisation (European Committee for Standardization) (French)
CENEL: Comité Européen de Coordination des Normes Électriques (European Electrical Standards Coordinating Committee) (French) (EC)
CENELEC: Comité Européen de Normalisation Électro-téchnique (European Community for Electrotechnical Standardization) (French) (EC)
CenHud: Central Hudson Gas & Electric Corp. (newspaper)
CenSoW: Central & South West Corp. (newspaper)
Centel: Centel Corp. (newspaper)
CentEn: Centerior Energy Corp. (newspaper)
Centex: Centex Corp. (newspaper)
CentGp: Centennial Group Inc., The (newspaper)
CentrCP: Centronics Data Computer Corp. (newspaper)
Centrst: CenTrust Savings Bank (newspaper)
CentSe: Central Securities Corp. (newspaper)
CenvD: Cenvill Development Corp. (newspaper)
Cenvill: Cenvill Investors Inc. (newspaper)
CEO: Chief Executive Officer
Comprehensive Electronics Office
CEP: Concentrated Employment Program
ConVest Energy Partners Ltd. (ASE)
Council on Economic Priorities
CEPS: Center for European Policy Studies (EC)
CEPT: Conférence Européenne des administration des Postes et des Télécommunications (European Conference of Postal and Telecommunications Administrations) (French)

CEQ: Centennial Group Inc., The (ASE)
Council on Environmental Quality

CER: CILCORP Inc. (NYSE)
Civil Engineering Report
Cost Estimated (Estimating) Report

CERC: Computer Entry and Readout Control

CERD: Committee for European Research and Development (EC)

CERDEC: Center for Research and Documentation in the European Community (EC)

CER-DIP: Ceramic Dual-In-Line Package

CERE: Computer Entry and Readout Equipment

CERN: Center Européen de Recherches Nucléaires (European Organization for Nuclear Research) (French)

cert: certificate
certification
certify

CERT: Constant Extension Rate Test

CES: Comité Économique et Social (Economic and Social Committee) (French) (EC)
Commonwealth Energy System (NYSE)

CESD: Composite External Symbol Dictionary

CESO: Council of Engineers and Scientists Organizations

CESSE: Council of Engineering and Scientific Society

CET: Central Securities Corp. (ASE)
Common External Tariff (EC)

CETA: Comprehensive Employment and Training Act

Cetec: Cetec Corp. (newspaper)

CETI: Committee for Energy Thrift in Industry (EC)

CETIA: Control, Electronics, Telecommunications, Instrument Automation

cf: certificates (in bond listings of newspapers)

C&F: Cost and Freight

CF: Cape Fear (railways)
Carried Forward
Cash Flow
Collins Foods International Inc. (NYSE)
Compagnie de Navigation Fraissinet (steamship)
Cost and Freight
Faucett (airline)

CFA: Cash Flow Accounting
Chartered Financial Analyst
Component Flow Analysis
Computer Factory, The (NYSE)

CFB: Citizens First Bancorp (ASE)

CFC: Chartered Financial Consultant
Consolidated Freight Classification

CFCda: Central Fund of Canada Ltd. (newspaper)

CFCF: Central Flow Control Facility

CF C-O: Chemin de Fer Congo-Ocean (French-Congo-Ocean Railroad) (Congo People's Republic) (Brazzaville)

CFE: Contractor Furnished Equipment

CFF/SFF/FFS: Chemins de fer Federaux Suisses/ Schweizerische Bundesbahnen/ Ferrovie Dederali Svizzere (French, German, Italian-Swiss Federal Railways)

CFG: Copelco Financial Services Group Inc. (ASE)
CFI: Cal Fed Income Partners LP (NYSE)
Cost, Freight, and Insurance
CFIA: Component Failure Impact Analysis
CFIUS: Committee on Foreign Investment in the United States
CFK: Comfed Bancorp Inc. (ASE)
CFL: Societé Nationale des Chemins de fer Luxembourgeois (French-Luxembourg National Railways)
CFM: Caminho de Ferro de Mocambique (Portuguese-Mozambique Railroad)
Chemin de Fer Madagascar (French-Madagascar Railroad)
Cubic Feet per Minute
CFMS: Chained File Management System
CFO: Cancel Form Order
Chief Financial Officer
Consolidated Functions Ordinary
CFP: Certified Financial Planner
Common Fisheries Policy (EC)
CFPO: Compagnie Française des Phosphates de l'Oceanie (French-Phosphate Company of Oceania) (steamship)
CFQ: Quaker Fabric Corp. (ASE)
CFR: Caile Ferate Ramane (Romanian-General Direction of the Romanian Railroads)
Code of Federal Regulations
CFRC: Chemins de Fer Royaux du Cambodge (French-Royal Cambodian Railways)
CFS: Combined File Search
CFSS: Combined File Search System
CFTC: Commodity Futures Trading Commission
C&G: Columbus & Greenville (railroad)
CG: Capital Gain
Capital Goods
Central of Georgia (railway)
Columbia Gas System Inc., The (NYSE)
Computer Graphics
CGBR: Central Government Borrowing Requirement
CGC: Cascade Natural Gas Corp. (NYSE)
CG&E: Cincinnati Gas and Electric Company
CGE: Carriage Industries Inc. (NYSE)
Chicago and Eastern Illinois (railroad)
CGEL&PB: Consolidated Gas, Electric Light and Power Company of Baltimore
CGI: Computer-Generated Image
CGL: Cagle's Inc. (ASE)
Canadian Gulf Line (steamship)
CGN: Cognitronics Corp. (ASE)
CGO: Chase Medical Group Inc. (ASE)
CGP: Coastal Corp., The (NYSE)
CGR: Ceylon Government Railway
Chariot Group Inc., The (ASE)
Cyrenaica Government Railways (Libya)
CGS: Central Gulf Steamships
Consolidated Oil & Gas Inc. (ASE)
CGSA: Computer Graphics Structural Analysis
CGT: Capital Gains Tax
Compagnie Generale Transatlantic (French-General Transatlantic Company)

C>R: Canada and Gulf Terminal Railway
CGTA: Compagnie Generale des Transports Aeriens (Algerian Air Lines)
CGW: Chicago Great Western (railroad)
ch: channel
clearinghouse
C&H: Cheswick and Harmer (railroad)
CH: Champion Products Inc. (ASE)
Chicago Helicopter Airways
Clearing House
Custom House
chair: chairperson (chairman) (chairwoman)
CHAMP: Character Manipulation Procedures
ChampSp: Champion Spark Plug Co. (newspaper)
CHAP: Champion International Corp. (NYSE)
CHAPS: Clearing House Automated Payments System (London) (UK)
char: character
Chariot: Chariot Group Inc., The (newspaper)
CHARM: Checking, Accounting and Reporting for Member firms (London Stock Exchange) (UK)
ChartC: Charter Co., The (newspaper)
Chase: Chase Manhattan Corp., The (newspaper)
CHAT: Cheap Access Terminal
Chaus: Bernard Chaus Inc. (newspaper)
CHB: Champion Enterprises Inc. (ASE)
CHD: Chelsea Industries Inc. (NYSE)
ChDev: Chambers Development Company Inc. (newspaper)
CHDL: Computer Hardware Description Language
CHE: Chemed Corp. (NYSE)
Chelsea: Chelsea Industries Inc. (newspaper)
Chemed: Chemed Corp. (newspaper)
Chevrn: Chevron Corp. (newspaper)
CHF: Chock Full O'Nuts Corp. (NYSE)
ChfDv: Chieftain Development Company Ltd. (newspaper)
chg: charge
CHG: Chicago Milwaukee Corp. (NYSE)
CHH: Carter Hawley Hale Stores Inc. (NYSE)
CHI: Computer Human Interaction
ChiMlw: Chicago Milwaukee Corp. (newspaper)
CHIPS: Clearing House Interbank Payments Systems (New York)
CHIRP: Confidential Human Factors Incident Report
ChiRv: Chicago Rivet & Machine Co. (newspaper)
CHITO: Container Handling In Terminal Operations
chk: check
ChkFull: Chock Full O'Nuts Corp. (newspaper)
chkpt: checkpoint
CHL: Chemical Banking Corp. (NYSE)
ChmBk: Chemical Banking Corp. (newspaper)
chmn: chairperson (chairman)
ChmpEn: Champion Enterprises Inc. (newspaper)
ChmpIn: Champion International Corp. (newspaper)
ChmpPd: Champion Products Inc. (newspaper)
chnl: channel

CHP: Charter Power Systems Inc. (ASE)
Council of Housing Producers
CH-P: Ferrocarril Chihuahua al Pacific (railroad)
CHPAE: Critical Human Performance and Evaluation
ChpStl: Chaparral Steel Co. (newspaper)
chq.: cheque
chr: character
CHR: Charter Co., The (NYSE)
Chestnut Ridge Railway
ChrisCr: Chris-Craft Industries Inc. (newspaper)
Christn: Christiana Companies Inc., The (newspaper)
CHRT: Coordinated Human Resource Technology
CHRYS: Chrysler
Chryslr: Chrysler Corp. (newspaper)
CHS: Bernard Chaus Inc. (NYSE)
ChsMed: Chase Medical Group Inc. (newspaper)
Chspk: Chesapeake Corp. (newspaper)
CHT: Collection, Holding, and Transfer
ChtMd: Charter Medical Corp. (newspaper)
ChtPwr: Charter Power Systems Inc. (newspaper)
CHTT: Chicago Heights Terminal Transfer (railroad)
Chubb: Chubb Corp., The (newspaper)
CHV: Chattahoochee Valley (railroad)
Chevron Corp. (NYSE)
CHW: Chemical Waste Management Inc. (NYSE)
Chesapeake Western (railroad)
ChWst: Chemical Waste Management Inc. (newspaper)
CHX: Pilgrim's Price Corp. (NYSE)
CHY: Chyron Corp. (NYSE)
Chyron: Chyron Corp. (newspaper)
C&I: Cambria and Indiana (railroad)
C/I: Certificate of Insurance
CI: Capital Intensive
Cash Items
Catalina Island Steamship Line
Certificate of Insurance
China Airlines
Christmas Island Phosphate Commission
CIGNA Corp. (NYSE)
Compounded Interest
Cost and Insurance
Current-awareness Information
Cia: Compañia (Spanish Company)
CIA: Cash In Advance
Certified Internal Auditor
Chemical Industries Association
Computer Industry Association
CIARB: Chartered Institute of Arbitrators (UK)
CIB: Centralized Intercept Bureau
Classification Internationale des Brevets (International Classification of Patents)
CIBS: Chartered Institution of Building Services
CIC: Cedar Rapids and Iowa City (railway)
Chartered Investment Counsel
Continental Corp., The (NYSE)
Custom-Integrated Circuit
CICA: Canadian Institute of Chartered Accountants
Construction Industry Computing Association
CICI: Confederation of Information Communication Industries (EC)
CICS: Customer Information Control System
CICS/VS: Customer Information Control System/Vertical Storage

CID: Charge-Injection Imaging Device
Chieftain Development Company Ltd. (ASE)
Component Identification Number
Compound Interest Deposit
CIDs: Civil Investigative Demands
Cie: Compagnie (French company)
CIE: Computer Interrupt Equipment
Control by Importance and Exception
Coras Iompair Eireann (Gaelic-Irish State Railways)
CIEC: Conference on International Economic Cooperation
CIF: Central Information File
Colonial Intermediate High Income Fund (NYSE)
Computer-Integrated Factory
Construction Industry Federation
Corporate Income Fund
Cost, Insurance, and Freight
CIF & C: Cost, Insurance, Freight and Commissions (Charges)
CIFC: Center for Inter-Firm Comparison
CIFE: Cost, Insurance, Freight and Exchange
CIFCI: Cost, Insurance, Freight (plus) Commission and Interest
CIFIE: Cost, Insurance, Freight, Interest and Exchange
CIG: Continental Graphics Corp. (ASE)
CIGNA: CIGNA Corp. (newspaper)
CIH: Continental Illinois Holding Corp. (NYSE)
CII: Center for Innovation in Industry
Chartered Insurance Institute (UK)
Collective Investment Institution
CRI Insured Mortgage Investments II Inc. (NYSE)
CI&L: Chicago, Indianapolis & Louisville (railroad)
CIL: Computer Interpreter Language
Continental Illinois Corp. (NYSE)
CILA: Casualty Insurance Logistics Automated
Cilcorp: CILCORP Inc. (newspaper)
CILOP: Conversion In Lieu Of Procurement
C&IM: Chicago & Illinois Midland (railroad)
CIM: Capital Investment Model
CIM High Yield Securities (ASE) (newspaper)
Computer Input Microfilm
Computer-Integrated Manufacturing
CIMA: Construction Industry Manufacturers Association
CIMAH: Control of Industrial Major Accident Hazards
CIMB: Construction Industry Manpower Board
CIME: Comité Intergouvernemental pour les Migrations Européennes (Intergovernmental Committee for European Migration) (French) (EC)
Council of Industry for Management Education
CIMG: Construction Industry Marketing Group
CIMS: Computer Installation Management System
Computer-Integrated Manufacturing System
Coordination and Interference Management System
Countermeasures Internal Management System

CIMTECH: Center for Information Media and Technology (EC)
CIN: Cincinnati Gas & Electric Co., The (NYSE)
CinBel: Cincinnati Bell Inc. (newspaper)
CIND: Central Indiana (railway)
CineOd: Cineplex Odeon Corp. (newspaper)
CinGE: Cincinnati Gas & Electric Co., The (newspaper)
CinMil: Cincinnati Milacron Inc. (newspaper)
CIO: Career Is Over
Chief Information Officer
Congress of Industrial Organizations
CIOB: Chartered Institute of Building (UK)
CIP: Central Illinois Public Service Co. (NYSE)
Complex Information Processing
CIPA: Chartered Institute of Patent Agents (UK)
CIPFA: Chartered Institute of Public Finance and Accountancy (UK)
CIPM: Council for International Progress in Management
CIPS: Canadian Information Processing Society
cir: circular
CIR: Circus Circuit Enterprises Inc. (NYSE)
Commission on Industrial Relations
Cost Information Report
Council of Industrial Relations
Current Instruction Register
CIRC: Centralized Information Reference and Control
CIRCA: Computerized Information Retrieval and Current Awareness
CIRCAL: Circuit Analysis
CircleK: Circle K Corp., The (newspaper)
CirCty: Circuit City Stores Inc. (newspaper)
Circus: Circus Circus Enterprises Inc. (newspaper)
CIRCUS: Circuit Simulator
CIRD: Research and Development Interservice Committee
CIRIA: Construction Industry Research and Information Association
C&IRR: Cambria and Indiana Railroad
CIRR: Chattahoochee Industrial Railroad
CIRT: Conference on Industrial Robot Technology
CIS: Concord Fabrics Inc. (ASE)
Control Indicator Set
Current Information Selection
Custom Integrated System
CISC: Complex Instruction Set Computing
Construction Industry Stabilization Committee
CISPI: Cast Iron Soil Pipe Institute
CISS: Conference on Information Science and Systems
CIT: Counselor In Training
CITA: Commercial Industrial Type Activities
Citadel: Citadel Holding Corp. (newspaper)
Citicrp: Citicorp (newspaper)
CITIES SERVICE: Cities Service Oil Company
CITS: Central Integrated Test System Multiplex
CityBcp: Citytrust Bancorp (newspaper)
CitzFst: Citizens First Bancorp (newspaper)
CIU: Computer Interface Unit
CIV: Columbia Real Estate Investments Inc. (ASE)

CIW: Chicago and Illinois Western (railroad)
CIWL: Compagnie Internationale des Wagon-Lits (French-International Sleeping Car Company) (railroad)
CJ: California Jocket Club (ASE)
CJA: Carpenters and Joiners of America
CJN: Caesars New Jersey Inc. (ASE)
ck: check
CK: Connair (airline)
CKC: Conchemco Inc. (ASE)
CKD: Completely Knocked-Down
Count-Key-Data Device
CKE: Castle & Cooke Inc. (NYSE)
CKL: Clark Equipment Co. (NYSE)
CKP: Circle K Corp., The (NYSE)
cks: checks
CKSO: Condon, Kinzua and Southern (railroad)
CKT: Continental Circuits Corp. (ASE)
cl: centiliter
clause
CL: Called (NYSE)
Call Loan
Capital Loss
Car Load
Cash Letter
Ceylon Lines (steamship)
Coast Lines (steamship)
Colgate-Palmolive Co. (NYSE)
Command Language
Common Law
Compiler Language
Current Liabilities
CLA: Computer Law Association
Copyright Licensing Agency
Clabir: Clabir Corp. (newspaper)
CLAD: Cover Layer Automated Design
ClairSt: Claire's Stores Inc. (newspaper)
CLAMP: Computer Listing and Analysis of Maintenance Programs
ClarkC: Clark Consolidated Industries Inc. (newspaper)
ClarkE: Clark Equipment Co. (newspaper)
Clarmt: Claremont Capital Corp. (newspaper)
CLASP: Circuit Layout, Automated Scheduling and Production
CLASS: Capacity Loading and Scheduling System
Closed Loop Accounting for Stores Sales
Container-Lights Aboard Ship System
CLAUDIUS: Coopers & Lybrand Accounting and Distributive Inventory System
ClayHm: Clayton Homes Inc. (newspaper)
CLC: CLC of America Inc. (NYSE) (newspaper)
Columbia and Cowlitz (railroad)
Cost of Living Council
Current Leading Components
CLCB: Committee of London Clearing Bank (UK)
CLCO: Claremont and Concord Railroad
cld: called (in stock listings of newspapers)
cancelled
cleared
CLD: Computerland Corp. (NYSE)
Current-Limiting Device
CLE: Claire's Stores Inc. (NYSE)
CLEAR: Closed Loop Evaluation And Reporting
ClearCh: Clear Channel Communications Inc. (newspaper)
CLEAT: Computer Language for Engineers and Technologists
CLEO: Clear Language for Expressing Orders

CLF: Cleveland-Cliffs Inc. (NYSE)
CLG: Clabir Corp. (NYSE)
CLGW: Cement, Lime and Gypsum Workers (union)
CLI: Cost-of-Living Index
CLIC: Command Language for Interrogating Computers
Computer Layout of Integrated Circuits
CLIMATE: Computer and Language Independent Modules for Automatic Test Equipment
CLIP: Computer Layout Installation Planner
CLIPPER LINE: Wisconsin and Michigan Steamship Company
CLIRA: Closed Loop In-Reactor Assembly
CLISP: Conversational LISP
clk: clock
CLK: Cadillac and Lake City (railway)
Clark Consolidated Industries Inc. (ASE)
CLM: Clemente Global Growth Fund Inc. (NYSE)
ClmGlb: Clemente Global Growth Fund Inc. (newspaper)
CLO: At The Close
Coleco Industries Inc. (NYSE)
CLOB: Composite Limit Order Book
CLOC: Clean Letter Of Credit
CLODS: Computerized Logic-Oriented Design System
CLOG: Computer Logic Graphics
Clorox: Clorox Co., The (newspaper)
CLP: Clarendon and Pittsford (railroad)
Current Line Pointer
clr: clear
CLR: Color Systems Technology Inc. (ASE)
Combined Line and Recording
CLRR: Camp Lejeune Railroad
CLS: Commercial Loan System
CLT: Cominco Ltd. (ASE)
Communications Line Terminals
CLU: Chartered Life Underwriter
ClubMd: Club Med Inc. (newspaper)
CLUSAN: Cluster Analysis
CLV: Ceiling Limit Value
ClvClf: Cleveland-Cliffs Inc. (newspaper)
CLX: Clorox Co., The (NYSE)
cm: centimeter
CM: Call Money
Call of More
Central Median
Cheap Money
Compania Maritima (Spanish-Maritime Company)
Configuration Management
COPA (Compania Panamena de Aviacion-Panamanian Aviation Company)
Core Memory
Corrective Maintenance
CMA: Canadian Manufacturers Association
Cash Management Account
Compania Mexicana de Aviacion
Computerized Management Account
Contractors Mutual Association
CMarc: Canadian Marconi Co. (newspaper)
CMARS: Cable Monitoring and Rating System
CMB: Chase Manhattan Corp., The (NYSE)
Compagnie Maritime Belge (French-Belgian Maritime Company)(Royal Belgian Lloyd Steamship)
Corrective Maintenance Burden

CMC: Commercial Metals Co. (NYSE)
Comparison Measuring Circuit
CM/CCM: Countermeasures/ Counter Countermeasures
CmcCrd: Commercial Credit Co. (newspaper)
CmceT: Commerce Total Return Fund Inc. (newspaper)
CMCR: Continuous Melting, Casting and Rolling
CMD: Charter Medical Corp. (ASE)
cmdty.: commodity
CME: Chicago Mercantile Exchange
CMEA: Council for Mutual Economic Assistance
CMF: Constant Magnetic Field
CmFct: Computer Factory Inc., The (newspaper)
CMH: Clayton Homes Inc. (NYSE)
CMI: Club Med Inc. (NYSE)
Computer-Managed Instruction
CMI Cp: CMI Corp. (newspaper)
CMIS: Common Manufacturing Information System
Computer-oriented Management Information System
CML: CML Group Inc. (NYSE) (newspaper)
Current Mode Logic
CMM: Coordinate Measuring Machine
CMMA: Concrete Mixer Manufacturers Association
CMMP: Commodity Management Master Plan
CmMtl: Commercial Metals Co. (newspaper)
cmn: commission
CMN: Callahan Mining Corp. (NYSE)
cmnd: command
CMO: CareerCom Corp. (NYSE)
Chicago, St.Paul, Minneapolis and Omaha (railroad)
Collaterized Mortgage Obligation
CMOS: Complementary Metal-Oxide Semiconductor
CMP: Comprehensive Care Corp. (NYSE)
Cost of Maintaining Product
CmpAs: Computer Associates International Inc. (newspaper)
CmpCn: Computer Consoles Inc. (newspaper)
CmpCre: Comprehensive Care Corp. (newspaper)
CMPM: Computer-Managed Parts Manufacture
CmpR: Campbell Resources Inc. (newspaper)
Cmptrc: CompuTrac Inc. (newspaper)
CmpTsk: Computer Task Group Inc. (newspaper)
CMR: Code Matrix Reader
Committee on Manpower Resources
Commtron Corp. (ASE)
CMRA: Chemical Marketing Research Association
CMS: Circuit Maintenance System
CMS Energy Corp. (NYSE)
Compiler Monitor System
Computer Management System
Construction Management System
Consumer and Marketing Service
CMS En: CMS Energy Corp. (newspaper)
CMSNC: China Merchants Steam Navigation Company
CMSP&P: Chicago, Milwaukee, St. Paul and Pacific (railroad)
CM StP&P: Chicago, Milwaukee, St. Paul and Pacific (railroad)

CMT: Computer-Managed Training
Computer-Mediated Teleconferencing
Construction Materials Testing
CMU: Colonial Municipal Income Trust (NYSE)
CMV: Current Market Value
CMW: Canadian Marconi Co. (ASE)
CmwE: Commonwealth Edison Co. (newspaper)
CMX: CMI Corp. (ASE)
CMX Cp: CMX Corp. (newspaper)
CMY: Community Psychiatric Centers (NYSE)
CMZ: Cincinnati Milacron Inc. (NYSE)
Compagnie Maritime du Zaiere
cn: consolidated
C&N: Carolina and Northwestern (railway)
CN: Calton Inc. (NYSE)
Canadian National (railway)
Circular Note
Contract Number
Coordination Number
Craft Airlines
Credit Note
CNA: CNA Financial Corp. (NYSE)
CNA Fn: CNA Financial Corp. (newspaper)
CNAI: CNA Income Shares Inc. (newspaper)
CNC: China Navigation Company
Computer Numerical Control
Conseco Inc. (NYSE)
Cnchm: Conchemco Inc. (newspaper)
cncl: cancel
cncld: canceled
CNE: Connecticut Energy Corp. (NYSE)
CNEP: Cable Network Engineering Program
CNF: Consolidated Freightways Inc. (NYSE)
CNG: Consolidated Natural Gas Co. (NYSE)
CNH: Central Hudson Gas & Electric Corp. (NYSE)
CNJ: Central of New Jersey (railroad)
CNK: Crompton & Knowles Corp. (NYSE)
cnl: cancel
cancellation
CN&L: Columbia, Newberry & Laurens (railroad)
CNL: Central Louisiana Electric Company Inc. (NYSE)
CnLaEl: Central Louisiana Electric Company Inc. (newspaper)
CnIlPS: Central Illinois Public Service Co. (newspaper)
CNN: CNA Income Shares Inc. (NYSE)
CNO: Caspen Oil Inc. (ASE)
CNOP: Conditional Non-Operation
CNO&TPR: Cincinnati, New Orleans and Texas Pacific Railroad
CNP: Compagnie Navigation Paquet (French-Paquet Navigation Company) (steamship)
Crown Central Petroleum Corp. (ASE)
CnPacC: Central Pacific Corp. (newspaper)
CNR: Chiriqui National Railroad (Panama)
CNS: Canadian National Steamships
Communications Network Simulator
Consolidated Stores Corp. (NYSE)
Continuous Net Settlement
CnsEP: Consolidated Energy Partners LP (newspaper)
CnsFrt: Consolidated Freightways Inc. (newspaper)

CnStor: Consolidated Stores Corp. (newspaper)
cnt: count
CNT: Centel Corp. (NYSE)
CntCrd: Countrywide Credit Industries Inc. (newspaper)
cntl: control
CntlCp: Continental Corp., The (newspaper)
CntlInfo: Continental Information Systems Corp. (newspaper)
CNTP: Cincinnati, New Orleans and Texas Pacific (railroad)
cntr: counter
cntrl: control
CntrMt: Countrywide Mortgage Investments Inc. (newspaper)
CntryTl: Century Telephone Enterprises Inc. (newspaper)
CNV: Convertible Holdings Inc. (NYSE)
C&NW: Carolina & North Western (railroad)
Chicago & North Western (railroad)
CNY: Continental Information Systems Corp. (NYSE)
c/o: Care Of
co: coinsurance
company
C&O: Chesapeake and Ohio (railroad)
CO: Call Option
Carried Over
Cash Order
Central Office
Certificate of Origin (EC)
Chesapeake and Ohio (railway)
Continental Airlines
Contracting Office
Cost Of
Covered Option
COA: Coachmen Industries Inc. (NYSE)
Coachm: Coachmen Industries Inc. (newspaper)
COAM: Customer-Owned And Maintained
COAMP: Computer Analysis of Maintenance Policies
Coastal: Coastal Corp., The (newspaper)
CoastR: Coast R.V. Inc. (newspaper)
CoastSL: Coast S&L Assn. (California) (newspaper)
COAX: Coaxial Cable
COB: Close Of Business (with date)
Commission des Operations de Bourse
Coordination Of Benefits
COBLOS: Computer-Based Loans System
COBOL: Common Business-Oriented Language
COBRA: Consolidated Omnibus Budget Reconciliation Act
COC: Comptroller of the Currency
CocaCl: Coca-Cola Co., The (newspaper)
CocCE: Coca-Cola Enterprises Inc. (newspaper)
COCCEE: Comité des Organisations Commerciales des Pays de la CE (Committee of Commercial Organizations in the European Community) (French) (EC)
COCOM: Coordinating Committee on Multilateral Export Controls (EC)
COCS: Container Operating Control System
COD: Cash On Delivery
Cargo On Deck
CODAP: Client-Oriented Displacement Application
Comprehensive Occupa-

tional Data Analysis Program
CODAS: Customer-Oriented Data System
CODASYL: Conference on Data Systems Language (EC)
CODEC: Coder-Decoder
Coding-Decoding Device
CODEM: Coded Modulator-Demodulator
CODEST: European Development of Science and Technology (EC)
CODILS: Commodity-Oriented Digital Input Label System
COE: Crude Oil Equivalent
Current Operations Expenditures
COEA: Cost and Operational Effectiveness Analysis
COEES: Central Office Equipment Estimation System
Coeur: Coeur d'Alene Mines Corp. (newspaper)
COFACE: Compagnie Francaise pour l'Assurance du Commerce Exterieure
COFACTS: Cost Factoring System
COFAD: Computerized Facilities Design
COG: Customer-Owned Goods
COGAP: Computer Graphics Arrangement Program
COGENT: Compiler and Generalized Translator
Cognitr: Cognitronics Corp. (newspaper)
COGO: Coordinate Geometry
COGP: Commission on Government Procurement
COH: Cash-On-Hand
Cohu Inc. (ASE)
Cohu: Cohu Inc. (newspaper)
COI: Central Office of Information
Certificate Of Incorporation
Certificate Of Indebtedness
COIE: Committee on Invisible Exports
COINS: Computer and Information Sciences
Coordinated Inventory Control System
COIU: Congress of Independent Unions
col: column
COL: Computer-Oriented Language
COLA: Cost-Of-Living Adjustment (Allowance)
COLC: Cost-Of-Living Council
COLDEMAR: Compania Colombiana de Navegacion Maritima (Colombian Maritime Navigation Company) (steamship)
Coleco: Coleco Industries Inc. (newspaper)
ColFds: Collins Food International Inc. (newspaper)
ColGas: Columbia Gas System Inc., The (newspaper)
ColgPal: Colgate-Palmolive Co. (newspaper)
CollHI: Colonial-Intermediate High Income Fund (newspaper)
Coll: collateral
collator
collect
collection
Collat: collateral
Collins: Collins Industries Inc. (newspaper)
Coll L: Collection Letter
Coll Tr: Collateral Trust (bond)
ColMu: Colonial Municipal Income Trust (newspaper)
ColorSy: Color Systems Technology Inc. (newspaper)
ColPr: Colorado Prime Corp. (newspaper)
ColREI: Columbia Real Estate Investments Inc. (newspaper)

CO LTD: Closed Corporation
ColumS: Columbia S&L Assn. (newspaper)
com: commerce
commercial
commission
committee
COM: Computer Output Microfilm
Computer Output Microfilmer
Crowley Milner & Co. (ASE)
COMAC: Continuous Multiple Access Collator
COMAT: Computer-Assisted Training
comb: combination
COMCAN: Common Cause Analysis
Comdis: Comdisco Inc. (newspaper)
Comdre: Commodore International Ltd. (newspaper)
ComES: Commonwealth Energy System (newspaper)
COMECON: Council for Mutual Economic Assistance
COMETT: Community Program in Education and Training for Technology (EC)
COMEX: Commodity Exchange, Inc.
COMEXT: External statistics of the European Community (EC)
COMFd: Comfed Bancorp Inc. (newspaper)
COMFOR: International Computer Forum and Exposition
COMICS: Computer-Oriented Managed Inventory Control System
Cominc: Cominco Ltd. (newspaper)
COMITEXTIL: Comité de Coordination des Industries Textiles de la CE (Coordinating Committee of the Textile Industry in the European Community) (French) (EC)
coml: commercial
Com'l Ppr: Commercial Paper
comm: commercial
commission
committee
COMMANDS: Computer-Operated Marketing, Mailing and News Distribution System
COMMEND: Computer-Aided Mechanical Engineering Design
COMMS: Central Office Maintenance Management System
Comp: compatible
composite
compound
computer
computerization
computerize
computerized
COMP: Council on Municipal Management
Compaq: COMPAQ Computer Corp. (newspaper)
COMPARE: Computer-Oriented Method of Program Analysis, Review and Evaluation
COMPAS: Computer Acquisition System
COMPASS: Central Office Maintenance Printout Analysis and Suggestion System
Computer-Assisted Classification and Assignment System
compd: compound
CompD: CompuDyne Corp. (newspaper)
COMPENDEX: Computerized Engineering Index
COMPETA: Computer and Peripherals Equipment Trade Association

COMPROC: Command Processor
CompSc: Computer Sciences Corp. (newspaper)
compt: comptroller
Comptek: Comptek Research Inc. (newspaper)
compu: computability
computable
computer
COMRADE: Computer-Aided Design Environment
COMS: Computer-based Operations Management System
COMSAC: Computerized Measurements for Safeguards and Accountability
COMSAT: Communications Satellite
Communications Satellite Corporation (newspaper)
COMSEQUN: Component Sequencing and Insertion
comsn: commission
COMSOAL: Computer Method of Sequencing Operations for Assembly Lines
Comstk: Comstock Partners Strategy Fund Inc. (newspaper)
ComSy: COM Systems Inc. (newspaper)
comt: comptroller
comte: committee
Comtrn: Commtron Corp. (newspaper)
CON: Connelly Containers Inc. (ASE)
CONACS: Contractors Accounting System
ConAg: ConAgra Inc. (newspaper)
ConcdF: Concord Fabrics Inc. (newspaper)
Con Cr: Contra Credit
Cond: condition
CONDOC: Consortium to Develop an Online Catalog (EC)
Con Ed: Consolidated Edison
CONEX: Container Express
conf: conference
confer: conference
Cong: Congress
CONIT: Connector for Network Information Transfer
ConnE: Connecticut Energy Corp. (newspaper)
Connly: Connelly Containers Inc. (newspaper)
ConnNG: Connecticut Natural Gas Corp. (newspaper)
Conqst: Conquest Exploration Co. (newspaper)
CONRAD: Conversational On-line Real-time Algorithm Definition
Conrail: Consolidated Rail Corp. (newspaper)
Cons: console
consolidate
consolidated
Consec: Conseco Inc. (newspaper)
consgt: consignment
Consid: consideration
ConsNG: Consolidated Natural Gas Co. (newspaper)
ConsOG: Consolidated Oil & Gas Inc. (newspaper)
CONSOLS: Consolidated Annuities
CONSORT: Conversation System with On-line Remote Terminals
const: constant
Constn: Conston Corp. (newspaper)
Constr: Constar International Inc. (newspaper)
CONSUL: Control Sub-routine Language
consult: consultant
Cont: contract
controller
CONT: Continental Airlines

CONTAX: Consumers and Taxpayers
Contel: Contel Corp. (newspaper)
ContGr: Continental Graphics Corp. (newspaper)
ContIll: Continental Illinois Corp. (newspaper)
ContMtl: Continental Materials Corp. (newspaper)
CONUS: Continental United States
Conv: conversion
convertible
ConvHld: Convertible Holdings Inc. (newspaper)
Convsn: Conversion Industries Inc. (newspaper)
Convst: ConVest Energy Partners Ltd. (newspaper)
COO: Chief Operating Officer
Cooper Companies Inc., The (NYSE)
CoopCo: Cooper Companies Inc., The (newspaper)
Cooper: Cooper Industries Inc. (newspaper)
cop: copyright
COP: Calculator-Oriented Processor
City of Prineville (railroad)
Coefficient of Performance
Control-Oriented Processor
Copley Properties Inc. (ASE)
Customer Order Processing
Customer Owned Property
COPA: Comité des Organisations Professionnelles Agricoles de la CE (Committee of Agricultural Organizations in the European Community) (French) (EC)
Compania Panamena de Aviacion (Panamanian Air Lines)
COPE: Committee on Paperless Entries (Atlanta)
Committee on Political Education
Copelc: Copelco Financial Services Group Inc. (newspaper)
COPES: Computer-Oriented Purchasing and Engineering System
COPILOT: Cost-Oriented Production and Inventory Loading Operations Technique Works
Copley: Copley Properties Inc. (newspaper)
COPMEC: Comité des Petites et Moyennes Enterprises Commerciales des pays de la CE (Committee of Small and Medium Sized Commercial Enterprises of the European Community) (French) (EC)
COPR: Copper Range Railroad
CoprTr: Cooper Tire & Rubber Co. (newspaper)
COPS: Costing Out Policy Systems
Copwld: Copperweld Corp. (newspaper)
copy: copyright
COQ: Cost-of-Quality
cor: corpus
correspondent
COR: Crystal Oil Co. (ASE)
CORAL: Computer On-Line Realtime Applications Language
CORBFUS: Copy Of Reply to Be Furnished Us
CorBlk: Corroon & Black Corp. (newspaper)
Corcp: Corcap Inc. (newspaper)
CORD: Computer-Reinforced Design
Computer with On-line Remote Devices
CORE: Congress of Racial Equality
Contingency Response Program

CoreIn: Core Industries Inc. (newspaper)
COREPER: Comité des Représentants Permanents de la CE (Committee of Permanent Representatives of the European Community) (French) (EC)
CornGl: Corning Glass Works (newspaper)
corp: corporate
corporation
CORPORAL: Corporate Resource and Allocation
CORTEX: Communications-Oriented Real-Time Executive
COS: Cash On Shipment
Central Operations System
Communications-Oriented System
Copperweld Corp. (NYSE)
Corporation for Open Systems
COSA: Chairman of the Office of Savings Association
Cost-Of-Sales Adjustment
COSI: Committee on Scientific Information
COSIRA: Council for Small Industries in Rural Areas
CosmCr: Cosmopolitan Care Corp. (newspaper)
COSMIC: Computer Systems for Management Information Services
COSMO: Communications Simulation Model
COSMOS: Computer Optimization and Simulation Modeling for Operating Supermarkets
COST: Congressional Office of Science and Technology
Co-opération Européenne dans le Domaine de la Recherche Scientifique et Technique (European Co-operation in Science and Technology) (French) (EC)
COSTAR: Conversational On-line Storage and Retrieval
COSTER: Cost Optimizing System to Evaluate Reliability
COTR: Contracting Officer's Technical Representative
COTRAN: Code-Transformation
COTS: Container Off-loading and Transfer System
COU: Courtaulds PLC (ASE)
COURT: Cost Optimization Utilizing Reference Techniques
Courtld: Courtaulds PLC (newspaper)
COW: Crude Oil Washing
United Stockyards Corp. (NYSE)
COWPS: Council on Wage and Price Stability
C&P: Cumberland & Pennsylvania (railroad)
CP: Call Processor
Canadian Pacific Airlines
Canadian Pacific Ltd. (NYSE)
Canadian Pacific Railway Co.
Card Punch
Central Processor
Character Printer
Closing Price
Closing Purchase
Collar Pricing
Command Processor
Commercial Paper
Companhia des Caminhos de Ferro Portuguese Railways (Portuguese)
Condition Precedent
Conference Paper
Conference Proceedings
Construction Permit
Contract Price
Control Program

Corporate Planning
Critical Path

C-P: Colgate-Palmolive

C&PA: Coudersport & Port Allegany (railroad)

CPA: Canadian Pacific Airways
Certified Public Accountant
Chartered Public Accountant
Chicago Pacific Corp. (NYSE)
Consumer Protection Agency
Cost, Planning and Appraisal
Coudersport and Port Allegany (railroad)
Critical Path Analysis

CPACS: Comprehensive Payroll Accounting System

CPAF: Cost-Plus-Award Fee

CP AIR: Canadian Pacific Airlines

CPB: Campbell Soup Co. (NYSE)
Corporation for Public Broadcasting
Critical Path Bar chart

CPC: Card Programmed Calculator
Computerized Production Control
Computer Production Control
CPC International Inc. (NYSE)

CPCU: Chartered Property & Casualty Underwriter

CPD: Continuing Professional Development

CPE: Colorado Prime Corp. (ASE)
Customer Premises Equipment

CPF: Comstock Partners Strategy Fund Inc. (NYSE)
Cotton Plant-Fargo (railway)

CPFF: Cost Plus Fixed Fee

CPH: Capital Holding Corp. (NYSE)

CPI: Characters Per Inch
Commercial Performance Index
Consumer Price Index

CPIF: Cost Plus Incentive Fee

CPIS: Computerized Personnel Information System

CPL: Carolina Power & Light Co. (NYSE)

CP<: Camino, Placerville and Lake Tahoe (railroad)

CP/M: Control Program Microcomputer

CPM: Cards Processed per Minute
Computer Performance Monitor
Continuous Processing Machine
Contract Planning Model
Critical Path Method

CPN: Commercial Paper Note
CP National Corp. (NYSE)

CPO: Commodity Pool Operator
Concurrent Peripheral Operations
Cost Proposal Outline

CPP: Calprop Corp. (ASE)
Critical Path Plan
Current Purchasing Power

CPPC: Cost Plus a Percentage of Cost

CPPS: Critical Path Planning and Scheduling

CPQ: COMPAQ Computer Corp. (NYSE)

CPR: Canadian Pacific Railroad
Cost Performance Report

CP Rail: Canadian Pacific Railroad

cps: coupons

CPS: Characters Per Second
Consolidated Energy Partners LP (ASE)
Contingency Planning System
Controlled Path System
Convertible Preferred Stock
Critical Path Scheduling
Cumulative Preferred Stock

CPSC: Consumer Product Safety Commission

CP Ships: Canadian Pacific Steamships

CPSK: Coherent Phase-Shift Keying

CPsys: Community Psychiatric Centers (newspaper)
CPT: Chicago Produce Terminal
Chief Programmer Team
Continuous Performance Test
CptInd: Computerland Corp. (newspaper)
CPU: Central Processing Unit
CPV: Corporacion Peruana de Vapores (Peruvian Steamship Corporation)
CPX: Cineplex Odeon Corp. (NYSE)
CQ: Aero-Chaco (airlines)
Communications Satellite Corp. (NYSE)
CQA: Computer-aided Question Answering
CQMS: Circuit Quality Monitoring System
CQX: Conquest Exploration Co. (ASE)
cr: credit
creditor
CR: Card Reader
Carriage Return
Carrier's Risk
Cash Reserve
Commonwealth Railways
Commuter Airlines
Company Risk
Conference Report
Contract Report
Contractor Report
Copper Range (railroad)
Cost Reimbursement
Crane Co. (NYSE)
Critical Ratio
CRA: Community Redevelopment Agency
Computer Retailers Association
Contemporaneous Reserve Accounting
Craig Corp.(NYSE)
CRAFTS: Central Regional Automated Funds Transfer System
Craig: Craig Corp. (newspaper)
CRAM: Card Random Access Memory (Method)
Computerized Reliability Allocation Method
CRAMM: Coupon Reading and Marking Machine
CRANDIC: Cedar Rapids and Iowa City (railway)
Crane: Crane Co. (newspaper)
CrayRs: Cray Research Inc. (newspaper)
CRC: Cameroon Railways Corporation (West Africa)
Carolco Pictures Inc. (NYSE)
Carrier Return Character
Civil Rights Commission
Cumberland Railway Company (Nova Scotia)
Cyclic Redundancy Check
CrCPB: Crown Central Petroleum Corp. (newspaper)
CRD: Computer Read-out Device
CRDS: Certified Reliability Data Shell
CRE: Care Enterprises Inc. (ASE)
Commercial Relations and Exporters
cred: credit
creditor
CREDD: Customer-Requested Earlier Due Date
CREDIT: Cost Reduction Early Decision Information Techniques
CREF: Commingled Real Estate Funds
CREST: Comité de Recherche Scientifique et Technique (Committee of Scientific and Technological Research) (French) (EC)
CRF: Capital Recovery Factor
Cross Reference File
CR-HI: Channel Request-High Priority

CRI: Chicago River and Indiana (railroad)
Core Industries Inc. (NYSE)
CRI Insured Mortgage Investments Inc. (newspaper)

CR&IC: Cedar Rapids and Iowa City (railway)

CRIIM: CRI Insured Mortgage Investments LP (newspaper)

CRILA: Credit Insurance Logistics Automated

CRI&P: Chicago, Rock Island & Pacific (railroad)

CR&IR: Chicago River and Indiana Railroad

CRIS: Current Research Information System

CRJE: Conversational Remote Job Entry

CR-LO: Channel Request-Low Priority

CRM: Computer Resources Management
CRI Insured Mortgage Investments LP (NYSE)

CR-MED: Channel Request-Medium Priority

CrmpK: Crompton & Knowles Corp. (newspaper)

CRN: Carolina and Northwestern (Southern Railway)

CROM: Control Read-Only Memory

CRONOS: Community Statistical Office computerized economic data bank (EC)

CROP: Compliance Registered Options Principal

Crosby: Philip Crosby Associates Inc. (newspaper)

Cross: A.T. Cross Co. (newspaper)

CrowlM: Crowley, Milner & Co. (newspaper)

CRP: Central Railway of Peru
Combined Refining Process
Counter-Rotation Platform

CRR: Clinchfield Railroad
Consolidated Rail Corp. (NYSE)

CRRNJ: Central Railroad of New Jersey

CRS: Carpenter Technology Corp. (NYSE)

CRSI: Concrete Reinforcement Steel Institute

CRSS: CRS Sirrine Inc. (newspaper)

CRT: Cathode Ray Tube
Computer Remote Terminal

CRU: Collective Reserve Unit
Control and Reporting Unit

CRUSADER: Crusader Line (steamship)

CRV: Coast R. V. Inc. (ASE)

CRW: Crown Crafts Inc. (ASE)

CrwnCk: Crown Cork & Seal Company Inc. (newspaper)

CrysBd: Crystal Brands Inc. (newspaper)

CrystO: Crystal Oil Co. (newspaper)

C&S: Colorado & Southern (railroad)

C/S: Certificate of Service

CS: Cambrian Airways
Capital Stock
Carolina Southern (railroad)
Car Service
Closing Sale
Common Stock
Computer Science
Condition Subsequent

CSA: Ceskoslovenski Aerolinia (Czechoslovakian Airlines)
Coast S&L Assn. (California) (NYSE)

CSAR: Central South African Railways
Communication Satellite Advanced Research

CSAV: Compania Sud-Americana de Vapores (South American Steamship Company) (Chile)

CSC: Civil Service Commission
Clyde Shipping Company
Computer Sciences Corp. (NYSE)

CSCC: Cumulative Sum Control Chart

CSCE: Conference on Security and Cooperation in Europe

CSCS: Cost, Schedule, and Control System

CSD: Ceskoslovenske Statni Drahy (Czechoslovakian State Railways)
Closed System Delivery
Computerized Standard Data

CSE: Cincinnati Stock Exchange

CSEA: Civil Service Employees' Association

CSECT: Control Section

CSF: Critical Success Factor

CshAm: Cash America Investments Inc. (newspaper)

CSI: Council for the Securities Industry

CSK: Chesapeake Corp. (NYSE)

CSL: Canada Steamship Lines
Carlisle Companies Inc. (NYSE)
Chicago Short Line (railway)
Context-Sensitive Language
Control and Simulation Language
Current Switch Logic

CSM: Chaparral Steel Co. (NYSE)
Computer System Manual

CSMA: Communications Systems Management Association

CSMS: Computerized Specification Management System

CSN: Card Security Number
Cincinnati Bell Inc. (NYSE)

CSO: Central Statistical Office
Cities Service Oil

CSP: Camas Prairie (railroad)
Combustion Engineering Inc. (NYSE)

CSPC: Cost and Schedule Planning and Control

CSR: Central & South West Corp. (NYSE)

CSROEPM: Communication, System, Results, Objectives, Exception, Participation, Motivation

CSS: Central Certificate Service
Chicago South Shore and South Bend (railroad)
Commodity Stabilization Service
Computer Systems Simulator
CSS Industries Inc. (ASE) (newspaper)

CSSCO: Cunard Steamship Company

CSS&SBR: Chicago South Shore and South Bend Railroad

CST: Central Standard Time
Christiana Companies Inc., The (NYSE)
Consolidated Schedule Technique
Cumulative Sum Techniques

Cstam: CoastAmerica Corp. (newspaper)

C-store: Convenience Store

C St.PM&O: Chicago, St. Paul, Minneapolis and Omaha (railroad)

CSTS: Computer Sciences Teleprocessing System

CSU: Channel Service Unit
Circuit Switching Unit

CSV: Cash Surrender Value
Columbia S&L Assn. (NYSE)

CSVLI: Cash Surrender Value of Life Insurance

CSW: Channel Status Word

CSX: CSX Corp. (NYSE) (newspaper)

ct: court

C&T: Classification and Testing

CT: Air Commuter (airlines)
Cable Transfer

California Real Estate Investment Trust (NYSE)
Cash Trade
Central Time
Certificate (NYSE)
Cleveland Tankers
Compania Transmediterranea (Transmediterranean Company)

CTA: Central Pacific Corp. (ASE)
Chicago Transit Authority
Commodity Trading Adviser

CTAB: Commerce Technical Advisory Board

CTB: Collateral Trust Bond
Concentrator Terminal Buffer
Cooper Tire & Rubber Co. (NYSE)

CTC: Canadian Transport Commission
Cincinnati Transit Company
Contel Corp. (NYSE)

CTCA: Channel-To-Channel Adapter

CTCM: Computer Timing and Costing Model

CTCS: Component Time Control System

CTD: Certificate of Tax Deposit

CtData: Control Data Corp. (newspaper)

CTE: Compania Transatlantica Espanola (Spanish Transatlantic Line) (steamship)
Computer Telex Exchange

CTF: Counsellors Tandem Securities Fund Inc. (NYSE) (newspaper)

CTFC: Central Time and Frequency Control

ctfs: certificates

CTG: Connecticut Natural Gas Corp. (NYSE)

ctge: cartage

CTH: CRI Insured Mortgage Investments III LP (NYSE)

C 3 Inc.: C3 Inc. (newspaper)

CTI: Charge Transfer Inefficiency

CTK: Comptek Research Inc. (ASE)

CTL: Century Telephone Enterprises Inc. (NYSE)
Coastal Transport Limited (steamship)
Compiler Target Language

CtlCrc: Continental Circuits Corp. (newspaper)

CtlIHld: Continental Illinois Holding Corp. (newspaper)

CTM: Composite-Tape Memory
COM Systems Inc. (ASE)

CTMA: Commercial Truck Maintenance Association

CTN: Canton Railroad

CTO: Commerce Total Return Fund Inc. (ASE)

CTP: Central Maine Power Co. (NYSE)

ctr: counter

CTR: Constar International Inc. (NYSE)

ctrl: control

CTRS: Computerized Test-result Reporting System

Cts.: cents

CTS: Clear To Send
Cleveland Transit System
Commercial Transaction System
Communications Technology Satellite
CTS Corp. (NYSE) (newspaper)

CTT: Capital Transfer Tax

CTU: Commercial Telegraphers' Union

CTV: Cable Television

CTX: Centex Corp. (NYSE)

CTY: Century Communications Corp. (ASE)

CtyCom: Century Communications Corp. (newspaper)

CU: Consumers' Union
Container Unit
Control Unit

Credit Union
Cubana Airlines
CUA: Circuit Unit Assembly
CUAG: Computer Users Associations Group
CUB: Cubic Corp. (ASE)
Cubic: Cubic Corp. (newspaper)
CUC: Culbro Corp. (NYSE)
CUCV: Commercial Utility and Cargo Vehicle
CUDN: Common User Data Network
CUE: Computer Updating Equpment
Correction-Update-Extension
Quantum Chemical Corp. (NYSE)
CUG: Closed User Group
Culbro: Culbro Corp. (newspaper)
CULPRIT: Cull and Print
cum: cumulative
CUM: Central-Unit Memory
Cummins Engine Company Inc. (NYSE)
CumEn: Cummins Engine Company Inc. (newspaper)
CUNA: Credit Union National Association
CUNARD: Cunard Steam-Ship Company, Limited
CUO: Continental Materials Corp. (ASE)
CUPID: Create, Update, Interrogate and Display
Cuplex: Cuplex Inc. (newspaper)
CUR: Current Income Shares Inc. (NYSE)
CurInc: Current Income Shares Inc. (newspaper)
curr: currency
Curtce: Curtice-Burns Foods Inc. (newspaper)
CurtW: Curtiss-Wright Corp. (newspaper)
CUS: Customedix Corp. (ASE)
Cus Ho: Custom House
CUSIP: Committee on Uniform Securities Identification Procedures
cust: custom(s)
Custmd: Customedix Corp. (newspaper)
CUSUM: Cumulative Sum
CUT: Chartered Union of Taxpayers (UK)
CUTC: Cincinnati Union Terminal Company
CUTS: Cassette User Tape System
Computer User Tape System
CUUS: Consumers Union of the United States
CUV: Current Use Value
CUVA: Cuyahoga Valley (railroad)
cv: convertible
CV: Central Vermont Public Service Corp. (NYSE)
Central Vermont (railroad)
Collection Voucher
Constant Value
Convertible (NYSE)
CVA: Current Value Accounting
CVC: Cablevision Systems Corp. (ASE)
Convertible Security (in bond and stock listings of newspapers)
CVF: Castle Convertible Fund Inc. (ASE)
CVI: Cenvill Investors Inc. (NYSE)
CVL: Cenvill Development Corp. (ASE)
CVP: Cost-Volume-Profit
CVR: Chicago Rivet & Machine Co. (ASE)
Continuous Video Recorder
CVRY: Cuyahoga Valley Railway
CVS: Constant Volume Sampling
cvt: convertible
CVT: TCW Convertible Securities Fund Inc. (NYSE)
CVtPS: Central Vermont Public Service Corp. (newspaper)

cw: clockwise
C&W: Charleston and Western Carolina (railway)
Colorado & Wyoming (railroad)
CW: Channel Airways
Chesapeake Western (railroad)
Control Word
Curtiss-Wright Corp. (NYSE)
CWA: Communication Workers of America (union)
C&WC: Charleston & Western Carolina (railroad)
CWD: Clerical Work Data
CWE: Commonwealth Edison Co. (NYSE)
CWI: Chicago and Western Indiana (railroad)
CWine: Canandaigua Wine Company Inc. (newspaper)
CWM: Clerical Work Measurement
Convertible Wraparound Mortgage
Countrywide Mortgage Investments Inc. (NYSE)
CwnCr: Crown Crafts Inc. (newspaper)
CWO: Cash With Order
CWP: Chicago, West Pullman and Southern (railroad)
CWR: California Western Railroad
CWS: Cooperative Wage Study
CWSA: Contract Work Study Association
cwt: hundredweight
CX: Cathay Pacific Airways
Centerior Energy Corp. (NYSE)
Colorado and Southern Railway
CXC: CMX Corp. (ASE)
CXI: Cuplex Inc. (ASE)
CXR: CXR Telecom Corp. (ASE) (newspaper)
CXT: Common External Tariff (EC)
CXV: Cavalier Homes Inc. (ASE)
cxy: carrier
CXY: Canadian Occidental Petroleum Ltd. (ASE)
cy: carry
currency
cycle
CY: Current Year
Current Yield
Cyprus Airways
Cycare: CyCare Systems Inc. (newspaper)
cyl: cylinder
CyprFd: Cypress Semiconductor Corp. (newspaper)
CYR: Cray Research Inc. (NYSE)
CYS: CyCare Systems Inc. (NYSE)
CZ: Canal Zone
Air Champagne Ardennes (airline)
CZM: CalMat Co. (NYSE)
CZMS: Canal Zone Merit System

d: data
deci
decimal
delivery
destination
digit
digital
discount
displacement
dollar
domain
pence

D: Checkable Deposits of depository institutions
Dominion Resources Inc. (NYSE)
The price that is the low for the past year (in stock tables)

D/A: Digital to Analog (converter)
Documents for (against) Acceptance

DA: CRS Sirrine Inc. (NYSE)
Dan-Air Services (airline)
Data Administrator
Days after Acceptance
Demand Assigned
Department of Agriculture
Department of the Army
Depletion Allowance
Deposit Account
Destination Address
Development Assistance (Fund)
Direct Action
Directory Assistance
Discharge Afloat
Discretionary Account
Documents Attached
Documents for (against) Acceptance
Dollar Averaging
Dominion Atlantic (railroad)
Dormant Account

D of A: Department of the Army

DAA: Data Access Arrangement
Direct Access Arrangement

DAC: Data Analysis and Control
Design Augmented by Computer
Development Assistance Committee
Digital-to-Analog Converter

D ACC: Doctor of Accountancy

DACE: Data Acquisition and Control Executive

DACOR: Data Correction

DADEC: Design And Demonstration Electronic Computer

DADEE: Dynamic Analog Differential Equation Equalizer

DADIOS: Direct Analog To Digital Input-Output System

D ADM: Doctor of Administration

DADS: Data Acquisition and Display System

DAF: Data Acquisition Facility
Described As Follows

DAFA: Data Accounting Flow Assessment

DAFC: Digital Automatic Frequency Control

DAI: Direct Access Information

DAIS: Direct Access Intelligence Systems

DAISY: Decision Aiding Information System

DAL: Delta Air Lines Inc. (NYSE)
Deutsche-Afrika Linien (German African Line) (steamship)

Dallas: Dallas Corp. (newspaper)

DAM: Damson Oil Corp. (ASE)
Data Addressed Memory

Diagnostic Acceptability Measure
DAMA: Demand Assigned Multiple Access
DamCr: Damon Creations Inc. (newspaper)
DamE: Damson Energy Company LP (newspaper)
DAME: Digital Automatic Measuring Equipment
D'AMICO: D'Amico Line (steamship)
DAMID: Discounting Analysis Model for Investment Decisions
DAMOS: Data Moving System
Damson: Damson Oil Corp. (newspaper)
DAN: Daniel Industries Inc. (NYSE)
DanaCp: Dana Corp. (newspaper)
Danhr: Danaher Corp. (newspaper)
Daniel: Daniel Industries Inc. (newspaper)
DAP: Do Anything Possible
D A Plan: Deposit Administration Plan
DAPS: Direct Access Programming System
DART: Daily Automatic Rescheduling Technique
Design Automation Routing Tool
Detection, Action and Response Technique
DAS: Data Acquisition System
Data Analysis System
Data Automation System
Delivered Alongside Ship
Design Analysis System
DASD: Direct Access Storage Device
DASM: Direct Access Storage Media
DAT: Data Abstract Tape
Desk-top Analysis Tool
Digital Audio Tape
Dynamic Address Translation
DATACOM: Data Communication
DATACOR: Data Correction
DataGn: Data General Corp. (newspaper)
Datamet: Datametrics Corp. (newspaper)
DatAn: Data Analysis
DataNet: Data Network
DataPd: Dataproducts Corp. (newspaper)
Datapt: Datapoint Corp. (newspaper)
DATAR: Digital Automatic Tracking and Ranging
Datarm: Dataram Corp. (newspaper)
DATAS: Data in Associative Storage
DATEL: Data Telecommunication
DATICO: Digital Automatic Tape Intelligence Checkout
DatIn: Data Inserter
DaTran: Data Transmission
D/Atchd: Draft Attached
DAU: Data Adapter Unit
DAV: Data Above Voice
DavWtr: Davis Water & Waste Industries Inc. (newspaper)
Daxor: Daxor Corp. (newspaper)
DAY LINE: Hudson River Day Line
DaytHd: Dayton Hudson Corp. (newspaper)
db: daybook
debenture
decibel
D&B: Dun and Bradstreet
DB: Data Base
Data Bus
Deutsche Bundesbahn (German Railways)
DBA: Data-Base Administrator
Doctor of Business Administration
Doing Business As
DBAM: Data Base Access Method

DBD: Diebold Inc. (NYSE)
D B ED: Doctor of Business Education
DBF: Drexel Bond-Debenture Trading Fund (NYSE)
DBK: Daiichi Bussan Kaisha (steamship)
DBL: Data Base Language
DBMS: Data-Base Management System
DB RTS: Debenture Rights
DBS: Direct Broadcast System
DC: Da Capo (from the beginning)
Daisy Chain
Data Channel
Data Classifier
Data Code
Data Communication
Datametrics Corp. (ASE)
Delray Connecting (railroad)
Digital Computer
Direct Current
Double Column
DCA: Digital Communications Associates Inc. (NYSE)
DCATA: Drug, Chemical, and Allied Trades Association
DCB: Data Control Block
DCC: Development Coordination Committee
Device Cluster Controller
DCCA: Design Change Cost Analysis
DCDS: Digital Control Design System
DCE: Data Communications Equipment
Domestic Credit Expansion
DCF: Discounted Cash Flow
DCFM: Discounted Cash Flow Method
DCH: Data Channel
DCI: Des Moines and Central Iowa (railroad)
Donaldson Company Inc. (NYSE)
DckM: Dickenson Mines Ltd. (newspaper)
dcl: declaration
DCL: Diners' Club, Inc.
Discretionary Credit Limit
DCN: Dana Corp. (NYSE)
DCNY: DCNY Corp. (newspaper)
DCO: Ducommun Inc. (ASE)
D COM: Doctor of Commerce
DCR: Delray Connecting Railroad
DC&S: Detroit, Caro & Sandusky (railroad)
DCS: Data Control System
Doctor of Commercial Science
DCT: Digital Communications Terminal
Diversified Cooperative Training
Washington, D.C. Transit
DCY: DCNY Corp. (NYSE)
DD: Command Airways
Data Definition
Data Dictionary
Data Division
Day's (Days after) Date
Declaration Date
De Dato (of this Date)
Deferred Delivery
Delayed Delivery
Demand Draft
Double Deck
Double Draft
Dry Dock
Due Date
E. I. du Pont de Nemours & Co. (NYSE)
DDA: Demand Deposit Accounts
Digital Differential Analyzer
DDAM: Dynamic Design-Analysis Method
DDAS: Digital Data Acquisition System
DDB: Double-Declining-Balance (depreciation method)
DDC: Direct Digital Control

DDD: Comprehensive Dishonesty, Disappearance, and Destruction policy
Death, Dismemberment, or Disability (insurance)
Direct Deposit of Dividends
Direct Distance Dialing

DDL: Data-Description Language
Data-Design Laboratories Inc. (NYSE)
Digital Data Link

DDName: Data-Definition Name

DDP: Direct Deposit of Payroll
Distributed Data Processing

DDR: Dynamic Device Reconfiguration

DDS: Dataphone Digital Service
Digital Data System
Dillard Department Stores Inc. (ASE)

DD Statement: Data-Definition Statement

ddt: deduct

DDT&E: Design, Development, Test, and Evaluation

D&E: De Queen and Eastern (railroad)

DE: Data Entry
Deere & Co. (NYSE)
Double Entry

DeanFd: Dean Foods Co. (newspaper)

deb: debenture

dec: decimal
decoder
decrement

DEC: Detroit Edison Company
Digital Equipment Corp. (NYSE)

DECA: Descent Engine Control Assembly

deck: deque

Decorat: Decorator Industries Inc. (newspaper)

decr: decrement

deduct: deduction

DEE: Dee Corp. PLC (NYSE)
Digital Evaluation Equipment

DeeCp: Dee Corporation PLC (newspaper)

Deere: Deere & Co. (newspaper)

def: deferred
deficit
definition

DEFRA: Deficit Reduction Act

DFU: Data File Utility

DEG: De Laurentiis Entertainment Group Inc. (ASE)

DEI: Diversified Energies Inc. (NYSE) (newspaper)

del: delete

DEL: Direct Exchange Line

DeLau: De Laurentiis Entertainment Group Inc. (newspaper)

DelLab: Del Laboratories Inc. (newspaper)

Delmed: Delmed Inc. (newspaper)

DelmP: Delmarva Power & Light Co. (newspaper)

DELTA: Delta Air Lines
Development of Learning through Technological Advance (EC)

DeltaAr: Delta Air Lines Inc. (newspaper)

Deltona: The Deltona Corp. (newspaper)

Deluxe: Deluxe Corp. (newspaper)

DelVal: Del-Val Financial Corp. (newspaper)

dely: delivery

dem: demand
demurrage

DEMA: Data Entry Management Association

DEMS: Digital Electronic Message Service

demur: demurrage

denom: denomination

DensMf: Dennison Manufacturing Co. (newspaper)
dep: depart
department
deposit
depositary
depositor
DEP: Damson Energy Company LP (ASE)
Displaced Employee Program
Dep Ctf: Deposit Certificate
depo: deposit
deq: dequeue
DeRose: De Rose Industries Inc. (newspaper)
DES: Data Enryption Standard
Design and Evaluation System
Desgnl: Designcraft Industries Inc. (newspaper)
DeSoto: DeSoto Inc. (newspaper)
desp: despatch
dest: destination
DeTab: Decision Table
DetEd: Detroit Edison Co., The (newspaper)
DEU: Data Exchange Unit
DEW: Delmarva Power & Light Co. (NYSE)
DEX: Dexter Corp., The (NYSE)
Dexter: Dexter Corp., The (newspaper)
D&F: Determination and Findings
DF: Data Field
Dean Foods Co. (NYSE)
Destination Field
Device Flag
D-F: Dansk-Franske (Danish-French Line) (steamship)
DFC: Data-Flow Control
DFI: Duty Free International Inc. (ASE)
DFM: Design For Manufacturability
DFP: De Laurentiis Film Partners LP (ASE)
DFR: Decreasing Failure Rate
DFT: Diagnostic Function Test
Digital Facility Terminal
dg: datagram
DGN: Data General Corp. (NYSE)
DGR: Denver and Rio Grande Western (railroad)
dh: deadhead
D&H: Delware and Hudson (railroad)
DH: Dayton Hudson Corp. (NYSE)
Design Handbook
DHR: Danaher Corp. (NYSE)
Darjeeling Himalayan Railway
DHS: Data Handling System
DHUD: Department of Housing and Urban Development
DHV: Design Hourly Volume
DI: Department of the Interior
Device Independence
Disability Insurance
Dresser Industries Inc. (NYSE)
DIA: Design and Industries Association
Diasonics Inc. (ASE)
Dulles International Airport
Diag: Diagnostic/Retrieval Systems Inc. (newspaper)
DiagPr: Diagnostic Products Corp. (newspaper)
DIAL: Draper Industrial Assembly Language
DIAN: Digital Analog
DianaCp: Diana Corp., The (newspaper)
DIANE: Direct Information Access Network for Europe (EC)
DIANESGUIDE: Online guide to European database producers, hosts, databases and databanks (EC)
DiaSo: Diamond Shamrock Offshore Partners LP (newspaper)
Diasonc: Diasonics Inc. (newspaper)

DIBOL: Digital Business-Oriented Language
DIC: Dependency and Indemnity Compensation
Digital Incremental Computer
Digital Integrating Computer
dict: dictionary
DIDC: Depository Institutions Deregulation Committee
DI/DO: Data Input/Data Output
DIDS: Decision Information Distribution System
Digital Information Display System
Diebold: Diebold Inc. (newspaper)
diff: difference
differential
dig: digit
DIG: Di Giorgio Corp. (NYSE)
DiGior: Di Giorgio Corp. (newspaper)
Digital: Digital Equipment Corp. (newspaper)
DigtlCm: Digital Communications Associates Inc. (newspaper)
DII: Decorator Industries Inc. (ASE)
DI IND: DI Industries Inc. (newspaper)
Dillard: Dillard Department Stores Inc. (newspaper)
DimeNY: Dime Savings Bank of New York FSB (newspaper)
DIMS: Data Information and Manufacturing System
DIN: Data Identification Number
DINER: Dining Car
DIO: Diodes Inc. (ASE)
Diodes: Diodes Inc. (newspaper)
DIOS: Distributed Input/Output System
DIP: Dual In-line Package
dir: director
directory
DIRAC: Direct Access
DirActn: Direct Action Marketing Inc. (newspaper)
dis: disconnect
discount
DIS: Walt Disney Co., The (NYSE)
disb: disburse
disbursement
disbmt: disbursement
disc: discount
DISC: Distribution Stock Control System
Domestic International Sales Corporation
disct: discount
DISLAN: Display Language
dism: dismiss
dismissal
Disney: Walt Disney Co., The (newspaper)
disp: displacement
display
dist: discount
district
DIST: Distributed (NYSE)
div: dividend
division
divisional
DIV: Data In Voice
PLC Diversifund (ASE)
DIVA: Digital Inquiry-Voice Answerback
divd: dividend
DiviHtl: Divi Hotels N.V. (newspaper)
Divrsln: Diversified Industries Inc. (newspaper)
divs: dividends
DIX: Dixieline Products Inc. (ASE)
Dixilne: Dixieline Products Inc. (newspaper)
DixnGp: Dixons Group PLC (newspaper)
DisnTi: Dixon Ticonderoga Co. (newspaper)
diy: Do It Yourself

D&J: December and June (securities)
DJ: Air Djibouti (airline)
Dow-Jones & Company Inc. (NYSE)
D-J: Dow-Jones (average)
DJA: Dow-Jones Averages
DJI: Designcraft Industries Inc. (ASE)
Dow-Jones Industrial (average)
DJIA: Dow-Jones Industrial Average
DJNR: Dow-Jones News Retrieval
DJTA: Dow-Jones Transportation Average
DJUA: Dow-Jones Utility Average
dk: dock
DK: Don't Know (A stock transaction between a broker and another broker in which there is some discrepancy in the records)
DKS: Doniphan, Kensett and Searcy (railway)
DL: Data Link
Data List
Day Letter
Delta Airlines
Demand Loan
Department of Labor
Dominion Shipping (steamship)
DLauF: De Laurentiis Film Partners LP (newspaper)
DLC: Data-Link Control (character)
dld: delivered
DLD: Deadline Date
DLE: Data-Link Escape (character)
DLF: Development Loan Fund
DLI: Del Laboratories Inc. (ASE)
DLP: CenTrust Savings Bank (ASE)
Dynamic Limit Programming
dlr: dealer
dls: dollars
DLS: Dallas Corp. (NYSE)
Debt Liquidation Schedule
DLS/SHR: Dollars per Share
DLT: Data-Loop Transceiver
Decision Logic Table
Deltona Corp., The (NYSE)
DL&W: Delaware, Lackawanna & Western (railroad)
DLX: Deluxe Corp. (NYSE)
dm: decimeter
D&M: Detroit and Mackinac (railroad)
DM: Data Management
Data Manager
Design Manual
Deutsche Mark (currency of Germany)
Maersk Air (airline)
DMA: Direct Memory Access
DMAA: Direct Mail Advertising Association
DMAC: Direct Memory Access Channel
DMC: Direct Manufacturing Cost
Diversified Industries Inc. (NYSE)
DMD: Delmed Inc. (ASE)
DME: Dime Savings Bank of New York FSB (NYSE)
Distance Measuring Equipment
DM&IRR: Duluth, Missabe & Iron Range Railroad
DMJS: December, March, June, September (securities)
DMK: Direct Action Marketing Inc. (ASE)
DML: Data Manipulating Language
Dickenson Mines Ltd. (ASE)
DMM: Dansville and Mount Morris (railroad)
DMO: Data Management Officer
dmp: dump
DMR: Data Management Routines
DMS: Data Management System
Data Multiplexer
Digital Multiplex Switching (System)

DMU: Data Management Unit
Des Moines Union (railway)
DMWR: Des Moines Western Railway
DN: Data Name
Debit Note
DNA: Diana Corp., The (NYSE)
Does Not Answer
Does Not Apply
DNB: Dun & Bradstreet Corp., The (NYSE)
DNC: Direct Numerical Control
DNE: Duluth and Northeastern (railroad)
DNF: Did Not Finish
DNI: Damon Creations Inc. (ASE)
Distributable Net Income
DNIC: Data Network Identification Code
DNL: Do Not Load
DNP: Duff & Phelps Selected Utilities (NYSE)
DNR: Do Not Reduce (order)
Do Not Renew (policy)
DNY: R.R. Donnelley & Sons Co. (NYSE)
do: ditto (same)
DO: Day Order
Delivery Order
Direct Orient (Orient Express)
Disbursing Office (Officer)
District Office
DOA: Date Of Availability
Department Of Agriculture
DOB: Date Of Birth
Disbursed Operating Base
doc: document
DOC: Department Of Commerce
Direct Operating Costs
DOD: Department Of Defense
DODC: Double (Dual) Overhead Camshaft
DOE: Department Of Energy
DOES: Direct Order Entry System
DOF: Degree Of Freedom
DOG: Days Of Grace
DOI: Department Of the Interior
DOJ: Department Of Justice
dol: dollar
DOL: Department Of Labor
DOLARS: Disk On-line Accounts Receivable System
Dom Ex: Domestic Exchange
DOMINA: Distribution-Oriented Management Information Analyzer
DomRs: Dominion Resources Inc. (newspaper)
Domtr: Domtar Inc. (newspaper)
DON: Donnelly Corp. (ASE)
Donald: Donaldson Company Inc. (newspaper)
Donley: R.R. Donnelley & Sons Co. (newspaper)
DonlyC: Donnelly Corp. (newspaper)
DOP: Developing Out Paper
DORACE: Design Organization, Record, Analyze, Charge, Estimate
DORR: Delaware Otsego Railroad
DOS: Date Of Shipment
Disk Operating System
DOSES: Development Of Statistical Expert Systems
DOS/VS: Disk Operating System with Virtual Storage
DOT: Date Of Trade
Department Of the Treasury
Department Of Transportation
Designated Order Turnaround
Double-B: Double-Banked
Double-Bonded
DOV: Dover Corp. (NYSE)
Dover: Dover Corp. (newspaper)
DOW: Dow Chemical Co., The (NYSE)
Dow-Jones Averages
DowCh: Dow Chemical Co., The (newspaper)

DowJns: Dow Jones & Company Inc. (newspaper)
Downey: Downey S&L Assn. (newspaper)
DP: Data Processing
Data Processor
Diagnostic Products Corp. (NYSE)
Distribution Point
Documents against Payment
Due Process
Dynamic Programming
DPA: Deferred Payment Account
Doctor of Public Administration
DPB: Deposit PassBook
DPC: Data Processing Center
Dataproducts Corp. (ASE)
DPE: Data Processing Equipment
DPF: Deferred Pay Fund
DPG: Development Program Grant
DPI: Domestic Product of Industry
DP&L: Dallas Power and Light
DPL: DPL Inc. (NYSE) (newspaper)
DPMA: Data Processing Management Association
DPPP: Deferred Premium Payment Plan
DPS: Data-Processing Station
Dividends Per Share
DPSK: Differential Phase-Shift Keying
dpst: deposit
dpt: depth
DPT: Datapoint Corp. (NYSE)
DPW: Department of Public Works
DPX: Duplex Products Inc. (ASE)
DQ: Colony Airlines
DQ&E: Dequeen & Eastern (railroad)
DQU: Duquesne Light Co. (NYSE)
dr: debit
debtor
divisor
D&R: Dardanelle and Russellville (railroad)
DR: Daily Report
Data Report
Deposit Receipt
Discount Rate
DRAM (D-RAMS): Dynamic Random Access Memory (chip)
Dravo: Dravo Corp. (newspaper)
DRAW: Direct Read After Write
DRCS: Dynamically Redefinable Character Set
DRE: Duke Realty Investments (NYSE)
DREAM: Design Realization, Evaluation and Modelling
Digital Recording and Measurement
Dresr: Dresser Industries Inc. (newspaper)
DrexB: Drexel Bond-Debenture Trading Fund (newspaper)
Dreyfus: Dreyfus Corp., The (newspaper)
DRG: Detroit Rubber Group
D&RGW: Denver & Rio Grande Western (railroad)
DRH: Driver-Harris Co. (ASE)
DRI: Davenport, Rock Island and North Western (railway)
De Rose Industries Inc. (ASE)
DRIVE: Dedicated Road Infrastructure of Vehicle Safety (EC)
DrivHar: Driver-Harris Co. (newspaper)
DRL: DI Industries Inc. (ASE)
DRM: Diamond Shamrock R&M Inc. (NYSE)
Direct Reduction Mortgage
DRO: Digital Read-Out
DRON: Data Reduction
DRP: Distribution Resource Planning
Dividend-Reinvestment Plan
DRR: Discounted Rate of Return

DRS: Diagnostic/Retrieval Systems Inc. (ASE)
DRV: Dravo Corp. (NYSE)
DRY: Devco Railway
Dreyfus Corp., The (NYSE)
DryStGn: Dreyfus Strategic Government Income Fund (newspaper)
DryStr: Dreyfus Strategic Municipals Inc. (newspaper)
D&S: Durham & Southern (railroad)
DS: Air Senegal (airline)
Data Set
Days after Sight
Debenture Stock
Dominion Shipping (steamship)
Draft Stop
D-S: Ditley-Simonsen, Halfdan and Company (steamship)
DSB: Danske Statsbaner (Danish State Railways)
DSBAM: Double SideBand Amplitude Modulation
DSC: Detroit Stock Exchange
DSCB: Data-Set Control Block
DSDD: Double-Sided Double-Density
DSDT: Data-Set Definition Table
DSE: Data-Switching Exchange
Distributed Systems Environment
DSECT: Dummy Control Section
DSG: Designatronics Inc. (ASE)
Dsgntrn: Designatronics Inc. (newspaper)
DShRM: Diamond Shamrock R&M Inc. (newspaper)
DSI: Dreyfus Strategic Government Income Fund (NYSE)
dsk: disc (disk)
DSL: Downey S&L Assn. (NYSE)
dsmd: dismissed
DSN: Data-Set Name
Dennison Manufacturing Co. (NYSE)
DSO: Days Sales Outstanding
DeSoto Inc. (NYSE)
DSP: Diamond Shamrock Offshore Partners LP (NYSE)
Digital Signal Processing
DSP Chip: Digital Signal Processing Chip
dspl: display
DSR: Data Set Ready
Detroit Street Railways
DSRO: Designated Self-Regulatory Organization
DSS: Decision Support System
Distribution Scheduling System
Dynamic Support System
DSS&A: Duluth, South Shore & Atlantic (railroad)
DSSD: Double-Sided Single-Density
DST: Daylight Saving Time
dstr: distribution
distributor
DSU: Data Service Unit
DT: Data Terminal
Department of Transportation
Department of the Treasury
Detroit Terminal (railroad)
Dial Tone
Dow Theory
DTA: Direccao de Exploracao dos Transportes Aereos (Angola Airlines)
DtaDsg: Data-Design Laboratories Inc. (newspaper)
DTAS: Data Transmission And Switching (System)
DTC: Dallas Transit Company
Department of Trade and Commerce (UK)
Depositary Trust Company
Deposit-Taking Company
Design To Cut
Desk Top Computer
Direct-To-Consumer
Domtar Inc. (NYSE)
dtd: dated

DTE: Data-Terminal Equipment
Detroit Edison Co., The (NYSE)
DTG: Date-Time Group
DTI: Detroit, Toledo and Ironton (railroad)
DTM: Dataram Corp. (ASE)
DTR: Data Terminal Ready
D&TSL: Detroit & Toledo Shore Line
DTUPC: Design-to-Unit Production Cost
DtyFr: Duty Free International Inc. (newspaper)
DU: Del Air-Air Cargo (airline)
Ducom: Ducommun Inc. (newspaper)
Du Dat: Due Date
DuffPh: Duff & Phelps Selected Utilities (newspaper)
DUK: Duke Power Co. (NYSE)
DukeP: Duke Power Co. (newspaper)
DukeRln: Duke Realty Investments Inc. (newspaper)
dun: dunnage
DunBd: Dun & Bradstreet Corp., The (newspaper)
DUNS: Data Universal Numbering System (Dun's Number)
dup: duplicate
Duplex: Duplex Products Inc. (newspaper)
duPont: E.I. du Pont de Nemours & Co. (newspaper)
DuqLt: Duquesne Light Co. (newspaper)
DUT: Device Under Test
DUV: Data Under Voice
DV: Dependent Variable
dvc: device
DVCDN: Console Command-Device Down
DVCUP: Console Command-Device Up
DVH: Divi Hotels NV (ASE)
DVL: Del-Val Financial Corp. (NYSE)
DVP: Delivery Versus Payment
Discounted Present Value
DVS: Delta Valley and Southern (railway)
DVST: Direct View Storage Tube
D&W: Danville & Western (railroad)
DW: Cross Sound Commuter Airlines
Daisy Wheel
Dead Weight
Dock Warrant
Double-Word
DWG: DWG Corp. (ASE) (newspaper)
DWGI: Dean Witter Government Income Trust (newspaper)
DWIM: Do What I Mean
DW&P: Duluth, Winnipeg & Pacific (railroad)
DWP: Del E. Webb Investment Properties Inc. (ASE)
DwT: Deadweight Tonnage
DWW: Davis Water & Waste Industries Inc. (NYSE)
DX: Aerotaxi de Colombia (airline)
DXC: Data Exchange Control
DXN: Dixons Group PLC (NYSE)
DXR: Daxor Corp. (ASE)
DXT: Dixon Ticonderoga Co. (ASE)
DYA: Dynamics Corporation of America (NYSE)
DYN: DynCorp. (NYSE)
DynAm: Dynamics Corporation of America (newspaper)
DYNAMIT: Dynamic Allocation of Manufacturing Inventory and Time
Dyncrp: DynCorp (newspaper)
DYSTAL: Dynamic Storage Allocation

e: error
execute
execution
expended
exponent
expression
extended

E: European Community (stamp)
Declared or Paid in the preceding 12 months (in stock listings of newspapers)
Transco Energy Co. (NYSE)

EA: Edge Act
Effective Address
Electronic Associates Inc. (NYSE)
Element Activity
Energy Analysis
Environmental Analysis
Environment Analysis

EAA: Electrical Appliance Association

EAAA: European Association of Advertising Agencies

EABS: Published results of scientific and technical research programs (EC)

EAC: EAC Industries Inc. (ASE) (newspaper)
East Asiatic Company (steamship)
Equity Appreciation Certificate

EACEM: European Association of Consumer Electronic Manufacturers

EAD: Equipment Allowance Document
Estimated Availability Date

EADAS: Engineering and Administration Data Acquisition System

EAE: Extended Arithmetic Element

EAEL: European Atomic Energy Community (Euratom)

EAGGF: European Agricultural Guidance and Guarantee Fund (EC)

EAGL: Eagle Financial Corp. (ASE)

EaglCl: Eagle Clothes Inc. (newspaper)

EagleP: Eagle-Picher Industries Inc. (newspaper)

EaglFn: Eagle Financial Corp. (newspaper)

EAM: Electrical Accounting Machine

EAN: European Article Numbering

EAP: Employee Assistance Program
Emulator Application Program
Extended Arithmetic Processor

EAPM: European Association for Personnel Management

EAPROM: Electrically Alterable Programmable Read-Only Memory

EAR: East African Railways
Extended Address Register

EARC: East African Railways Corporation

EAR&H: East African Railways and Harbours

EARL: Easy Access Report Language

EAROM: Electrically Alterable Read-Only Memory

EAS: Energy Audit Scheme

EASAL: Easy Application Language
easemt: easement
EastGF: Eastern Gas & Fuel Associates (newspaper)
EastUtl: Eastern Utilities Associates (newspaper)
EASY: Exception Analysis System
Eaton: Eaton Corp. (newspaper)
EAU: Extended Arithmetic Unit
EAX: Electronic Automatic Exchange
E&B: Ellerman and Bucknall Steamship Company
EB: Ehrlich Bober Financial Corp. (ASE)
Metro-Aire Commuter Airlines
EBAM: Electron Beam Addressable Memory
EBC: Electronic Business Communications
EBCD: Extended Binary-Code Decimal
EBCDIC: Extended Binary-Coded Decimal Interchange Code
E BEAM: Electronic Beam
EBES: Electron Beam Exposure System
EBF: Ennis Business Forms Inc. (NYSE)
EBIT: Earnings Before Interest and Taxes
EBM: Extended Branch Mode
EBR: Electron Beam Recording
Emu Bay Railway (Tasmania)
EBRD: European Bank for Reconstruction and Development
EBRY: Eastern Bengal Railway
EBS: Edison Brother Stores Inc. (NYSE)
Emergency Broadcast System
EBU: European Broadcasting Union
EBV: Extended Binary Vectors
ec: economics
EC: East African Airways
East Carolina (railroad)
Electronic Computer
Engelhard Corp. (NYSE)
Engineering Change
Error Correcting
Ex-Coupon
Extended Control
Extended Coverage
European (Communities) Community
ECA: Economic Cooperation Administration
Electronics Control Assembly
ECAC: European Civil Aviation Conference
ECAM: Extended Content-Addressable Memory
ECAP: Electronic Circuit Analysis Program
ECB: Event Control Block
ECC: ECC International Corp. (NYSE) (newspaper)
Error Check and Control
Error Checking and Correction
Error Correction Code
Error Correction Control
ECCM: Electronic Counter Counter Measures
ECD: Estimated Completion Date
ECDIN: Environmental Data and Information Network on Chemicals (EC)
ECE: Economic Commission for Europe
Executive Communication Exchange
Extended Coverage Endorsement
ECF: Ellsworth Convertible Growth & Income Fund Inc. (ASE)
ECFTUC: European Confederation of Free Trade Union in the Community (EC)

ECGD: Export Credits Guarantee Department
ECH: Echlin Inc. (NYSE)
Echlin: Echlin Inc. (newspaper)
EchoB: Echo Bay Mines Ltd. (newspaper)
ECI: European Cooperation in Informatics
Export Consignment Identifying number
ECIF: Electronic Components Industry Federation
ECIN: Economic Indicators
ECITO: European Central Inland Transport Organization
ECL: Ecolab Inc. (NYSE)
Emitter-Coupled Logic
Executive Control Language
ECLA: Economic Commission for Latin America
ECLAIR: European Collaboration Linkage of Agriculture and Industry through Research (EC)
ECM: Electric Coding Machine
Electronic Counter Measures
European Common Market
ECMA: European Computer Manufacturers' Association
ECMRA: European Chemical Marketing Research Association
ECMT: European Conference of Ministers of Transport
ECN: Ecogen Inc. (ASE)
Engineering Change Notice
ECO: Echo Bay Mines Ltd. (ASE)
Engineering Change Order
ECOA: Equal Credit Opportunity Act
Ecofin: Council of finance ministers (EC)
Ecogn: Ecogen Inc. (newspaper)
Ecolab: Ecolab Inc. (newspaper)
EcolEn: Ecology & Environment Inc. (newspaper)
ECOM: Electronic Computer-Originated Mail
ECOMA: European Computer Measurement Association
econ: economics
economist
economy
ECON: Extended Console System
ECONOMAN: Effective Control of Manpower
ECOS: Extended Communications Operating System
ECOW: Metropolitan Realty Corp. (ASE)
ECOWAS: Economic Community of West African States
ECP: Emulator Control Program
Engineering Change (Cost) Proposal
ECPS: Extended Control Program Support
ECPT: European Conference of Posts and Telecommunications
ECR: Electronic Cash Register
Embossed Character Reader
ECREEA: European Conference of Radio and Electronic Equipment Association
ECS: Energy Conversion System
European Communication Satellite
Extended Control Storage
Extended Core Store
ECSA: European Computing System Simulator
ECSC: European Coal and Steel Community (EC)
ECSS: Extendable Computer System Simulator
ECSW: Extended Channel Status Word
ECT: Earliest Completion Time
Environment Control Table
Estimated Completion Time

ECTEL: European Telecommunications and Professional Electronics Industry
ECTL: Emitter Coupled Transistor Logic
ECU: European Currency Unit (EC)
ECVP: European Community's Visitors Program (EC)
ECYO: European Community Youth Orchestra (EC)
ed: editor
extra
E/D: Encode/Decode
ED: Consolidated Edison Company of New York Inc. (NYSE)
Encryption Device
Extra Dividend
EDA: Economic Development Administration
Electronic-Design-Automation
European Area of Development (EC)
EDAC: Error Detection and Correction
EDAMA: European Domestic Appliance Manufacturers Association
EDBMS: Engineering Data Base Management System
EDBS: Educational Data Base Management System
EDC: Electronic Digital Computer
Estimated Date of Completion
European Defense Community
Export Development Corporation
Extended Device Control
External Disk/Drum Channel
EDD: Envelope Delay Distortion
Estimated Delivery Date
Expected Date of Delivery
Expert Data base Designer
EDE: Empire District Electric Co., The (NYSE)
EDF: European Development Fund (EC)
EDFM: Extended Disk File Management System
EDGAR: Electronic Data Gathering And Retrieval
edi: editor
EDI: Electronic Document Interchange
EDIS: Engineering Data Information System
EdisBr: Edison Brothers Stores Inc. (newspaper)
edit: editor
EDL: Emulation Design Language
EDLR: Egyptian Delta Light Railways
EDM: Electrical Discharge Machining
Event Driven Monitor
EDMA: Extended Direct Memory Access
EDMS: Extended Data Base Management System
EDO: EDO Corp. (NYSE) (newspaper)
EDOS: Extended Disk Operating System
EDP: Electronic Data Processing
Energy Development Partners Ltd. (ASE)
EDPE: Electronic Data Processing Equipment
EDPM: Electronic Data Processing Machine
EDPS: Electronic Data Processing System
EDR: European Depositary Receipt
EDS: Electronic Data Switching
Electronic Data System
EDS: Engineering Data System
Exchangeable Disk Store
EDSAC: Electronic Delay Storage Automatic Computer
edt: editor

EDT: Eastern Daylight Time
Engineering Design Text
EDVAC: Electronic Discrete Variable Automatic Computer
EDW: El Dorado and Wesson (railroad)
Edward: A.G. Edwards Inc. (newspaper)
EDX: Event Driven Executive
EE: Electrical Engineer
Equity Earnings
Errors Excepted
Esquire Radio & Electronics Inc. (ASE)
E-E: End-to-End
EEA: European Environment Agency (EC)
EEC: East Erie Commercial (railroad)
EECO Inc. (ASE)
European Economic Community
EECA: European Electronic Component Manufacturers Association
EECL: Emitter to Emitter Coupled Logic
EECO: EECO Inc. (newspaper)
EEE: Ensource Inc. (NYSE)
EEG: Europese Economische Gemeenschap (European Economic Community) (Dutch) (EC)
EEI: Ecology & Environment Inc. (ASE)
Essential Elements of Information
EEIC: Elevated Electrode Integrated Circuit
EEIG: European Economic Interest Group (Grouping) (EC)
EEO: Equal Employment Opportunity
EEOC: Equal Employment Opportunities Commission
EEP: Electronic Evaluation and Procurement
Electronic Event Programmer
EE-PROMs: Electrically Erasable, Programmable Read-Only Memories
EES: European Economic Space (EC)
EEZ: Exclusive Economic Zone
E&F: Elders and Fyffes Limited (steamship)
EF: Execution Function
Extended Facility
External Flag
EFA: Empresa Ferrocarriles Argentinos (Argentine Railways Enterprise)
EFE: Empresa de los Ferrocarriles del Estado (State Railways Enterprise) (Chile)
EFEE: Empresa de los Ferrocarriles del Estado Ecuatoriano (Ecuadorian State Railways Enterprise)
EFF: Exchange For Futures
Expandable File Family
effect: effective
EFG: Equitec Financial Group Inc. (NYSE)
EFH: E.F. Hutton Group Inc., The (NYSE)
EFIC: Export Finance & Insurance Corporation
EFL: Emitter-Follower Logic
Error Frequency Limit
EFM: Export-Financiering-Maatschappij
EFMA: European Financial Marketing Association
EFMD: European Foundation for Management Development
EFOP: Economic Feasibility of Projects and Investments
Expanded Function Operator Panel

EFP: European Federation of Purchasing
Exchange For Physical
EFS: Error Free Seconds
External Function Store
EFT: Electronic Financial Transaction
Electronic Funds Transfer
EFTA: European Free Trade Association
EFTPOS: Electronic Funds Transfer at Point of Sale
EFTS: Electronic Funds Transfer System
EFU: Eastern Gas & Fuel Associates (NYSE)
EFX: Equifax Inc. (NYSE)
EG: Exempli Gratia (for example)
GCS Air Service (airline)
EGA: EQK Green Acres LP (NYSE)
EGCI: Export Group for the Construction Industry
EGCM: European Group for Cooperation in Management
E/GCR: Extended Group Coded Recording
EGF: European Guarantee Fund (EC)
EGG: EG&G Inc. (NYSE) (newspaper)
EGKS: Europäische Gemeinschaft für Kohle und Stahl (European Coal and Steel Community) (German) (EC)
EGL: Eagle Clothes Inc. (ASE)
EGM: Enhanced Graphics Module
EGN: Energen Corp. (NYSE)
EGP: EastGroup Properties (ASE)
EGX: Engex Inc. (ASE)
EHCN: Experimental Hybrid Computer Network
EHF: Extra High Frequency
EHP: Effective HorsePower
Emerald Homes LP (NYSE)
EHPM: Electro-Hydraulic Pulse Motor
EhrBbr: Ehrlich Bober Financial Corp. (newspaper)
EHV: Extra High Voltage
EI: Aer Lingus (Irish Airline)
Earned Income
Enable Interrupt
Endevco Inc. (ASE)
Error Indicator
Exact Interest
Ex-Interest
EIA: Electronic Industries Association
Environmental Impact Analysis (Assessment)
EIB: European Investment Bank
Export-Import Bank
EIBW: Export-Import Bank of Washington
EIC: Equipment Identification Code
EIEMA: Electrical Installation Equipment Manufacturers Association
EIES: Electronic Information Exchange System
EIN: European Informatics Network
EIOS: Extended Input/Output System
EIRENE: European Information Researchers Network (EC)
EIRMA: European Industrial Research Management Association
EIRP: Effective Isotropic Radiated Power
EIS: Excelsior Income Shares Inc. (NYSE)
Executive Information System
Extended Instruction Set
EIT: Emplacement, Installation, and Test(ing)
EITS: Express International Telex Service
EJ: Everest & Jennings International Ltd. (ASE)
EJ&E: Elgin, Joliet & Eastern (railway)

EJR: East Jersey Railroad
EK: Eastman Kodak Co. (NYSE)
Masling Airlines
EKodk: Eastman Kodak Co. (newspaper)
EKR: EQK Realty Investors I (NYSE)
EL: Elevated Railroad
End-of-Line
Erie Lackawanna (railway)
Even Lots
External Link
ELA: Equipment Leasing Association
Extended Line Adapter
EL AL: El Al Israel Airlines
ELAN: Error Logging and Analysis
ELB: Eldorado Bancorp (ASE)
ELC: Europe's Largest Companies
Elcor: Elcor Corp. (newspaper)
ELD: Eldon Industries Inc. (NYSE)
ELDO: European Launcher Development Organization (EC)
Eldon: Eldon Industries Inc. (newspaper)
Eldorad: Eldorado Bancorp (newspaper)
ELE: Empress Nacional de Electricidad S.A. (NYSE)
ELEC: European League for Economic Cooperation
ElecAs: Electronic Associates Inc. (newspaper)
ElecSd: ElectroSound Group Inc. (newspaper)
elem: element
ELF: Extensible Language Facility
Extra Low Frequency
Elgin: Elgin National Industries Inc. (newspaper)
ELINT: Electronic Intelligence
ELK: Elcor Corp. (NYSE)
ELMA: Empresa Lineas Maritimas Argentinas (Argentine Ship Lines) (steamship)
ELP: Electronic Line Printer
ELR: Error Logging Register
E&LS: Escanaba & Lake Superior (railroad)
ELS: Economic Lot Size
Elsinore Corp. (ASE)
Entry Level System
Elscint: Elscint Ltd. (newspaper)
ELSI: Extremely Large Scale Integration
Elsinor: Elsinore Corp. (newspaper)
Elswth: Ellsworth Convertible Growth & Income Fund Inc. (newspaper)
elt: element
ELT: Elscint Ltd. (NYSE)
E&M: Edgmoor and Manetta (railroad)
EM: East Mark
Electronic Mail
End-of-Medium (character)
Entertainment Marketing Inc. (ASE)
European Movement
Extended Memory
EMA: European Marketing Association
European Monetary Agreement (EC)
Extended Memory Area
EMAD: Engine Maintenance, Assembly, and Disassembly
EMB: Emulator Board
EMC: Electromagnetic Compatibility
EMC Corp. (NYSE) (newspaper)
Emitter Coupled Logic
Export Management Company
External Multiplexer Channel
EmCar: Empire of Carolina Inc. (newspaper)
EMCF: European Monetary Cooperation Fund (EC)
EME: Emerson Radio Corp. (NYSE)

EMF: Electromagnetic Interference
Templeton Emerging Markets Fund Inc. (ASE)
EMI: Electromagnetic Interference
Encore Marketing International Inc. (ASE)
EMIND: European Modular Interactive Network Designer (EC)
EML: Eastern Co., The (ASE)
Emulator Machine Language
EMMS: Electronic Mail and Message System
EMP: Electromagnetic Pulse
Empire of Carolina Inc. (ASE)
End-of-Month Payment
Energy Management Program
European Member of Parliament (EC)
Emp Agcy: Employment Agency
empd: employed
EmpDs: Empire District Electric Co., The (newspaper)
EmpirA: Empire of America Federal Savings Bank (newspaper)
empl: employee
employer
employment
EMPL: Extensible Microprogramming Language
EmpNa: Empress Nacional de Electricidad S.A. (newspaper)
EMQ: Economic Manufacturing Quantity
EMR: Emerson Electric Co. (NYSE)
EmRad: Emerson Radio Corp. (newspaper)
Emrld: Emerald Homes LP (newspaper)
EmrsE: Emerson Electric Co. (newspaper)
EM&S: Equipment Maintenance and Support
EMS: Electronic Mail System
Electronic Message Service
European Monetary System (EC)
Extended Main Store
EMSS: Electronic Message Service System
EMSU: European Medium and Small Business Union
EMT: Emulator Trap
EMTS: Electronic Money Transfer System
EMU: Economic and Monetary Union (EC)
Electromagnetic Unit
European Monetary Union (EC)
Extended Memory Unit
EMUA: European Monetary Unit of Account (EC)
EMUG: European Manufacturing Automation Protocol Users' Group (EC)
EMV: Expected Monetary Value
E&N: Esquimalt & Manaimo (railroad)
EN: Enterra Corp. (NYSE)
ENALIM: Evolving Natural Language Information Model
enbl: enable
encl: enclosure
EncrM: Encore Marketing International Inc. (newspaper)
end: endorsement
End Guar: Endorsement Guaranteed
ENDOC: Directory of environmental information and documentation centers (EC)
ENDS: Euratom Nuclear Documentation System (EC)
Endvco: Endevco Inc. (newspaper)
EnDvl: Energy Development Partners Ltd. (newspaper)
ENE: Enron Corp. (NYSE)

Energen: Energen Corp. (newspaper)
ENF: Empresa Nacional de Ferrocarriles (National Railways Enterprise) (Bolivia)
ENFIA: Exchange Network Facilities for Interstate Access
ENG: Enron Oil & Gas Co. (NYSE)
Engex: Engex Inc. (newspaper)
EnglC: Engelhard Corp. (newspaper)
ENIAC: Electronic Numerical Integrator And Calculator (computer)
EnisBu: Ennis Business Forms Inc. (newspaper)
ENLG: Enable Level Group
ENN: Expand Nonstop Network
enq: enquiry
ENREP: Directory of environmental research projects (EC)
EnrOG: Enron Oil & Gas Co. (newspaper)
Enron: Enron Corp. (newspaper)
ENS: ENSERCH Corp. (NYSE)
Extended Network Services
ENSCO: Energy Service Company Inc. (newspaper)
EnsExp: Ensearch Exploration Partners Ltd. (newspaper)
ENSR: ENSR Corp. (newspaper)
Ensrce: Ensource Inc. (newspaper)
Ensrch: ENSERCH Corp. (newspaper)
ENT: Equivalent Noise Temperature
Entera: Enterra Corp. (newspaper)
EntMkt: Entertainment Marketing Inc. (newspaper)
ENV: Enviropact Inc. (ASE)
Envrpct: Enviropact Inc. (newspaper)
EnvSys: Environmental Systems Co. (newspaper)
EnvTrt: Environmental Treatment & Technologies Corp. (newspaper)
ENW: Elgin National Industries Inc. (NYSE)
ENX: ENSR Corp. (ASE)
ENZ: Enzo Biochem Inc. (ASE)
EnzoBi: Enzo Biochem Inc. (newspaper)
EO: Davey Air Services (airline)
Enable Output
Engineering Order
Executive Order
Ex Officio (by virtue of the office)
EOA: Effective On (Or) About
Empire of America Federal Savings Bank (ASE)
End-Of-Address
EOB: End-Of-Block
EOC: Economic Opportunity Commission
End-Of-Character
End-Of-Conversion
EOD: End-Of-Data
End-Of-Day
Entry-On-Duty
Every-Other-Day
E&OE: Errors and Omissions Excepted
EOE: End-Of-Extent
EOF: End-Of-File
Europaeiske okonomiske Faelleskab (European Economic Community) (Danish) (EC)
EOI: End-Of-Inquiry
EOJ: End-Of-Job
EOL: End-Of-Line
EOLM: End-Of-Line Marker
EOM: End-Of-Medium
End-Of-Message (code)
End-Of-Month
EON: End-Of-Number
EOP: End-Of-Page
EOQ: Economical Ordering Quantity
End-Of-Query

EOR: End-Of-Record
Exclusive OR
EOS: Electronic Office System
End-Of-Screen
End-Of-Segment
End-Of-Sequence
End-Of-Step
EOST: Electrical Output Storage Tube
EOT: End-Of-Tape
End-Of-Test
End-Of-Text
End-Of-Transmission (character)
EOV: End-Of-Volume
EOW: End-Of-Word
EP: Aerolineas Peruanas (airline)
Earning Power
Effective Par
Emulator Program
Enserch Exploration Partners Ltd. (NYSE)
Environmental Protection
European Parliament (EC)
EPA: Environmental Protection Agency
Estimated Profile Analysis
European Productivity Agency (EC)
Extended Performance Analysis
EPBX: Electronic Private Branch Exchange
EPC: Economic and Policy Council
Editorial Processing Center
European Political Cooperation (EC)
EPCI: Entry Point Control Item
EPF: Employee Partnership Fund
EPI: Eagle-Picher Industries Inc. (NYSE)
EPIC: Exchange Price Information Computer
EPL: Electronic Switching Systems Programming Language
Encoder Programming Language
EPLANS: Engineering, Planning and Analysis Systems
EPO: Emergency Power Off
European Patents Office (EC)
EPOS: Electronic Point-of-Sale
EPR: Earnings-Price Ratio
Error Pattern Register
EPROM: Electrically Programmable Read-Only Memory
EPS: Earnings Per Share
Electronic Payments System
European Political System (EC)
Even Parity Select
EPSCS: Enhanced Private Switched Communications Service
EPT: Excess Profits Tax
Executive Process Table
EPU: European Parliamentary Union (EC)
European Payments Union (EC)
Execution Processing Unit
EQ: Equal (to)
EQK: Equimark Corp. (NYSE)
EQK G: EQK Green Acres LP (newspaper)
EQK Rt: EQK Realty Investors I (newspaper)
eql: equal
EQM: Equitable Real Estate Shopping Centers LP (NYSE)
eqpt: equipment
EQT: Equitable Resources Inc. (NYSE)
EqtRes: Equitable Resources Inc. (newspaper)
EqtRl: Equitable Real Estate Shopping Centers LP (newspaper)
equ: equal
equity
EQUATE: Electronic Quality Assurance Test Equipment

Equifax: Equifax Inc. (newspaper)
Equimk: Equimark Corp. (newspaper)
equip: equipment
Equitec: Equitec Financial Group Inc. (newspaper)
equiv: equivalent
er: error
ER: Caribbean Executive Airlines
Earnings Record
Earnings Report
Egyptian Railways
Established Reliability
Excess Reserves
Exponent Register
Ex-Rights
E-R: Entity-Relationship
ERASMUS: European Community Action Scheme for the Mobility of University Students (EC)
ERB: Erbamont NV (NYSE)
Erbmnt: Erbamont N.V. (newspaper)
ERBR: Eastern Region of British Railways
ERC: ERC International Inc. (NYSE) (newspaper)
ERCC: Error Checking and Correction
ERDA: Energy Research and Development Administration (EC)
ERDF: European Regional Development Fund (EC)
EREP: Environmental Recording, Editing, and Printing
ERF: European Reserve Fund (EC)
ERIE: Erie Railroad
ERISA: Employee Retirement Income Security Act
ERJE: Extended Remote Job Entry
ERLS: Economic Release Lot-Sizes
ERM: Exchange-Rate Mechanism
ERMA: Electronic Recording Machine Accounting
ERMES: European Radio Messaging System (EC)
ERO: Ero Industries Inc. (ASE) (newspaper)
EROM: Erasable Read-Only Memory
ERP: Effective Radiated Power
Error Recovery Procedures
European Recovery Program
err: error
ERRC: Expandability, Recoverability, Repairability Cost
ERT: European Round Table (EC)
Expected Run-Time
ERTA: Economic Recovery Tax Act
ERU: External Run Unit
ES: Earned Surplus
Exempt Securities
Expert System
External Store
Seagreen Air Transport-Air Cargo (airline)
ESA: Employee Spending Account
EURATOM Supply Agency (EC)
European Space Agency (EC)
Externally Specified Address
ESB: Electrical Standards Board
Esselte Business Systems Inc. (NYSE)
esc: escape
ESC: Environmental Systems Co. (NYSE)
European Security Community
European Space Conference (EC)
Escagn: Escagenitics Corp. (newspaper)
ESCB: European System of Central Banks
ESD: Electrostatic Discharge
Engineered Systems & Development Corp. (ASE) (newspaper)

Estimated Shipping Date
Ex-Stock Dividend
External Symbol Dictionary
ESDS: Entry Sequenced Data Set
ESE/VM: Expert System Environment/VM
EsexCh: Essex Chemical Corp. (newspaper)
ESF: European Social Fund (EC)
Extended Spooling Facility
ESG: ElectroSound Group Inc. (ASE)
ESH: Earl Scheib Inc. (ASE)
ESI: ESI Industries Inc. (ASE) (newspaper)
Externally Specified Index
ESL: Esterline Corp. (NYSE)
European Systems Language (EC)
ESLAB: European Space Laboratory (EC)
ESLJ: East St. Louis Junction (railroad)
ESN: Escagenitics Corp. (ASE)
External Segment Name
ESOP: Employee Stock Ownership Plan
ESOT: Employee Stock Ownership Trust
ESP: Electrosensitive Paper
Espey Manufacturing & Electronics Corp. (ASE)
Exchange Stock Portfolio
Espey: Espey Manufacturing & Electronics Corp. (newspaper)
ESPL: Electronic Switching Programming Language
Esprit: Esprit Systems Inc. (newspaper)
ESPRIT: European Strategic Program for Research and Development in Information Technology (EC)
EsqRd: Esquire Radio & Electronics Inc. (newspaper)
ESR: Electronic Send/Receive
Equivalent Series Resistance
ESRO: European Space Research Organization (EC)
ESS: Electronic Switching System
Event Scheduling System
EssBus: Esselte Business Systems Inc. (newspaper)
ESSO: Esso Petroleum Company
est: estate
estimated
EST: Earliest Start Time
Eastern Standard Time
ESTEC: European Space Technical Organization (EC)
Estgp: EastGroup Properties (newspaper)
ESTI: European Solar Testing Installation (EC)
European Space Technology Institute (EC)
EstnCo: Eastern Co., The (newspaper)
Estrlne: Esterline Corp. (newspaper)
ESTV: Error Statistics by Tape Volume
EST Wgt: Estimated Weight
ESU: Electrostatic Unit
ESV: Energy Service Company Inc. (ASE)
Error Statistics by Volume
ESX: Essex Chemical Corp. (NYSE)
ESY: E-Systems Inc. (NYSE)
E Syst: E-Systems Inc. (newspaper)
ET: Eastern Time
Emerging Technology
End of Text
Estate Tax
Ethiopian Airlines
Executive Team
ETA: Energy Tax Act
Estimated Time of Arrival
ET AL: Et Alia (and others)
ETB: End-of-Transmission-Block

ETC: Estimated Time of Completion
Et Cetera (and other things; and so forth)
European Trade Commission
Export Trading Company
ETD: Estimated Time of Departure
ET/GTS: Electronic Text and Graphics Transfer System
Ethyl: Ethyl Corp. (newspaper)
ETI: Esprit Systems Inc. (ASE)
E-TIME: Execution Time
ETL: Essex Terminal (railway)
ETLG: Enable This Level Group
ETLT: Equal To or Less Than
ETMF: Elapsed Terminal Measurement System
ETN: Eaton Corp. (NYSE)
ETOC: Expected Total Operating Cost
ETOS: Extended Tape Operating System
ETP: Electrical Tough Pitch
ETR: Expected Time of Response
ETRO: Estimated Time of Return to Operation
ETS: Electronic Translator System
Electronic Typing System
Engine Test Stand
ET SEQ: And Following
ETSI: European Telecommunications Standards Institute (EC)
ETSP: Entitled To Severance Pay
ETSPL: Extended Telephone Systems Programming Language
ETSS: Entry Time-Sharing System
ETT: Environmental Treatment & Technologies Corp. (NYSE)
Expected Test Time
ETUC: European Trade Union Confederation
ETUI: European Trade Union Institute
ET&WNC: East Tennessee & Western North Carolina (railroad)
ETX: End-of-Text
End-of-Transmission
ETX/ACK: End-of-Text/Acknowledge
ETZ: Etz Lavud Ltd. (ASE)
EtzLav: Etz Lavud Ltd. (newspaper)
EU: Compania Ecuatoriana de Aviacion (Ecuadorean Aviation Company) (airline)
End-User
Exchange Unit
Execution Unit
EUA: Eastern Utilities Associates (NYSE)
European Unit of Account (EC)
EUCATEL: European Conference of Association of Telecommunications Industries (EC)
EUCLID: Easily Used Computer Language for Illustration and Drawing (EC)
EUF: End User Facility
EUR: Unit of Account (EC)
EUR-6: Original members of the European Economic Community
EUR-9: Nine members of the European Community
EUR-10: Ten members of the European Community
EUR-12: Twelve members of the European Community
EURAILPASS: European Railroad Pass
EURAM: European Research in Advanced Materials (EC)
EURATOM: European Atomic Energy Community (EC)
EURCO: European Composite Unit (EC)

EURET: Recherche dans le Transport en Europe (EC)
EURISTOTE: Directory of university thesis and studies on European integration (EC)
EUROCOOP: European Community of Consumers' Co-operatives (EC)
EUROCRAT: European Civil Servant (EC)
EURODICAUTOM: Online terminology databank (EC)
EUROFINAS: European Federation of Finance House Association
EUROMART: European Common Market (EC)
European Cooperative Measures for Aeronautical Research and Technology (EC)
EUROMICRO: European Association for Microprocessing and Microprogramming (EC)
EURONET: European Information Network (EC)
EURONET DIANE: Direct Information Access Network for Europe (EC)
EURONORMS: European standards (EC)
EUROPAT: European Patent (EC)
EUROSTAT: Statistical Office of the European Community (EC)
EUROSYNDICAT: Index number for European stock exchange securities (EC)
EUROTOX: European standing committee for the protection of populations against the long-term risks of intoxication (EC)
EUROTRA: Program Europeen de Traduction automatique de conception Avancee (EC)
EURYDICE: European Community's Educational Information Network (EC)
EV: Elivie (airline)
End Vector
EVA: Error Volume Analysis
EVDS: Electronic Visual Display Subsystem
EVFU: Electronic Vertical Format Unit
EVG: Europäische Verteidigungsgemeinschaft (European Defense Community) (German)
EVHA: European Port Data Processing Association (EC)
evid: evidence
EVIL: Extensible Video Interactive Language
EVM: Extended Virtual Machine
EVMA: Expanded Virtual Machine Assist
EVR: Electronic Video Recording
EvrJ: Everest & Jennings International Ltd. (newspaper)
EW: East Washington (railway)
East-West Airlines
Ex-Warrants
EWG: Europäische Wirtschaftliche Gemeinschaft (European Economic Community) (German)
EWOS: European Workshop for Open Systems (EC)
ex: exchange
exchequer
execute
executor
without

EX: Executive Airlines
ExAcct: Expense Account
Ex B/L: Exchange Bill of Lading
EXC: Excel Industries Inc. (ASE)
Excel: Excel Industries Inc. (newspaper)
Excelsr: Excelsior Income Shares Inc. (newspaper)
exch: exchange
exchequer
Ex Cp: Ex Coupon
EXCP: Execute Channel Program
excpt: exception
exctr: executor
EXD: External Device
Ex D: Ex-Dividend
Without Dividend
EXDAMS: Extendable Debugging and Monitoring System
Ex Div: Ex-Dividend
Without Dividend
exec: execute
executive
Exec: Executive Officer
execs: executives
EXF: External Function
EXIM: Export-Import Bank (United States or Japan)
EXIMBANK: Export-Import Bank (of the United States or Japan)
Ex Int: Ex-Interest (NYSE)
EXLST: Exit List
exmr: examiner
Ex O: Executive Officer
Executive Order
exor: executor
EXOR: Exclusive OR
exp: expense
exponent
export
exporter
express
expression
EXP: Transco Exploration Partners Ltd. (NYSE)
ExPlan: Exercise Plan
EXPLOR: Explicit Patterns, Local Operations, and Randomness
expnd: expenditure
expo: exposition
expr: expression
Ex R: Ex-Rights
Ex-Rights: Without the Rights
ext: external
extd: extended
EXTM: Extended Telecommunications Module
EXTRA: Extra Dividend (NYSE)
EXTRAN: Expression Translator
EXTRN: External Reference
Ex-Warrants: Without Warrants
Exxon: Exxon Corp. (newspaper)
EY: Ethyl Corp. (NYSE)
Europe Aero Service (airline)
EYB: Europa Year Book (EC)
EYE: European Year of the Environment (EC)
EZU: Europäische Zahlungs-union (European Payments Union) (German) (EC)

f: false
farad
fetch
file
fixed
flag
frequency
function

F: Flat (in bonds listings in newspapers)
Ford Motor Co. (NYSE)
Franc
On a ticker tape after a foreign stock symbol showing that the stock has been sold by a foreign owner

F&A: February and August (securities)
Finance and Accounting

FA: Face Amount
Facilitating Agency
Factory Automation
February and August (securities)
Field Address
Fixed Assets
Floating Assets
Florida Airlines
Free Alongside
Freight Agent
Frozen Assets
Full Adder

FAA: Faculty of Accountants and Auditors
Federal Aviation Administration (Agency)
Finska Angfartygs Aktiebolaget (Finnish Steamship Company)
Free of All Average

FabCtr: Fabri-Centers of America Inc. (newspaper)

FabInd: Fab Industries Inc. (newspaper)

fac: facsimile
factory

FAC: Face-Amount Certificate
Federal Advisory Council
Federal Aviation Commission
File Access Channel
Floating Accumulator

FACE: Field Alterable Control Element

FACS: Financial Accounting and Control System

fact: factory

FACT: Facility for Automation, Control and Test
Factor Analysis Chart Technique
Factory Automation, Control, and Test Facility
Fully Automatic Compiling Technique

FacTs: Facsimile Transmission

facty: factory

FADS: Force Administration Data System

FAIR: Free from tax Affordable, Insured Rewarding

Fairfd: Fairfield Communities Inc. (newspaper)

FAK: Freight All Kinds

FAL: Falcon Cable Systems Company LP (ASE)
File Access Listener

FalCbl: Falcon Cable Systems Company LP (newspaper)

FALLINE: Federal Atlantic-Lakes Line (steamship)

FAM: Fast Auxiliary Memory
File Access Manager
FamDlr: Family Dollar Stores Inc. (newspaper)
FAMEM: Federation of Associations of Mining Equipment Manufacturers
FAMHEM: Federation of Associations of Materials Handling Equipment Manufacturers
FAMIS: Financial And Management Information System
FAMOS: Floating-gate Avalanche-injection Metal-oxide Semiconductor
FAMS: Forecasting and Modeling System
FANF: Flota Argentina de Navegacion Fluvial (Argentine River Navigation Fleet) (steamship)
FANNIE MAE: Federal National Mortgage Association
Fanstel: Fansteel Inc. (newspaper)
FANU: Flota Argentina Nevegacion Ultramar (Argentine Ship Line) (steamship)
FAP: Failure Analysis Program
FAPS: Financial Application Preprocessor System
FAQ: Fair Average Quality
Free Alongside Quay
Free At Quay
FAQS: Fast Queuing System
FAR: File Address Register
Fisheries and Aquaculture Research (EC)
Farah: Farah Manufacturing Company Inc. (newspaper)
FarWst: Far West Financial Corp. (newspaper)
FAS: Financial Analysis System
Free Alongside Ship
FASB: Financial Accounting Standards Board
FASCIA: Fixed Asset System Control Information and Accounting
FASR: Forward Acting Shift Register
FAST: Fast Access Storage Technology
Forecasting and Assessment in the field of Science and Technology (EC)
FASTER: Filing and Source Data Entry Techniques for Easier Retrieval
FAT: Fixed Asset Transfer
FATAL: Fit Anything to Anything you Like
FATAR: Fast Analysis of Tape and Recovery
FATS: Fast Analysis of Tape Surfaces
FAU: Freeport-McMoRan Gold Co. (NYSE)
FAVER: Fast Virtual Export/Restore
fax: facsimile
FAX: First Australia Prime Income Fund (ASE)
FAY: Fay's Drug Company Inc. (NYSE)
F/B: Foreground/Background
FB: Fidelity Bond
File Block
Fixed Block
Foreign Bond
Freight Bill
FBA: Farm Bankruptcy Act
Fixed-Block Architecture
FBC: First Boston Inc. (NYSE)
FBD: Fibreboard Corp. (ASE)
Full Business Day
FBF: First Boston Income Fund Inc. (NYSE)
FBH: Frank B. Hall & Company Inc. (NYSE)

FBI: First Boston Strategic Income Fund Inc. (NYSE)
FBM: Foreground and Background Monitor
FBO: Federal Paper Board Company Inc. (NYSE)
FBosIF: First Boston Income Fund Inc. (newspaper)
FBosSt: First Boston Strategic Income Fund Inc. (newspaper)
FBostn: First Boston Inc. (newspaper)
FBS: First Bank System Inc. (NYSE)
FBT: First City Bancorporation of Texas Inc. (NYSE)
F&C: Frankfort & Cincinnati (railroad)
F de C: Ferrocarriles de Cuba (Cuban Railroads)
FC: Fixed Capital
Fixed Charges
Floating Capital
Flow Controller
Flux Change
Font Change
Ford Motor Company of Canada Ltd. (ASE)
Front End Computer
Function Code
Futures Contract
Manufacturers Air Transport Service (airline)
FCA: Fabri-Centers of America Inc. (NYSE)
Farm Credit Administration
Fellow of the Institute of Chartered Accountants (UK)
Functional Configuration Audit
FCAB: Ferrocarril Antofagasta-Bolivia (Antofagasta and Bolivia Railway)
FCapHd: First Capitol Financial Corp. (Colorado) (newspaper)
FCB: File Control Block
Foote Cone & Belding Communications Inc. (NYSE)
Forms Control Buffer
FCBA: Fair Credit Billing Act
FCC: Federal Communications Commission
First Central Financial Corp. (ASE)
FCCFF: First Check Character Flip Flop
FCDN Ferrocarril del Nacozari (Nacozari Railroad) (Mexico)
FCE: Foreign Currency Exchange
Forest City Enterprises Inc. (ASE)
FCF: Free Cash Flow
FCFO: Full Cycling File Organization
FCFS: First Come, First Serve(d)
FC&G: Fernwood, Columbia & Gulf (railroad)
FCH: First Capital Holding Corp. (NYSE)
FCI: Fairfield Communities Inc. (NYSE)
Federal Crime Insurance
Flux Changes Per Inch
FCIA: Foreign Credit Insurance Association
FCIC: Federal Crop Insurance Company
FCIM: Farm, Construction and Industrial Machinery
FCIN: Frankfort and Cincinnati (railroad)
FCL: Format Control Language
Functional Capabilities List
FCM: Ferrocarriles Nacionales de Mexico (Mexican National Railways)
Firmware Control Memory

FCO: First Connecticut Small Business Investment Co., The (ASE)
FCP: Ferrocarril del Pacifico (Pacific Railroad)
File Control Processor
File Control Program
FC del P: Ferrocarril Central del Peru (Central Railway of Peru)
FCPA: Foreign Corrupt Practice Act
FCPI: Flux Changes Per Inch
FC/PM: Facility Control/Power Management
FCPU: Flexible Central Processing Unit
FCR: Firstcorp Inc. (ASE)
FCRA: Fair Credit Reporting Act
FCRAM: File Create And Maintenance
fcs: franc (currency of France)
FCS: Financial Control System
Fixed Control Storage
Foreign Commercial Service
Frame Check Sequence
FCSC: Foreign Claims Settlement Commission
fct: function
fcty: factory
FCU: Federal Credit Union
File Control Unit
FCUS: Federal Credit Union System
FCX: Freeport-McMoRan Copper Co. (NYSE)
FCY: First City Industries Inc. (NYSE)
FCZ: Ferrocarril Coahuila-Zacatecas (Coahuila-Zacatecas Railway) (Mexico)
fd: fund
funding
F&D: Freight and Demurrage
FD: File Definition
File Description
Flexible Disk
Floppy Disk
Freight Department
Fourth Day
Freight Department
Full Duplex
FDA: Food and Drug Administration
FDB: File Data Block
FD&C: Food, Drug and Cosmetic Act (U.S.)
FDC: Floppy Disk Controller
Fully Distributed Costs
FDCPA: Fair Debt Collection Practices Act
FDCS: Functionally Distributed Computing System
FDCT: Factory Data Collection Terminal
FDD: Floppy Disk Drive
FDDL: File Data Description Language
FDDM: Fort Dodge, Des Moines and Southern (railway)
fdg: funding
FDIC: Federal Deposit Insurance Corporation
FDL: Forms Description Language
FDM: Frequency Division Multiplex
FDMA: Frequency Division Multiple Access
FDMI: Function Management Data Interpreter
FdMog: Federal-Mogul Corp. (newspaper)
FDO: Family Dollar Stores Inc. (NYSE)
FDOS: Floppy Disk Operating System
FDR: File Data Register
FDS: Flexible Disk System
Floppy Disk System
FdSgnl: Federal Signal Corp. (newspaper)
FDSR: Floppy Disk Send/Receive
FDT: Functional Description Table

FDU: Form Description Utility
FDX: Federal Express Corp. (NYSE)
Full Duplex
F&E: Facilities and Equipment
FE: Foreign Exchange
Format Effector
Framing Error
Front End
Futures Exchange
FEA: Federal Energy Administration
FEAMIS: Foreign Exchange Accounting and Management Information System
FEAT: Frequency of Every Allowable Term
FEBI: Fédérations Européennes des Branches d'Industries (European Federations of Branches of Industry) (French)
FEC: Front-End Computer
Florida East Coast Railroad
Forward Error Correction
FECDBA: Foreign Exchange and Currency Deposit Brokers Association
FECOM: European Monetary Cooperation Fund
FECP: Front End Communications Processor
FED: Federal Reserve System
FirstFed Financial Corp. (NYSE)
Feders: Fedders Corp. (newspaper)
FedExp: Federal Express Corp. (newspaper)
Fed Funds: Federal Funds
FedlPB: Federal Paper Board Company Inc. (newspaper)
FedNM: Federal National Mortgage Assn. (newspaper)
FEDPAC: Federal Pacific Lakes Line (steamship)
FedRlty: Federal Realty Investment Trust (newspaper)
FEDS: Fixed/Exchangeable Disk Store
FEDSEA: Federal South East Asia Line (steamship)
FEEDBAC: Foreign Exchange, Eurodollar and Branch Accounting
FEFO: First-Ended, First-Out
FEGUA: Ferrocarriles de Guatemala (Railroads of Guatemala)
FEI: Financial Executives Institute
Frequency Electronics Inc. (ASE)
FEIA: Foreign Earned Income Act
FEM: Finite Element Modeling
FEMA: Foundry Equipment Manufacturers Association
FEmp: First Empire State Corp. (newspaper)
FEOGA: Fond Européen d'Orientation et de Garantie Agricole (European Agricultural Guidance and Guarantee Fund) (French) (EC)
FEP: Ferrocarril Electrico al Pacifico (Pacific Electric Railway) (Costa Rica)
Front End Processor
FEPA: Fair Employment Practices Act
FEPC: Fair Employment Practices Committee
FEPEM: Federation of European Petroleum Equipment Manufacturers
FER: Franco-Ethiopian Railway
FERA: Federal Emergency Relief Administration
Ferro: Ferro Corp. (newspaper)
FERST: Freight and Equipment Reporting System for Transportation (EC)
FES: Ferrocarril de El Salvador (El Salvador Railway)

First Empire State Corp. (ASE)
Forms Entry System
FESCO: Far East Steamship Company
FET: Federal Excise Tax
Field-Effect Transistor
FEX: Foreign Exchange
FEXT: Far-End Cross Talk
FF: Fast Forward
First Financial Fund Inc. (NYSE)
Flip-Flop
Folded Flat
Form-Feed
FFA: FirstFed America Inc. (ASE)
Foreign Freight Agent
Free From Alongside (ship)
FFB: Federal Financing Bank
First Fidelity Bancorporation (New Jersey) (NYSE) (newspaper)
FFBcp: First Federal Bancorp Inc. (Michigan) (newspaper)
FF&C: Full Faith and Credit
FFC: Fireman's Fund Corp. (NYSE)
FFI: Finance For Industry
FFinFd: First Financial Fund Inc. (newspaper)
FFLA: Federal Farm Loan Act
FFMC: Federal Farm Mortgage Corporation
FFMED: Fixed Format Message Entry Device
FFN: Full Function Node
FFP: FFP Partners LP (ASE) (newspaper)
Firm Fixed Price
FFS: First Federal Bancorp Inc. (Michigan) (ASE)
Formatted File System
fg: foreground
FG: Ariana Afghan Airlines
USF & G Corp. (NYSE)
FGE: Fitchburg Gas & Electric Light Co. (ASE)
FGI: Foothill Group Inc., The (NYSE)
FGL: FMC Gold Co. (NYSE)
F de G a LP: Ferrocarril de Guayaquil-La Paz (Guayaquil-La Paz Railway) (Peru)
fgn: foreign
foreigner
FGN: Flow General Inc. (NYSE)
FGT: Foreground Table
FH: Field Handler
Fixed Head
FHA: Federal Housing Administration
FHB: Federal Home Bank
FHD: Fixed Head Disk
FHDS: Fixed Head Disk/Drum Store
FHF: Fixed Head File
FHLBA: Federal Home Loan Bank Administration
FHLBB: Federal Home Loan Bank Board
FHLBS: Federal Home Loan Bank System
FHLMC: Federal Home Loan Mortgage Corporation
FHO: Frederick's of Hollywood Inc. (ASE)
FHR: Fisher Foods Inc. (NYSE)
FHSF: Fixed Head Storage Facility
FHW: Flexible Working Hours
FHWA: Federal Highway Administration
FI: Flugfelag-Icelandair (airline)
Foreign Investment
Format Identifier
Front End Processor Interface
FIA: Factory Insurance Association
Financial Inventory Accounting
Full Interest Admitted
FIB: File Information Block
Fibrbd: Fibreboard Corp. (newspaper)

FIBV: Fédération International des Bourses de Valeurs (International Federation of Stock Exchanges)
FIC: Federal Insurance Contribution
First-In-Chain
Freight, Insurance, Carriage
FICA: Federal Insurance Contributions Act
Ferrocarriles Internacionales de Centro America (International Railways of Central America)
FICB: Federal Intermediate Credit Bank
FICON: File Conversion
FICS: Factory Information Control System
Financial Information and Control System
Forecasting and Inventory Control System
fid: fidelity
fiduciary
FID: Fidata Corp. (ASE)
Forecasts-In-Depth
Format Identification
FIDAC: Film Input to Digital Automatic Computer
FIDAS: Forms-Oriented Interactive Data Base System
FIDIC: Fédération International des Ingenieurs Consultatifs (International Federation of Consulting Engineers)
FidlFn: Fidelity National Financial Inc. (newspaper)
FIF: Family Information Facility
Financial News Composite Fund Inc. (NYSE)
FIFO: First In, First Out
FIGED: Fédération Internationale des Grande Entreprises de Distribution (Federation of Large Retail Distributors) (French)
FIGS: Figures Shift
FILEX: File Exchange
FILO: First In, Last Out
FILSYS: File System
Filtrk: Filtertek Companies, The (newspaper)
FILU: Four-Bit Interface Logic Unit
FIMS: Financial Information Management System
Functionally Identification Maintenance System
fin: finance
financial
FIN: Financial Corporation of America (NYSE)
FINAC: Fast Interline Non-active Automatic Control
FINAR: Financial Analysis and Reporting
FINMAN: Financial Management
FINNAIR: Finnish Airlines
FinNws: Financial News Composite Fund Inc. (newspaper)
Finstat: Financial Times database of key statistical information
Fintste: First Interstate Bancorp. (newspaper)
FINUFO: First In Not Used First Out
Finvst: Finevest Foods Inc. (newspaper)
FIO: For Information Only
Free In and Out
FIP: Finance Image Processor
FIPC: Ferrocarril Industrial del Potosi y Chihuahua (Industrial Railways of Potosi and Chihuahua) (Mexico)
FIPS: Federation Information Processing Standard
FIR: File Indirect Register
Floating-In Rates

FireFd: Fireman's Fund Corp. (newspaper)
FIRM: Financial Information for Resource Management
FIRREA: Financial Institutions Reform, Regulation and Enforcement Act
FIS: Feasible Ideal System
Fischbach Corp. (NYSE)
Fischb: Fischbach Corp. (newspaper)
FischP: Fischer & Porter Co. (newspaper)
FishFd: Fisher Foods Inc. (newspaper)
FIS: Floating (point) Instruction Set
FISSL: Finite State Specification Language
FIST: Feasible Ideal System Target
FIT: Fab Industries Inc. (ASE)
Federal Income Tax
File Inquiry Technique
Free In Truck
Free of Income Tax
Functional Industrial Training
FITAL: Financial In Terminal Application Language
FITCE: Fédération des Ingénieurs des Télécommunications de la Communauté Européenne (Federation of Telecommunications Engineers in the European Community) (French) (EC)
FitcGE: Fitchburg Gas & Electric Light Co. (newspaper)
FITW: Federal Income Tax Withholding
FIU: Federation of Information Users
FIXBLK: Fixed Blocked
FIXUNB: Fixed Unblocked
FJ: Fiji Airways
FJA: Functional Job Analysis
FJ&G: Fonda, Johnstown & Gloversville (railroad)
FJQ: Fedders Corp. (NYSE)
FKL: Franklin Corp., The (ASE)
FKM: John Fluke Manufacturing Company Inc. (ASE)
F/L: Fetch/Load
FL: Fesco Pacific Line (steamship)
Field Length
FLA: Florida East Coast (railway)
Florida East Coast Industries Inc. (NYSE)
FlaEC: Florida East Coast Industries Inc. (newspaper)
FLAIR: Food Linked Agro-Industrial Research program
Flanign: Flanigan's Enterprises Inc. (newspaper)
FLAP: Flow Analysis Program
FlaPrg: Florida Progress Corp. (newspaper)
FlaRck: Florida Rock Industries Inc. (newspaper)
FlaStl: Florida Steel Corp. (newspaper)
FLB: Federal Land Bank
Federal Loan Bank
FLCN: Field Length Condition Register
fld: field
FLD: Fieldcrest Cannon Inc. (NYSE)
Fldscrst: Fieldcrest Cannon Inc. (newspaper)
FLE: Fleetwood Enterprises Inc. (NYSE)
FLEE: Fast Linkage Editor
FleetEn: Fleetwood Enterprises Inc. (newspaper)
Flemng: Fleming Companies Inc. (newspaper)
FLEXIMIS: Flexible Management Information System
flg: flag
FlghtSf: FlightSafety International Inc. (newspaper)
FLIH: First-Level Interrupt Handler

FLIM: Fast Library Maintenance
FLIP: Flexible Loan Insurance Plan
FLIT: Fault Location by Interpretive Testing
FLM: Fleming Companies Inc. (NYSE)
FLO: Flowers Industries Inc. (NYSE)
FloatPt: Floating Point Systems Inc. (newspaper)
FLOP: Floating Point Operation per second
Flower: Flowers Industries Inc. (newspaper)
FLOWGEN: Flowchart Generator
FLP: Floating Point
Floating Point Systems Inc. (NYSE)
FLPAU: Floating Point Arithmetic Unit
FLR: Fayum Light Railways (Egypt)
Flag Register
Fluor Corp. (NYSE)
FLRA: Federal Labor Relations Authority
FLS: Florida Steel Corp. (NYSE)
FLSA: Fair Labor Standards Act
flt: float
FLT: Fault Locating Test
Fleet Norstar Financial Corp. (NYSE)
FltNors: Fleet Norstar Financial Corp. (newspaper)
Fluke: John Fluke Manufacturing Company Inc. (newspaper)
Fluor: Fluor Corp. (newspaper)
FLV: Finite Logical View
FlwGen: Flow General Inc. (newspaper)
FLY: Airlease Ltd. (NYSE)
FM: Facilities Management
File Management
File Manager
Format Manager
Frequency Modulation
FMA: Fabricating Machinery Association
FMAN: February, May, August, November (securities)
FMC: Federal Maritime Commission
FMC Corp. (NYSE) (newspaper)
FMCC: Freeport-McMoRan Copper Co. (newspaper)
FMC G: FMC Gold Co. (newspaper)
FMCS: Federal Mediation and Conciliation Service
FMD: Flota Mercante Dominicana (Dominican Merchant Fleet) (steamship)
Function Management Data
FME: Foundation for Management Education
FMEP: Freeport-McMoRan Energy Partners Ltd. (newspaper)
FMFB: Frequency Modulation Feedback
FMG: Flota Mercante Grancolombiana (Great Colombian Merchant Fleet) (steamship)
FMGC: Freeport-McMoRan Gold Co. (newspaper)
FmHA: Farmers Home Administration
FML: File Manipulation Language
FMLF: File Management Loading Facility
FMO: Federal-Mogul Corp. (NYSE)
FMOG: Freeport-McMoRan Oil & Gas Royalty Trust (newspaper)
FMP: Freeport-McMoRan Energy Partners Ltd. (NYSE)
FMPP: Flexible Multipipeline Processor
FMPS: Functional Mathematical Programming System
FMR: Facility Management Reporting

Freeport-McMoRan Oil & Gas Royalty Trust (NYSE)

FMRP: Freeport-McMoRan Resource Partners LP (newspaper)

FMRS: Federal Mediation and Reconciliation Service

FMS: File Management System
Financial Management System
Flexible Manufacturing System
Fort Meyers Southern (railroad)

FMV: Fair Market Value

FN: Ferrocarriles Nacionales (National Railways of Argentina, Chile, Colombia, Cuba, Ecuador, Honduras, Mexico, Panama, and Venezuela)
First National Corp. (California) (ASE)
Functional Network
St. Louis-San Francisco (railway)

F del N: Ferrocarriles del Norte (Northern Railways) (Paraguay)

FNB: File Name Block
First Chicago Corp. (NYSE)

FNC: Ferrocarriles Nacionales de Cuba (National Railroads of Cuba)

FNF: Fidelity National Financial Inc. (ASE)
First Normal Form

FN de H: Ferrocarriles Nacionales de Honduras (National Railways of Honduras)

FNL: Fansteel Inc. (NYSE)

FNM: Federal National Mortgage Association (NYSE)
Ferrocarriles Nacionales de Mexico (National Railways of Mexico)

FNMA: Federal National Mortgage Association

FNP: Front End Network Processor

FNPA: Foreign Numbering Plan Area

FNS: Feedback Node Set

FnSBar: Financial Corporation of Santa Barbara (newspaper)

FNT: File Name Table

FntCal: First National Corp. (California) (newspaper)

FO: Fjellfly (airlines)

FOB: Free On Board
Freight On Board

FOC: Fiber Optics Communications

FOCAL: Formula Calculator

FOCH: Forward Channel

FOCIS: Financial On-line Central Information System

FOCS: Freight Operation Control System

FOCUS: Financial and Operational Combined Uniform Single (report)

FOD: Function Operational Design

FOE: Ferro Corp. (NYSE)

FOIA: Freedom of Information Act

fol: folio
following

FOL: Function of Lines

FOM: Ferrocarril Occidental de Mexico (Western Railway of Mexico)
Fiber - Optic Modem

FOMC: Federal Open Market Committee

FONASBA: Federation of National Associations of Ship Brokers and Agents

Foodmk: Foodmaker Inc. (newspaper)

Foodrm: Foodarama Supermarkets Inc. (newspaper)

FOOF: Fanout-Observed Output Function

FOPC: First Order Predicate Calculus

FOPIC: Fiber Optic Modem

FOPS: Forecast Operating System
FOQ: Free On Quay
for: foreign
FOR: Farmer-Owned Reserve
Fore River (railroad)
Free On Rail
FORATOM: Forum Atomique Européen (European Atomic Forum) (French) (EC)
FordCn: Ford Motor Company of Canada Ltd. (newspaper)
FordM: Ford Motor Co. (newspaper)
FOREM: File Organization Evaluation Model
FOREX: Foreign Exchange
forg: forgery
FORGE: File Organization Generator
FORMAC: Formula Manipulation Compiler
FORMS: Forms Management System
ForstC: Forest City Enterprises Inc. (newspaper)
ForstL: Forest Laboratories Inc. (newspaper)
FORT: FORTRAN
FORTE: File Organization Techniques
FORTRA: Federation of Radio and Television Retailers Association
FORTRAN: Formula Translation
FOS: Function Operational Specification
Free (Freight) On Shipboard (Steamer)
FostWh: Foster Wheeler Corp. (newspaper)
FOT: Free On Truck
FOTS: Fiber-Optic Transmission System
FOW: Free On Wagon
FOX: Foxboro Co., The (NYSE)
Foxbro: Foxboro Co., The (newspaper)
FP: Faithful Performance
File Processor
Fischer & Porter Co. (ASE)
Fixed Price
Floating Point
Fully Paid
Function Processor
F del P: Ferrocarril del Pacifico (Pacific Railroad) (Mexico)
FPA: Floating Point Arithmetic
FPA Corp. (newspaper)
Free of Particular Average
FPAL: Floating Point Arithmetic Library
FPB: Floating Point Board
FPC: Federal Power Commission
Florida Progress Corp. (NYSE)
Functional Processor Cluster
FPCAL: Ferrocarriles President Carlos Antonio Lopez (President Carlos Antonio Lopez Railways) (Paraguay)
FPE: Fairport, Painesville and Eastern (railroad)
FP&ER: Fairport, Painesville and Eastern Railway
FPGA: Field Programmable Gate Array
FPI: Fixed Price Incentive
FPIL: Full Premium If Lost
FPIS: Fixed Price Incentive with Successive Targets
FPL: FPL Group Inc. (NYSE)
FPLA: Field-Programmable Logic Array
FPL Gp: FPL Group Inc. (newspaper)
FPM: File Protect Memory
FPMIS: Federal Personnel Management Information System
FPMR: Federal Property Management Regulation
FPN: Ferrocarril del Pacifico de Nicaragua (Pacific Railway of Nicaragua)

FPO: Fixed Price Open
FPA Corp. (ASE)
FPP: Fixed-Path Protocol
Floating-Point Package
Floating-Point Processor
FPPU: Floating-Point Processor Unit
FPR: Federal Procurement Regulations
Fixed Price Redeterminable
Floating-Point Register
FPROM: Field Programmable Read-Only Memory
FPS: Financial Planning System
First Preferred Stock
Frames Per Second
FPSI: Floriday Payment System, Inc.
FPU: File Processing Unit
Floating-Point Unit
FQA: Fuqua Industries Inc. (NYSE)
FQL: Formal Query Language
FQR: Formal Qualification Review
FQT: Formal Qualification Test
fr: franc
F/R: Failure and Recovery
FR: Feather River (railway)
Federal Register
Federal Reserve
File Register
Final Report
Floating-Point Register
Freight Release
FRA: Farah Manufacturing Company Inc. (NYSE)
Federal Reserve Act
FRACA: Failure Reporting, Analysis and Corrective Action
fract: fraction
Franc: France Fund Inc., The (newspaper)
FRB: Federal Reserve Bank (Board)
FRBK: Federal Reserve Bank
FRC: First Republic Bancorp Inc. (California) (ASE)
FRCD: Floating-Rate Certificate of Deposit
FRCS: Federal Reserve Communications System
FRD: Friedman Industries Inc. (ASE)
Functional Requirements Document
FrdHly: Frederick's of Hollywood Inc. (newspaper)
FR DIST: Federal Reserve District
FRDN: Ferdinand Railroad
FRED: Front End for Databases
FREDDIE MAC: Federal Home Loan Mortgage Corporation
freebd: freeboard
FREITS: Finite-life Real-Estate Investment Trusts
freq: frequency
FreqEl: Frequency Electronics Inc. (newspaper)
frgt: freight
Friedm: Friedman Industries Inc. (newspaper)
FriesEn: Fries Entertainment Inc. (newspaper)
FRIMP: Flexible Reconfigurable Interconnected Multiprocessor System
FRISCO: St. Louis-San Francisco (railway)
FRK: Florida Rock Industries Inc. (ASE)
FRL: Frame Representation Language
FRM: First Mississippi Corp. (NYSE)
Functional Requirements Model
FRMS: Financial Resources Management System
FRN: Floating-Rate Note
France Fund Inc., The (NYSE)

Frnkln: Franklin Corp., The (newspaper)
FrnkR: Franklin Resources Inc. (newspaper)
FROM: Fusable Read-Only Memory
FRP: Freeport-McMoRan Resource Partners LP (NYSE)
FrptMc: Freeport-McMoRan Inc. (newspaper)
FRR: Functional Recovery Routines
FRS: Federal Reserve System
Financial Reporting System
Financial Results Simulator
Frisch's Restaurants Inc. (ASE)
FRSS: Financial Results Simulator System
Frstm: Forstmann & Company Inc. (newspaper)
frt: freight
FRT: Federal Realty Investment Trust (NYSE)
Frt Ppd: Freight Prepaid
FRTRA: Federation of Radio and Television Retailers Association
FRU: Field Replaceable Unit
FruhfB: Fruehauf Corp. (newspaper)
FruitL: Fruit of the Loom Inc. (newspaper)
FRUMP: Fast Reading and Understanding Memory Program
FRV: Fur Vault Inc., The (ASE)
FRX: Forest Laboratories Inc. (ASE)
fry: fried
FS: Ferrovie dello Stato (Italian State Railway)
Field Separator
Field Service
File Separator
Financial Statement
Finite State
Full Scale
Function Select
Futures Spread
Key Airlines
FSA: Farm Security Administration
Finite State Automation
Flexible Spending Account
FSB: Federal Specifications Board
Financial Corporation of Santa Barbara (NYSE)
FSBC: Ferrocarril Sonora-Baja California (Sonora-Baja California Railroad)
FSC: Federal Supply Code
Foreign Sales Corporations
FSCB: File System Control Block
FSCM: Federal Supply Code for Manufacturers
FSCR: Field Select Command Register
FSD: Full-Scale Deflection
FSF: Forward Space File
FSI: Flight Safety International Inc. (NYSE)
FSIM: Functional Simulation
FSK: Frequency-Shift Keying
FSL: Formal Semantic Language
FSLA: Federal Savings and Loan Association
FSLIC: Federal Savings and Loan Insurance Corporation
FSM: Finite State Machine
Foodarama Supermarkets Inc. (ASE)
FSOS: Free Standing Operating System
FSP: Full-Screen Processing
FS del P: Ferrocarril del Sur del Peru (Southern Railway of Peru)
FSR: Feedback Shift Register
Forward Space Record
Full-Scale Range
FSS: Federal Signal Corp. (NYSE)
Federal Supply Service
Flying Spot Scanner

FST: File Status Table
Forstmann & Company Inc. (ASE)
Fstcrp: Firstcorp Inc. (newspaper)
FstFd: FirstFed America Inc. (newspaper)
FstFed: FirstFed Financial Corp. (newspaper)
FSU: Facsimile Switching Unit
Field Select Unit
FSVB: Fort Smith and Van Buren (railway)
FT: Financial Times (UK)
Flying Tiger Line (Air Cargo) (airline)
Format Type
Frequency and Time
FTA: Freight Transport Association
FtAust: First Australia Fund Inc., The (newspaper)
FtBkSy: First Bank System Inc. (newspaper)
FtbTex: First City Bankcorporation of Texas (newspaper)
FTC: Fault Tolerant Computer
Federal Trade Commission
Foreign Trading Company
FTCA: Federal Tort Claims Act
FtCity: First City Industries Inc. (newspaper)
FtCntrl: First Central Financial Corp. (newspaper)
FtConn: First Connecticut Small Business Investment Co., The (newspaper)
FTD: Fort Dearborn Income Securities Inc. (NYSE)
FTD DM&S: Fort Dodge, Des Moines and Southern (railway)
FtDear: Fort Dearborn Income Securities Inc. (newspaper)
FTF: Factory Terminal Facility
File To File
FthillG: Foothill Group Inc., The (newspaper)
FTI: Financial Times Index (UK)
Fixed Time Interval
FtIber: First Iberian Fund (newspaper)
FTK: Filtertek Companies, The (NYSE)
FTL: Fast Transient Loader
Fruit of the Loom Inc. (ASE)
FTMA: Federation of Textile Manufacturers Associations
FtMiss: First Mississippi Corp. (newspaper)
FTN: FORTRAN
FTP: File Transfer Program
File Transfer Protocol
FTPI: Flux Transitions Per Inch
FTR: Foreign Trade Reports
Fruehauf Corp. (NYSE)
Funds Transfer
FtRpBc: First Republic Bancorp Inc. (California) (newspaper)
FTS: Federal Telecommunication System
Free Time System
FTSC: Federal Telecommunications Standards Committee
FTSE: Financial Times Stock Exchange Index (UK)
FTT: Financial Transaction Terminal
FTU: First Union Corp. (NYSE)
FtVaBk: First Virginia Banks Inc. (newspaper)
FtWach: First Wachovia Corp. (newspaper)
FtWisc: First Wisconsin Corp. (newspaper)
FTX: Freeport-McMoRan Inc. (NYSE)
FTZ: Foreign-Trade Zone
FU: Field Unit
Functional Unit
FUD: Ferrocarriles Unidos Dominicanos (United Do-

minican Railways) (Dominican Republic)

FUN: Cedar Fair LP (NYSE)

func: function

FUND: International Monetary Fund

FUnRl: First Union Real Estate Equity & Mortgage Investments (newspaper)

Fuqua: Fuqua Industries Inc. (newspaper)

FUR: First Union Real Estate Equity & Mortgage Investments (NYSE)

FurrsB: Furr's/Bishop's Cafeterias LP (newspaper)

FurVlt: Fur Vault Inc., The (newspaper)

FUS: Ferrocarriles Unidos del Sureste (United Railways of the Southeast)

FUTA: Federal Unemployment Tax Act

FUTC: Fidelity Union Trust Company

FUY: Ferrocarriles Unidos de Yucatan (United Railways of Yucatan) (Mexico)

FV: Face Value

F-V: Frequency to Voltage

FVB: First Virginia Banks Inc. (NYSE)

FVU: File Verification Utility

fw: firmware

FW: First Wachovia Corp. (NYSE)
First Word
Furness, Withy and Company (steamship)
Wright Airlines

FWA: Federal Works Agency

FWB: First Wisconsin Corp. (NYSE)
Fort Worth Belt (railway)

FWC: Foster Wheeler Corp. (NYSE)

fwd: forward

FW&D: Fort Worth and Denver (railroad)

fwdg: forwarding

fwdr: forwarder

FWF: Far West Financial Corp. (NYSE)

FWH: Flexible Working Hours

FWL: Furness Warren Line (steamship)

FWO: First Wyoming Bancorporation (ASE)

FWP: First Word Pointer

FWT: Flexible Working Time

FWymB: First Wyoming Bancorporation (newspaper)

FX: Foreign Exchange

FXPALU: Fixed Point Address Arithmetic Logic Unit

FY: Fiscal Year

FYI: For Your Information

FYIG: For Your Information and Guidance

G

g: gain
giga-
gold
group

G: Dividends and Earnings in Canadian Dollars (stock listings of newspapers)
Greyhound Corp., The (NYSE)

GA: Garuda Indonesian Airways
General Account
General Agent
General Automation Inc. (ASE)
General Average
Georgia Railroad
Global Address
Gross Asset

GAAC: Graphic Arts Advertisers Council

GAAP: Generally Accepted Accounting Principles

GaAs: Gallium Arsenide Chips

GAAS: Generally Accepted Auditing Standards

GAASS: Government Agency Arbitrage and Swap System

GAB: Gabelli Equity Trust Inc., The (NYSE)
General Arrangements to Borrow
Graphic Adapter Board

Gabeli: Gabelli Equity Trust Inc., The (newspaper)

GAC: General Acceptance Corporation
General Access Copy

GACHA: Georgia Automated Clearing House Association

GAD: Graphic Active Device

GADS: Geographical Analysis and Display System

GAFTA: Grain And Feed Association

GaGulf: Georgia Gulf Corp. (newspaper)

GAI: Grand Auto Inc. (ASE)
Guaranteed Annual Income

GAIC: Gallium Arsenide Integrated Circuit

Gainsco: Gainsco Inc. (newspaper)

GAInv: General American Investors Company Inc. (newspaper)

gal: gallon

GAL: Generalized Assembly Language
German Atlantic Line (steamship)
Lewis Galoob Toys Inc. (NYSE)

GalaxC: Galaxy Carpet Mills Inc. (newspaper)

GalHou: Galveston-Houston Co. (newspaper)

Gallagr: Arthur J. Gallagher & Co. (newspaper)

Galoob: Lewis Galoob Toys Inc. (newspaper)

GALPAT: Galloping Pattern

GalxCbl: Galaxy Cablevision LP (newspaper)

GAM: General American Investors Company Inc. (NYSE)
Graphic Access Method

GAMA: Gas Appliance Manufacturers Association
General Aviation Manufacturers Association

GAMTA: General Aviation Manufacturers and Traders Association

GAN: Garan Inc. (ASE)
Gannet: Gannett Company Inc. (newspaper)
GANO: Georgia Northern (railway)
GAO: General Accounting Office
Gap: Gap Inc., The (newspaper)
GAP: Graphics Application Program
Great Atlantic & Pacific Tea Company Inc., The (NYSE)
GaPac: Georgia-Pacific Corp. (newspaper)
GAPM: Generalized Access Path Method
Garan: Garan Inc. (newspaper)
GAS: NICOR Inc. (NYSE)
GAS&C: Georgia, Ashburn, Sylvester & Camilla (railroad)
GASP: General Activity Simulation Program
Generalized Audit Software Package
GAT: Greenwich Apparent Time
GATS: General Acceptance Test Software
GATT: General Agreement on Tariffs and Trade
GATX: GATX Corp. (newspaper)
GAUGE: General Automation Users Group Exchange
GAW: Guaranteed Annual Wage
GaylC: Gaylord Container Corp. (newspaper)
GB: Air Gabon (airline)
Gigabit
Gigabyte
Government Bond
Great Britain
Guaranteed Bond
Guardian Bancorp (ASE)
GBE: Grubb & Ellis Co. (NYSE)
GBF: Geographic Base File
GBIT: Gigabit
GBMP: General Benchmark Program
GBS: General Business System
GBTS: General Banking Terminal System
GB&W: Green Bay & Western (railroad)
g-byte: gigabytes
GC: Gaylord Container (railroad)
General Counsel
Gigacycle
Graham County (railroad)
Linacongo (airline)
GCA: GCA Corp. (NYSE) (newspaper)
GCB: General Circuit Breaker
GCC: Gulf Cooperation Council
GCCA: Graphic Communications Computer Association
GCda: Gulf Canada Corp. (newspaper)
GCE: Ground Communication Equipment
GCFI: Gulf and Caribbean Fisheries Institute
GCH: Gigacharacters
GCI: Gannett Company Inc. (NYSE)
Generalized Communication Interface
GCinm: General Cinema Corp. (newspaper)
GCLA: Group Carry Look-Ahead
GCMA: Government Contract Management Association of America
GCMI: Glass Container Manufacturers' Institute
GCN: General Cinema Corp. (NYSE)
GCO: Genesco Inc. (NYSE)
GCOS: General Comprehensive Operating Supervisor
GCR: Gaylord Container Corp. (ASE)
Group Coded Recording
GCS: Graphics Compatibility System
GCT: Graphics Communications Terminal
Greenwich Civil Time

GCW: Garden City Western (railway)
GD: Air Antilles (airline)
General Debt
General Dynamics Corp. (NYSE)
Good Delivery
Graphics Display
Gross Debt
GDA: Global Data Administrator
GDB: Global Database
GDBMS: Generalized Database Management System
GDBS: Global Database System
GDC: General DataComm Industries Inc. (NYSE)
Guidance Display Computer
GDD: General Design Document
GDDL: Graphical Data Definition Language
GD/DS: Generalized Dictionary/Directory System
GDE: Generalized Data Entry
GDF: Group Distribution Frame
GDG: Generation Data Group
GDI: Generalized Database Interface
GDL: Graphic Display Library
GDMS: Generalized Data Management Systems
GDP: Goal Directed Programming
Gross Domestic Product
GDR: German Democratic Republic
Gdrich: B.F. Goodrich Co., The (newspaper)
GDS: Glenmore Distilleries Co. (ASE)
Graphic Data Sysytem
Graphic Design System
GDSDF: Generalized Data Structure Definition Facility
GDU: Graphic Display Unit
GDV: General Development Corp. (NYSE)
GDW: Golden West Financial Corp. (NYSE)
GDX: Genovese Drug Stores Inc. (ASE)
GE: General Electric Co. (NYSE)
Greater than or Equal to
Gross Earnings
GEB: Gerber Products Co. (NYSE)
GEC: GEICO Corp. (NYSE)
GED: General Energy Development Ltd. (NYSE)
GEDIT: General Purpose Text Editor
GEF: Nicholas-Applegate Growth Equity Fund Inc. (NYSE)
GEICO: GEICO Corp. (newspaper)
Government Employees' Insurance Co.
GEL: General Emulation Language
GelmS: Gelman Sciences Inc. (newspaper)
GEM: Gas Equipment Manufacturers' Group
Gemco: GEMCO NATIONAL INC. (newspaper)
GEMCOS: Generalized Message Control System
gen: general
generate
generation
GEN: GenRad Inc. (NYSE)
GenDev: General Development Corp. (newspaper)
GenEl: General Electric Co. (newspaper)
Genetch: Genentech Inc. (newspaper)
GENIE: General Information Extractor
Genisco: Genisco Technology Corp. (newspaper)
GENISYS: Generalized Information System
genl: general
Gen Led: General Ledger
Gen Mtge: General Mortgage
GenRe: General Re Corp. (newspaper)
Gensco: Genesco Inc. (newspaper)

GENTRAS: General Training System
GenuP: Genuine Parts Co. (newspaper)
GenvD: Genovese Drug Stores Inc. (newspaper)
GEO: GEO International Corp. (newspaper)
Geothermal Resources International Inc. (ASE)
GeoRes: Geothermal Resources International Inc. (newspaper)
GER: Germany Fund Inc., The (NYSE)
GerbPd: Gerber Products Co. (newspaper)
GerbSc: Gerber Scientific Inc. (newspaper)
GerFd: Germany Fund Inc., The (newspaper)
GERT: Graphical Evaluation and Review Technique
GERTS: General Remote Terminal System
GES: Genisco Technology Corp. (ASE)
Gold Exchange Standard
GET: Gross Error Test
GETMA: GET from local Manufacturer
Getty: Getty Petroleum Corp. (newspaper)
G&F: Georgia & Florida (railroad)
GF: America First Guaranteed Income Fund (ASE)
Gulf Aviation (airline)
GFA: General Freight Agent
GFB: GF Corp. (NYSE)
GFC: Gibraltar Financial Corp. (NYSE)
GF Cp: GF Corp. (newspaper)
GFD: Guilford Mills Inc. (NYSE)
GFE: Government-Furnished Equipment
GFI: Graham Field Health Products Inc. (ASE)
Guided Fault Isolation
GFM: Government-Furnished Material
GFO: Gulf, Mobile & Ohio (railroad)
GFP: Generalized File Processor
GFS: General Financial System
Giant Foods Inc. (ASE)
Grand Falls Central (railway)
GFTU: General Federation of Trade Unions
GG: Golden Pacific Airlines
Guinea Gulf Line (steamship)
GGC: Georgia Gulf Corp. (NYSE)
GGF: Global Growth & Income Fund Inc. (NYSE)
GGG: Graco Inc. (NYSE)
GGInc: Global Growth & Income Fund Inc. (newspaper)
GH: General Host Corp. (NYSE)
Ghana Airways
GH&H: Galveston, Houston and Henderson (railroad)
GHM: Graham Corp. (ASE)
GHO: General Homes Corp. (NYSE)
GHW: General Houseware Corp. (NYSE)
GHX: Galveston-Houston Co. (NYSE)
GHZ: GigaHertz
GI: Air Guinee (airline)
Government Initiated
Gross Inventory
GIANT: GIANT GROUP LTD. (newspaper)
GiantF: Giant Food Inc. (newspaper)
GibCR: C. R. Gibson Co. (newspaper)
GibrFn: Gibraltar Financial Corp. (newspaper)
GIBS: C. R. Gibson Co. (ASE)
GIC: General Input/Output Channel
GICs: Guaranteed Income Contracts

Guaranteed Investment Contracts
GIDEP: Government Industry Data Exchange Program
GIGO: Garbage In, Garbage Out
GII: Greiner Engineering Inc. (ASE)
GIIP: Groupement International de l'Industrie Pharmaceutique des pays de la CE (International Pharmaceutical Industry Group for the European Community) (French) (EC)
GIL: General Purpose Interactive Programming Language
Gillete: Gillette Co., The (newspaper)
GIM: Generalized Information Management
GIncPl: Global Income Plus Fund Inc. (newspaper)
GINO: Graphical Input and Output
GIOP: General Purpose Input/Output Processor
GIPSY: General Information Processing System
GIRL: Generalized Information Retrieval Language
GIRLS: Graphical Data Interpretation and Reconstruction in Local Satellite
GIRO: European Style Credit-Based Payments System (EC)
GIRS: Generalized Information Retrieval System
GIS: Generalized Information System
General Mills Inc. (NYSE)
GJ: Airlines of South Australia
Graphic Job (processor)
Greenwich and Johnsonville (railway)
GJP: Graphic Job Processor
GL: General Ledger
General Letter
Go Long
Good Luck
Greek Line (steamship)
Greenlandair (airline)
Glatflt: P. H. Glatfelter Co. (newspaper)
Glaxo: Glaxo Holdings PLC (newspaper)
GlbGvt: Global Government Plus Fund Inc., The (newspaper)
GlbM: Global Marine Inc. (newspaper)
GLD: Gould Inc. (NYSE)
GldFld: Goldfield Corp., The (newspaper)
GldNug: Golden Nugget Inc. (newspaper)
GldWF: Golden West Financial Corp. (newspaper)
GLE: Gleason Corp. (NYSE)
GleasC: Gleason Corp. (newspaper)
Glenfed: GLENFED Inc. (newspaper)
GL/FICS: General Ledger/Financial Information and Control System
GlfStUt: Gulf States Utilities Co. (newspaper)
GLI: Global Income Plus Fund Inc. (NYSE)
GLK: Great Lakes Chemical Corp. (NYSE)
GLM: Global Marine Inc. (NYSE)
GLN: GLENFED Inc. (NYSE)
Glnmr: Glenmore Distilleries Co. (newspaper)
GlobNR: Global Natural Resources Inc. (newspaper)
GlobYld: Global Yield Fund Inc., The (newspaper)
GLP: Gould Investors LP (ASE)
GLT: P. H. Glatfelter Co. (ASE)
GLW: Corning Glass Works (NYSE)
GLX: Glaxo Holdings PLC (NYSE)
GM: Gainesville Midland (railroad)
General Manager

General Mortgage
General Motors Corp. (NYSE)
Great Northern Airways
Group Mark

GMA: Grocery Manufacturers of America

GMAC: General Motors Acceptance Corp.

GMAP: General Macroassembly Program

GMAT: Greenwich Mean Astronomical Time

GMB: Good Merchandise Brand

GmbH: Gesellschaft mit beschränkter Haftung (Company with limited liability) (German)

GMC: Gruen Marketing Corp. (ASE)

GME: General Motors Class E Common Stock (NYSE) (newspaper)

GMH: General Motors Class H Common Stock (NYSE) (newspaper)

GMIS: Generalized Management Information System
Government Management Information Sciences

GML: Generalized Mark-up Language
Graphic Machine Language

GMN: Greenman Brothers Inc. (ASE)

GM&O: Gulf, Mobile & Ohio (railroad)

GMot: General Motors Corp. (newspaper)

GMP: Good Manufacturing Practice
Green Mountain Power Corp. (NYSE) (newspaper)

GMQ: Good Merchantable Quality

GMRC: Green Mountain Railroad Corporation

GMS: General Maintenance System

GMSS: Graphical Modeling and Simulation System

GMT: GATX Corp. (NYSE)
Generalized Multitasking
Greenwich Mean Time

GMW: General Microwave Corp. (ASE)

G&N: Greenville & Northern (railroad)

GN: Georgia Northern (railroad)
Great Northern (railway)

GN&A: Graysoñia, Nashville & Ashdown (railroad)

GNA: Gainsco Inc. (ASE)

GnAuto: General Automation Inc. (newspaper)

GNCrp: GenCorp Inc. (newspaper)

GnData: General DataComm Industries Inc. (newspaper)

GnDyn: General Dynamics Corp. (newspaper)

GNE: Genentech Inc. (NYSE)

GnEmp: General Employment Enterprises Inc. (newspaper)

GnEngy: General Energy Development Ltd. (newspaper)

GNG: Golden Nugget Inc. (NYSE)

GnHme: General Homes Corp. (newspaper)

GnHost: General Host Corp. (newspaper)

GnHous: General Housewares Corp. (newspaper)

GNI: Generation of New Ideas
Great Northern Iron Ore Properties (NYSE)
Gross National Income

GnInst: General Instrument Corp. (newspaper)

GNIrn: Great Northern Iron Ore Properties (newspaper)

GNL: GEMCO NATIONAL Inc. (ASE)

GNMA: Government National Mortgage Association

GnMicr: General Microwave Corp. (newspaper)

GnMills: General Mills Inc. (newspaper)
GNP: Gross National Product
GNR: Global Natural Resources Inc. (ASE)
GnRad: GenRad Inc. (newspaper)
GnRefr: General Refractories Co. (newspaper)
GnSignl: General Signal Corp. (newspaper)
GNT: Green Tree Acceptance Inc. (NYSE)
GntYl: Giant Yellowknife Mines Ltd. (newspaper)
GNW: Genesee and Wyoming (railroad)
GO: Collins Industries Inc. (ASE)
General-Obligation (bond)
General Office
General Order
General Organization
Generated Output
Government Obligations
Gulf Oil (steamship)
GOC: Gulf Canada Corp. (ASE)
GOCO: Government-Owned Contractor-Operated (production plant)
GOI: Gearhart Industries Inc. (NYSE)
GOL: Goal-Oriented Language
Goodyr: Goodyear Tire & Rubber Co., The (newspaper)
GOP: Graham-McCormick Oil & Gas Partnership (ASE)
GOR: General Operations Requirement
GorRup: Gorman-Rupp Co., The (newspaper)
GOS: Grade Of Service
Graphics Operating System
GOT: Gottschalks Inc. (NYSE)
Gotchk: Gottschalks Inc. (newspaper)
Gould: Gould Inc. (newspaper)
GOV: Global Government Plus Fund Inc., The (NYSE)
GP: General Purpose
Georgia-Pacific Corp. (NYSE)
Going Public
Gold Points
Grace Periods
Graphic Processor
Gross Profits
Growth in total Profit
GPA: Gas Processors Association
General Purpose Array
GPAC: Graphics Package
GPACK: General Utility Package
GPAM: Graduated-Payment Adjustable Mortgage
GPC: General Peripheral Controller
General Purpose Computer
Genuine Parts Co. (NYSE)
GPCA: General Purpose Communications Adapter
GPCB: General Purpose Communications Base
GPCF: General Purpose Computing Facility
GPC/P: General Purpose Controller/ Processor
GPD: General Protocol Driver
GPDC: General Purpose Digital Computer
GPDS: General Purpose Display System
GPH: Gallons Per Hour
GPI: Guardsman Products Inc. (NYSE)
GPIA: General Purpose Interface Adapter
GPIB: General Purpose Interface Bus
GPIC: General Purpose Intelligent Cable
GPIO: General Purpose Input/ Output
GPL: General Price Level
General Purpose Language
GPLA: General Price Level Adjusted (Accounting)
GPLAN: Generalized Plan

GPM: Gallons Per Minute
General Purpose Macrogenerator
General Purpose Module
Graduated-Payment Mortgage
Gross Processing Margin

GPO: General Post Office
Giant Group Ltd. (NYSE)
Government Printing Office

GPOS: General Purpose Operating System

GPP: General Purpose Processor
General Purchasing Power

GPR: General Purpose Register

GPRL: Gulf Puerto Rico Lines (steamship)

GPS: Gallons Per Second
Gap Inc., The (NYSE)
General Problem Solver
General Programming Subsystem
Graphic Programming Services

GPSA: Gas Processors Suppliers Association

GPSCS: General Purpose Satellite Communications System

GPSS: General Purpose Systems Simulator

GPU: General Postal Union
General Processing Unit
General Public Utilities Corp. (NYSE) (newspaper)

G&Q: Guayaquil and Quito (railroad)

GQ: Golden West Airlines
Grumman Corp. (NYSE)

gr: gross

GR: B. F. Goodrich Co. (NYSE)
General Air (airline)
General Register
Gross Receipts
Gross Revenue

GRA: W. R. Grace & Co. (NYSE)

Grace: W.R. Grace & Co. (newspaper)

GRACE: Grace Line (steamship)

Graco: Graco Inc. (newspaper)

Graham: Graham Corp. (newspaper)

GrahMc: Graham-McCormick Oil & Gas Partnership (newspaper)

Graingr: W. W. Grainger Inc. (newspaper)

GRAN FLOTA BLANCA: Great White Fleet (United Fruit Company) (steamship)

Grang: Granges Exploration Ltd. (newspaper)

GRANIS: Graphical Natural Inference System

GRASP: Generalized Read and Simulate Program
Generalized Remote Acquisition and Sensor Processing
Graphics Subroutine Package

GRB: Gerber Scientific Inc. (NYSE)

GRC: Gorman-Rupp Co., The (ASE)

GrdnB: Guardian Bancorp. (newspaper)

GrdPrd: Guardsman Products Inc. (newspaper)

GRE: Gulf Resources & Chemical Corp. (NYSE)

Greiner: Greiner Engineering Inc. (newspaper)

GrenTr: Green Tree Acceptance Inc. (newspaper)

Grenm: Greenman Brothers Inc. (newspaper)

Greyh: Greyhound Corp., The (newspaper)

GRF: Geographic Reference File

GRG: Graphical Rewriting Grammar

GrhmFld: Graham Field Health Products Inc. (newspaper)
GRI: G. R. I. Corp. (newspaper)
GRINDER: Graphical Interactive Network Designer
GRIP: Graphics Interactive Programming
GRIT: Grantor Retained Income Trust
GRL: General Instrument Corp. (NYSE)
GRN: General Re Corp. (NYSE)
Greenville and Northern Railway
grnd: ground
GrndAu: Grand Auto Inc. (newspaper)
GRNR: Grand River Railway
GRO: Grow Group Inc. (NYSE)
GrowGp: Grow Group Inc. (newspaper)
GR&PA: Ghana Railway and Port Authority
GRR: Georgetown Railroad
G. R. I. Corp. (ASE)
GRS: General Records Schedule
General Reporting System
GRSS: Guyana Railways and Shipping Services
GRT: Graphic Technology Inc. (ASE)
Greater Than
Gross Register(ed) Tonnage
GrTch: Graphic Technology Inc. (newspaper)
GrtLkC: Great Lakes Chemical Corp. (newspaper)
GRTS: General Remote Terminal Supervisor
GrubEl: Grubb & Ellis Co. (newspaper)
Gruen: Gruen Marketing Corp. (newspaper)
Grumn: Grumman Corp. (newspaper)
GRX: General Refractories Co. (NYSE)
GS: Air Vosges (airline)
General Secretary
Gillette Co., The (NYSE)
Glamour Stock
Government Securities
Gross Sales
Gross Spread
Group Separator
Growth Stock
GSA: General Services Administration
Glass-Steagal Act
Gulf and South American Steamship Company
GSAM: Generalized Sequential Access Method
GSBCA: General Services Board of Contract Appeals
GSC: Gelman Sciences Inc. (ASE)
Group Switching Center
GSE: Government Sponsored Enterprise
Ground Support Equipment
GSF: ACM Government Securities Fund Inc. (NYSE)
Georgia Southern and Florida (railroad)
GSI: Grand Scale Integration
GSIU: Ground Standard Interface Unit
GSL: Guaranteed Student Loan
GSM: Graphics System Module
GSO: Growth Stock Outlook Trust Inc. (NYSE)
GSP: Generalized Scheme of Preferences
Generalized System of Tariff Preferences
Graphics Subroutine Package
Gross State Product
GSR: Global-Shared Resources
GSS: Graphic Support Software
GST: Generation-Skipping Transfer (tax)
GSTP: Generalized System of Tariff Preferences

GSU: Gulf States Utilities Co. (NYSE)
GSVC: Generalized Supervisor Call
GSW: Great Southwest (railroad)
GSX: General Signal Corp. (NYSE)
G/T: Gain-to-noise-Temperature ratio
GT: Gas Turbine Engine
Gibraltar Airways
Gift Tax
Goodyear Tire & Rubber Co., The (NYSE)
Grand Trunk (railroad)
Graphics Terminal
Greater Than
Gross Tonnage
Gross Tons
GTA: Great American First Savings Bank (NYSE)
GtAFst: Great American First Savings Bank (newspaper)
GtAtPc: Great Atlantic & Pacific Tea Company Inc., The (newspaper)
GTC: Good Till Cancelled (Countermanded)
gtd: guaranteed
GT&E: General Telephone and Electronics Corp.
GTE: GTE Corp. (NYSE) (newspaper)
GTF: Generalized Trace Facility
Greater Than Flag
GthStk: Growth Stock Outlook Trust Inc. (newspaper)
GTI: GTI Corp. (ASE) (newspaper)
GTM: Good-This-Month order
GTP: Graphic Transform Package
GTV: Galaxy Cablevision LP (ASE)
GTW: Good-This-Week order
Grand Trunk Western (railroad)
GtWash: Greater Washington Investors Inc. (newspaper)
GtWFn: Great Western Financial Corp. (newspaper)
GTY: Getty Petroleum Corp. (NYSE)
G&U: Grafton and Upton (railroad)
GU: Aviateca (airline)
guar: guarantee
GUC: Good-Until-Canceled order
GUD: Gestion de l'Union Douaniére (Organization of the European Commission responsible for the administration of the Customs Union) (French) (EC)
GuldLP: Gould Investors LP (newspaper)
GULF: Gulf Oil Corporation (steamship)
Gulfrd: Guilford Mills Inc. (newspaper)
GulfRs: Gulf Resources & Chemical Corp. (newspaper)
GULP: Group Universal Life Policy
GUN: Gundle Environmental Systems Inc. (ASE)
Gundle: Gundle Environmental Systems Inc. (newspaper)
GV: Territory Airlines
Goldfield Corp., The (ASE)
GVO: Gross Value of Output
GVT: Dean Witter Government Income Trust (NYSE)
G&W: Genesee and Western (railroad)
GWA: Golden West Airlines
GWF: Great Western Financial Corp. (NYSE)
GWI: Greater Washington Investors Inc. (ASE)
GWP: Gross World Product
GWR: Great Western Railway
GWT: GW Utilities Ltd. (ASE)
GW Ut: GW Utilities Ltd. (newspaper)
GWW: W. W. Grainger Inc. (NYSE)
GWWDR: Great Winnipeg Water District Railway

GX: GEO International Corp. (NYSE)
Great Lakes Air Service (airline)

GXL: Granges Exploration Ltd. (ASE)

GXY: Galaxy Carpet Mills Inc. (ASE)

GY: Aurigny Air Services (airline)
GenCorp Inc. (NYSE)

GYK: Giant Yellowknife Mines Ltd. (ASE)

GYSCO: Great Yarmouth Shipping Company

GZT: Greenwich Zone Time

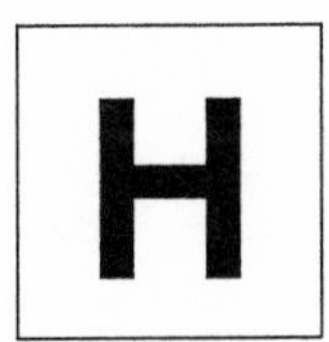

h: hardware
head
hecto
host
hour

H: Declared or paid stock dividend or split-up (stock listings of newspapers)
Half-Adder
Hawaiian Airlines
HelmResources Inc. (ASE)
Home Address

HA: HAL Inc. (ASE)
Half-Adder
Hazard Analysis
Home Address
House Account
Human Adaptability

HAA: Human Asset Accounting

HAB: Home Address Block

HAC: Hierarchical Abstract Computer
House Appropriations Committee

HAD: Hadson Corp. (NYSE)
Herein After Described

Hadson: Hadson Corp. (newspaper)

HAG: Home Address Gap

HAI: Hampton Industries Inc. (ASE)

H&A Ins: Health and Accident Insurance

HAL: HAL Inc. (newspaper)
Halliburton Co. (NYSE) (newspaper)
Holland-American Line (steamship)

Halifax: Halifax Engineering Inc. (newspaper)

HallFB: Frank B. Hall & Company Inc. (newspaper)

Halmi: Robert Halmi Inc. (newspaper)

Halwod: Hallwood Group Inc., The (newspaper)

HAM: Hierarchical Access Method

HampH: Hampton Healthcare Inc. (newspaper)

Hamptl: Hampton Industries Inc. (newspaper)

HAMT: Human-Aided Machine Translation

HAN: Hanson Trust PLC (NYSE)

hand: handling

HandH: Handy & Harman (newspaper)

Handlm: Handleman Co. (newspaper)

HanFb: Hancock Fabrics Inc. (newspaper)

Hanfrd: Hannaford Brothers Co. (newspaper)

HanJI: John Hancock Investors Trust (newspaper)

HanJS: John Hancock Income Securities Trust (newspaper)

Hanna: M. A. Hanna Co. (newspaper)

HANSA: Hansa Line (steamship)

Hanson: Hanson Trust PLC (newspaper)

HAPAG: Hamburg-Amerika Paket Aktiengessllschaft (German-Hamburg-America Packet Company) (steamship)

HAPAG-LLOYD: Hamburg-Amerika (North German Lloyd Lines) (steamship)

HAR: Harman International Industries Inc. (NYSE)
Home Address Register
HarBrJ: Harcourt Brace Jovanovich Inc. (newspaper)
HARDMON: Hardware Monitor
hardwr: hardware
Harley: Harley-Davidson Inc. (newspaper)
Harlnd: John H. Harland Co., The (newspaper)
Harman: Harman International Industries Inc. (newspaper)
Harnish: Harnischfeger Industries Inc. (newspaper)
Harris: Harris Corp. (newspaper)
Harsco: Harsco Corp. (newspaper)
Hartmx: Hartmarx Corp. (newspaper)
Harvey: Harvey Group Inc., The (newspaper)
HAS: Hasbro Inc. (ASE)
Hasbr: Hasbro Inc. (newspaper)
HASQ: Hardware-Assisted Software Queue
Hasting: Hastings Manufacturing Co. (newspaper)
HAT: Hatteras Income Securities Inc. (NYSE)
HATRS: High-Altitude Transmit/Receive Satellite
HattSe: Hatteras Income Securities Inc. (newspaper)
HawEl: Hawaiian Electric Industries Inc. (newspaper)
hb: handbook
H&B: Hampton & Branchville (railroad)
HB: Air Melanesiae (airline)
Hillenbrand Industries Inc. (NYSE)
HBAR: Head Bar Address Register
HBC: Hudson's Bay Company (steamship)
HBE: Honeybee Inc. (ASE)
HBEN: High Byte Enable
HBJ: Harcourt Brace Jovanovich Inc. (NYSE)
HBLRR: Harbor Belt Line Railroad
HBR: Harvard Business Review
HBS: Harvard Business School
Hoboken Shore (railroad)
HBT: Houston Belt and Terminal (railroad)
H&BTM: Huntington & Broad Top Mountain Railroad & Coal Co.
HBW: Howard B. Wolf Inc. (ASE)
HC: Held Covered
Helene Curtis Industries Inc. (NYSE)
Historical Cost
Holding Company
Host Computer
HCA: Hospital Care Corporation of America (NYSE) (newspaper)
HCF: Host Command Facility
HCFA: Health Care Financing Administration
HCH: Health-Chem Corp. (ASE)
HCI: Host Computer Interface
Hybrid Computer Interface
HCL: Hamburg-Chicago Line (steamship)
High Cost of Living
HCM: Health-Care Management
HCMTS: High-Capacity Mobile Telecommunications System
HCMW: Hatters, Cap and Millinery Workers (union)
HCN: Health Care REIT Inc. (ASE)
HCO: HUBCO Inc. (ASE)
HCP: Hard Copy Printer
Health Care Property Investors Inc. (NYSE)
HCR: Hardware Check Routine
HCRST: Hardware Clipping, Rotation, Scaling and Translation

HCS: Hard Copy System
Hundred Call Seconds
HD: Aero Servicios (airline)
Half-Duplex
Hierarchical Direct
High Density
Home Depot Inc., The (NYSE)
HDA: Head/Disk Assembly
HDAM: Hierarchical Direct Access Method
HDAS: Hybrid Data Acquisition System
HDC: High-Speed Data Channel
Holder in Due Course
HDDR: High-Density Digital Recording
HDF: High-Density Flexible
HDI: Harley-Davidson Inc. (NYSE)
HDL: Handleman Co. (NYSE)
HDLA: High-Level Data Link Control Adapter
HDLC: High-Level Data Link Control
HDLM: High-Level Data Linkage Module
HDMR: High-Density Multitrack Recording
HDOS: Hard Disk Operating System
hdr: header
HDR: Heldor Industries Inc. (ASE)
High-Density Recording
HDS: Hills Department Stores Inc. (NYSE)
HDT: High-Density Tape
HDTV: High-Definition Television
hdw: hardware
HDX: Half-Duplex
HE: Hawaiian Electric Industries Inc.
Hollis and Eastern (railroad)
Hecks: Heck's Inc. (newspaper)
HeclaM: Hecla Mining Co. (newspaper)
HEI: HEICO Corp. (ASE)
Heico: HEICO Corp. (newspaper)
Heilig: Heilig-Meyers Co. (newspaper)
HeinWr: Hein-Werner Corp. (newspaper)
Heinz: H. J. Heinz Co. (newspaper)
Heldor: Heldor Industries Inc. (newspaper)
HelmP: Helmerich & Payne Inc. (newspaper)
HelmR: HelmResources Inc. (newspaper)
HelneC: Helene Curtis Industries Inc. (newspaper)
HelthM: Health-Mor Inc. (newspaper)
Helvet: Helvetia Fund Inc., The (newspaper)
HEMT: High-Electron-Mobility Transistors
HER: Hellenic Electric Railway
Human Error Rate
Herculs: Hercules Inc. (newspaper)
HeritEn: Heritage Entertainment Inc. (newspaper)
HershO: Hershey Oil Corp. (newspaper)
HEW: Department of Health, Education, and Welfare (defunct)
HewlPk: Hewlett-Packard Co. (newspaper)
HEX: Heck's Inc. (NYSE)
Hexadecimal
Hexcel: Hexcel Corp. (newspaper)
H/F: Held For
HF: High Frequency
HFC: Household Finance Corp.
HFD: Home Federal S&L Assn. (California) (NYSE)
HFDF: High-Frequency Distribution Frame
HFE: Human Factors Engineering
HFI: Hudson Foods Inc. (ASE)
HFIA: Heat and Frost Insulators and Asbestos Workers (union)

HFL: Hawaii Freight Lines (steamship)
Homestead Financial Corp. (NYSE)
HFM: Hold For Money
HFR: Hold For Release
HGC: Hudson General Corp. (ASE)
hgt: height
H/H: Host to Host
HH: Hamburger Hochbahn (Hamburg Elevated Railway)
Hetch Hetchy (railroad)
H. Hogarth and Sons (steamship)
Hooper Homes Inc. (ASE)
Somalia (airlines)
HHA: H.H. Anderson Line (steamship)
Humphrey-Hawkins Act
HHC: Horizon Healthcare Corp. (NYSE)
HHFA: Housing and Home Finance Agency
HHG: Household Goods
HHH: Heritage Entertainment Inc. (ASE)
HHI: Hampton Healthcare Inc. (ASE)
HI: Holton Inter-Urban (railway)
Hot Issue
Household International Inc. (NYSE)
HIA: Holiday Corp. (NYSE)
HIC: Hybrid Integrated Circuit
HICS: Hierarchical Information Control System
HIDAM: Hierarchical Indexed Direct Access Method
HIFT: Hardware Implemented Fault Tolerance
HII: Healthcare International Inc. (ASE)
HiIncO: High Income Advance Trust (newspaper)
HillDp: Hills Department Stores Inc. (newspaper)
Hillnbd: Hillenbrand Industries Inc. (newspaper)
Hilton: Hilton Hotels Corp. (newspaper)
HIM: Hardware Interface Module
Hierarchy of Interpretive Modules
Himont: HIMONT Inc. (newspaper)
H In DC: Holder In Due Course
Hindrl: Hinderliter Industries Inc. (newspaper)
HINIL: High-Noise-Immunity Logic
HIP: Health Insurance Plan
Hipotronics Inc. (ASE)
Host Interface Processor
HIPO: Hierarchy, Input, Process, Output
Hiptron: Hipotronics Inc. (newspaper)
hir: hierarchy
HI-RES: High-Resolution
HISAM: Hierarchical Indexed Sequential Access Method
HISDAM: Hierarchical Indexed Sequential Direct Access Method
HiShear: Hi-Shear Industries Inc. (newspaper)
HIT: High Isolation Transformer
Hitachi Ltd. (NYSE)
Hitachi: Hitachi Ltd. (newspaper)
HI-TECH: High Technology
HITS: Hobbyist's Interchange Standard
HiYld: High Yield Income Fund Inc., The (newspaper)
HiYldPl: High Yield Plus Fund Inc. (newspaper)
HJ: Toa Airways
HJR: Hedjaz Jorday Railway
HK: Cogeair (airline)
HKF: Hancock Fabrics Inc. (NYSE)
HKIBOR: Hong Kong Inter-Bank Offered Rate
HL: Hecla Mining Co. (NYSE)
Holiday Airlines

Home Lines (steamship)
Host Language
HLA: High-Speed Line Adapter
HLAIS: High-Level Analog Input Subsystem
HLBB: Home Loan Bank Board
HLDA: Hold Acknowledge
HLDTL: High-Level Diode Transistor Logic
HII: Healthcare International Inc. (newspaper)
HLI: Host Language Interface
HLL: High-Level Language
HLML: High-Level Microprogramming Language
HLMPL: High-Level Microprogramming Language
HLNE: Hillsboro and Northeastern (railroad)
HLPI: High-Level Programming Interface
HLQL: High-Level Query Language
HLR: High-Level Representation
hlt: halt
HLT: Highly Leveraged Transaction
Hilton Hotels Corp. (NYSE)
HlthCh: Health-Chem Corp. (newspaper)
HlthCP: Health Care Property Investors Inc. (newspaper)
HlthCr: Health Care REIT Inc. (newspaper)
HlthMn: Health Management Associates Inc. (newspaper)
HltRhB: Health & Rehabilitation Properties Trust (newspaper)
HLTU: Hierarchized Threshold Logic Unit
Hltvst: HealthVest (newspaper)
HM: Hypothetical Machine
HMA: Hardware Manufacturers Association
Health Maintenance Act
Health Management Associates Inc. (ASE)
HMC: Honda Motor Company Ltd. (NYSE)
HME: Home Group Inc., The (NYSE)
HmeD: Home Depot Inc., The (newspaper)
HmeGp: Home Group Inc., The (newspaper)
HMF: Hastings Manufacturing Co. (ASE)
HmFB: Homestead Financial Corp. (newspaper)
HmFSD: Home Federal S&L Assn. (California) (newspaper)
HMG: Hedge Mutual Fund
HMG Property Investors Inc. (ASE) (newspaper)
HMI: Hardware Monitor Interface
Health-Mor Inc. (ASE)
HMM: Hardware Multiply Module
HMO: Hardware Microcode Optimizer
Health Maintenance Organization
HMPL: High-Level Microprogram Language
HmpU: Hampton Utilities Trust (newspaper)
HMPY: Hardware Multiplier
HMS: Her (His) Majesty's Ship (UK)
HmstF: Homestead Financial Corp. (newspaper)
Hmstke: Homestake Mining Co. (newspaper)
HMT: HIMONT Inc. (NYSE)
HMY: Heilig-Meyers Co. (NYSE)
HN: Host to Network
Hutchinson and Northern (railroad)
KLM-Dutch Airlines
HNA: Hierarchical Network Architecture
HND: Hinderliter Industries Inc. (ASE)

HNE: Harriman and Northeastern (railroad)
HNH: Handy & Harman (NYSE)
HNIL: High-Noise-Immunity Logic
HNM: M.A. Hanna Co. (NYSE)
HNPA: Home Numbering Plan Area
HNPL: High-Level Network Processing Language
HNW: Hein-Werner Corp. (ASE)
HNZ: H.J. Heinz Co. (NYSE)
HO: Head Office
Home Office
Houston Oil Trust (ASE)
HOC: Holly Corp. (ASE)
HOF: Hofmann Industries Inc. (ASE)
Hofman: Hofmann Industries Inc. (newspaper)
HOI: House Of Issue
HOKEYS: Home Owners' Loan Corporation Bonds
HOL: High-Order Language
Holco Mortgage Acceptance Corp. (ASE)
HOLC: Home Owners' Loan Corporation (defunct)
Holco: Holco Mortgage Acceptance Corp. (newspaper)
HOLDET: Higher Order Language Development and Evaluation Tool
Holidy: Holiday Corp. (newspaper)
HollyCp: Holly Corp. (newspaper)
HOLWG: High-Order Language Working Group
HomeSh: Home Shopping Network Inc. (newspaper)
HON: Honeywell Inc. (NYSE)
hon'd: honored
Honda: Honda Motor Company Ltd. (newspaper)
Honwell: Honeywell Inc. (newspaper)
Honybe: Honeybee Inc. (newspaper)
HoopHl: Hooper Holmes Inc. (newspaper)
HoprSol: Hopper Soliday Corp. (newspaper)
HOR: Holder Of Record
Horn & Hardart Co., The (ASE)
HO&RC: Humble Oil and Refining Company
Horizon: Horizon Corp. (newspaper)
Hormel: George A. Hormel & Co. (newspaper)
HOS: Higher Order Software
Hosp Ins: Hospital Insurance
HOT: Hotel Investors Trust/Corporation (NYSE)
HotlInv: Hotel Investors Trust/Corporation (newspaper)
HOU: Houston Industries Inc. (NYSE)
HouFab: House of Fabrics Inc. (newspaper)
HougM: Houghton Mifflin Co. (newspaper)
HouInd: Houston Industries Inc. (newspaper)
HouOR: Houston Oil Royalty Trust (newspaper)
HouOT: Houston Oil Trust (newspaper)
HousInt: Household International Inc. (newspaper)
HOV: Hovnanian Enterprises Inc. (ASE)
HovnE: Hovnanian Enterprises Inc. (newspaper)
HOW: Howell Industries Inc. (ASE)
HoweRh: Howe Richardson Inc. (newspaper)
HowlCp: Howell Corp. (newspaper)
HowlIn: Howell Industries Inc. (newspaper)
Howtk: Howtek Inc. (newspaper)
HP: Apollo Airways
Helmerich & Payne Inc. (NYSE)

High Power
Horsepower
Host Processor

HPA: High-Power Amplifier

HPAA: High-Performance Antenna Assembly

HPC: Hercules Inc. (NYSE)

HPCA: High-Performance Communications Adapter

HPF: High Pass Filter
Host Preparation Facility

HPGS: High-Performance Graphics System

HPH: Harnischfeger Industries Inc. (NYSE)

HPPL: Host Program Preparation Facility

HPT: Head Per Track

HPT&D: High Point, Thomasville & Denton (railroad)

hq: headquarters

HQ: Valley Airlines

HQH: H & Q Healthcare Investors (NYSE)

HQ Hlt: H & Q Healthcare Investors (newspaper)

HR: Hit Ratio
House of Representatives
Human Relations
Pennsylvania Commuter (airlines)

HRA: Harvey Group Inc. (ASE)
Health Resources Administration

HRB: H & R Block Inc. (NYSE)

HRD: Hannaford Brothers Co. (NYSE)

HrdRk: Hard Rock Cafe PLC (newspaper)

HRE: HRE Properties (NYSE) (newspaper)

HREU: Hotel and Restaurant Employees Union

HRI: Howe Richardson Inc. (ASE)

HRK: Hard Rock Cafe PLC (ASE)

HRL: George A. Hormel & Co. (ASE)

HRM: Hardware Read-In Mode
Human Resources Management

HRMR: Human Read/Machine Read

HRN: Highest Response-Ratio Next

HRNES: Host Remote Node Entry System

HrnHar: Horn & Hardart Co., The (newspaper)

HRP: Health & Rehabilitation Properties Trust (NYSE)
Human Resources Planning

HRS: Harris Corp. (NYSE)
Human Resources System

Hrshey: Hershey Foods Corp. (newspaper)

HRSS: Host Resident Software System

HRT: Harwell Railway

HR-10: Keogh Plan

HrzHlt: Horizon Healthcare Corp. (newspaper)

HS: Half-Subtracter
Hartford and Slocomb (railroad)
Hierarchical Sequential
Hopper Soliday Corp. (NYSE)
Scenic Airlines

HSA: Hawley-Smoot Act

HSAL: Hamburg South American Line (steamship)

HSAM: Hierarchical Sequential Access Method

HSB: High-Speed Buffer

HSBA: High-Speed Bus Adapter

HSC: Harsco Corp. (NYSE)
High-Speed Concentrator

HSDB: High-Speed Data Buffer

HSDG: Hamburg-Sudamerikanische Dampfs Gesell (Columbus Line) (steamship)

HSDMS: Highly Secure Database Management System

HSE: High-Speed Signal Control Equipment
HSEL: High-Speed Selector Channel
HSI: Hi-Shear Industries Inc. (NYSE)
HSLC: High-Speed Single Line Controller
HSM: Hierarchical Storage Manager
High-Speed Memory
HSN: Home Shopping Network Inc. (ASE)
HSO: Hershey Oil Corp. (ASE)
HSP: High-Speed Printer
HSR: High-Speed Reader
HSS: Hierarchical Service System
HSW: Helena Southwestern (railroad)
HSY: Hershey Foods Corp. (NYSE)
H/T: Head per Track
HT: Air Chad (airline)
Hand-Held Terminal
Horizontal Tabulation (character)
HTB: Hexadecimal to Binary
HTC: Hybrid Technology Computer
HTG: Heritage Media Corp. (ASE)
HtgMd: Heritage Media Corp. (newspaper)
HTK: Howtek Inc. (ASE)
HTL: High Threshold Logic
HTN: Houghton Mifflin Co. (NYSE)
HTS: Head, Track, and Sector
Host To Satellite
HT&W: Hoosac Tunnel & Wilmington (railroad)
HU: Cascade Airways
Hampton Utilities Trust (ASE)
HUB: Hubbell Inc. (ASE)
HUBCO: HUBCO Inc. (newspaper)
Hubel: Hubbell Inc. (newspaper)
HUD: Department of Housing and Urban Development
HudFd: Hudson Foods Inc. (newspaper)
HudGn: Hudson General Corp.
HUF: Huffy Corp. (NYSE)
Huffy: Huffy Corp. (newspaper)
HUG: Hughes Supply Inc. (NYSE)
HughSp: Hughes Supply Inc. (newspaper)
HUM: Humana Inc. (NYSE)
Human: Humana Inc. (newspaper)
Human Eng: Human Engineering
HumInt: Human Intelligence
HUN: Hunt Manufacturing Co. (NYSE)
HuntM: Hunt Manufacturing Co. (newspaper)
HUT: High-Usage Intertoll Trunk
Homes Using Television
HuttEF: E.F. Hutton Group Inc., The (newspaper)
HV: High Voltage
HVR: Hardware Vector to Raster
HVT: HealthVest (ASE)
HVTS: High-Volume Time-Sharing
hw: hardware
H&W: Holm and Wonsild (steamship)
HWAL: Holland West-Afrika Line (steamship)
HWG: Hallwood Group Inc., The (NYSE)
HWI: Hardware Interpreter
HWL: Howell Corp. (NYSE)
HWP: Hewlett-Packard Co. (NYSE)
HX: Halifax Engineering Inc. (ASE)
Virginia Air Cargo (airline)
HXL: Hexcel Corp. (NYSE)
HY: Houston Metro Airlines
Hydral: Hydraulic Co., The (newspaper)
HYI: High-Yield Income Fund Inc., The (NYSE)
HYP: High-Yield Plus Fund Inc. (NYSE)
HY&T: Hooppole, Yorktown & Tampico (railroad)
hz: hertz
HZN: Horizon Corp. (NYSE)

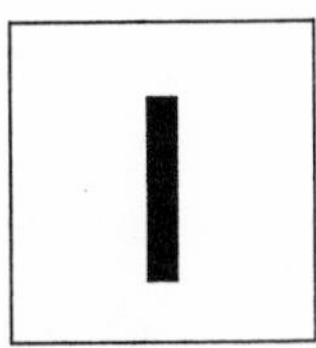

i: information
input
instruction
interest (rate of) (symbol)
interrupt

I: First Interstate Bancorp. (NYSE)
Interest rate (nominal market)
Paid this year, dividend omitted, deferred, or no action taken at dividend meeting (stock listings in newspapers)

I&A: Indexing and Abstracting

IA: Immediately Available
Inactive Account
Income Averaging
Indian Airlines (India)
Institute of Actuaries
Institutional Advertising
Instruction Addresss
Intangible Asset
Integrated Adapter
Interim Audit
Iraqi Airways

IAA: Insurance Accountants Association
International Advertising Association
Investment Advisers Act

IAB: Inter-American Bank
International Air Bahama (airline)
Interrupt Address to Bus

IABB: Inter-American Bank Bonds

IAC: Integration, Assembly, Checkout
Interactive Array Computer
International Association for Cybernetics

IACA: International Association of Consulting Actuaries

IACHA: Iowa Automated Clearing House Association

IACP: International Association of Computer Programmers

IAD: Initial Address Designator
Inland Steel Industries Inc. (NYSE)
Integrated Automatic Documentation

IADB: Inter-American Development Bank

IADR: Instruction Address

IAEA: International Atomic Energy Agency

IAF: First Australia Fund Inc., The (ASE)
Interactive Facility

IAI: Israel Aircraft Industries

IAL: International Algebraic Language
International Aluminum Corp. (NYSE)

IALE: Instrumented Architectural Level Emulation

IAM: Innovation Access Method
Institute of Administrative Management
International Association of Machinists

IANET: Integrated Access Network

IAP: Image Array Processor
Internal Array Processor

IAPW: International Association of Personnel Women

IAR: Instruction Address Register
Interrupt Address Register

IARIW: International Association for Research on Income and Wealth

IAS: Immediate Access Storage
Interactive Application System

IASA: Insurance Accounting and Statistical Association

IASC: International Accounting Standards Committee
International Association for Statistical Computing

IASG: Inflation Accounting Steering Group

IATA: International Air Transport Association

IATV: Income Approach To Value

IAU: Interface Adaptor Unit

IAW: In Accordance With

ib: ibidem (in the same place)

I&B: Improvements and Betterments

IB: Iberia (airline)
Identifier Block
In Bond
Income Bond
Industrialized Building
Input Bus
Instruction Bus
Insurance Broker
Interface Bus
International Bank Bonds
Introducing Broker
Investment Banker
Investment Banking
Is Between

IBA: Independent Bankers Association of America
International Banking Act
Investment Bankers Association

IBAA: Independent Bankers Association of America

IBAM: Institute of Business Administration and Management (Japan)

IBB: International Bank Bonds

IBC: Integrated Block Channel
Integrated Broadband Communications
Interstate Bakeries Corp. (NYSE)

IBCC: International Bureau of Chambers of Commerce

IBE: Inventory By Exception

IBEC: International Bank for Economic Cooperation

IBELs: Interest-Bearing Eligible Liabilities

IBES: Institutional Broker's Estimate System

IBEW: International Brotherhood of Electrical Workers (union)

IBF: First Iberian Fund (ASE)
Input Buffer Full
International Banking Facility

IBFO: International Brotherhood of Firemen and Oilers (union)

IBFS: International Banking Facilities

IBG: Inter Block Gap

ibid: ibidem (in the same place)

IBIS: International Bank Information System

IBK: International Banknote Company Inc. (ASE)

IBL: Iroquois Brands Ltd. (ASE)

IBM: International Business Machines Corp. (NYSE) (newspaper)

IBNR: Incurred But Not Reported

IBO: Invoice Book, Outward

IBOL: Interactive Business Oriented Language

IBOLS: Integrated Business Oriented Language Support

IBOP: International Brotherhood of Operative Potters (union)

IBP: IBP Inc. (NYSE) (newspaper)

IBRD: International Bank for Reconstruction and Development

IBS: International Bank for Settlements

IBSAC: Industrialized Building Systems and Components
IBT: Integrated Business Terminal
International Brotherhood of Teamsters (union)
IBTCWH: International Brotherhood of Teamsters, Chauffeurs, Warehousemen, and Helpers (union)
IBU: International Broadcasting Union
I&C: Installation and Checkout
IC: Identification Code
Income Capital
Index of Coincidence
Indian Airlines
Industrial Concentration
Industrialized Country
Information Circular
Instruction Counter
Instrumentation Control
Integrated Circuit
Investment Counselor
ICA: Imperial Corporation of America (NYSE) (newspaper)
Intercomputer Adapter
International Communication Association
Interstate Commerce Act
Investment Company Act
I of CA: Institute of Chartered Accountants (UK)
ICAD: Integrated Control and Display
ICAE: Integrated Communications Adapter Extension
ICAM: Integrated Computer-Aided Manufacturing
ICAO: International Civil Aviation Organization
ICB: Information Collection Budget
InterCapital Income Securities Inc. (NYSE)
Internal Common Bus
ICBS: Interconnected Business System
IC&C: Invoice Cost and Charges
ICC: International Chamber of Commerce
Interstate Commerce Commission
ICCA: Independent Computer Consultants Association
ICCAD: International Center for Computer-Aided Design
ICCDP: Integrated Circuit Communications Data Processor
ICCF: Interactive Computing and Control Facility
ICCH: International Commodities Clearing House
ICCP: Institute for the Certification of Computer Professionals
ICCU: Intercomputer Communications Unit
Intercomputer Control Unit
ICD: Interface Control Document
ICDB: Integrated Corporated Data Base
ICDDB: Internal Control Description Data Base
ICDL: Integrated Circuit Description Language
Internal Control Description Language
ICDLA: Internal Control Description Language Analyzer
ICDR: Inward Call Detail Recording
ICDS: Integrated Circuit Design System
ICE: Artice Alaska Fisheries Corp. (ASE)
Incircuit Emulator
International Commercial Exchange
ICEA: International Consumer Electronics Association
ICEE: ICEE-USA (newspaper)
ICFC: Industrial and Commercial Finance Corporation

ICFTU: International Confederation of Free Trade Unions

ICG: Interactive Computer Graphics
Inter-City Gas Corp. (ASE)

ICH: I.C.H. Corp. (ASE) (newspaper)

ICI: Imperial Chemical Industries (steamship)
Imperial Chemical Industries PLC (NYSE)
Intelligent Communications Interface
Investment Company Institute

IC Ind: IC Industries Inc. (newspaper)

ICL: Insurance, Casualty and Liability
Intercommunication Logic
Intercomputer Communication Link
Interpretive Coding Language

ICM: ICM Property Investors Inc. (NYSE) (newspaper)
Institute of Credit Management
Instruction Control Memory

ICMA: Institute of Cost and Management Accountants

ICMS: Integrated Circuit and Message Switch

ICMUP: Instruction Control Memory Update Processor

ICN: ICN Pharmaceuticals Inc. (NYSE)
Integrated Computer Network

ICN Bio: ICN Biomedicals Inc. (newspaper)

ICN Ph: ICN Pharmaceuticals Inc. (newspaper)

ICOR: Incremental Capital Output Ratios

ICOS: Interactive COBOL Operating System

ICP: Initial Connection Protocol
Inventory Control Point

ICR: Indirect Control Register
Input Control Register
Interrupt Control Register

ICS: Industrial Control System
Information Control System
Institute of Computer Science
Interactive Communications Software
International Chamber of Shipping
International Communications System
Interpretive Computer Simulation
Issued Capital Stock

ICSID: International Center for the Settlement of Investment Disputes

ICSN: Indo-China Steam Navigation Company (steamship)

ICT: InComing Trunk

ICTB: International Customs Tariffs Bureau

ICU: Industrial Control Unit
Instruction Control Unit
Interface Control Unit
Interrupt Control Unit

ICV: Initial Chaining Value

ICW: Initial Condition Word
Interface Control Word

ICWU: International Chemical Workers' Union

ICX: IC Industries Inc. (NYSE)

ICY: ICEE-USA (ASE)

id: identification
identifier

ID: Immediate Delivery
Import Duty
Income Debenture
Industrial Dynamics
Inelastic Demand
Intelligent Digitizer
Interim Dividend
Item Descriptor
Interlocking Directors
The discount rate

IDA: Idaho Power Co. (NYSE)
Integrated Data Analysis
Interactive Data Analysis
Interactive Debugging Aid
International Development Association

IDAB: Industrial Advisory Board

IDAC: Instant Data Access and Control

IdahoP: Idaho Power Co. (newspaper)

IDAM: Indexed Direct Access Method

IDAS: Industrial Data Acquisition System
International Database Access Service

IDB: Industrial Development Bond
Input Data Buffer
Integrated Database
InterAmerican Development Bank

IDBMS: Integrated Database Management System

IDBR: Input Data Buffer Register

IDC: Internal Data Channel

IDCA: International Development Cooperation Agency

IDCC: Integrated Data Communications Controller

IDCMA: Independent Data Communication Manufacturers Association

IDD: Integrated Data Dictionary
International Direct Dialing

IDDD: International Direct Distance Dialing

IDDL: Interactive Database Design Laboratory

IDDS: International Digital Data Service

IDE: Interactive Data Entry

IDEA: Interactive Data Entry/Access

IdealB: Ideal Basic Industries Inc. (newspaper)

IDEAS: Integrated Design and Analysis System
Integrated Design and Engineering Automated System

IDEN: Interactive Data Entry Network

ident: identification

IDES: Interactive Data Entry System

IDF: Image Description File
Intermediate Distributing Frame

IDI: Improved Data Interchange
Intelligent Dual Interface

IDIS: Interbourse Data Information System (EC)

idl: idle

IDL: Ideal Basic Industries Inc. (NYSE)
Information Description Language
Instruction Definition Language
Intermediate Data Description Language

IDM: Interactive Decision Making

IDMAS: Interactive Database Manipulator and Summarizer

IDMH: Input Destination Message Handler

IDMS: Integrated Database Management System

IDN: Intelligent Data Network

IDO: Internal Distribution Only
Isolated Digital Output

IDOS: Interrupt Disk Operating System

IDP: Integrated Data Processing
Interactive Database Processor
International Data Processing

IDPS: Interactive Direct Processing System

IDR: Information Descriptor Record
International Depositary Receipt

IDRS: Integrated Data Retrieval System

IDS: Information Display System
Integrated Data Store
Intelligent Display System
Interactive Display System

IDT: Intelligent Data Terminal
Interactive Data Terminal

IDU: Industrial Development Unit
Interactive Database Utilities

I&E: Income and Expense
Information and Education

IE: Interrupt Enable
Solomon Islands Airways

IEA: International Executives Association

IEC: PEC Israel Economic Corp. (ASE)

IEEE: Institute of Electrical and Electronics Engineering

IEEPA: International Emergency Economic Powers Act

IEI: Indiana Energy Inc. (NYSE)

IE Ind: IE Industries Inc. (newspaper)

IEL: IE Industries Inc. (NYSE)

IES: Income and Expense Statement
Inventory of publicly funded information technology R&D projects, research sites, and electronic mail addresses (EC)

IESC: International Executive Service Corps

IET: Interest Equalization Tax

IEX: Institute of Export

if: interface

IF: Instruction Field
Insufficient Funds
Interflug (airline) (now part of Lufthansa Airlines)
Intermediate Frequency

IFA: Information Flow Analysis
International Fiscal Association
International Franchise Association

IFAC: International Federation of Accountants

IFALPA: International Federation of Air Line Pilots Association (union)

IFAM: Inverted File Access Method

IFB: Invitation For Bid

IFC: Interface Clear
International Finance Corporation

IFCTU: International Federation of Christian Trade Unions

IFDO: International Federation of Data Organizations

IFE: Institute of Financial Education

IFEBS: Integrated Foreign Exchange and Banking System

IFF: International Flavors & Fragrances Inc. (NYSE)

IFG: Inter-Regional Financial Group Inc. (NYSE)

IFI: Inter-Freight International (steamship)
International Financial Institution
Interfault Interval

IFIPS: International Federation of Information Processing Societies

IFL: IMC Fertilizer Group Inc. (NYSE)

IFLA: International Finance and Leasing Association

IFLWU: International Fur and Leather Workers Union

IFM: Interactive File Manager

IFMS: Integrated Financial Management System

IFP: Integrated File Processor
International Federation of Purchasing
IFPCW: International Federation of Petroleum and Chemical Workers (union)
IFPMM: International Federation of Purchasing and Materials Management
IFPS: Interactive Financial Planning System
IFR: Interface Register
IFRA: Increasing Failure Rate Average
IFS: Institute of Fiscal Studies
Interactive File Sharing
IFTDO: International Federation of Training and Development Organizations
IFTU: International Federation of Trade Unions
IFU: Instruction Fetch Unit
IG: Alisarda (airline)
IGI Inc. (ASE)
Industrial Goods
IGAS: Interactive General Accounting System
IGC: Interstate General Company LP (ASE) (newspaper)
IGF: India Growth Fund (NYSE)
IGI: IGI Inc. (newspaper)
IGL: Interactive Graphics Language
International Minerals & Chemical Corp. (NYSE)
IGN: International Great Northern (railroad)
IGS: Information Group Separator
Interactive Graphics System
IGT: Interactive Graphics Terminal
IGU: International Gas Union
IGWF: International Garment Workers Federation (union)
IGWUA: International Glove Workers Union of America
IH: Industrialized Housing
Interrupt Handler
Itavia (airline)
IHB: Indiana Harbor Belt (railroad)
IHS: IPCO Corp. (NYSE)
IHSR: Improved High Speed Rail
IHY: I Heard You
II: Imperial Airlines
Institutional Investor
Interrupt Inhibit
Inventory and Inspection
IIA: Information Industries Association
Institute of Internal Auditors
Insurance Institute of America
IIAS: International Institute of Administrative Sciences
International Institute of Administrative Services
IIB: International Investment Bank (COMECON)
IID: Investment In Default
III: Insteel Industries Inc. (ASE)
IIL: Integrated Injection Logic
IIOP: Integrated Input/Output Processor
IIP: Index of Industrial Production
International Income Property Inc. (ASE) (newspaper)
IIPACS: Integrated Information Presentation And Control System
IIPF: International Institute of Public Finance
IIRA: International Industrial Relations Association
IIS: INA Investment Securities Inc. (NYSE)
Interactive Instructional System
Investment Income Surcharge
IISI: International Iron and Steel Institute
IISWM: Institute of Iron and Steel Wire Manufacturers
IIU: Instruction Input Unit

IJC: Interjob Communications
IJS: Interactive Job Submission
IK: Interlake Corp. (NYSE)
IKB: Intelligent Keyboard
IL: Instruction List
Intermediate Language
LANSA (Lineas Aereas Nacionales, SA-National Air Lines Corporation)
ILA: Insurance Logistics Automated
Intelligent Line Adapter
Intermediate Level Amplifier
ILACIF: Latin America Institute of Auditing Sciences
ILAH: Insurance, Life, Accident and Health
ILB: Initial Load Block
ILC: Indirect Labor Cost
Instruction Length Code
Instruction Location Counter
Irrevocable Letter of Credit
ILD: Intersection Loop Detection
ILE: Interface Latching Element
ILGWU: International Ladies' Garment Workers' Union
IllPowr: Illinois Power Co. (newspaper)
ILM: Intermediate Language Machine
ILO: Individual Load Operation
International Labor Organization
ILOC: Internal Location
ILP: Intermediate Language Program
ILU: Institute of Life Insurance
Institute of London Underwriters (UK)
ILWU: International Longshoremen's and Warehousemen's Union
IM: Index Marker
Idle Money
Information Management
Institute of Marketing and Sales Management
Instruction Memory
Instrumentation and Measurement
Integrated Modem
Interrupt Mask
Massachusetts Air Industries (airline)
IMA: Input Message Acknowledgment
International Management Association
Invalid Memory Address
IMACHA: Intermountain Automated Clearing House Association
IMARS: Information Management and Retrieval System
IMB: Intermode Bus
IMC: Institute of Management Consultants
International Multifoods Corp. (NYSE)
IMC F: IMC Fertilizer Group Inc. (newspaper)
IMCO: Intergovernmental Maritime Consultative Organization
IMCS: Interactive Manufacturing Control System
IMD: Imo Delaval Inc. (NYSE)
IMF: International Marketing Federation
International Monetary Fund
IMG: International Mail Gram
IMH: Institute of Materials Handling
IMI: Intermark Inc. (ASE)
IMIS: Integrated Management Information System
IML: Information Manipulation Language
Initial Microcode (Microprogram) Load
imm: immediate
IMM: Intelligent Memory Manager
International Monetary Market
International Money Management

IMMAC: Inventory Management and Material Control
IMO: Imperial Oil Ltd. (ASE)
ImoDv: Imo Delaval Inc. (newspaper)
IMOS: Interactive Multiprogramming Operating System
imp: import
importer
improvement
IMP: Industry Market Potential
Information Management Package
Integrated Mediterranean Program (EC)
Interface Message Processor
Inventory Management Package
IMPAC: Information for Management Planning Analysis and Coordination
IMPACT: Information Market Policy Actions (EC)
Integrated Management Planning and Control Techniques
ImpCh: Imperial Chemical Industries PLC (newspaper)
IMPEL: Insurance Management Performance Evaluation, Life
IMPL: Initial Microcode (Microprogram) Load
ImpOil: Imperial Oil Ltd. (newspaper)
IMPROVE: Inventory Management, Product Replenishment and Order Validity Evaluation
IMR: Interrupt Mask Register
IMRA: Industrial Marketing Research Association
International Market Research Association
IMRADS: Information Management, Retrieval and Dissemination System
IMS: Industrial Management Society
Information Management System
Institute of Management Services
Integrated Manufacturing System
Inventory Management System
IMSI: Information Management System Interface
IMSP: Integrated Mass Storage Processor
IMS/VS: Information Management System/Virtual Storage
IMTS: Improved Mobile Telephone Service
IMU: Increment Memory Unit
Instruction Memory Unit
International Mailers Union
International Maritime Union
IMX: In-Line Multiplexer
Inquiry Message Exchange
in: inch
income
increase
input
IN: Aerlinte (Irish airline)
Illinois Northern (railroad)
Income (NYSE)
Index Number
Installment Note
INA: Integrated Network Architecture
INAIn: INA Investment Securities Inc. (newspaper)
INAS: Interbank National Authorization System
inc: income
incorporate
incorporated
increment
INCA: Inventory Control and Analysis
incl: including
inclusive

INCO: Inco Ltd. (newspaper)
International Chamber of Commerce
INCOS: Integrated Control System
incr: increment
incre: increment
Incstar: Incstar Corp. (newspaper)
ind: indicator
industrial
industry
INDAC: Industrial Data Acquisition and Control
indent: indenture
INDEX: Indiana Exchange Inc.
India: India Growth Fund (newspaper)
IndiEn: Indiana Energy Inc. (newspaper)
Ind Led: Individual Ledger
indm: indemnity
indus: industrial
industry
INERT: Index of National Enervation and Related Trends
INET: Interbank Network Electronic Transfer
info: inform
information
INFOL: Information-Oriented Language
INFONET: Information Network
INFOR: Information Network and File Organization
INFORMAC: Immediate Information For Merchant and Customer
INFOTEX: Information Via Telex
INFRAL: Information Retrieval Automatic Language
INFUT: Information Utility
INGA: Interactive Graphic Analysis
IngerR: Ingersoll-Rand Co. (newspaper)
INGRES: Interactive Graphic and Retrieval System
IngrTec: Ingredient Technology Corp. (newspaper)
inher: inheritance
init: initialize
inj: injunction
InldStl: Inland Steel Industries Inc. (newspaper)
inp: input
INP: Integrated Network Processor
Intelligent Network Processor
Intelligent Systems Master LP (ASE)
INR: Insilco Corp. (NYSE)
ins: insurance
INS: International Seaway Trading Corp. (ASE)
INSA: International Shipowners Association
INSAR: Instruction Address Register
insce: insurance
INSCO: Intercontinental Shipping Corporation
Insd Val: Insured Value
INSEAD: Institut Européen d'Administration des Affaires (European Institute of Business Administration) (French)
InSeT: In-Service Training
Insilco: Insilco Corp. (newspaper)
INSIS: Intern-Institutional Information System (EC)
InspRs: Inspiration Resources Corp. (newspaper)
inst: installment (instalment)
instant
instruction
instrument
Insteel: Insteel Industries Inc. (newspaper)
INSTINET: Institutional Networks Corporation
instl: installment (instalment)
INSTPS: Institute of Purchasing and Supply

InstPw: Interstate Power Co. (newspaper)
instr: instruction
Instron: Instron Corp. (newspaper)
InstSy: Instrument Systems Corp. (newspaper)
insur: insurance
INSYD: Instantaneous Systems Display
int: integer
interest
internal
international
interrupt
INT: International Recovery Corp. (ASE)
Interstate (railroad)
INTA: Interrupt Acknowledge
INTABS: International Terminal Accounting and Banking Service
IntAlu: International Aluminum Corp. (newspaper)
IntBknt: International Banknote Company Inc. (newspaper)
IntBkr: Interstate Bakeries Corp. (newspaper)
IntCty: Inter-City Gas Corp. (newspaper)
INTE: Interrupt Enable
INTELSAT: International Telecommunications Satellite (consortium)
inten: intensity
Interco: INTERCO INCORPORATED (newspaper)
intermed: intermediate
interp: interpreter
INTERTEST: Interactive Test Controller
IntFlav: International Flavors & Fragrances Inc. (newspaper)
INTFU: Interface Unit
INTGEN: Interpreter-Generator
IntgRsc: Integrated Resources Inc. (newspaper)
INTI: Industrial and Technological Information
INTIP: Integrated Information Processing
intl: international
IntlgSy: Intelligent Systems Master LP (newspaper)
Intlog: Interlogic Trace Inc. (newspaper)
Intmed: Intermedics Inc. (newspaper)
IntMin: International Minerals & Chemical Corp. (newspaper)
IntMult: International Multifoods Corp. (newspaper)
IntPap: International Paper Co. (newspaper)
IntpbG: Interpublic Group of Companies Inc., The (newspaper)
IntProt: International Proteins Corp. (newspaper)
IntPwr: International Power Machines Corp. (newspaper)
intr: interrupt
INTR: Interrupt Register
Interrupt Request
IntRec: International Recovery Corp. (newspaper)
IntRect: International Rectifier Corp. (newspaper)
Int Rev: Internal Revenue
IntRFn: Inter-Regional Financial Group Inc. (newspaper)
Intrlke: Interlake Corp. (newspaper)
Intrmk: Intermark Inc. (newspaper)
intro: introduction
INTRQ: Interrupt Request
IntSeaw: International Seaway Trading Corp. (newspaper)

IntSec: Interstate Securities Inc. (newspaper)
IntTch: International Telecharge Inc. (newspaper)
IntThr: International Thoroughbred Breeders Inc. (newspaper)
inv: invoice
INWATS: Inward Wide Area Telecommunications Service
INX: Index Character
I&O: Individual and Organization performance
I/O: Input/Output
IO: Immediate Order
Out Island Airways
IOA: Input/Output Adapter
Institute of Outdoor Advertising
IOAU: Input/Output Access Unit
IOB: Input/Output Block
Input/Output Buffer
Insurance Ombudsman Bureau
IOC: Immediate-Or-Cancel
Indirect Operating Costs
Initial Operational Capacity
Input/Output Channel
Input/Output Controller
IOCS: Input/Output Control System
IOCU: Input/Output Control Unit
IOD: Input/Output Device
IOE: International Organization of Employers
IOF: Input/Output Front End
IOGEN: Input/Output Generation
IOI: Indication Of Interest
IOIH: Input/Output Interrupt Handler
IOLA: Input/Output Link Adapter
IOLC: Input/Output Link Control
IO LTD: Imperial Oil Ltd. (steamship)
IOM: Input/Output Module
Input/Output Multiplexer
Institute of Marketing and Sales Management
IOMS: Input/Output Management System
IOM SPC: Isle of Man Steam Packet Company (steamship)
ION: Ionics Inc. (ASE)
Ionics: Ionics Inc. (newspaper)
IOP: Input/Output Processor
Institute of Packaging
IOPS: Input/Output Program System
IOQ: Input/Output Queue
IOR: Input/Output Read
Input/Output Register
Institute for Operational Research
Iowa Resources Inc. (NYSE)
IOS: Interactive Operating System
IOSYS: Input/Output System
IOT: Input/Output Transfer
Interoffice Trunk
Iron Ore Transport (steamship)
IOU: Input/Output Unit
I Owe you
IOW: Input/Output Wire
IowaRs: Iowa Resources Inc. (newspaper)
IowIlg: Iowa-Illinois Gas & Electric Co. (newspaper)
IOWQ: Input/Output Wait Queue
IOX: Input/Output Executive
IP: Impact Printer
Incentive Pay
Information Processor
Initial Phase
Input/Output Processor
Instruction Pointer
Interchangeable Parts
Interface Processor
International Paper Co. (NYSE)
Issue Price
IPA: Institute for Production and Automation
Institute of Practitioners in Advertising
Institutional Patent Agreement

Integrated Peripheral Adapter
Integrated Printer Adapter
Intermediate Power Amplifier
Ipalco: IPALCO Enterprises Inc. (newspaper)
IPB: Integrated Processor Board
Interprocessor Buffer
IPC: Illinois Power Co. (NYSE)
Industrial Process Control
IpcoCp: IPCO Corp. (newspaper)
IPCS: Interactive Problem Control System
IPD: Information Processing Department
IPE: Indian-Pacific Express (Perth to Sydney) (railroad)
Industrial Plant Equipment
IPF: Information Processing Facility
IPG: Interpublic Group of Companies Inc., The (NYSE)
IPI: Implicit Price Index
Intelligent Printer Interface
International Petroleum Institute
IPIC: Initial Production and Inventory Control
IPICS: Initial Production and Inventory Control System
IPL: Information Processing Language
Initial Program Load
Initial Program Loader
IPALCO Enterprises Inc. (NYSE)
Ital Pacific Line (steamship)
IPM: Institute of Personnel Management
Integrated Manufacturing Planning
Inventory Policy Model
IPM Technology Inc. (ASE) (newspaper)
IPMA: International Personnel Management Association
IP/MP: Inphase/Midphase
IPO: Initial Public Offering
Input, Process, and Output
Installation Productivity Option
IPO/E: Installation Productivity Option/Extended
IPOT: Inductive Potentiometer
IPP: Imminent Peril to the Public
IPPF: Instruction Preprocessing Function
IPR: Imposter Pass Rate
Intellectual Property
IPRA: International Public Relations Association
IPS: American Income Properties LP (ASE)
Index Participation
Information Processing System
Installation Performance Specifications
Institute of Purchasing and Supply
IPSB: Interprocessor Signal Bus
IPSO: Initiating Production by Sales Order
IPSS: Information Processing System Simulator
IPSX: Interprocessor Switch Matrix
IPSY: Interactive Planning System
IPT: Improved Productivity Techniques
IP Timberlands Ltd. (NYSE)
IPTim: IP Timberlands Ltd. (newspaper)
IPU: Instruction Processing Unit
Integrated Processor Unit
Interprocessor Unit
IPW: Interstate Power Co. (NYSE)
IQ: Import Quota
Information Quick
Intelligence Quotient
IQA: Institute of Quality Assurance
IQE: Interruption Queue Element
IQF: Interactive Query Facility
IQL: Interactive Query Language

IQMH: Input Queue Message Handler

I&R: Information and Retrieval

IR: Index Register
Industrial Relations
Informal Report
Information Retrieval
Ingersoll-Rand Co. (NYSE)
Inland Revenue (UK)
Instruction Register
Interim Report
Internal Revenue
Interrupt Request
Investor Relations
Iran National Airlines
Israel Railways

IRA: Individual Retirement Account
International Rubber Association
Investment-Return Assumption

IRAM: Indexed Random Access Method

IRAN: Inspection and Repair As Necessary

IRB: Industrial Revenue Bond
Interruption Request Block

IRC: Inspiration Resources Corp. (NYSE)
Internal Revenue Code
International Record Carrier

IRCA: International Railways of Central America

IR&D: Independent Research and Development

IRD: Income in Respect of a Decedent
Internal Research and Development

IRE: Integrated Resources Inc. (NYSE)

IREDA: International Radio and Electrical Distributors Association

IREP: Internal Representation

IRF: Input Register Full
International Rectifier Corp. (NYSE)

IRG: InterRecord Gap

IRH: Inductive Recording Head

IRI: Industrial Research Institute
Interreference Interval

IRIS: Industrial Relations Information System

IRJE: Interactive Remote Job Entry

IRL: Information Retrieval Language

IRM: Information Resources Management
Inspection, Repair and Maintenance
Intelligent Remote Multiplexer
Interim Research Memorandum

IRN: Internal Routing Network
Ironton (railroad)

IRO: Industrial Relations Officer

IroqBrd: Iroquois Brands Ltd. (newspaper)

IROS: Increased Reliability of Operational Systems

IRP: Inventory and Requirements Planning

IRQ: Interrupt Request

IRR: Internal Rate of Return
Interrupt Return Register

IRRA: Industrial Relations Research Association

irred: irredeemable

irreg: irregular

IRRYS: Iraqi Republic Railways

IRS: Information Retrieval System
Internal Revenue Service
Iranian State Railway

IRT: Index Return (character)
IRT Property Co. (NYSE) (newspaper)

IRT Cp: IRT Corp. (newspaper)

IRTU: Intelligent Remote Terminal Unit

IRV: Interrupt Request Vector

IrvBnk: Irving Bank Corp. (newspaper)
IRW: Indirect Reference Word
IRX: Interactive Resource Executive
I&S: Investigation and Suspension
IS: Income Statement
Income Stocks
Indexed Sequential
Information Science
Information Separator
Information System
International Standard
Interstate Securities Inc. (NYSE)
ISAL: Information System Access Line
ISAM: Indexed Sequential Access Method
ISAR: Information Storage And Retrieval
ISB: Investors Service Bureau
ISBL: Information System Base Language
ISBN: International Standard Book Number
ISC: Ideal Standard Cost
Interstate Commerce
I-S CURVE: Investment Should Absorb Savings
ISD: Information Structure Design
Intermediate Storage Device
International Subscriber Dialing
ISDN: Integrated Services Digital Network
ISDOS: Information System Design and Optimization System
ISDS: Instruction Set Design System
Integrated Software Development System
ISE: Insystem Emulator
Interrupt System Enable
ISEM: Improved Standard Electronic Module
ISEP: International Standard Equipment Practice
I-SEQ: Indexed Sequential
ISEU: International Stereotypers' and Electrotypers Union
ISF: Individual Store and Forward
Insurance, Surety and Fidelity
Interdistrict Settlement Fund
International Shipping Federation
ISFD: Integrated Software Functional Design
ISFM: Indexed Sequential File Manager
ISFMS: Indexed Sequential File Management System
ISFSM: Incompletely Specified Finite State Machine
ISG: Intersubblock Gap
ISI: Information Structure Implementation
Instrument Systems Installation
Internally Specified Index
Iron and Steel Institute
ISS-International Service Systems Inc. (ASE)
ISIC: International Standard Industrial Classification
ISIS: Instant Sales Indicator System
Integrated Software Invocation System
ISI Sy: ISI Systems Inc. (newspaper)
ISK: Instruction Space Key
ISL: Interactive Simulation Language
Intersatellite Link
Intersystem Link
ISM: Institute of Supervisory Management
ISMH: Input Source Message Handler
ISMS: Image Store Management System
ISN: Initial Sequence Number
Instron Corp. (ASE)
ISNOT: Is Not Equal To
ISO: Incentive Stock Options
Information Systems Office

International Standards Organization (International Organization for Standardization)
International Sugar Organization

ISOC: Individual System/Organization Cost

ISP: Instruction Set Processor

ISPC: International Sound Program Center

ISPICE: Interactive Simulation Program with Integrated Circuit Emphasis

IS&R: Information Storage and Retrieval

ISR: Incstar Corp. (ASE)
Information Storage and Retrieval
Interrupt Service Routine

ISRAD: Integrated Software Research and Development

ISS: Integrated Support System
Intelligent Support System
INTERCO INCORPORATED (NYSE)
ISS-International Service System Inc. (newspaper)

ISSN: International Standard Serial Number

ISSR: Information Storage, Selection, and Retrieval

ISSS: Integrated Support System Sort

ISSUE: Information System and Software Update Environment

IST: Internal Standard

ISTA: International Society for Technology Assessment

ISTR: Indexed Sequential Table Retrieval

ISU: Instruction Storage Unit
Interface Sharing Unit

ISY: Instrument Systems Corp. (ASE)

it: item

IT: Air Inter (airline)
Immediate Transportation
Income Tax
Indent Tab (character)
Information Technology
Input Terminal
Inspection Tag
Intelligent Terminal
Interlogic Trace Inc. (NYSE)
International Trade
Inventory Transfer
Inventory Turnover

ITA: Interface Test Adapter
Italy Fund Inc., The (NYSE)

ITALIA: Italian Line (steamship)

Italy: Italy Fund Inc., The (newspaper)

ITAM: Interdata Telecommunications Access Method

ITAVS: Integrated Testing, Analysis and Verification System

ITB: Intermediate Text Block
International Thoroughbred Breeders Inc. (ASE)
Interstate Trade Barriers
Invisible Trade Balance

ITC: Illinois Terminal Company
Income Tax Credit
Ingredient Technology Corp. (NYSE)
Installation Time and Cost
Integrated Transaction Controller
Intelligent Transaction Controller
Interdata Transaction Controller
International Tea Council
International Tin Council
Investment Tax Credit

ITcpSE: InterCapital Income Securities Inc. (newspaper)

IT Crp: International Technology Corp. (newspaper)

ITDF: Interactive Transaction Dump Facility

ITDM: Intelligent Time Division Multiplexor
ITDNS: Integrated Tour Operating Digital Network Service
ITDS: Integrated Technical Data Systems
ITEM: Integrated Test and Maintenance
ITEMS: Incoterm Transaction Entry Management System
ITER: International Thermonuclear Experimental Reactor (EC)
ITF: Integrated Test Facility
ITFS: Instructional Television Fixed Service
ITI: Inagua Transports Incorporated (steamship)
Interactive Terminal Interface
International Telecharge Inc. (ASE)
I-TIME: Instruction Time
itin: itinerary
ITL: Intermediate Transfer Language
ITM: Indirect Tag Memory
Intermedics Inc. (NYSE)
ITN: Integrated Teleprocessing Network
ITO: International Trade Organization
ITOS: Interactive Terminal-Oriented Software
ITP: Income Tax Plan
Integrated Transaction Processor
Interactive Terminal Protocol
ITRA: Interdata Transaction Controller
ITRC: Iowa Transfer Railway Company
ITRI: International Tin Research Institute
ITS: Institute for Telecommunication Science
Interactive Terminal Support
Intermarket Trading System
International Trade Secretariats
Invitation To Send
Iowa Transfer System
ITT: International Telephone and Telegraph Corp.
Intertoll Trunk
ITT Corp. (NYSE)
ITT Cp: ITT Corp. (newspaper)
ITU: International Telecommunication Union
International Typographical Union
ITV: Instructional Television
ITW: Illinois Tool Works Inc. (NYSE) (newspaper)
ITWF: International Transport Workers Federation (union)
ITX: International Technology Corp. (NYSE)
IU: Indiana Union (railway)
Information Unit
Input Unit
Instruction Unit
Interface Unit
IU International Corp. (NYSE) (newspaper)
Midstate Air Commuter (airline)
IUBSSA: International Union of Building Societies and Savings Associations
IUE: International Union of Electrical Workers
IUMI: International Union of Maritime Insurance
IUMMSW: International Union of Mine, Mill and Smelter Workers
IUMSWA: Industrial Union of Marine and Shipbuilding Workers of America
IUOE: International Union of Operating Engineers
IUPW: International Union of Petroleum Workers

IUR: International Union of Railways
IURP: Integrated Unit Record Processor
IUS: Information Unit Separator
Interchange Unit Separator
IUUCLGW: International Union, United Cement, Lime & Gypsum Workers
IUWWML: International Union of Wood, Wire, and Metal Lathers
IV: Independent Verification and Validation
Interface Vector
Intrinsic Value
Invoice Value
Lineas Aereas Guinea Ecuatorial (Equatorial Guinea Airlines)
IVA: Inventory Valuation Adjustment
IvaxCp: IVAX Corp. (newspaper)
IVDTS: Integrated Voice/Data Terminal
Iverson: Iverson Technology Corp. (newspaper)
IVG: Interrupt Vector Generator
IVM: Interface Virtual Machine
IVP: Installation Verification Procedure
IVT: Integrated Video Terminal
Iverson Technology Corp. (ASE)
IV & V: Independent Verification and Validation
IVX: IVAX Corp. (ASE)
IW: International Air Bahama (airline)
IWA: International Wheat Agreement
International Woodworkers of America (union)
IWB: Industry-Wide Bargaining
IWC: International Wheat Council
IWDS: Interactive Wholesale Distribution System
IWG: Iowa-Illinois Gas & Electric Co. (NYSE)
IWISTK: Issue While In StocK
IWIU: Insurance Workers International Union
IWS: Instruction Work Stack
Interactive Work Station
IWW: Industrial Workers of the World (union)
IX: INAIR (Internacional de Aviacion) (airline)
Index Register
IRT Corp. (ASE)
IXC: Interexchange Channel
IXM: Index Manager
IXU: Index Translation Unit
IY: Swift Airlines
IZ: Arkia-Israel Inland Airlines

j: judgment
JA: Job Analysis
Joint Account
Junior Accountant
JAB: Job Analysis and Billing
JAC: Johnstown American Co. (ASE)
JACK: Jackpot Enterprises Inc. (NYSE)
Jackpot: Jackpot Enterprises Inc. (newspaper)
Jaclyn: Jaclyn Inc. (newspaper)
Jacobs: Jacobs Engineering Group Inc. (newspaper)
JAF: Job Accounting Facility
JAI: Job Accounting Interface
JAJO: January, April, July, October (securities)
JAL: Japan Air Lines
jam: jammed
Jamsw: Jamesway Corp. (newspaper)
JanBel: Jan Bell Marketing Inc. (newspaper)
Japinfo: A database of Japanese statistical information
JAR: Jump Address Register
JARS: Job Accounting Report System
JAS: Job Analysis System
JAT: Job Accounting Table
Jugoslovenski Aero Transport (Yugoslavian Airlines)
JB: Aeronaves del Norte (airline)
Junior Bond
JBM: Jan Bell Marketing Inc. (ASE)
JBPS: Jamaica Banana Producers' Steamship Company
JBS: Japanese Broadcast Satellite
JC: Jewelcor Inc. (NYSE)
Job Classification
Just Compensation
JCB: Job Control Block
JCC: Job Control Card
JCI: Johnson Controls Inc. (NYSE)
JCL: Job Control Language
JCLGEN: Job Control Language Generation
JCLPREP: Job Control Language Preprocessor
JCM: Job Cylinder Map
JCP: J. C. Penney Company Inc. (NYSE)
Job Control Processor
JCS: Job Control Statement
jct: junction
JCT: Job Control Table
Johnstown/Consolidated Realty Trust (NYSE)
J&D: June and December (securities)
JD: Japan Domestic Airlines
Job Description
June and December (securities)
JDI: Joint Declaration of Intent (EC)
JDL: Job Description Library
JDS: Job Data Sheet
JE: Jerseyville and Eastern (railroad)
Job Enlargement
Job Enrichment
JEA: Joint Export Agent
JEC: Jacobs Engineering Group Inc. (ASE)
Joint Economic Committee
JECL: Job Entry Control Language

JeffPl: Jefferson-Pilot Corp. (newspaper)
JEM: Jewelmasters Inc. (ASE)
JEPS: Job Entry Peripheral Services
JES: Job Entry System
JESSI: Joint European Submicron Silicon (EC)
JET: Jetronic Industries Inc. (ASE)
Job Economic Training
Joint European Torus (EC)
Journal Entries Transfer
JetCa: Jet Capital Corp. (newspaper)
Jetron: Jetronic Industries Inc. (newspaper)
JETS: Job Executive and Transport Satellite
JFCB: Job File Control Block
JFET: Junction Field Effect Transistor
JFN: Job FIle Number
JH: Smyer Aircraft
John H. Harland Co., The (NYSE)
JHI: John Hancock Investors Trust (NYSE)
JhnCn: Johnson Controls Inc. (newspaper)
JhnCRt: Johnstown/Consolidated Realty Trust (newspaper)
JHS: John Hancock Income Securities Trust (NYSE)
JHSC: Johnstown and Stony Creek (railroad)
JI: Aeronaves del Este (airline)
JIB: Foodmaker Inc. (NYSE)
JIC: Joint Information Center
JII: Johnston Industries Inc. (NYSE)
JIRA: Japanese Industrial Robot Association
JIS: Japanese Industrial Standard
Job Information System
Job Input Station
JIT: Job Instruction Training
JJ: January and July (securities)
Josephson Junction
JJS: Jumping-Jack Shoes Inc. (ASE)
JL: Japan Air Lines
Job Lot
JLN: Jaclyn Inc. (ASE)
JLPT: Japanese Long Term Prime Rate
JLT: Job Lot Trading
JM: Air Jamaica (airline)
JMadsn: James Madison Ltd. (newspaper)
JMEM: Job Memory
JML: James Madison Ltd. (ASE)
jmp: jump
JMP: J. M. Peters Company Inc. (ASE)
JMSX: Job Memory Switch Matrix
JMT: Job Methods Training
JMY: Jamesway Corp. (NYSE)
JN: Sun Valley Air (airline)
JNJ: Johnson & Johnson (NYSE)
JNR: Japanese National Railways
JNT STK: JoiNT STocK
JO: Aeronaves del Oeste (airline)
Joint Ownership
JOB: General Employment Enterprises Inc. (ASE)
JOBDOC: Job Documentation
JOBLIB: Job Library
JOBS: Job Opportunities in the Business Sector
JOC: Job Order Costing
JOCE: Journal Officiel des Communautés Européennes (Official Journal of the European Communities) (French) (EC)
JohnAm: Johnstown American Companies (newspaper)
JohnInd: Johnston Industries Inc. (newspaper)
JohnJn: Johnson & Johnson (newspaper)

JohnPd: Johnson Products Company Inc. (newspaper)
JOJA: July, October, January, April (securities)
JOL: Job Organization Language
Joule Inc. (ASE)
JOMO: Job Mix Optimization
JOR: Earle M. Jorgensen Co. (NYSE)
Jorgen: Earle M. Jorgensen Co. (newspaper)
JOS: Jostens Inc. (NYSE)
Josten: Jostens Inc. (newspaper)
Joule: Joule Inc. (newspaper)
JOULE: Joint Opportunities for Unconventional or Long-term Energy supply (EC)
jour: journal
JOVIAL: Jules' Own Version of International Algorithmic Language
JP: Jefferson-Pilot Corp. (NYSE)
Job Processor
JPA: Job Pack Area
JPC: Johnson Products Company Inc. (ASE)
JPI: J. P. Industries Inc. (NYSE)
JP Ind: J. P. Industries Inc. (newspaper)
JPM: Joint Profit Maximization
J. P. Morgan & Company Inc. (NYSE)
JPU: Job Processing Unit
JQ: TAA (Trans-Australia Airlines)
jr: junior
JR: ACSA Airlines
James River Corporation of Virginia (NYSE)
Job Rotation
Joint Return
JRC: Jamaica Railway Corporation
Joint Research Center (Euratom)
JRiver: James River Corporation of Virginia
JRT: Job Relations Training
JS: Air Champagne Ardennes (airline)
Job Specification
JSC: Joint Stock Company
JSCS: Job Shop Control System
JSDM: June, September, December, March (securities)
JSF: Job Services File
JSI: Job Satisfaction Inventory
JSL: Job Specification Language
JSWAP: Job Swapping Memory
JT: Jamaica Air Service (airline)
Joint Tenancy
JTC: Jacksonville Terminal Company (railroad)
Jet Capital Corp. (ASE)
JTIDS: Joint Tactical Information Distribution System
JTPS: Job and Tape Planning System
JU: Jugoslavian Air Transport (airline)
JUG: Joint Users Group
JumpJk: Jumping-Jack Shoes Inc. (newspaper)
junc: junction
juris: jurisdiction
JV: Joint Venture
Jwlcr: Jewelcor Inc. (newspaper)
Jwlmst: Jewelmasters Inc. (newspaper)
JW&NW: Jamestown, Westfield & Northwestern (railroad)
JWP: JWP Inc. (NYSE) (newspaper)
JY: Air Caicos (airline)
JZ: Aeronaves del Centro (airline)

k: kelvin
key
keyboard

K: Declared or paid this year on a cumulative issue with dividends in arrears (stock listings of newspapers)
Kellogg Co. (NYSE)
Measured Computer Storage Capacity

ka: kiloampere

KAB: Kaneb Services Inc. (NYSE)

KACHA: Kentuckiana Automated Clearing House Association

Kaisrtc: Kaisertech Ltd. (newspaper)

KAL: Korean Air Lines

KambEn: Kaneb Energy Partners Ltd. (newspaper)

KAN: Kansas Power & Light Co., The (NYSE)

Kaneb: Kaneb Services Inc. (newspaper)

KanGE: Kansas Gas & Electric Co. (newspaper)

KanPL: Kansas Power & Light Co., The (newspaper)

Kappa: Kappa Networks Inc.

KATY: Missouri-Kansas-Texas Railroad

Katyln: Katy Industries Inc. (newspaper)

KaufB: Kaufman & Broad Inc. (newspaper)

KaufBH: Kaufman & Broad Home Corp. (newspaper)

KAY: Kay Corp. (ASE)

KayCp: Kay Corp. (newspaper)

KayJw: Kay Jewelers Inc. (newspaper)

kb: keyboard

KB: Kaufman & Broad Inc. (NYSE)
kickback
Kitsap Aviation (airline)

KBA: Kleinwort Benson Australian Income Fund Inc. (NYSE)

KBAukst: Kleinwort Benson Australian Income Fund Inc. (newspaper)

kbd: keyboard

KBE: Keyboard Entry

KBH: Kaufman & Broad Home Corp. (NYSE)

KBI: Key Buying Influence

kbit: kilobit

KBL: Keyboard Listener

KBPS: KiloBITs Per Second

KBR: Kankakee Belt Route (railroad)

kbs: kilobyte

kc: kilocycle

KC: Key Co., The (ASE)
Kiting Checks

KCBT: Kansas City Board of Trade

KCC: Kansas City Connecting (railroad)

kch: kilocharacter

KCH: Ketchum & Company Inc. (ASE)

kchr: kilocharacter

KCL: Keystation Control Language

KCMO: Kansas City, Mexico and Orient (railway)

KCNW: Kelley's Creek and Northwestern (railroad)

KCPSFO: Kansas City Public Service Freight Operation

KCR: Kanawha Central Railway

K-C RY: Kowloon-Canton Railway (Hong Kong)
KCS: Conston Corp. (ASE)
Kansas City Southern (railroad)
Kilocharacters Per Second
KCSou: Kansas City Southern Industries Inc. (newspaper)
KCS/SO: Keyboard Class Select/ Statistics Output
KCT: Kansas City Terminal (railway)
KCtyPL: Kansas City Power & Light Co. (newspaper)
KCU: Keyboard Control Unit
KD: Keyboard and Display
Key Definition
Knocked Down (price)
Kuwaiti dinar
KDCD: Kuwaiti Dinar Certificate of Deposit
KDE: Keyboard Data Entry
KDF: Knocked Down Flat
KDI: KDI Corp. (NYSE) (newspaper)
KDLCL: Knocked Down in Less than Carload Lots
KDOS: Key Display Operating System
Key to Disk Operating System
KDP: Keyboard, Display, and Printer
KDS: Key Display System
Key-to-Diskette System
KDSS: Key to Disk Subsystem
KDT: Key Data Terminal
KE: Koger Equity Inc. (ASE)
Korean Air Lines
KearNt: Kearney-National Inc. (newspaper)
KEC: Kent Electronics Corp. (ASE)
KEG: Key Gap
KEI: Keithly Instruments Inc. (ASE)
Keithly: Keithly Instruments Inc. (newspaper)
Kellogg: Kellogg Co. (newspaper)
Kellwd: Kellwood Co. (newspaper)
Kenmt: Kennametal Inc. (newspaper)
KentEl: Kent Electronics Corp. (newspaper)
Kenwin: Kenwin Shops Inc. (newspaper)
KEP: Kaneb Energy Partners Ltd. (NYSE)
Key Entry Processing
Kerkhf: Kerkhoff Industries Inc. (newspaper)
KerrGl: Kerr Glass Manufacturing Corp. (newspaper)
KerrMcv: Kerr-McGee Corp. (newspaper)
KES: Keystone Consolidated Industries Inc. (NYSE)
Keslr: Kessler Products Ltd. (newspaper)
Ketchm: Ketchum & Company Inc. (newspaper)
KEX: Kirby Exploration Company Inc. (ASE)
KEY: KeyCorp. (NYSE)
keybd: keyboard
KeyCa: Keystone Camera Products Corp. (newspaper)
KeyCo: Key Co., The
Keycp: KeyCorp (newspaper)
KeyInt: Keystone International Inc. (newspaper)
KeysCo: Keystone Consolidated Industries Inc. (newspaper)
KF: Catskill Airways
Key Field
Korea Fund Inc., The (NYSE)
KFAED: Kuwait Fund for Arab Economic Development
KFAS: Keyed File Access System
KFV: Quest For Value Dual Purpose Fund Inc. (NYSE)

KfW: Kreditanstalt Fur Wiederaufbau
kg: kilogram
KG: Koctug Line (steamship)
KGB: Kewaunee, Green Bay and Western (railroad)
KGE: Kansas Gas & Electric Co. (NYSE)
KGM: Kerr Glass Manufacturing Corp. (NYSE)
Key Generator Module
kh: kilohour
KH: Time Airways
KHI: Kemper High Income Trust (NYSE)
kHz: kilohertz
KI: Key Industry
KIBOR: Kuwait Interbank Offered Rate
KICU: Keyboard Interface Control Unit
KII: Keystone International Inc. (NYSE)
KIL: Keyed Input Language
Kilern: Killearn Properties Inc. (newspaper)
kilopac: kilopackets
KimbC: Kimberly-Clark Corp. (newspaper)
KIN: Kinark Corp. (ASE)
Kinark: Kinark Corp. (newspaper)
KIPS: Knowledge Information Processing Systems
Thousands of Instructions Per Second
Kirby: Kirby Exploration Company Inc. (newspaper)
KISS: Keyed Indexed Sequential Search
KIT: Kentucky and Indiana Terminal (railroad)
Kit Manufacturing Co. (ASE)
Kit Mfg: Kit Manufacturing Co. (newspaper)
KIX: Kerkhoff Industries Inc. (ASE)
KJI: Kay Jewelers Inc. (NYSE)
KK: Kabushiki-Kaisha (Japanese stock company)
Karlander Kangaroo Line (steamship)
Shawnee Air (airline)
KKR: Kohlberg Kravis Roberts
KL: Key Length
KLM (Koninklijke Luchtvaart Maatschappij-Royal Dutch Airlines)
KleerV: Kleer-Vu Industries Inc. (newspaper)
K LINE: Kawasaki Kisen Kaisha (steamship)
K of L: Knights of Labor
KLM: KLM Royal Dutch Airlines (NYSE) (newspaper)
klooj: kludge
KLT: Kansas City Power & Light Co. (NYSE)
KLU: Kaisertech Ltd. (NYSE)
KLY: Kelley Oil & Gas Partners Ltd. (ASE)
KlyOG: Kelley Oil & Gas Partners Ltd. (newspaper)
km: kilometer
K&M: Kansas and Missouri Railway and Terminal Company
KM: K mart Corp. (NYSE)
KMB: Kimberly-Clark Corp. (NYSE)
KMG: Kerr-McGee Corp. (NYSE)
KML: Carmel Container Systems Ltd. (ASE)
KMON: Keyboard Monitor
KmpHi: Kemper High Income Trust (newspaper)
K mrt: K mart Corp. (newspaper)
KMRT: Kansas and Missouri Railway and Terminal Company
KMT: Kennametal Inc. (NYSE)
KMW: KMW Systems Corp. (ASE) (newspaper)
KNC: Kingcome Navigation Company (steamship)
KNE: KN Energy Inc. (NYSE)

KN Eng: KN Energy Inc. (newspaper)
KnghtR: Knight-Ridder Inc. (newspaper)
KngWld: King World Productions Inc. (newspaper)
KNO: Knogo Corp. (NYSE)
Knogo: Knogo Corp. (newspaper)
KNR: Klamath Northern Railway
Korean National Railways
KNSM: Koninklijke Nederlandsche Stoomboot Maatschappij (Dutch-Royal Netherlands Steamship Company)
KNY: Kearney-National Inc. (ASE)
KO: Kodiak Airways
Coca-Cola Co., The (NYSE)
KOBOL: Key Station On-line Business-Oriented Language
KO&G: Kansas, Oklahoma & Gulf (railroad)
KOG: Koger Properties Inc. (NYSE)
Koger: Koger Properties Inc. (newspaper)
KogrEq: Koger Equity Inc. (newspaper)
KOL: Kollmorgen Corp. (NYSE)
Kolmor: Kollmorgen Corp. (newspaper)
KOP: Koppers Company Inc. (NYSE)
Kopers: Koppers Company Inc. (newspaper)
KOPS: Thousands of Operations Per Second
Korea: Korea Fund Inc., The (newspaper)
kp: keypunch
KP: Air Cape (airline)
Keogh Plan
Key Personnel
KPA: Kappa Networks Inc. (ASE)
KPC: Keyboard/Printer Control
KPI: Killearn Properties Inc. (ASE)
KPR: Keypunch Replacement
KPT: Kenner Parker Toys Inc. (NYSE)
KPToy: Kenner Parker Toys Inc. (newspaper)
KQ: King Airlines
KR: Dar-Air (airline)
Kennedy Round
Key Register
Kroger Co., The (NYSE)
KRA: Kraft Inc. (NYSE)
Kraft: Kraft Inc. (newspaper)
KRI: Knight-Ridder Inc. (NYSE)
KRL: Knowledge Representation Language
Kroger: Kroger Co., The (newspaper)
KS: Kiting Stocks
KSAM: Keyed Sequential Access Method
KSDS: Key Sequenced Data Set
KSF: Quaker State Corp. (NYSE)
KSH: Key Strokes Per Hour
KSN: Karachi Steam Navigation Line (steamship)
KSR: Keyboard Send/Receive
KSR/T: Keyboard Send/Receive Terminal
KSS: Kessler Products Ltd. (ASE)
KST: Known Segment Table
KSU: Kansas City Southern Industries Inc. (NYSE)
K&T: Kentucky and Tennessee (railroad)
KT: Katy Industries Inc. (NYSE)
Key Tape
KTDS: Key-to-Disc Software
KTL: KEY-EDIT Terminal Language
KTM: Key Transport Module
KU: Kentucky Utilities Co. (NYSE)
KUB: Kubota Ltd. (NYSE)
Kubota: Kubota Ltd. (newspaper)
KUH: Kuhlman Corp. (NYSE)
Kuhlm: Kuhlman Corp. (newspaper)
kV: kilovolt
KV: KV Pharmaceutical Co. (ASE)

KVA: Kilovolt-Ampere
KV Ph: KV Pharmaceutical Co. (newspaper)
KVU: Kleer-Vu Industries Inc. (ASE)
kw: kiloword
kW: kilowatt
KW: Dorado Wings (airline)
KWD: Kellwood Co. (NYSE)
KWH: Kilowatt Hour
KWIC: Key Word In Context
KWN: Kenwin Shops Inc. (ASE)
KWOC: Keyword Out of Context
KWP: King World Productions Inc. (NYSE)
KXU: Keyword Transformation Unit
KYC: Keystone Camera Products Corp. (ASE)
Know Your Customer
KYO: Kyocera Corp. (NYSE)
Kyocer: Kyocera Corp. (newspaper)
Kysor: Kysor Industrial Corp. (newspaper)
KyUtil: Kentucky Utilities Co. (newspaper)
KZ: Kysor Industrial Corp. (NYSE)

l: language
length
link
liter
local

L: Liquid assets of money supply
Listed (securities)

L&A: Louisiana & Arkansas (railroad)

LA: LAN - Linea Aerea Nacional de Chile (National Air Line of Chile)
Legal Asset
Letter of Authority
Line Adapter
Liquid Assets
Local Address
Local Agent

LAA: Los Angeles Airways

LAAD: Latin American Agribusiness Development Corporation

LAB: Lloyd Aereo Boliviano (Bolivian Airline)
Nichols Institute (ASE)

LaBarg: LaBarge Inc. (newspaper)

LAC: LAC Minerals Ltd. (NYSE) (newspaper)

LaclGs: Laclede Gas Co. (newspaper)

LACSA: Lineas Aereas Costarricenses Sociedad Anonima (Costa Rican Airlines)

LADDER: Language Access to Distributed Data with Error Recovery
Life Assurance Direct Entry and Retrieval

LADS: Local Area Data Set

LAER: Lowest Achievable Emission Rate

LAF: Lafarge Corp. (NYSE)

Lafarge: Lafarge Corp. (newspaper)

LAFTA: Latin American Free Trade Association

LaGenl: Louisiana General Services Inc. (newspaper)

LAI: Linee Aeree Italiane (Italian airline)

LAIA: Latin American Integration Area

LAIRS: Labor Agreement Information Retrieval System

LAJ: Los Angeles Junction (railway)

Lajolla: La Jolla Bancorp. (newspaper)

LaLand: Louisiana Land & Exploration Co., The (newspaper)

LA&LR: Livonia, Avon and Lakeville Railroad

LAMA: Local Automatic Message Accounting

LAMACHA: Louisiana-Alabama-Mississippi Automated Clearing House Association

LAMCO: Liberian America Swedish Minerals Company (Liberian Railways)

LAMP: Logic Analysis for Maintenance Planning

LamSes: Lamson & Sessions Co., The (newspaper)

LAN: Lancer Corp. (ASE)
Linea Aerea Nacional (Chile National Airline)
Local Area Network

Lancer: Lancer Corp. (newspaper)
LANDAC: Land Development Accounting System
LANICA: Lineas Aereas de Nicaragua (Nicaraguan Airline)
LAO: Lead Agency Official
LAP: Lineas Aerias Paraguayas (Paraguay National Airline)
Link Access Procedure
LaPac: Louisiana-Pacific Corp. (newspaper)
LaPnt: La Pointe Industries Inc. (newspaper)
LAR: Limit Address Register
Larizz: Larizza Industries Inc. (newspaper)
LARPS: Local and Remote Printing Station
LAS: Laser Industries Ltd. (ASE)
Legal Aid Society
Local Address Space
LASCOT: Large Screen Color Television
Laser: Laser Industries Ltd. (newspaper)
LASER: Light Amplification by Stimulation of Emitted Radiation
LASH: Lighter Aboard Ship Handling
LASL: Los Alamos Scientific Laboratory
LASP: Local Attached Support Processor
LASS: Logistics Analysis Simulation System
LAT: Latshaw Enterprises Inc. (ASE)
LATA: Local Access and Transport Areas
Latshw: Latshaw Enterprises Inc. (newspaper)
LAU: Line Adapter Unit
Lauren: Laurentian Capital Corp. (newspaper)
LAV: Linea Aeropostal Venezolana (Venezuelan Air Line)
LAVA: Look Ahead Variable Acceleration
LAW: Lawter International Inc. (NYSE)
LawrG: Lawrence Insurance Group Inc. (newspaper)
Lawsn: Lawsen Mardon Group Ltd. (newspaper)
Lawtlnt: Lawter International Inc. (newspaper)
LAWV: Lorain and West Virginia (railway)
Laz By: La-Z-Boy Chair Co. (newspaper)
LazKap: Lazare Kaplan International Inc. (newspaper)
LB: LaBarge Inc. (ASE)
Legal Bond
Line Buffer
Lloyd Aero Boliviano (airline)
Lloyd Brasileiro (steamship)
Logical Block
Lower Bound
LBA: Lease Brokers Association
Linear Bounded Automation
Local Bus Adapter
LBC: Landbank Bancshares Corp. (NYSE)
Left Bounded Context
Local Bus Controller
LBE: Long Bill of Exchange
LBEN: Low Byte Enable
lbl: label
LBMI: Lease Base Machine Inventory
LBO: Leveraged Buyout
Line Build-Out
libr: librarian
LBR: Lowville and Beaver River (railroad)
LbtyAS: Liberty All-Star Equity Fund (newspaper)

L&C: Lancaster & Chester (railroad)
LC: Late Charge
Legal Capital
Letter of Credit
Leverage Contract
Liberty Corp., The (NYSE)
Lineas Aeras del Estade-State Air Lines
Line Concentrator
Line Control
Line of Credit
Listed Company
Loan Capital
Loan Crowd
Location Counter
Lower Case
L/C: Letter of Credit
Line Control
LCA: Lake Central Airlines
Line Control Adapter
Low Cost Automation
LCB: Line Control Block
Link Control Block
Logic Control Block
LCBX: Large Computerized (Private) Branch Exchange
LCC: Ledger Card Computer
Life Cycle Cost (Costing)
LCCPMP: Life Cycle Computer Program Management Plan
LCD: Least Common Denominator
Liquid Crystal Display
LCDHWIU: Laundry, Cleaning, and Dye House Workers International Union
LCDS: Low-Cost Development System
LCE: London Commodity Exchange (UK)
Lone Star Industries Inc. (NYSE)
LCES: Least Cost Estimating and Scheduling
LCF: Least Common Factor
Logical Channel Fill
LCFS: Last-Come, First Served
LCH: Logical Channel
LCHILD: Logical Child
LCL: Less than Carload Lot
Limited Channel Logout
Lower Control Limit
LCM: Large Core Memory
Least Common Multiple
Line Concentrator Module
Line Control Module
LCNTR: Location Counter
LCP: Language Conversion Program
Laws for Construction of Programs
Link Control Procedure
Local Control Point
Logical Construction of Programs
L/CR: Letter of Credit
LCR: Least Cost Routing
LCRR: Low Cost Risk Reduction
LCS: Large Core Storage
LCSP: Logical Channels Switching Program
LCT: Latest Completing Time
Less than Truckload Lot
Line Control Table
Logical Channel Termination
Low-Cost Technology
LC/TC: Line Control/Task Control
LCU: Level Converter Unit
Line Control Unit
Local Control Unit
LCW: Line Control Word
L&D: Loans and Discounts
Loss and Damage
LD: Labor Day
Labor Dispute
LADE (Lineas Aeras del Estrade-State Airlines)
Logical Design
Long Distance

LDA: Local Data Administrator
Local Display Adapter
Logical Device Address
LDB: Large Database
Logical Database
LDBS: Local Data Base System
LDC: Less-Developed Country
Local Display Controller
Low-Density Center
Low-Speed Data Channel
LDCS: Long Distance Control System
LDD: Local Data Distribution
LDG: Longs Drug Stores Corp. (NYSE)
Ld Gt: Land Grant
LDL: Logical Database Level
Lydall Inc. (ASE)
LDLA: Limited Distance Line Adapter
LDM: Limited Distance Modem
Linear Delta Modulation
Local Data Manager
LDMA: London Discount Market Association (UK)
LdmkSv: Landmark Savings Assn. (Pennsylvania) (newspaper)
LDMS: Laboratory Data Management System
LDMX: Local Digital Message Exchange
LDO: Logical Device Order
LDT: Language Dependent Translator
LDU: Line Drive Unit
LE: Lake Geneva Airways
Lands' End Inc. (NYSE)
Leading Edge
Less than (Equal to)
LEAA: Law Enforcement Assistance Administration
LEAD: Learn, Execute, and Diagnose
LEADS: Law Enforcement Automated Data System
Learnl: LeaRonal Inc. (newspaper)
LearPP: Lear Petroleum Partners LP (newspaper)
LearPt: Lear Petroleum Corp. (newspaper)
LEAS-FACS: Lease-Financial Accounting Control System
LECE: Ligue Européenne de Coopération Économique (European League for Economic Cooperation) (French)
led: ledger
LED: Light-Emitting Diode
LEE: Lake Erie and Eastern (railroad)
Lee Enterprises Inc. (NYSE)
LeeEnt: Lee Enterprises Inc. (newspaper)
LeePhr: Lee Pharmaceuticals (newspaper)
LEF: Lake Erie, Franklin and Clarion (railroad)
Line Expansion Function
LE&FW: Lake Erie and Fort Wayne (railroad)
LEG: Leggett & Platt Inc. (NYSE)
LegMas: Legg Mason Inc. (newspaper)
LegPlat: Leggett & Platt Inc. (newspaper)
Lehmn: Lehman Corp., The (newspaper)
LEIN: Law Enforcement Information Network
Leiner: P. Leiner Nutritional Products Corp. (newspaper)
LeisurT: Leisure & Technology Inc. (newspaper)
LEL: Lower Earnings Limit
LEM: Lehman Corp., The (NYSE)
Logical End of Media
Logic Enhanced Memory
len: length

LEN: Lake Erie and Northern (railway)
Lennar Corp. (NYSE)
Lennar: Lennar Corp. (newspaper)
LEO: Dreyfus Strategic Municipals Inc. (NYSE)
LEQ: Less than (Equal to)
LES: Leslie Fay Companies, The (NYSE)
LeslFay: Leslie Fay Companies Inc., The (newspaper)
LESS: Least Cost Estimating and Scheduling
let: letter
LeucNt: Leucadia National Corp. (newspaper)
lev: level
Levitt: Levitt Corp. (newspaper)
LEVTAB: Level Table
LEX: Line Exchanger
LF: Labor Force
Laissez-Faire
Ledger Folio
Line Feed
Linjeflyg (airline)
Low Frequency
LFA: Littlefield Adams & Co. (ASE)
Local Freight Agent
LFC: Local Form Control
LFD: Local Frequency Distribution
Lfetime: Lifetime Corp. (newspaper)
LFF: Limited Fanout-Free
LFM: Local File Manager
LFN: Logical File Name
LFS: Local Format Storage
LFSR: Linear Feedback Shift Register
lft: left
LFT: Lifetime Corp. (ASE)
LFU: Least Frequently Used
lg: large
LG: Laclede Gas Co. (NYSE)
Luxair-Luxembourg Airlines
LGA: Landrum-Griffin Act
LGFS: Local Government Financial System
LGI: Linear Gate and Integrator
LGL: Lynch Corp. (ASE)
LGN: Logical Group Number
Logicon Inc. (NYSE)
LGS: Louisiana General Services Inc. (NYSE)
LG TN: Long Ton (2240 lbs.)
L + H: Lamport and Holt Line (steamship)
LH: Legal Holiday
Lufthansa German Airlines
LHC: Left Hand Chain
L & N Housing Corp. (NYSE)
LHF: List Handling Facility
L&HR: Lehigh & Hudson River (railroad)
LHS: Left-Hand Side
li: liability
liabilities
L/I: Letter of Intent
LI: Labor Intensive
Leeward Islands Air Transport (airline)
Long Island (railroad)
LIA: Laser Industry Association
Laser Institute of America
Loop Interface Address
Low-Speed Input Adapter
LIAT: Leeward Islands Air Transport
lib: librarian
LIB: Line Interface Base
Line-Item Budget
LIBE: Library Editor
LIBEDIT: Library Editor
LIBMAN: Library Management
LIBO: London Inter-Bank Offered (rate)
LIB/OL: LIBRARIAN/Online
LIBOR: London Inter-Bank Offered Rate
libr: librarian
LIBRIS: Library Information System
LibtyCp: Liberty Corp., The (newspaper)

LIC: Less Industrialized Country
LIDO: Logic In, Documents Out
LIED: Linkage Editor
LIF: Line Interface Feature
LIFER: Language Interface Facility with Ellipsis and Recursion
LIFFE: London International Financial Futures Exchange (UK)
LIFO: Last In, First Out
LIG: Liggett Group Inc. (NYSE)
Ligget: Liggett Group Inc. (newspaper)
LIH: Line Interface Handler
LII: Larizza Industries Inc. (ASE)
LIL: Long Island Lighting Co. (NYSE)
LILA: Life Insurance Logistics Automated
LILCo: Long Island Lighting Co. (newspaper)
Lilly: Eli Lilly & Co. (newspaper)
LILO: Last In, Last Out
LilVer: Lillian Vernon Corp. (newspaper)
LIM: Language Interpretation Module
Linear-Induction-Motion engine
Line Interface Module
LIMA: Logic-In-Memory Array
Limean: The mean of London interbank bid and offer rates
LIMIT: Lot-size Inventory Management Interpolation Technique
Limited: Limited Inc., The (newspaper)
LIML: Linear Propagation Time Immediate Language
LincNtl: Lincoln National Corp. (newspaper)
LincPl: Lincoln National Direct Placement Fund Inc. (newspaper)
LINDI: Line to Disk
LINED: Line Editor
LinPro: Linpro Specific Properties (newspaper)
LINUS: Logical Inquiry and Update System
LIO: Lionel Corp., The (ASE)
Lionel: Lionel Corp., The (newspaper)
LIOP: Local Input/Output Processor
Low-Speed Input/Output Processor
LIPID: Logical Page Identifier
LIPS: Laboratory Interconnecting Programming System
liq: liquid
LIQT: Liquid Transient
liquid: liquidation
lir: lira (currency of Italy)
LIRC: Low-Interest Rate Currency
LIRR: Long Island Railroad
LIRS: Library Information Retrieval System
LISA: Linked Index Sequential Access
LISH: Last In, Still Here
LISP: List Processing
lit: literal
LIT: Life Insurance Trust
Litton Industries Inc. (NYSE)
Local Income Tax
Litfld: Littlefield, Adams & Co. (newspaper)
Litton: Litton Industries Inc. (newspaper)
LIU: Line Interface Unit
LJ: Sierra Leone Airways
LJC: La Jolla Bancorp. (ASE)
LJE: Local Job Entry
LK: Alag-Alpine Lift-Trans (airline)
Lockheed Corp. (NYSE)
LKI: Lazare Kaplan International Inc. (ASE)
LKM: Low Key Maintenance
LK&PRR: Lahaina-Kaanapal and Pacific Railroad (Hawaii)

LL: Icelandic Airlines
Lauro Line (steamship)
Leased Line
Limited Liability
Link Line (steamship)
Lloyd's of London (UK)
Local Line
Local Loopback
LLA: Leased Line Adapter
Long Line Adapter
Low-Speed Line Adapter
LLB: CompuTrac Inc.
LLBA: Language and Language Behavior Abstracts
LLE Ry: LL & E Royalty Trust (newspaper)
LLG: Logical Line Group
LLI: Low-Level Interface
LLIB: Load Module Librarian
LLL: Lawrence Livermore Laboratory
LLM: Low-Level Multiplexer
LLN: Line-Link Network
LLOYD'S: Lloyd's Register of Shipping (UK)
LLRR: Log-Likelihood Ratio Representation
LLX: Louisiana Land & Exploration Co., The (NYSE)
LLY: Eli Lilly & Co. (NYSE)
LM: ALM-Dutch Antillean Airlines
Labor Market
Labor Movement
Legg Mason Inc. (NYSE)
Leningrad Metro
Link Manager
Litchfield and Madison (railway)
Local Memory
Logic Module
Loop Multiplexer
Louisiana Midland (railroad)
LMB: Left Most Bit
LMBI: Local Memory Bank Interface
Local Memory Bus Interface
LMC: Liberia Mining Company (railroad)
Lomas Mortgage Corp. (NYSE)
LMCSS: Letter Mail Code Sort System
LME: London Metal Exchange (UK)
LMEC: London Metal Exchange (UK)
LMG: Lawsen Mardon Group Ltd. (ASE)
LMI: Local Memory Image
LML: Landmark Land Company Inc. (ASE)
Logical Memory Level
LMOS: Loop Maintenance Operations System
LMRA: Labor Management Relations Act (Taft-Hartley Act)
LMRBR: London Midland Region of British Railways (UK)
LMRDA: Labor Management Reporting & Disclosure Act
LMS: Lamson & Sessions Co., The (NYSE)
List Management System
LMT: Local Mean Time
Logical Mapping Table
LMU: Line Monitor Unit
LMV: Long Market Value
LMX: Local Multiplexer
ln: line
L&N: Louisville & Nashville (railroad)
LN: Libyan Arab Airlines
Link Number
LNA: Low-Noise Amplifier
LNAC: Louisville, New Albany and Corydon (railroad)
LNB: Local Name Base
LNC: Lincoln National Corp. (NYSE)
LncNC: Lincoln N. C. Realty Fund (newspaper)

LncNtC: Lincoln National Convertible Securities Fund Inc. (newspaper)
LND: Lincoln National Direct Placement Fund Inc. (NYSE)
LndBnc: Landbank Bancshares Corp. (newspaper)
LndEd: Lands' End Inc. (newspaper)
Lndmk: Landmark Land Company Inc. (newspaper)
LndPc: Landsing Pacific Fund (newspaper)
L&NE: Lehigh & New England (railroad)
LNE: Local Network Emulator
LNF: Lomas & Nettleton Financial Corp. (NYSE)
LNG: Liquefied Natural Gas
LN Ho: L & N Housing Corp. (newspaper)
LNM: Logical Network Machine
LNN: Linear Nearest Neighbor
LNO: Liaison Officer
LNP&W: Laramie, North Park & Western (railroad)
L&NR: Ludington and Northern Railway
LNR: Low-Noise Receiver
L&NRY: Laona and Northern Railway
LnStar: Lone Star Industries Inc. (newspaper)
LNV: Lincoln National Convertible Securities Inc. (NYSE)
L&NW: Louisiana & North West (railroad)
lo: low
L/O: Letter of Offer
LO: Letter of Offer
Limit (limited) Order
Line Organization
Local Oscillator
Lowest Offer
Polish Airlines
LOA: Leave Of Absence
Length Overall
Low-Speed Output Adapter
LOAP: Length of Adjacency Process
loc: local
location
LOC: Letter Of Credit
Lines Of Communication
Location Counter
Location Dependent
Loctite Corp. (NYSE)
Lockhd: Lockheed Corp. (newspaper)
LOCPURO: Local Purchase Order
Loctite: Loctite Corp. (newspaper)
Loews: Loews Corp. (newspaper)
LOF: Look Ahead on Fault
LOFAR: Low-Frequency Analysis Recording
LOG: Rayonier Timberlands LP (NYSE)
LOGFED: Log File Editor
Logicon: Logicon Inc. (newspaper)
LOGIK: Logical Organizing and Gathering of Information Knowledge
LOGO: Limit Of Government Obligation
LOI: Letter Of Instruction
LOM: Lomas & Nettleton Mortgage Investors (NYSE)
LOMA: Life Office Management Association
LomasM: Lomas Mortgage Corp. (newspaper)
LomFn: Lomas & Nettleton Financial Corp. (newspaper)
LOMI: Letter Of Moral Intent
LomMt: Lomas & Nettleton Mortgage Investors (newspaper)
LongDr: Longs Drug Stores Corp. (newspaper)
LOP: Line Oriented Protocol
LOP&G: Live Oak, Perry & Gulf (railroad)

LOR: Level Of Repair
Look Ahead on Request
Loral Corp. (NYSE)
Loral: Loral Corp. (newspaper)
LoriCp: Lori Corp., The (newspaper)
LOS: Length Of Service
Line Of Sight
Loss Of Signal
LOSR: Limit Of Stack Register
LOT: Light Operated Typewriter
LOTIS: Logic, Timing and Sequencing
LOTS: Low-Overhead Time-Sharing System
LOU: Louisville Gas & Electric Co. (NYSE)
LouvGs: Louisville Gas & Electric Co. (newspaper)
LOW: Lowe's Companies Inc. (NYSE)
Lowes: Lowe's Companies Inc. (newspaper)
LOWL: Low-Level Language
LP: Air Alpes (airline)
Lead Programmer
Light Pen
Limited Partner
Linear Programming
Line Printer
Line Protocol
Logic Probe
Long Position
LPA: Lease Purchase Agreement
Link Pack Area
LPB: Louisiana and Pine Bluff (railway)
LPC: Linear Predictive Coding
LPCM: Linear Phase Code Modulation
LPE: Layer Primitive Equation
LPF: Landsing Pacific Fund (ASE)
Low Pass Filter
LPG: Liquefied Petroleum Gas
Petrolane Partners LP (NYSE)
LPH: Lee Pharmaceuticals (ASE)
LPI: La Pointe Industries Inc. (ASE)
Lines Per Inch
LPID: Logical Page Identifier
LPIU: Lithographers and Photoengravers International Union
LPL: List Processing Language
LPM: Lines Per Minute
LPN: Logical Page Number
Longview, Portland and Northern (railway)
LPO: Linpro Specific Properties (ASE)
LPP: Latest Precedence Partition
Lear Petroleum Partners LP (ASE)
LPS: Language for Programming-in-the-Small
Linear Programming System
Lines Per Second
Low-Priced Stock
LPT: Largest Processing Time First
Lear Petroleum Corp. (NYSE)
Line Printer
LPTTL: Low-Power Transistor-Transistor Logic
LPTV: Low-Power Television service
LPU: Language Processor Unit
Line Printer Unit
Line Processing Unit
LPVT: Large-Print Video Terminal
LPX: Louisiana-Pacific Corp. (NYSE)
LQ: Laurentian Capital Corp. (ASE)
LQM: La Quinta Motor Inns Inc. (NYSE)
LQP: La Quinta Motor Inns LP (NYSE)
LQuint: La Quinta Motor Inns Inc. (newspaper)
LQuMt: La Quinta Motor Inns LP (newspaper)
LR: LACSA (Lineas Aereas Costarricenses-Costa Rican Airlines)

Left to Right
Legal Reserve
Lending Rate
Limited Response
Limit Register
Listing Requirements
Lloyd's Register (UK)
Loan Rate
Logical Record

L-R: Left to Right

LRA: Lagged Reserve Accounting
Lease Rental Agreement
Logical Record Access

LRAC: Long Run Average Cost curve

LRB: Labor Relations Board

LRBC: Left-Right Bounded-Context

LRC: Longitudinal Redundancy Check
Lori Corp., The (ASE)

LRCC: Longitudinal Redundancy Check Character

LRCR: Longitudinal Redundancy Check Register

LRECL: Logical Record Length

LREP: Left-Bracketed Representation

LRF: Lincoln N.C. Realty Fund (ASE)

LRI: Lawndale Transportation Company
LeaRonal Inc. (NYSE)

LRIC: Long Run Incremental Costing

LRIP: Low Rate Initial Production

LRL: Linking Relocating Loader
Logical Record Length
Logical Record Location

LRMC: Low-Run Marginal Cost

LROI: Legal Rate Of Interest

LRP: Long-Range Planning

LRPE: Long-Range Procurement Estimate

LRR: Loop Regenerative Repeater

LRS: Laurinburg and Southern Railroad
Lloyd's Register of Shipping (UK)

LRSP: Long Range Strategic Planning

LRT: LL & E Royalty Trust (NYSE)

LRU: Least Recently Used

L&S: Laurinburg and Southern (railroad)

LS: Labor Shift
Least Significant
Legal Signature
Letter Stock
Listed Securities (Stock)
Little Stock
Local Store
Louisiana Southern (railroad)
Low Speed

LSA: Landmark Savings Assn. (Pennsylvania) (ASE)
Line-Sharing Adapter
Lump-Sum Appropriation

LSAR: Local Storage Address Register

LSB: Least Significant Bit
Lock, Stock and Barrel
LSB Industries Inc. (ASE)

LS&BC: La Salle and Bureau County (railroad)

LSB Ind: LSB Industries Inc. (newspaper)

LSC: Loop Station Connector
Low-Speed Interface Control
Low-Speed Concentrator
Shopco Laurel Centre LP (ASE)

LSD: Language for Systems Development
Least-Significant Difference
Least-Significant Digit
Line Signal Detector

LSDB: Launch Support Data Base

LSDR: Local Store Data Register

LSE: London School of Economics and Political Science (UK)
London Stock Exchange (UK)

LSFR: Local Storage Function Register
Lshld: leasehold
L&SH: Long and Short Haul
LS&I: Lake Superior and Ishpeming (railroad)
LSI: Large-Scale Integration
LSIC: Large-Scale Integrated Circuit (Circuitry)
LSID: Local Session Identification
LSL: Ladder Static Logic
Link and Selector Language
LSM: Labor Saving Machine (Machinery)
Letter Sorting Machine
Line Select Module
LSMA: Low-Speed Multiplexer Arrangement
LSMLC: Low-Speed Multiline Controller
LSO: Louisiana Southern (railway)
LSP: Local Store Pointer
LSQA: Local System Queue Area
LSR: Lebanese State Railroads
Local Storage Register
Low-Speed Reader
LSS: Language for Symbolic Simulation
LST: Landing Ship Tank
Landing Ship Transport
Latest Starting Time
Local Standard Time
LST&TRC: Lake Superior Terminal and Transfer Railway Company
LSU: Least Significant Unit
Library Storage Unit
Line-Sharing Unit
Load Storage Unit
Local Storage Unit
LSUP: Loader Storage Unit Support Program
LSX: LSI-UNIX System
L&T: Language and Terminal
LT: Lake Terminal (railroad)
Land Tax
Lead Time
Legal Tender
Legal Title
Less Than
Letter of Trust
Line Terminator
Lloyd Triestino (Italian-Trieste Line) (steamship)
Long Term
Long Ton
Luxury Tax
LTA: Logical Transient Area
LTB: Logical Twin Backward Pointer
London Transport Board (UK)
LTBL: Level Table
LTC: Less Than Carload
Line Time Clock
Local Terminal Controller
Long-Term Contract
Long-Term Credit
LTCG: Long-Term Capital Gain
LTCL: Long-Term Capital Loss
Ltd: Limited (Company limited in its liability) (Irish) (British) (UK)
LTD: Limited (to any security or purpose)
Limited Inc., The (NYSE)
Line Transfer Device
LTF: Logical Twin Forward Pointer
LTFV: Less Than Fair Value
LTG: Catalina Lighting Inc. (ASE)
ltge: lighterage
LTH: Logical Track Header
Long-Term Holiday
LTI: Level Term Insurance
Long-Term Income (benefits)
LTL: Less-than-Truckload
LTM: Leverage Transaction Merchant
Long-Term Memory
LTOC: Lowest Total Overall Cost
LTPD: Lot Tolerance Percent Defective

ltr: letter
lighter
LTR: Loew's Corp. (NYSE)
LTRS: Letters Shift
LTS: Line Transient Suppression
LTT: Long-Term Trend
LTU: Line Termination Unit
LTV: LTV Corp., The (newspaper)
LU: Logical Unit
LUB: Logical Unit Block
Luby's Cafeterias Inc. (NYSE)
Lubrzl: Lubrizol Corp., The (newspaper)
Lubys: Luby's Cafeterias Inc. (newspaper)
LUC: Lukens Inc. (NYSE)
LUCRE: Lower Unit Costs and Related Earnings
LUCS: Land Use Cost Studies
LUE: Link Utilization Efficiency
LUF: Limiting System Utilization Factor
LUK: Leucadia National Corp. (NYSE)
Lukens: Lukens Inc. (newspaper)
LU-LU: Logical Unit to Logical Unit
LUM: Lumex Inc. (ASE)
Lumex: Lumex Inc. (newspaper)
LUN: Logical Unit Number
LUR: L. Luria & Son Inc. (ASE)
Luria: L. Luria & Son Inc. (newspaper)
LUSVC: Logical Unit Services Manager
LUV: Southwest Airlines Co. (NYSE)
LUX: Leisure & Technology Inc. (NYSE)
LUXIBOR: Luxembourg Inter-Bank Offered Rate
L/V: Loader/Verifier
LV: LAV (Lineas Aeropostal Venezolana) (Venezuelan Aeropostal Airlines)
Lehigh Valley (railroad)
LVA: Line Voltage Analyzer
Local Virtual Address
LVC: Lillian Vernon Corp. (ASE)
LVI: LVI Group Inc., The (NYSE)
LVI Gp: LVI Group Inc., The (newspaper)
LVT: Levitt Corp. (ASE)
L&W: Louisville & Wadley (railroad)
LW: Last Word
Lien Waivers
Living Wage
LWA: Last Word Address
LWB: Lower Bound
LWC: Loop Wiring Connector
LWOP: Leave Without Pay
LWP: Leave With Pay
LWR: Lawrence Insurance Group Inc. (ASE)
LWU: Leather Workers Union
LWV: Lackawanna & Wyoming Valley (railroad)
LXMAR: Load External Memory Address Register
LY: El Al Israel Airlines
Last Year (Year's)
Lydal: Lydall Inc. (newspaper)
LynchC: Lynch Corp. (newspaper)
LYONS: Liquid Yield Option Note
LZ: Bulgarian Airlines
Lubrizol Corp., The (NYSE)
LZB: La-Z-Boy Chair Co. (NYSE)

m: machine
magnetization
mantissa
master
matured
mega
memory
meter
milli
mode
modem
monitor
multiplier

M: MCorp. (NYSE)
Matured bonds (in bond listings in newspapers)
The equilibrium nominal Money stock

ma: milliampere

M&A: Maintenance and Administration
Mississippi & Alabama (railroad)
Missouri and Arkansas (railroad)

MA: Machine Account
Magyan Allamvasutak (Hungarian State Railways)
Malev (Hungarian Air Transport) (airline)
Manufacturer's Agent
Manufacturing Assembly
Margin Account
Market Averages
Memory Address
Moving Average

MAB: Macroaddress Bus

MAC: Machine-Aided Cognition
Maintenance Allocation Chart
Maximum Allowable Cost
Memory Access Controller
Monthly Availability Charge
Multiaccess Computing (Computer)
Municipal Assistance Corporation

MACC: Micos Asynchronous Communications Controller

MACDAC: Man Communication and Display to Automatic Computer

MACE: Management Applications in a Computer Environment

MacGrg: MacGregor Sporting Goods Inc. (newspaper)

mach: machine
machinery
machinist

MACHA: Michigan Automated Clearing House Association
Mid-America Automated Clearing House Association
Mid-Atlantic Automated Clearing House Association
Midwest Automated Clearing House Association

maclib: macrolibrary

Macmil: Macmillan Inc. (newspaper)

MacNSc: MacNeal-Schwendler Corp., The (newspaper)

MACOM: M/A-Com Inc. (newspaper)

macp: macroprocessor
MACR: Minneapolis, Anoka and Guyana Range (railroad)
macro: macroassembler
macroprocessor
macrol: macrolanguage
MACS: Monitoring and Control Station (System)
Multiline Automatic Calling System
MACSYM: Measurement and Control System
MAD: Mean Absolute Deviation
MADCAP: Mathematical Problems and Set Operations
MADR: Microprogram Address Register
MAE: Master of Aeronautical Engineering
Memory Address Extension
MAFIA: Multiaccess Executive with Fast Interrupt Acceptance
mag: macrogenerator
magnetic
MAGEN: Matrix and Report Generator
MAGPIE: Machine Automatically Generating Production Inventory Evaluation
MAHR: Milliampere Hour
MAI: Machine Aided Indexing
M/A-Com Inc. (NYSE)
Multiple Access Interface
MAIBF: MAI Basic Four Inc. (newspaper)
maint: maintenance
maj: majority
MAJSR: Major State Register
MAL: Maximal Acceptable Load
Memory Access Logic
Meta Assembly Language
Malart: Malartic Hygrade Gold Mines Ltd. (newspaper)
Malaysa: Malaysia Fund Inc., The (newspaper)
MAM: Memory Allocation Manager
Mid-America Industries Inc. (ASE)
Multiapplication Monitor
MAMENIC: Marina Mercante Nicaraguense (Nicaraguan Merchant Marine) (steamship)
MAMS: Manufacturing Applications Management System
man: manual
manufacture
MAN: Manville Corp. (NYSE)
MANDATE: Multiline Automatic Network Diagnostic and Transmission Equipment
manf: manufacture
manufacturer
manufacturing
MANF: May, August, November, February (securities)
ManfHo: Manufactured Homes Inc. (newspaper)
ManhNt: Manhattan National Corp. (newspaper)
MANIAC: Mathematical Analyzer Numerical Integrator And Computer
Mechanical And Numerical Integrator And Computer
MANMAN: Manufacturing Management
ManrCr: Manor Care Inc. (newspaper)
manuf: manufacture
manufacturing
MANUPACS: Manufacturing Planning and Control System
Manvl: Manville Corp. (newspaper)
MAO: Marathon Office Supply Inc. (ASE)
MAOS: Metal Alumina Dielectric Oxide Semiconductor

MAP: Macroassembly Program
Maine Public Service Co. (ASE)
Maintenance Analysis Procedures
Management Analysis and Projection
Marketing Assistance Program
Memory Allocation and Protection
Microprogrammed Array Processor
Minimum Annual Premium
Minimum Acceptable Rate of Return

MAPCO: MAPCO Inc. (newspaper)

MAPD: Maximum Allowable Percent Defective

MAPEX: Mid-America Payment Exchange

MAPGEN: Map Generator

MAPI: Machinery and Allied Products Institute

MAPICS: Manufacturing, Accounting, and Production Information Control System

MAPLE: Marketing and Product Line Evaluation

MAPS: Management Analysis and Planning System
Manufacturing and Production System
Mid-American Automated Payments System
Modern Accounts Payable System
Monetary and Payments System
Multivariate Analysis, Participation, and Structure

MAR: Macroaddress Register
Marcade Group Inc., The (NYSE)
Memory Address Register
Microprogram Address Register

MARC: Machine Readable Catalog

Marcde: Marcade Group Inc., The (newspaper)

marg: margin
marginal

MARGIE: Memory Analysis, Response Generation and Inference on English

MarionMDow: Marion Merrill Dow Laboratories Inc. (newspaper)

Maritrn: Maritrans Partners LP (newspaper)

mark: market
marketing

Marlton: Marlton Technologies Inc. (newspaper)

MARR: Magma Arizona Railroad

Marriot: Marriott Corp. (newspaper)

MarsG: Mars Graphic Services Inc. (newspaper)

MART: Maintenance Analysis and Review Technique
Mean Active Repair Time

MartM: Martin Marietta Corp. (newspaper)

MARY: Massawa-Agordad Railway (Ethiopia)

mas: macroassembler

MAS: Management Aid System
Management (Managerial) Appraisal System
Masco Corp. (NYSE)
Monetary Authority of Singapore

MASAR: Management Assurance of Safety, Adequacy and Reliability

MASC: Management Systems Concept

Masco: Masco Corp. (newspaper)

MASCOT: Modular Approach to Software Construction Operation and Test

MasCp: MassMutual Corporate Investors (newspaper)
MASER: Microwave Amplification by Stimulated Emission of Radiation
MasInc: MassMutual Income Investors Inc. (newspaper)
MASIS: Management and Scientific Information System
MASK: Multiple Amplitude Shift Keying
MASM: Meta Assembler
MASS: Multiple Access Switching System
MAST: Marine Science and Technology (EC)
MASTER: Multiple Access Shared-Time Executive Routines
mat: matured (stocks)
maturity
MAT: Mattel Inc. (NYSE)
Medial Axis Transformation
Memory Address Test
MATE: Modular Automatic Test Equipment System
Matec: MATEC Corp. (newspaper)
MATEX: Macrotext Editor
MATLAN: Matrix Manipulation Language
MATR: Management Access To Records
Matrix: Matrix Corp. (newspaper)
MatRsh: Materials Research Corp. (newspaper)
MATS: Multiple-Access Time Sharing
MatSci: Material Sciences Corp. (newspaper)
Matsu: Matsushita Electric Industrial Company Ltd. (newspaper)
Mattel: Mattel Inc. (newspaper)
MattW: Matthews & Wright Group Inc. (newspaper)
MATV: Master Antenna Television System
MAU: Memory Access Unit
Multiple Access Unit
MauLoa: Mauna Loa Macadamia Partners LP (newspaper)
max: maximum
MAX: Matrix Corp. (ASE)
Maxam: MAXXAM Group Inc. (newspaper)
Maxphrm: MaxPharma Inc. (newspaper)
Maxus: Maxus Energy Corp. (newspaper)
Maytag: Maytag Co., The (newspaper)
mb: megabit
megabyte
M&B: Marianna & Blountstown (railroad)
Meridan and Bigbee (railroad)
Metes and Bounds
MB: Member Bank
Memory Buffer
Memory Bus
Merchant Bank
Municipal Bond
MBA: Master of Business Administration
Mortgage Bankers Association (of America)
MBC: Memory Bus Controller
Mickelberry Corp. (NYSE)
Multiple Basic Channel
MBCD: Modified Binary Coded Decimal
MBD: Magnetic Bubble Domain Device
Million Barrels per Day
MBDA: Metal Building Dealers Association
MBDOE: Million Barrels per Day Oil Equivalent
MBE: Management By Exception
Molecular Beam Epitaxy

MBE-ARMS: Multiple Business Entity-Accounts Receivable Management System
MBEO: Minority Business Enterprise Office
MBF: MAI Basic Four Inc. (NYSE)
Monotonic Boolean Function
MBI: Marianna and Blountstown (railroad)
MBIA Inc. (NYSE)
Memory Bank Interface
MBIA: MBIA Inc. (newspaper)
Municipal Bond Insurance Association
MBIO: Microprogrammable Block Input/Output
mbit: megabit
MBM: Magnetic Bubble Memory
MBN: Metrobank NA (California) (ASE)
MBO: Management By Objectives
mbr: member
M&BR: Meridian & Bigbee River (railroad)
MBR: Memory Base Register
Memory Buffer Register
MBS: Modular Banking System
Mutual Broadcasting System
MBT: Marianna and Blountstown (railroad)
MBTA: Massachusetts Bay Transportation Authority
MBU: Memory Buffer Unit
MBWA: Management By Walking Around
MBY: Middleby Corp. (ASE)
m-byte: megabyte
mc: megacycle
MC: Magnetic Card
Maine Central (railroad)
Marginal Cost
Margin Call
Master Control
Matsushita Electric Industrial Company Ltd. (NYSE)
Memory Control
Michigan Central (railroad)
Middle Creek Railroad
Mississippi Central (railroad)
Mortgage Company
Motor Carrier
Municipal Code
MCA: Management Consultants Association
MCA Inc. (NYSE) (newspaper)
Monetary Compensatory Amount (EC)
Multiprocessor Communications Adapter
MCAR: Machine Check Analysis and Recording
MCB: Microcomputer Board
MCBF: Mean Characters Between Failures
Mean Cycles Between Failure
MCC: Mestek Inc. (NYSE)
Miscellaneous Common Carrier
Multichannel Communications Controller
Multichip Carrier
Mutual Capital Certificate
MCCD: Message Cryptographic Check Digits
McCla: McClatchy Newspapers Inc. (newspaper)
MCCU: Multiple Channel Control Unit
MCD: McDonald's Corp. (NYSE)
Monitor Console Routine Dispatcher
MCDBSU: Master Control and Data Buffer Storage Unit
McDerl: McDermott International Inc. (newspaper)
McDld: McDonald's Corp. (newspaper)
McDnD: McDonnell Douglas Corp. (newspaper)

McDnl: McDonald & Company Investments Inc. (newspaper)
MCDS: Management Control Data System
MCE: Master of Civil Engineering
MCEL: Machine Check Extended Logout
MCF: Magnetic Card File
McFad: McFaddin Ventures Inc. (newspaper)
McGrH: McGraw-Hill Inc. (newspaper)
mch: megacharacter
MCH: Machine Check Handler
MedChem Products Inc. (ASE)
MCHB: Maintenance Channel Buffer Register
MCHC: Maintenance Channel Command Register
MchER: Michigan Energy Resources Co. (newspaper)
mchr: megacharacter
MCHTR: Maintenance Channel Transmit Receiver Register
MCI: Machine Check Interruption
MassMutual Corporate Investors (NYSE)
MCIC: Machine Check Interruption Code
Multichannel Interface Controller
McInt: McIntyre Mines Ltd. (newspaper)
MCIS: Maintenance Control Information System
Map and Chart Information System
Materials Control Information System
MCK: McKesson Corp. (NYSE)
McKes: McKesson Corp. (newspaper)
MCL: Microprogram Control Logic
Monitor Control Language
Moore Corporation Ltd. (NYSE)
MCLA: Microcoded Communications Line Adapter
McLe: McLean Industries Inc. (newspaper)
MCLK: Master Clock
MCM: Memory Control Module
Monte Carlo Method
MCMC: Multiple-Channel/Multiple-Choice
MCO: MCO Holdings Inc. (ASE)
Midland Continental (railroad)
MCOA/P: Multi-Company Accounts Payable
MCO Hd: MCO Holdings Inc. (newspaper)
MCorp: MCorp (newspaper)
MCO Rs: MCO Resources Inc. (newspaper)
MCOS: Microprogrammable Computer Operating System
MCP: Marginal-Cost Pricing
Maritime Company of the Philippines (steamship)
Master Control Program
Message Control Program
MCPG: Media Conversion Program Generator
MCPU: Multiple Central Processing Unit
MCR: Magnetic Card Reader
Master Control Register
Master Control Routine
McCloud River (railroad)
MCO Resources Inc. (ASE)
Memory Control Register
McRae: McRae Industries Inc. (newspaper)
MCRR: Machine Check Recording and Recovery
Maine Central Road Railroad

Monongahela Connecting Railroad

MCS: Maintenance Control System
Management Control System
Master Control System
Master of Commercial Science
Megacycles per Second
Message Control System
Microcomputer System
Microprogram Certification System
Multichannel Communications Support
Multiple Console Support

MCSA: Moscow, Camden and San Augustine (railroad)

MCST: Magnetic Card Selectric Typewriter

MCU: Maintenance Control Unit
Management Control Unit
Master Control Unit
Memory Control Unit
Microprocessor Control Unit
Microprogram Control Unit
Multiprocessor Communications Unit
Multisystem Communications Unit

MCUSR: Memory Control Unit Special Register

mcz: mechanized

md: Demand for nominal Money

MD: Air Madagascar (airline)
Management Development
Mark Down
Maturity Date
McDonnell Douglas Corp. (NYSE)
Memorandum of Deposit
Memory Data Register
Memory Decrement
Midnight Dumping
Months after Date
Municipal Docks Railway of the Jacksonville Port Authority

MDA: MAPCO Inc. (NYSE)
Multidimensional Access

MDAC: Multiplying Digital to Analog Converter

MDAP: Machining and Display Application Program

MDB: Master Data Bank
Multilateral Development Bank

MDC: M.D.C. Holdings Inc. (NYSE) (newspaper)
Memory Disk Controller
Microcomputer Development Center
Multiple Device Controller

MDCA: M.D.C. Asset Investors Inc. (newspaper)

Mdcore: Medicore Inc. (newspaper)

MDC&R: Management Data Collection and Reporting

MDCU: Magnetic Disk Control Unit
Multidisplay Control Unit

MDD: Magnetic Disk Drive
McDonald & Company Investments Inc. (NYSE)

MDES: Multidata Entry System

MDF: Main Distributing Frame
Microcomputer Development Facility

MDK: Medicore Inc. (ASE)

MDL: Macrodata Language
Maintenance Diagnostic Logic
Microprocessor Development Lab

MDLC: Multiple Data Link Controller

MDM: Multiplexer/Demultiplexer

MdMgt: Medical Management of America Inc. (newspaper)

MDNA: Machinery Dealers National Association

MDNF: Minimal Disjunctive Normal Form

MDO: Monthly Debit Ordinary
MDP: Meredith Corp. (NYSE)
Microdisplay Processor
MDPS: MICR Document Processing System
MDQS: Management Data Query System
MDR: McDermott International Inc. (NYSE)
Memory Data Register
Minimum Daily Requirement
Miscellaneous Data Record
MD&S: Macon, Dublin & Savannah (railroad)
MDS: Maintenance Data System
Management Decision System
Management Display System
Microcomputer Development System
Microprocessor Development System
Modular Data System
Multipoint Distribution Service
mdse: merchandise
mdsg: merchandising
MDSS: Microprocessor Development Support System
MDT: Mean Down Time
Medtronic Inc. (NYSE)
Merchant Deposit Transmittal
Mountain Daylight Time
MDU: Maintenance Diagnostic Unit
MDU Resources Group Inc. (NYSE) (newspaper)
MDW: Midway Airlines Inc. (NYSE)
MdwAir: Midway Airlines Inc. (newspaper)
M&E: Morristown and Erie (railroad)
ME: Managing Editor
Master of Engineering
Memory Element
Mercantile Exchange
Middle East Airlines
Movement Européen (European Movement) (French) (EC)
MEA: Master of Engineering Administration
Mead Corp., The (NYSE)
Memory Inspection Ending Address
Middle East Airlines (Lebanon)
Mead: Mead Corp., The (newspaper)
MEB: Modem Evaluation Board
MEC: Mail Exchange Center
Maine Central (railroad)
Mercato Comune Europeo (European Common Market) (Italian) (EC)
MECO: Measurement and Control
MED: MEDIQ Inc. (ASE)
Medch: MedChem Products Inc. (newspaper)
Media: Media General Inc. (newspaper)
MEDIA: Measures to Encourage the Development of the Community Audiovisual Industry (EC)
Mediq: MEDIQ Inc. (newspaper)
MedPr: Medical Properties Inc. (newspaper)
MEDREP: Inventory of biomedical and health care research projects (EC)
Medtrn: Medtronic Inc. (newspaper)
meg: megabyte
MEG: Media General Inc. (ASE)
MEI: MEI Diversified Inc. (NYSE)
MEL: Mellon Bank Corp. (NYSE)
MELCO: Mitsubishi Electric Corporation (Japan)
MELCU: Multiple External Line Control Unit
Mellon: Mellon Bank Corp. (newspaper)
Melvill: Melville Corp. (newspaper)

mem: memorandum
memory
Mem: MEM Company Inc. (newspaper)
MEM: MEM Company Inc. (ASE)
MEMA: Motor and Equipment Manufacturers Association
ME/ME: Multiple Entry/Multiple Exit
memo: memorandum
MEMR: Memory Read
MEMSEL: Memory Select
MEMW: Memory Write
MEP: Member of the European Parliament (EC)
Microfiche Enlarger Printer
MEPA: Master of Engineering and Public Administration
MePS: Maine Public Service Co. (newspaper)
MER: Merrill Lynch & Company Inc. (NYSE)
merc: mercantile
MERCATOR: Information and Documentation on Minority Languages (EC)
Merck: Merck & Company Inc. (newspaper)
MercSL: Mercury S&L Assn. (newspaper)
MercSt: Mercantile Stores Company Inc. (newspaper)
Merdth: Meredith Corp. (newspaper)
MERLIN: Machine Readable Library Information
MerLyn: Merrill Lynch & Company Inc. (newspaper)
MERM: Multilateral Exchange Rate Model
Mermc: Merrimac Industries Inc. (newspaper)
MES: Melville Corp. (NYSE)
Metal Semiconductor
Multiple Earning Statement
MESA: Mining and Enforcement and Safety Administration
Modularized Equipment Storage Assembly
Mesab: Mesabi Trust (newspaper)
MesaLP: Mesa Limited Partnership (newspaper)
MesaOf: Mesa Offshore Trust (newspaper)
MesaR: Mesa Royalty Trust (newspaper)
mesg: message
MESOP: Management Enrichment Stock Ownership Plan
Mesrx: Measurex Corp. (newspaper)
Mestek: Mestek Inc. (newspaper)
MET: Management Engineering Team
METC: Medesto and Empire Traction Company
Metex: Metex Corp. (newspaper)
MetPro: Met-Pro Corp. (newspaper)
Metrbkj: Metrobank N.A. (California) (newspaper)
MetrFn: Metropolitan Financial Corp. (North Dakota) (newspaper)
MetRlt: Metropolitan Realty Corp. (newspaper)
MEU: Memory Expansion and Protection Unit
MEUA: Million European Units of Account (EC)
MEWT: Matrix Electrostatic Writing Technique
MEX: Mississippi Export (railroad)
MexFd: Mexico Fund Inc., The (newspaper)
mf: microfarad
MF: Malaysia Fund Inc., The (NYSE)
Master File
Medium Frequency
Middle Fork (railroad)
Mutual Fund
MFA: Multifibre (MultiFibre) Arrangements (EC)
MFBM: Thousand Feet, Board Measurement

MFC: Maritime Fruit Carriers (steamship)
Metropolitan Financial Corp. (North Dakota) (NYSE)
MFCA: Multifunction Communications Adapter
M&FCS: Management and Financial Control System
MFCU: Multifunction Card Unit
mfd: manufactured
MFD: Master File Directory
Munford Inc. (NYSE)
MFDSUL: Multifunction Data Set Utility Language
MFE: Multifunction Executive
MFF: Match Flip Flop
mfg: manufacturing
MFG: Message Flow Graph
MFI: Metal Fabricating Institute
MFLD: Message Field
MFLOPS: Million Floating Point Operations Per Second
MFLP: Multifile Linear Programming
MFM: MFS Municipal Income Trust (NYSE) (newspaper)
Modified Frequency Modulation
MFN: Most-Favored-Nation
MFO: MFS Income & Opportunity Trust (NYSE) (newspaper)
MFP: Multiform Printer
MFPC: Multifunction Protocol Converter
MFPE: Minimum Final Prediction Error
mfr: manufacture
manufactured
manufacturer
MFR: Multifrequency Receiver
MfrHan: Manufacturers Hanover Corp. (newspaper)
MFS: Message Format Services
MFSK: Multiple Frequency Shift Keying
MFSL: Mathematical and Functional Subroutine Library
mfst: manifest
MFT: Master of Foreign Trade
Metallic Facility Terminal
MFS Multimarket Total Return Trust (NYSE) (newspaper)
Most-Favorable-Terms
Mutiprogramming with a Fixed Number of Tasks
mg: milligram
M&G: Mobile & Gulf (railroad)
MG: Malta Airlines
Managerial Grid
Motor Generator
MGA: Monongahela (railway)
MGC: Morgan Grenfell SMALLCap Fund Inc. (NYSE)
MGD: Million Gallons per Day
MGG: Matrix Generator Generator
MGI: MGI Properties (NYSE)
MGI Prp: MGI Properties (newspaper)
MGM: MGM/UA Communications Co. (NYSE)
mgmt: management
MGMUA: MGM/UA Communications Co. (newspaper)
MGN: Morgan Products Ltd. (NYSE)
MGP: Merchants Group Inc. (ASE)
Multiple Goal Programming
mgr: manager
MGS: MacGregor Sporting Goods Inc. (ASE)
mgt: management
MGU: Mobile and Gulf (railroad)
MH: Air Manila (airline)
Materials Handling
Message Handler
MHC: Manufacturers Hanover Corp. (NYSE)
MHD: Moving Head Disk
MHE: Materials Handling Equipment
MHG: Malartic Hygrade Gold Mines Ltd. (Canada) (ASE)
MHI: Materials Handling Institute

MHI Gp: MHI Group Inc. (newspaper)
MHM: Mount Hope Mineral (railroad)
MHMA: Mobile Home Manufacturers Association
M&HMRR: Marquette and Huron Mountain Railroad
MHP: McGraw-Hill Inc. (NYSE)
Message Handling Processor
MHR: Machine Hour Rate
MHS: Marriott Corp. (NYSE)
Multiple Host Support
MHSDC: Multiple High Speed Data Channel
MHz: megahertz
mi: microinstruction
MI: Machine-Independent
Mackey International Air Commuter (airline)
Maintenance Interface
Marshall Industries (NYSE)
Maskable Interrupt
Memory Input Register
Memory Interface
Merit Increase
Minority Interest
Miscellaneous Income
Missouri-Illinois (railroad)
MIA: Multiplex Interface Adapter
MIAC: Marketing Information Analysis Center
MIACS: Manufacturing Information and Control System
MIAR: Microaddress Register
MIARS: Maintenance Information Automated Retrieval System
MIAS: Management Information and Accounting System
MIAT: Mean Interarrival Time
MIB: Marketing of Investments Board
Microinstruction Bus
MIBOR: Madrid Interbank Offered Rate
MIC: Management Investment Company
Military Industrial Complex
Mortgage Insurance Company
MICALL: Microprocedure Call
MichStr: Michaels Stores Inc. (newspaper)
Micklby: Mickelberry Corp. (newspaper)
MICO: Midland Continental (railroad)
MICOT: Minimum Completion Time
MICR: Magnetic Ink Character Recognition
micro: microcomputer
microprocessor
MICROM: Microinstruction Read Only Memory
micron: micrometer
Micron Products Inc. (newspaper)
MICROSIM: Microinstruction Simulator
MICS: Management Information and Control System
micsim: microsimulator
MID: Message Input Description
Midway (railroad)
MidAM: Mid-America Industries Inc. (newspaper)
MIDAR: Microdiagnostics for Analysis and Repair
MIDAS: Digital Stimulated Analog Computing program
Management Interactive Data Accounting System
Memory Implement Data Acquisition Systems
Microprogrammable Integrated Data Acquisition System
MIDDLE: Microprogram Design and Description Language
MIDEF: Microprocedure Definition
Midlby: Middleby Corp. (newspaper)
Midlnd: Midland Co., The (newspaper)

MIDMS: Machine Independent Data Management System
MIDS: Management Information and Decision System
Mode Indicator Levels
Multimode Information Distribution System
MidSUt: Middle South Utilities Inc. (newspaper)
MIE: Master of Industrial Engineering
Military-Industrial Establishment
MIF: Master Index File
MuniInsured Fund Inc. (ASE)
MIG: Moody's Investment Grade
MIGET: Miniature Interface General-Purpose Economy Terminal
MIH: Missing Interruption Handler
Multiplex Interface Handler
MII: McLean Industries Inc. (NYSE)
MIKADOS: Mini Instant Keyboard Assembler, Debug and Operating System
mil: One thousandth of an inch
MIL: Microimplementation Language
Millipore Corp. (NYSE)
Module Interconnection Language
MILI: Micronesia Interocean Line Incorporated (steamship)
Millipre: Millipore Corp. (newspaper)
MILR: Master of Industrial Relations
MiltnR: Milton Roy Co. (newspaper)
MILW: Chicago, Milwaukee, St. Paul and Pacific (railroad)
MIM: Modem Interface Module
MIMD: Multiple Instruction, Multiple Data
MIMOLA: Machine Independent Microprogramming Language
min: minimum
minority
minute
MIN: MFS Intermediate Income Trust (NYSE) (newspaper)
MIND: Modular Interactive Network Designer
MINDD: Minimum Due Date
MINE: Minneapolis Eastern (railway)
mini: minicomputer
MINI: Minicomputer Industry National Interchange
MINIT: Minimum Idle Time
MinnPl: Minnesota Power & Light Co. (newspaper)
MINOS: Modular Input/Output System
MINSD: Minimum Planned Start Date
MINSOP: Minimum Slack Time Per Operation
MINTS: Mutual Institutions National Transfer System
MIN WT: Minimum Weight
MIO: Multiple Input/Output
MIOP: Multiplexer Input/Output Processor
MIOS: Metal Insulator Oxide Silicon
Modular Input/Output System
MIP: Marine Insurance Policy
Material In Process
Mixed Integer Programming
Monthly Investment Plan
Mortgage Insurance Premium
Mortgage Investments Plus Inc. (ASE)
Multipurpose Information Processor
MIPAS: Management Information Planning and Accountancy Service
MIPS: Million Instructions Per Second

MIR: M.D.C. Asset Investors Inc. (NYSE)
Memory Input Register
Microinstruction Register
MIRA: Motor Industry Research Association
MIRAC: Master Index Remote Access Capability
MIRAS: Mortgage Interest Relief At Source
MIRR: Material Inspection and Retrieval Report
MIS: Management Information Service
Management Information System
Marketing Information System
Merchandise Information Systems
Metal-Insulator-Semiconductor
Moody's Investor Service
MISAM: Multiple Index Sequential Access Method
misc: miscellaneous
MISD: Multiple Instruction, Single Data
MISE: Mean Integrated Square Error
MISER: Minimum Size Executive Routines
MIS-MDS: Multiple Instruction Streams-Multiple Data Streams
MIS-SDS: Multiple Instruction Streams-Single Data Streams
MISSION: Manufacturing Information System Support Integrated Online
MissnW: Mission West Properties (newspaper)
MISTI: Multipurpose International Securities Trading Information
MISTR: Management Items Subject To Repair
MIT: Market-If-Touched order
Master Instruction Tape
Modern Investment Theory
Modular Intelligent Terminal
Municipal Investment Trust
MITA: Microcomputer Industry Trade Association
MITE: Microprocessor Industrial Terminal
Mitel: Mitel Corp. (newspaper)
MITI: Ministry of International Trade and Industry (Japan)
MITROPA: Mitteleuropaische Schlaf und Speiswagen (Middle-European Sleeping Car and Dining Car)
MITS: Management Information and Text System
MITSUI: Mitsui OSK Lines (steamship)
MIU: Modem Interface Unit
MIV: MassMutual Income Investors Inc. (NYSE)
MIW: Microinstruction Word
MIX: Microprogram Index Register
MJ: Manufacturers' Junction (railway)
SMB State Lines (airline)
MJD: Management Job Description
MJMT: Mean Job Mill Time
MJSD: March, June, September, December (securities)
mk: marks
mask
MK: Air Mauritius (airline)
MKC: Marion Merrill Dow Laboratories Inc. (NYSE)
McKeesport Connecting (railroad)
mkd: marked
MKE: Michaels Stores Inc. (ASE)
MKH: Multiple Key Hashing
mkr: maker
MKS: Meter-Kilogram-Second
mkt: market
marketing

MKT: Missouri-Kansas-Texas (railroad)
ml: multileaving
M&L: Matched and Lost
ML: Machine Language
Malaysia-Singapore Airlines
Manchester Liners (steamship)
Martin Marietta Corp. (NYSE)
Maximum Likelihood
Memory Location
Microprogramming Language
Migrant Labor
MLA: Matching Logic and Adder
Midland Co., The (ASE)
Multiple Line Adapter
Mutual Loan Association
MLB: Maritime Labor Board
Multilayer Board
MLC: Magnetic Ledger Card
Manhattan National Corp. (NYSE)
Microprogram Location Counter
Multilayer Ceramic
Multiline Controller
MLCP: Multiline Communications Processor
MLCU: Magnetic Ledger Card Unit
MLD: Machine Language Debugger
Midland Railway of Manitoba
MLE: Maximum Likelihood Estimate (Estimation)
MLFS: Master Library File System
MLI: Machine Language Instruction
Multileaving Interface
MLIA: Multiplex Loop Interface Adapter
MLIM: Matrix Log-In Memory
MLL: Macmillan Inc. (NYSE)
MLM: Multileaving Line Manager
Multilevel Merchandise (Merchandiser)
MLP: Machine Language Program
Master Limited Partnership
Mesa Limited Partnership (NYSE)
MLPA: Modified Link Pack Area
MLR: Minimum Lending Rate
MLRC: Multilevel Rail Car
MLRTP: Multileaving Remote Terminal Processor
M&LS: Manistique & Lake Superior (railroad)
MLS: Microprocessor Line Set
MLT: Mitel Corp. (NYSE)
MLTA: Multiple Line Terminal Adapter
MLU: Memory Logic Unit
Multiple Logical Unit
mm: millimeter
M&M: Merchants and Manufacturers Association
MM: Main Memory
Maintenance Manual
Mass Memory
Master Mechanic
Materials Measurement
Memory Module
Messageries Maritimes (French) (steamship)
Middle Management
Money Market
Sociedad Aeronautica Medellin (airline)
MMA: Major Maintenance Availability
Management and Marketing Abstracts
Medical Management of America Inc. (ASE)
Multiple Module Access
MMAR: Main Memory Address Register
MMAS: Manufacturing Management Accounting Systems
MMB: Multiport Memory Bank
MMC: Main Memory Controller
Marsh & McLennan Companies Inc. (NYSE)
Money Market Certificate
Multiport Memory Controller

MMCA: Message-Mode Communications Adapter
MMCC: MultiMini Computer Compiler
MMD: Moore Medical Corp. (ASE)
MMDA: Money Market Deposit Account
MMDDYY: Designation of six character date field (month, day, and year)
MMDS: Multichannel Multipoint Distribution Service
MME: Master of Mechanical Engineering
Master of Mining Engineering
MMed: Moore Medical Corp. (newspaper)
MMF: Magnetomotive Force
Money Market Fund
MMH/OH: Maintenance Man-Hours per Operating Hour
MMI: Main Memory Interface
Man-Machine Interface
Multimessage Interface
Multiport Memory Interface
MMIS: Maintenance Management Information System
MMIU: Multiport Memory Interface Unit
MMM: Main Memory Module
Man-Machine Model
Minnesota Mining & Manufacturing Co. (NYSE) (newspaper)
Monolithic Main Memory
Multiport Memory Multiplexer
MMMC: Minimum Monthly Maintenance Charge
MMO: Monarch Machine Tool Co., The (NYSE)
MMOS: Message Multiplexer Operating System
MMP: Main Microprocessor
Multiple Microprocessors
MMPS: Manufacturing Material Planning System
MMPU: Memory Management and Protection Unit
MMR: Main Memory Register
Memory Management Register
Moscow Metro Railway
Multiple Match Resolver
MMS: Man-Machine System
Memory Management System
MMSE: Minimum Mean-Squared Error
MMSW: Mine, Mill and Smelter Workers (union)
MMT: MFS Multimarket Income Trust (NYSE) (newspaper)
MMU: Main Memory Unit
Memory Management Unit
Memory Mapping Unit
Million Monetary Units
mn: mnemonic
M&N: May and November (securities)
MN: Commercial Airways
Message Number
MNA: Multishare Network Architecture
MNC: Mediterranean Non-Candidates (EC)
Multinational Corporation
MNCS: Multipoint Network Control System
MND: Mitchell Energy & Development Corp. (ASE)
MNDP: Multinational Data Processing
mne: mnemonic
M&NE: Manistee & Northeastern (railroad)
MNE: Multi-National Enterprise
MNET: Measuring Network
M&NF: Morehead and North Fork (railroad)
MNF: Multisystem Networking Facility

mnfrs: manufacturers
mng: managing
MNH: Manufactured Homes Inc. (ASE)
MNI: McClatchy Newspapers Inc. (ASE)
MNJ: Middletown and New Jersey (railway)
MNOS: Metal-Nitride Silicon device
MNR: Manor Care Inc. (NYSE)
Maximum Number of Records
MN&S: Minneapolis, Northfield and Southern (railroad)
MNS: MacNeal-Schwendler Corp., The (ASE)
MNT: Montedison S.p.A. (NYSE)
mo: microoperation
month
M&O: Management and Organization
MO: Mail Order
Manually Operated
Memory Output
Money Order
Montreal Stock Exchange listings (in newspapers)
Moral Obligation
Philip Morris Companies Inc. (NYSE)
MOAT: Methods of Appraisal and Test
MOB: Mobil Corp. (NYSE)
Montreux-Oberland-Bernois (railway)
Mobil: Mobil Corp. (newspaper)
MobIC: Mobile Communications Corporation of America (newspaper)
MOC: Management-Oriented Computing
mod: model
modification
modulate
MOD: Message Output Description
MODAC: Modular Data Acquisition
MODACS: Modular Data Acquisition and Control Subsystem
MODE: Merchant-Oriented Data Entry
MODEM: Modulator-Demodulator
MODI: Modular Optical Digital Interface
MODUS: Modular One Dynamic User System
MOE: Measure of Effectiveness
Multiple Of Earnings
MOF: Ministry of Finance (Japan)
MOG: Moog Inc. (ASE)
MOH: Mohasco Corp. (NYSE)
MOHOL: Machine-Oriented Higher Order Language
Mohsc: Mohasco Corp. (newspaper)
MOL: Machine-Oriented Language
MOLE: Market Odd-Lot Execution system
MOM: Maintenance Of Membership
mon: monitor
MON: Monarch Capital Corp. (NYSE)
Monon (railroad)
MonCa: Monarch Capital Corp. (newspaper)
MONGEN: Monitor Generator
MONITOR: Strategic Analyses, Forecasting and Evaluation in Matters of Research and Technology (EC)
MonPw: Montana Power Co., The (newspaper)
Monrch: Monarch Machine Tool Co., The (newspaper)
MON RYS: Mongolian Railways
Monsan: Monsanto Co. (newspaper)
MonSt: Montgomery Street Income Securities Inc. (newspaper)
Monted: Montedison S.p.A. (newspaper)
MONY: MONY Real Estate Investors (newspaper)

Mutual Life Insurance Company of New York
Moog: Moog Inc. (newspaper)
Moore: Moore Corporation Ltd. (newspaper)
MOP: Margin Of Profit
Missouri Pacific (railroad)
MOPP: Mechanization of Planning Processes
MOPS: Mechanization Outside Plant Scheduling System
Million Operations Per Second
MOR: Management by Objectives and Results
Memory Output Register
Morgan Keegan Inc. (NYSE)
Morgan: J. P. Morgan & Company Inc. (newspaper)
MorgG: Morgan Grenfell SMALL-Cap Fund Inc. (newspaper)
MorgnF: Morgan's Foods Inc. (newspaper)
MorgnP: Morgan Products Ltd. (newspaper)
MorgSt: Morgan Stanley Group Inc. (newspaper)
MORIF: Microprogram Optimization Technique Considering Resource Occupancy and Instruction Formats
MorKeg: Morgan Keegan Inc. (newspaper)
MorKnd: Morrison Knudsen Corp. (newspaper)
Morton: Morton Thiokol Inc. (newspaper)
mos: months
MOS: Management Operating Systems
Manufacturing Operating Systems
Margin Of Safety
Memory Oriented System
Mesa Offshore Trust (NYSE)
Metal-Oxide Semiconductor
Microprogram Operating System
Multiprogramming Operating System
MOSFET: Metal Oxide Semiconductor Field Effect Transistor
MOS ROM: Metal-Oxide Semiconductor Read-Only Memory
MOSS: Market Oversight Surveillance System
MOST: Management Operation System Technique
Modular Office System Terminal
MOT: Motorola Inc. (NYSE)
MOTA: Mail Order Traders Association
Motel: Motel 6 LP (newspaper)
Motorla: Motorola Inc. (newspaper)
Motts: Mott's Super Markets Inc. (newspaper)
MOU: Memorandum Of Understanding
MOUTH: Modular Output Unit for Talking to Humans
mov: move
MOV: Moshassuck Valley (railroad)
MOW: Montana Western (railway)
M&P: Maryland & Pennsylvania (railroad)
mp: microprocessor
microprogram
multiprocessing
multiprocessor
MP: Mail Payment
Market Price
Mass Production
Master Plan
Mathematical Programming
McIntyre Mines Ltd. (NYSE)
Missouri Pacific (railroad)
MPA: Maryland and Pennsylvania (railroad)
Master of Public Accounting

Master of Public Administration
Multiple Peripheral Adapter

MPACT: Microprocessor Application to Control-Firmware Translator

MPAR: Microprogram Address Register

MPB: Montpelier and Barre (railroad)

MPC: Marginal Propensity to Consume
Microprogram Control
Microprogram Counter
Modular Peripheral Interface Converter

MPCC: Microprogrammable Communications Controller
Multiprotocol Communications Controller

MPCI: Multiport Programmable Communications Interface

MPCM: Microprogram Control Memory

MPCR: Microprogram Count Register

MPD: Missing Pulse Detector

MPDS: Market Price Display Service (London Stock Exchange) (UK)
Message Processing and Distribution System

MPE: Maximum Permitted Error
Memory Parity Error

MPES: Multiprogramming Executive System

MPF: Manufacturing Progress Function

MPGS: Microprogram Generating System

MPI: Marginal Propensity to Invest
Medical Payments Insurance
Microprocessor Interface

MPL: Macroprocedure Language
Message Processing Language
Microprogramming Language
Minnesota Power & Light Co. (NYSE)
Multischedule Private Line

mplx: multiplexer

mplxr: multiplexer

MPN: Most Probable Number

MPP: Medical Properties Inc. (ASE)
Message Processing Program
Multiple-Product Pricing

MPPR: Manitous and Pike's Peak Railway

MPR: Met-Pro Corp. (ASE)

MPS: Management Planning System
Marginal Propensity to Save
Multiprocessing System
Multiprogramming System

MPT: Modern Portfolio Theory

MPU: Microprocessing Unit

mpx: multiplexer

mpy: multiplier

M&R: Maintainability and Reliability
Maintainability and Repairs
Maintenance and Repair

MR: Air Mauritanie (airline)
Maintenance Report
Manufacturer's Representative
Marginal Revenue
Market Ratio
Mask Register
McCloud River (railroad)
Memorandum Report
Morgan's Foods Inc. (ASE)
Multiple Regression

M of R: Ministry of Railways (mainland China)

MRA: Malayan Railway Administration
Materials Requirement Analysis

MRC: Machine Readable Code
Milton Roy Co. (NYSE)

MrchGp: Merchants Group Inc. (newspaper)

MRDF: Machine Readable Data File

MRI: McRae Industries Inc. (ASE)

MRK: Merck & Company Inc. (NYSE)
MRL: Malawi Railways Limited
MRLE: Monthly Report of the Labor Force
MRM: Merrimac Industries Inc. (ASE)
MRN: Morrison Knudsen Corp. (NYSE)
MRO: Maintenance, Repair and Operating (Operational)
MRP: Manufacturing Resources Planning
Material Requirements Planning
Mission Resource Partners LP (ASE)
MRR: Mattagami Railroad
Mossi Railroad
MRS: Manufacturers Railway
Mrshln: Marshall Industries (newspaper)
MrshMc: Marsh & McLennan Companies Inc. (newspaper)
MRT: Maximum-Repair-Time
Mean-Repair-Time
Mortgage & Realty Trust (NYSE)
MrthOf: Marathon Office Supply Inc. (newspaper)
MRY: Malayan Railway
ms: millisecond
M&S: March and September (securities)
Materials and Services
MS: Main Storage
Maintenance and Service
Majority Stock (Stockholders)
Major Stockholder
Management Science
March and September (securities)
Margin of Safety
Mass Storage
Material Specification
Merit System
Metric System
Minority Stockholder
Money Supply
Months after Sight
Morgan Stanley Group Inc. (NYSE)
United Arab Airlines
MSA: Malaysia-Singapore Airlines
MSA Realty Corp. (newspaper)
MSACHA: Mid-South Automated Clearing House Association
MSAE: Master of Science in Aeronautical Engineering
MSAM: Master of Science in Applied Mechanics
MSB: Mesabi Trust (NYSE)
Most-Significant Bit
Mutual Savings Bank
MSBA: Master of Science in Business Administration
MSBY: Most Significant Byte
MSC: Material Sciences Corp. (ASE)
Mississippi Central (railroad)
Multisystem Coupling
MSCE: Master of Science in Civil Engineering
MS CO: Melbourne Steamship Company
MSD: Most Significant Digit
MSE: Master of Science in Engineering
Mexican Stock Exchange
Midwest Stock Exchange
Mississippi Export (railroad)
msec: millisecond
MSEE: Master of Science in Electrical Engineering
MSEL: Master Scenario Events List
MSEM: Master of Science in Engineering Mechanics
Master of Science in Engineering of Mines
msg: message
MSHA: Master of Science in Hospital Administration

Mine Safety and Health Administration

Mshp: Machine Shop

MSHP: Maintain System History Program

MSI: Medium Scale Integration
MSI Data Corp. (ASE)

MSI Dt: MSI Data Corp. (newspaper)

MSIE: Master of Science in Industrial Engineering

MSL: Mercury S&L Assn. (NYSE)
Minneapolis & St. Louis (railroad)

MSM: Mott's Super Markets Inc. (ASE)

MSME: Master of Science in Mechanical Engineering

MsmRs: Mission Resource Partners LP (newspaper)

MSOS: Mass Storage Operating System

MSP&SSM: Minneapolis, St. Paul & Sault Ste. Marie (railroad)

MSR: MSR Exploration Ltd. (ASE) (newspaper)

MSRB: Municipal Securities Rulemaking Board

MSS: Mass Storage System

MSSE: Master of Science in Sanitary Engineering

mssg: message

MST: Master Station
Mercantile Stores Company Inc. (NYSE)
Mountain Standard Time

MSTL: Minneapolis-St. Louis (railroad)

MSTR: Massena Terminal Railroad

MSTS: Military Sea Transportation Service

MSU: Middle South Utilities Inc. (NYSE)

M&SV: Mississippi & Skuna Valley (railroad)

MSW: Mission West Properties (ASE)

MT: Machine Translation
Magnetic Tape
Maximum Total
Midland Terminal (railroad)
Mountain Time

MTA: Miller-Tydings Act

MTBCD: Mean-Time-Between-Confirmed-Defects

MTBCF: Mean-Time-Between-Component-Failure

MTBD: Mean-Time-Between-Defects

MTBF: Mean-Time-Between-Failures

MTBM: Mean-Time-Between Maintenance

MTBO: Mean-Time-Between-Overhauls

MTBR: Mean-Time-Between-Repairs

MTBSF: Mean-Time-Between-Significant-Failures

MTBUM: Mean-Time-Between Unscheduled-Maintenance

MTBUR: Mean-Time-Between Unscheduled-Removal

MTC: Maintenance Time Constraint
Milwaukee Transport Company
Monsanto Co. (NYSE)
Montreal Transportation Commission
Mystic Terminal Company

MtchlE: Mitchell Energy & Development Corp. (newspaper)

MTF: Mean-Time-to-Failure

MTFR: Minnesota Transfer Railroad

mtg: mortgage

mtgd: mortgaged

mtge: mortgage

mtgee: mortgagee

mtgor: mortgagor

MtgPl: Mortgage Investments Plus Inc. (newspaper)

MtgRty: Mortgage & Realty trust (newspaper)
MTH: Mount Hood (railway)
mthly: monthly
MTI: Morton Thiokol Inc. (NYSE)
MTIRA: Machine Tool Industry Research Association
MTL: Materials Research Corp. (ASE)
MTM: Methods-Time Measurement
MtMed: Mountain Medical Equipment Inc. (newspaper)
MTN: Mountain Medical Equipment Inc. (ASE)
MTNs: Medium-Term Notes
Multinational Trade Negotiations
MTO: Made-To-Order
MTP: Montana Power Co., The (NYSE)
mtr: monitor
MTR: Mesa Royalty Trust (NYSE)
Montour Railroad
MTS: Manned Teller System
Member-Technical Staff
Message Telecommunication Service
Montgomery Street Income Securities Inc. (NYSE)
Monthly Treasury Statement
MTSF: Mean-Time-To-System-Failure
MTTF: Mean-Time-To-Failure
MTTFF: Mean-Time-To-First-Failure
MTTFSF: Mean-Time-To-First-System-Failure
MTTFSR: Mean-Time-To-First-System-Repair
MTTOP: Machine Tool Trigger Order Program
MTTR: Maximum Time to Repair
Mean-Time-To-Repair
Mean-Time-To-Restore
MTTSF: Mean-Time-To-System-Failure
MTU: Magnetic Tape Unit
MTUR: Mean-Time-To-Unscheduled-Replacement
MTW: Management Teamwork
Marinetee, Tomahawk and Western (railroad)
MTWCR: Mt. Washington Cog Railway
MTX: Metex Corp. (ASE)
mty: empty
MTY: Marlton Technologies Inc. (ASE)
MU: Memory Unit
Misair (airline)
Multiple Unit
MUF: Material Unaccounted For
Maximum Usable Frequency
Munivest Fund Inc. (ASE)
mul: multiplexer
MUL: Master Urgency List
mult: multiplier
MUM: Methodology for Unmanned Manufacturing
mun: municipal
MUN: Munsingwear Inc. (NYSE)
Munfrd: Munford Inc. (newspaper)
MUNI: Municipal Bond(s)
munic: municipal
MunIn: MuniInsured Fund Inc. (newspaper)
Munsng: Munsingwear Inc. (newspaper)
Munvst: Munivest Fund Inc. (newspaper)
MUO: Mutual of Omaha Interest Shares Inc. (NYSE)
MUP: Make-Up Pay
MUR: Murphy Oil Corp. (NYSE)
MurpO: Murphy Oil Corp. (newspaper)
MurryO: Murry Ohio Manufacturing Co. (newspaper)
Muscld: Musicland Group Inc., The (newspaper)
MutOm: Mutual of Omaha Interest Shares Inc. (newspaper)

mux: multiplexer
mV: millivolt
MV: Macrobertson Miller Airlines
Market Value
McFaddin Ventures Inc. (ASE)
Mean Variation
Midland Valley (railroad)
Motor Vehicle
MVMA: Motor Vehicles Manufacturers Association
MVT: Multiprogramming with a variable number of tasks
MW: Matthews & Wright Group Inc. (ASE)
Maya Airways
Migrant Worker
Minimum Wage
Minnesota Western (railroad)
Montana Western (railroad)
Montgomery Ward
MWE: Midwest Energy Co. (NYSE) (newspaper)
MWR: Muncie and Western Railroad
MX: Measurex Corp. (NYSE)
MXC: MATEC Corp. (ASE)
Multiplexer Channel
MXF: Mexico Fund Inc., The (NYSE)
MXM: MAXXAM Group Inc. (NYSE)
MXP: MaxPharma Inc. (ASE)
MXS: Maxus Energy Corp. (NYSE)
MY: Air Mali (airline)
MYE: Myers Industries Inc. (ASE)
Myerl: Myers Industries Inc. (newspaper)
MyerL: L. E. Meyers Company Group, The (newspaper)
MYG: Maytag Co., The (NYSE)
MYL: Mylan Laboratories Inc. (NYSE)
Mylan: Mylan Laboratories Inc. (newspaper)
Mylex: Mylex Corp. (newspaper)
MYM: MONY Real Estate Investors (NYSE)
MYO: Murry Ohio Manufacturing Co. (NYSE)
MYOB: Mind Your Own Business
MYR: L. E. Myers Company Group, The (NYSE)
MZ: Merpati Nusantara Airlines
M-ZONE: Manufacturing Zone

N

n: nano
negative
new
node
note
number
numeric

N: Inco Ltd. (NYSE)
New issue (stock listings of newspapers)

N/A: Name and Address

NA: National Airlines
National Association
Net Assets
New Account
No Account
No Action
No Advice
No Approval required
No Assets
Northern Alberta (railroad)
Nostro Account
Not Applicable
Not Appropriated
Not Authorized
Not Available

NAA: National Association of Accountants
Not Always Afloat

NAACPA: National Association of Asian American Certified Public Accountants

NAABSA: Not Always Afloat but Safe Aground

NAAD: National Association of Aluminum Distributors

NAAI: National Association of Accountants in Insolvencies

NAAIS: North American Association of Inventory Services

NAAN: National Advertising Agency Network

NAB: National Australia Bank Ltd. (NYSE)
Newspaper Advertising Bureau

NABA: National Association of Black Accountants

NABAC: National Association of Bank Auditors and Comptrollers

NABB: National Association of Business Brokers

NABCA: National Association for Bank Cost Analysis

NABET: National Association of Broadcast Engineers and Technicians

NABIS: National Association of Business and Industrial Saleswomen

NABM: National Association of Black Manufacturers
National Association of British Manufacturers

NABS: National Association of Business Services

NABW: National Association of Bank Women

NABWE: National Association of Black Women Entrepreneurs

NAC: National Airways Corporation (New Zealand) (airline)
Network Access Controller
New American Community
North Atlantic Coast

NACA: National Association of Cost Accountants

NACBFAA: National Association of Customs Brokers and Forwarders Association of America
NACCO: NACCO Industries Inc. (newspaper)
NACD: National Association of Corporate Directors
NACE: Nomenclature Générale des Activités Économique des Communautés (General Nomenclature of Economic Activities with the Community) (French) (EC)
NACH: Need for Achievement
NACHA: National Automated Clearing House Association
NACIS: National Credit Information Service
NACM: National Association of Credit Management
NACMB: National Association of Certified Mortgage Bankers
NACS: National Association for Check Safekeeping
NACSA: National Association of Casualty and Surety Executives
NACT: National Association of Chapter 13 Trustees
National Association of Corporate Treasurers
NACTP: National Association of Computerized Tax Processors
NAD: No Apparent Defect
NADA: National Automobile Dealers' Association
NADUG: National Data Manager Users' Group
NAE: National Academy of Engineering
NAEA: National Association of Estate Agents
NAEBM: National Association of Engine and Boat Manufacturers
NAES: National Association of Executive Secretaries
NAF: NAFCO Financial Group Inc. (NYSE)
National Association of Foremen
National Association of Independent Computer Companies
Nonappropriated Funds
NAFA: Net Acquisition of Financial Assets
NAFA: Nonappropriate Fund Activity
NAFBO: National Association for Business Organizations
NAFC: National Association of Food Chains
NAFCO: NAFCO Financial Group Inc. (newspaper)
National Airways and Finance Corporation (South Africa)
NAFE: National Association for Free Enterprise
NAFF: Need for Affiliation
NAFIN: Nacional Financiera (Mexico)
NAFMIS: Nonappropriated Funds Management Information System
NAFPB: National Association of Freight Payment Banks
NAFSONW: Nonappropriated Fund Statement of Operations and Net Worth
NAFTZ: National Association of Foreign-Trade Zones
NA&G: North Atlantic and Gulf Steamship Company
NAG: Net Annual Gain
NAHB: National Association of Home Builders

NAI: Net Annual Inflow
No Action Indicated

NAIA: National Association of Insurance Agents

NAIC: National Association of Investment Clubs

NAICC: National Association of Independent Companies

NAII: National Association of Independent Insurers

NAJ: Napierville Junction (railway)

NAK: Negative Acknowledge character

NAL: New Assembly Language
Norwegian American Line (steamship)

NALC: National Association of Letter Carriers

Nalco: Nalco Chemical Co. (newspaper)

NAM: National Association of Manufacturers
Network Access Machine

NAMA: National Automatic Merchandising Association

NAMAC: National Association of Merger and Acquisition Consultants

NAMB: National Association of Mortgage Brokers

NAMC: National Association of Minority Contractors

NAMF: National Association of Metal Finishers

NAMP: National Association of Meat Purveyors

NAMSB: National Association of Mutual Savings Banks

NAN: Nantucket Industries Inc. (ASE)
Network Application Node

NAND: Not-And

Nantck: Nantucket Industries Inc. (newspaper)

NAO: National Audit Office

NAP: Narragansett Pier (railroad)
Network Access Pricing
Network Access Protocol
Noise Analysis Program

NAPA: National Association of Purchasing Agents

NAPD: National Association for Personnel Directors

NAPE: National Association of Private Enterprise

NAPF: National Association of Pension Funds

NAPM: National Association of Purchasing Management

NAR: National Association of Realtors
No Action Required
Northern Alberta Railways
Northern Australia Railway

NARA: National Archives and Records Administration

NAREB: National Association of Real Estate Boards

NARI: National Association of Recycling Industries

NARM: National Association of Record Merchandisers

NARUC: National Association of Regulatory Utility Commissioners

NAS: Nasta International Inc. (ASE)
National Academy of Sciences
Non-Assessable Stock

NASA: National Aeronautics and Space Administration
National Association of Securities Administrators

NASAA: North American Securities Administrators Association

NASBIC: National Association of Small Business Investment Companies

NASBP: National Association of Surety Bond Producers

NASD: National Association of Securities Dealers
NASDAQ: National Association of Securities Dealers' Automated Quotations
NASDIM: National Association of Security Dealers and Investment Managers
Nashua: Nashua Corp. (newspaper)
NASS: National Association of Steel Stockholders
Nasta: Nasta International Inc. (newspaper)
nat: national
NAT: No Action Taken
NATA: North American Telephone Association
NatEdu: National Education Corp. (newspaper)
NATEX: National Stock Exchange (defunct)
NatFG: National Fuel Gas Co. (newspaper)
NATIONAL: National Airlines
natl: national
NATS: Negative Authorization Terminal System
NAU: Network Addressable Unit
NAV: Navistar International Corp. (NYSE)
Net Asset Value
Navistr: Navistar International Corp. (newspaper)
NAW: National Association of Wholesalers
NB: Narrow Band
National Bank
Navibel (Belgian Maritime Navigation Company)
Newport Air Park (airline)
No Bid (Bidder)
Northampton and Bath (railroad)
NBA: National Bankers Association
National Banking Association
National Bankruptcy Act
NBB: New Bedford Institutions for Savings (NYSE)
NBBS: National Better Business Bureau
NB&C: Norfolk, Baltimore and Carolina Line (steamship)
NBC: National Broadcasting Company
NBCD: Natural Binary Coded Decimal
NBD: NBD Bancorp Inc. (NYSE) (newspaper)
NBER: National Bureau of Economic Research
NBFA: National Business Forms Association
NBFI: Non-Bank Financial Intermediary
NBFM: Narrow Band Frequency Modulation
NBFS: New Balanced File Organization Scheme
NBNC: Noted But Not Corrected
NBPM: Narrow Band Phase Modulation
NBI: National BankAmericard Incorporated
NBI Inc. (NYSE) (newspaper)
NBL: Noble Affiliates Inc. (NYSE)
NBMS: National Bulk Mail System
nbr: number
NBR: Net Borrowing Requirement
Non-Borrowed Reserve
NBS: National Bureau of Standards (defunct) (now NIST)
Numeric Backspace character
NBSS: National Bank Surveillance System
NBU: National Billing Unit
NBV: Net Book Value
nc: non-callable
NC: NACCO Industries Inc. (NYSE)
Narrow Coverage
Net Capital
Net Cost

Network Control
No Charge
No Connection
Normally Closed
North Central Airlines
Numerical Control

NCA: Noise Control Act
Non-Contractual Authorization
Nuveen California Municipal Value Fund Inc. (NYSE)

NCAM: Network Communication Access Method

NCB: NCNB Corp. (NYSE)
Network Control Block
Non-Callable Bond

NCC: National Clearing Corporation
National Computer Center

NCCB: National Consumer Cooperative Bank

NCCF: Network Communications Control Facility

NCD: Negotiable Certificate of Deposit
No Claims Discount
Non-Cumulative Dividend
North Canadian Oils Ltd. (ASE)
Notice of Credit Due

NCdO: North Canadian Oils Ltd. (newspaper)

NCDS: Numerical Control Distribution System

NCE: Network Connection Element

NCEFT: National Commission on Electronic Funds Transfer

NCF: NCF Financial Corp. (newspaper)
Net Cash Flow

NCFA: National Consumers Finance Association

NCH: NCH Corp. (NYSE) (newspaper)
Network Connection Handler

N CHG: Normal Charge

NCI: New Community Instrument (EC)
No Common Interest
No-Cost Item
No Currency Involved
Non-Coded Information

NCIC: National Construction Industry Council

NCITD: National Committee on International Trade Documentation

NCL: Network Control Language
S. E. Nichols Inc. (ASE)

NCM: Nederlandsche Credietverzekering Maatschappij
Nuveen California Municipal Income Fund (NYSE)

NCMA: National Contract Management Association

NCMT: Numerical Control of Machine Tools

NCN: Network Control Node

NCNB: NCNB Corp. (newspaper)

NCO: Number Controlled Oscillator

NCP: Naviera Chilena del Pacifico (Chilean Shipping Company)
Network Control Program

NCR: National Cash Register
NCR Corp. (NYSE) (newspaper)

NCS: National Convenience Stores Inc. (NYSE)
Non-Callable Securities

NC&SL: Nashville, Chattanooga & St. Louis (railroad)

NCT: National Chamber of Trade
Non-Competitive Tenders

NCU: Number Crunching Unit

NCUA: National Credit Union Administration

NCV: No Commercial Value
No Core Value

ND: National Debt
Net Debt
New Deal
Next Day (newspaper)

No Date
No Defects
No Discount
Nordair (airline)
Not Dated

NDAC: Not Data Accepted
NDAM: New Disk Access Method
NDB: Net Debit Balance
NDBMS: Network Data Base Management System
NDC: Network Diagnostic Control
No Direct Charge
Normalized Device Coordinates
NDD: Non-Delivery Diagnostic
NDF: No Defect Found
Non-Deterministic FORTRAN
NDI: Nuclear Data Inc. (ASE)
NDIR: Non-Dispersive Infrared
NDLC: Network Data Link Control
NDMS: Network Design and Management System
NDP: Net Domestic Product
NDR: Non-Destructive Read
NDRO: Non-Destructive Readout
NDS: Network Data Series
NDT: Network Description Table
NE: Net Earnings
Northeast Airlines
Not Equal (to)
NEA: National Electronics Association
Northeast Airlines
NEACH: New England Automated Clearing House Association
NEAT: National Electronic Autocoding Technique
NEB: Bank of New England Corp. (NYSE)
NEBA: New England Bankcard Association
NEC: National Education Corp. (NYSE)
National Electrical Code
Not Elsewhere Classified
NECA: National Electrical Contractors Association
NECO: NECO Enterprises Inc. (newspaper)
NED: No Expiration Date
NEE: New England Express (steamship)
NEF: Noise Equivalent Flux
neg: negative
negb: negotiable
Neg Inst: Negotiable Instrument
negl: negligence
NEGTAX: Negative (income) Tax
NEI: National Enterprises Inc. (NYSE)
Not Elsewhere Indicated
NeimM: Neiman-Marcus Group Inc., The (newspaper)
NelsnH: Nelson Holdings International Ltd. (newspaper)
NEM: Newmont Mining Corp. (NYSE)
NEMA: National Electronics Manufacturers' Association
NEMS: National Exchange Market System
NeMtge: NorthEastern Mortgage Company Inc. (newspaper)
NEngEl: New England Electric System (newspaper)
NEP: New Economic Plan (Policy) (Soviet Union)
NEPA: National Environmental Policy Act
NER: NERCO Inc. (NYSE)
Nerco: NERCO Inc. (newspaper)
NES: New England Electric System (NYSE)
Not Elsewhere Specified
NestSv: Northeast Savings F.A. (newspaper)
net: network
NET: Next European Torus (EC)
North European Oil Royalty Trust (NYSE)
Not Earlier Than

NETA: New England Telecommunications Association
NETCON: Network Control
NETGEN: Network Generation
NETOP: Network Operator Process
NETS: Nebraska Electronic Transfer System
NETSET: Network Synthesis & Evaluation Technique
NETT: Network for Environmental Technology Transfer (EC)
NEurO: North European Oil Royalty Trust (newspaper)
NEV: Net Economic Value
NevPw: Nevada Power Co. (newspaper)
NEW: Net Economic Welfare
Newcor Inc. (ASE)
Newcor: Newcor Inc. (newspaper)
Newell: Newell Co. (newspaper)
Newhll: Newhall Land & Farming Co., The (newspaper)
NewLew: Newmark & Lewis Inc. (newspaper)
NewLine: New Line Cinema Corp. (newspaper)
NewsCp: News Corporation Ltd., The (newspaper)
NEXCO: National Association of Export Management Companies
NEXT: Near End Cross Talk
NEZP: Nezperce (railroad)
NF: No Funds
Non-Fundable
Normal Form
NFA: National Foundry Association
National Futures Association
Non-Financial Agreement
NFAI: No-Fault Auto Insurance
NFAM: Network File Access Method
NFAP: Network File Access Protocol
NFBI: Non-Residential Fixed Business Investment
NFC: National Freight Corporation
NCF Financial Corp. (ASE)
Not Favorably Considered
NFD: No Fixed Date
Norfolk, Franklin and Danville (railway)
NFE: Network Front End
NFEA: National Federated Electrical Association
NFETM: National Federation of Engineers' Tools Manufacturers
NFF: No Fault Found
NFFE: National Federation of Federal Employees
NFG: National Fuel Gas Co. (NYSE)
NFIB: National Federation of Independent Business
NFK: Norfolk and Western (railway)
NflkSo: Norfolk Southern Corp. (newspaper)
NFO: National Farmers' Organization
NFPA: National Fire Protection Association
NFRC: National Federation of Roofing Contractors
NFS: Not For Sale
NFSE: National Federation of Self-Employed
NFT: Networks File Transfer
NFTU: National Foreign Trade Council
NFU: National Farmers Union
NG: No (Not) Good (checks)
NGAA: Natural Gas Association of America
NGC: Newmont Gold Co. (NYSE)
NGE: New York State Electric & Gas Corp. (NYSE)
NGG: Neadymium Gallium Garnet
NGOs: Non-Governmental Organizations
NGP: Network Graphics Protocol

NGPA: Natural Gas Policy Act
Natural Gas Producers Association

NGR: Nepalese Government Railway

NGS: Niagara Share Corp. (NYSE)

NGT: Nominal Group Technique

NGTA: Non-Guaranteed Trade Arrears

NGX: Northgate Exploration Ltd. (NYSE)

NH: All Nippon Airways
New High
New York, New Haven and Hartford (railroad)
Not Held

NHA: National Housing Agency

NHI: National Health Insurance
Nelson Holdings International Ltd. (ASE)

NHIR: New Hope and Ivyland Railroad

NHL: Newhall Land & Farming Co., The (NYSE)

NHMA: National Housewares Manufacturers Association

NHPMA: Northern Hardwood and Pinewood Manufacturers Association

NHR: National Heritage Inc. (NYSE)

NHY: Norsk Hydro A.S. (NYSE)

nHz: NanoHertz

NI: LANICA (Lineas Aereas de Nicaragua-Air Lines of Nicaragua)
National Income
Negotiable Instrument
Net Income
Net Interest
Nielsen Index
NIPSCO Industries Inc. (NYSE)
Non-Inhibitable Interrupt
Not Issued

NIA: National Income Accounts
Newspaper Institute of America

NiagSh: Niagara Share Corp. (newspaper)

NiaMP: Niagara Mohawk Power Corp. (newspaper)

NIASA: National Insurance Actuarial and Statistical Association

NIB: Node Initialization Block

NIBL: National Industrial Basic Language

NIBOR: New York Interbank Official Rate

NIC: National Industrial Council
Net Interest Cost
Network Information Center
Network Interface Control
Newly Industrialized Country
Nicolet Instrument Corp. (NYSE)

NICB: National Industrial Conference Board

NichApl: Nichols-Applegate Growth Equity Fund Inc. (newspaper)

NICs: Newly Industrializing Countries

NichIn: Nichols Institute (newspaper)

Nichols: S.E. Nichols Inc. (newspaper)

Nicolet: Nicolet Instrument Corp. (newspaper)

NICOR: NICOR Inc. (newspaper)

NICS: Network Integrity Control System

NIEO: New International Economic Order

NIF: Network Information File

NIFs: Not In Files
Note Issuance Facilities

NIFO: Next-In, First-Out

NIGP: National Institute of Governmental Purchasing

NIH: Not Invented Here

NII: National Intergroup Inc. (NYSE) (newspaper)
NIICP: No Increase In Contract Price
NIL: Negotiable Instruments Law
NIM: Network Interface Machine (Monitor)
NIMEXE: Nomenclature for the External Trade Statistics of the Community (EC)
NINOW: Non-Interest bearing NOW account
NIOPSWL: New Input/Output Program Status Word Location
NIOSH: National Institute of Occupational Safety and Health
NIP: Newhall Investment Properties (NYSE)
Non-Impact Printer
Normal Investment Practice
Nucleus Initialization Program
NIPSCO: NIPSCO Industries Inc. (newspaper)
NIRA: National Industrial Recovery Act
NIS: National Information System
Network Information Service
Network Interface System
Not In Stock
NIST: National Institute of Standards & Technology
NIT: Negative Income Tax
Network Interface Task
New Investment Technology
NIW: National Industrial Workers (union)
NJ: Air South (airline)
Niagara Junction (railway)
NJCL: Network Job Control Language
NJE: Network Job Entry
NJI: Network Job Interface
NJI&I: New Jersey, Indiana and Illinois (railroad)
NJ&NY: New Jersey & New York (railroad)
NJOBS: Number of Jobs
NJR: New Jersey Resources Corp. (NYSE)
NJRsc: New Jersey Resources Corp. (newspaper)
NK: Namakwaland Lugdiens (airline)
NL: Liberian National Airlines
Net Loss
New-Line (character)
Night Letter
NL Industries Inc. (NYSE)
No Label
No-Load (funds)
NLA: Normalized Local Address
Norris-LaGuardia Act
NLB: National Labor Board
NLC: Nalco Chemical Co. (NYSE)
Network Language Center
New Orleans and Lower Coast (railroad)
NLF: No-Load Funds
NLG: National Gas & Oil Co. (ASE)
North Louisiana and Gulf (railroad)
NLI: Newmark & Lewis Inc. (ASE)
NL Ind: NL Industries Inc. (newspaper)
NLN: New Line Cinema Corp. (ASE)
NLO: No-Limit Order
NLP: National Realty LP (ASE)
NLRA: National Labor Relations Act
NLRB: National Labor Relations Board
NLT: Not Later Than
Not Less Than
N&M: November and May (securities)
NM: Mt. Cook Airlines
Narrow Market
Network Manager
NorthEastern Mortgage Company Inc. (ASE)

NMA: National Management Association
National Mortgage Association
NMAA: National Machine Accountants' Association
NMAM: National Market Advisory Board
NMB: National Mediation Board
Navigation Maritime Bulgare (Bulgarian Maritime Navigation)
NMC: Network Management Center
Numac Oil & Gas Ltd. (ASE)
NME: National Medical Enterprises Inc. (NYSE)
NMedE: National Medical Enterprises Inc. (newspaper)
NMF: New Master File
Non-Member Firm
NMFC: National Motor Freight Classification
NMG: Neiman-Marcus Group Inc., The (NYSE)
NMI: Non-Maskable Interrupt
Nuveen Municipal Income Fund (NYSE)
NMineS: National Mine Service Co. (newspaper)
NMK: Niagara Mohawk Power Corp. (NYSE)
NMO: Number of critical Microoperations
NMOS: N-Channel Metal Oxide Semiconductor
NMPA: National Meat Purveyor's Association
NMR: N-Modular Redundancy
NMRR: Normal Mode Rejection Ratio
NMS: National Market System
National Mines Service Co. (NYSE)
Network Management Services
NMTA: National Metal Trades Association
NMTBA: National Machine Tool Builders Association
NMU: National Maritime Union of America
NMxAr: New Mexico & Arizona Land Co. (newspaper)
NN: Nevada Northern (railroad)
NNA: New Network Architecture
NNBCLA: Negative Negabinary Carry-Look-Ahead Adder
NNC: Northern Navigation Company
NNI: Net-Net Income
Next Node Index
NNM: Nuveen N.Y. Municipal Income Fund (ASE)
NNN: Non-Normalized Number
NNP: Net National Product
New National Product
NNX: Northern Central Railway Company
NNY: Nuveen New York Municipal Value Fund Inc. (NYSE)
no: number
N/O: registered in Name Of
NO: Normally Open
NOA: Network-Oriented Analysis and Transformation Unit
Nullification Of Agreement
NOAB: National Outdoor Advertising Bureau
No AC: No Account
No Adv: No Advice
NOB: Northwest Corp. (NYSE)
NoblAf: Noble Affiliates Inc. (newspaper)
NOC: Northrop Corp. (NYSE)
Notation Of Content
Not-Carry
Not Otherwise Classified
NOCP: Network Operator Control Program
NODAL: Network-Oriented Data Acquisition Language

NODAS: Network-Oriented Data Acquisition System
NODM: Ferrocarril Noroeste de Mexico (Northwest Railway of Mexico)
NOE: Net Operating Earnings
Not Otherwise Enumerated
NoelInd: Noel Industries Inc. (newspaper)
NoestUt: Northeast Utilities (newspaper)
NOFI: National Oil Fuel Institute
NOHP: Not Otherwise Herein Provided
NOIBN: Not Otherwise Indexed By Name
NOK: Next Of Kin
NOL: Net Operating Loss
Noel Industries Inc. (ASE)
Norse Oriental Lines
NO&LC: New Orleans & Lower Coast (railroad)
NOMA: National Office Management Association
NOMDA: National Office Machine Dealers Association
non-can: non-cancellable
noncoll: non-collinear
non-cum: non-cumulative
NONE: New Orleans and Northeastern (railroad)
non-par: non-participating
NO OP: No-Operation instruction
NOP: Not Otherwise Provided for
NOPA: National Office Products Association
NOPB: New Orleans Public Service
NOR: Not OR
NORCACHA: North Carolina Automated Clearing House Association
NordRs: Nord Resources Corp. (newspaper)
NORM: Not Operationally Ready due to Maintenance
Not Operationally Ready Maintenance
NORRD: No Reply Received
NORS: Not Operationally Ready due to Supply
Not Operationally Ready Supply
Norsk: Norsk Hydro a.s. (newspaper)
Nortek: Nortek Inc. (newspaper)
NorTel: Northern Telecom Ltd. (newspaper)
NORTHWEST: Northwest Orient Airlines
Norton: Norton Co. (newspaper)
Nortrp: Northrop Corp. (newspaper)
Norwst: Northwest Corp. (newspaper)
nos: numbers
NOS: Network Operating System
Notice Of Sale
Not Otherwise Specified
NOSP: Network Operating Support Program
NoStPw: Northern States Power Co. (newspaper)
NOT: New Orleans Terminal (railroad)
noty: notary
Nova: Nova Corp. (newspaper)
Novo: Novo Industri A/S (newspaper)
NOW: Negotiable Order of Withdrawal
NOZ: New Process Co. (ASE)
NP: Narragansett Pier (railroad)
Net Position
Net Price
Net Proceeds
Net Profit
New Page
No Parity
No Protest
Normal Profit

Northern Pacific Railway Company
Notary Public
Note(s) Payable

N-P: Negative-Positive

NPA: National Petroleum Association
National Pharmaceutical Association
National Productivity Authority
Numbering Plan Area

N&PB: Norfolk and Portsmouth Belt Line (railroad)

NPC: Nanoprogram Counter
Non-Profit Corporation

NPCL: North Pacific Coast Line (steamship)

NPD: National Patent Development Corp. (ASE)
Network Protective Device

NPDA: Network Problem Determination Application

NPI: Nuveen Premium Income Municipal Fund Inc. (NYSE)

NPIU: Numerical Processing and Interface Unit

NPK: National Presto Industries Inc. (NYSE)

NPlnRl: New Plan Realty Trust (newspaper)

N-P-N: Negative-Positive-Negative

NPNA: No Protest Non-Acceptance

NPP: Network Protocol Processor

NPR: New Plan Realty Trust (NYSE)
Non-Processor Request

NPRA: National Petroleum Refiners Association

NProc: New Process Co. (newspaper)

NPS: Non-cumulative Preferred Stock
No-Par Stock
Numerical Plotting System

NPSM: Non-Productive Standard Minute

NPT: NECO Enterprises Inc. (ASE)
Network Planning Tool
Non-Packet Mode Terminal

NPTA: National Paper Trade Association

NPU: National Postal Union

NPV: Net Present Value
No Par Value

NPVS: No-Par-Value Stock

NQA: Net Quick Assets

NQB: National Quotation Bureau
No Qualified Bidders

NQR: Non-Quadratic Residues

NR: Newfoundland Railway
Newhall Resources (NYSE)
Northern Railway of Costa Rica
Northward Aviation Limited
Note(s) Receivable
Not Rated
Not Responsible for

NRA: National Recovery Administration

NRAB: National Railroad Adjustment Board

NRC: National Referendum Campaign
National Research Council
Networking Routing Center
Nigerian Railway Corporation
Nuclear Regulatory Commission

NRCA: National Retail Credit Association

NR/D: Not Required, but Desired

NRD: Nord Resources Corp. (NYSE)

NRDGA: National Retail Dry Goods Association

nretn: non-return

NRFD: Not Ready for Data

NRG: California Energy Co. (ASE)

NRI: Non-Recurring Investment

NRL: Network Restructuring Language
Normal Rated Load

NRLCA: National Rural Letter Carriers Association
NRM: National Railways of Mexico
Normal Response Mode
NRM Energy Company LP (ASE) (newspaper)
NRMA: National Retail Merchants' Association
NRO: Non-Resident-Owned (funds)
NRPC: National Railroad Passenger Corporation (Amtrak)
NRRC: National Railroad Company (Haiti)
NRT: Norton Co. (NYSE)
NRTZ: Non-Return to Zero
NRU: Network Resource Unit
NRX(C): Non-Return-to-Zero (change) Recording
NRZ: Non-Return-to-Zero Recording
NRZ(C): Non-Return-to-Zero (change) Recording
NRZI: Non-Return-to-Change-on-ones Recording
ns: nanosecond
NS: Nederlandsche Spoorwagen (Netherlands Railways)
Net Sales
Net Surplus
New Series
Non-cumulative Stock
Norfolk Southern (railroad)
Northeast Airlines
Not Specified
Not Sufficient
NSA: National Standards Association
NSB: Norges Statbaner (Norwegian State Railways)
Northeast Savings FA (NYSE)
NSC: Network Switching Center
Nodal Switching Center
Norfolk Southern Corp. (NYSE)
Normal Standard Cost
NSCC: National Securities Clearing Corporation
NSD: National-Standard Co. (NYSE)
N&SE: Nacogdoches & Southeastern (railroad)
NSE: National Stock Exchange
nsec: nanosecond(s)
NSF: (Non-) Not Sufficient Funds
NS Gp: NS Group Inc. (newspaper)
NSH: Nashua Corp. (NYSE)
NSI: National Service Industries Inc. (NYSE)
National Stock Exchange
Non-Standard Item
NSIA: National Security Industrial Association
NSK: Not Specified by Kind
N&SL: Norwood & St. Lawrence (railroad)
NSLI: National Service Life Insurance
NSM: National Semiconductor Corp. (NYSE)
NSN: National Stock Number
NSNP: No Space, No Print
NSP: Network Service Protocol
Northern States Power Co. (NYSE)
Numeric Space character
NSPF: Not Specifically Provided For
NSR: Norfolk Southern Railway
NSRB: National Security Resources Board
NSS: Newburgh and South Shore (railway)
NS Group Inc. (ASE)
NSSC: National Security Traders Association
NSTA: National Securities Trade Association
NStand: National-Standard Co. (newspaper)
NSTC: Not Subject To Call

NSTS: National Securities Trading System
NSW: Northwestern Steel & Wire Co. (NYSE)
NSWGR: New South Wales Government Railways
NSWMA: National Solid Wastes Management Association
N/T: Net Tonnage
NT: Net Ton
Northern Telecom Ltd. (NYSE)
Nuisance Tax
N de T: Nacional de Tehuantepec (Tehuantepec Railroad)
NTAust: National Australia Bank Ltd. (newspaper)
NTBs: Non-Tariff Barriers to Trade (EC)
NTC: National Transportation Center
NTCA: National Telephone Cooperative Association
NTE: Not To Exceed
NtEnt: National Enterprises Inc. (newspaper)
NTF: No Trouble Found
ntfy: notify
NTGB: North Thames Gas Board (steamship)
NtGsO: National Gas & Oil Co. (newspaper)
NtHert: National Heritage Inc. (newspaper)
Nthgat: Northgate Exploration Ltd. (newspaper)
NTIA: National Telecommunications and Information Administration
NTK: Nortek Inc. (NYSE)
NTL: National Training Laboratories
NtlCnv: National Convenience Stores Inc. (newspaper)
NTM: Non-Tariff Measure
NTO: No Try-On(s)
NtPatnt: National Patent Development Corp. (newspaper)
NtPrest: National Presto Industries Inc. (newspaper)
NtRty: National Realty LP (newspaper)
nts: notes
NT&SA: National Trust & Savings Association
NTSB: National Transportation Safety Board
NtSemi: National Semiconductor Corp. (newspaper)
NtSvIn: National Service Industries Inc. (newspaper)
NTU: Normal Trading Unit
NtWst: National Westminster bank PLC (newspaper)
NU: Northeast Utilities (NYSE)
Nothing Unsatisfactory
Southwest Airlines
NUA: Network User Address
NUAAW: National Union of Agricultural and Allied Workers
NuclDt: Nuclear Data Inc. (newspaper)
Nucor: Nucor Corp. (newspaper)
NUE: Nucor Corp. (NYSE)
NUH: Nu Horizons Electronics Corp. (ASE)
NuHrz: Nu Horizons Electronics Corp. (newspaper)
NUI: Network User Identity
NUI Corp. (NYSE) (newspaper)
nul: null
NUL: No Upper Limit
Null character
NULS: Net Unit-Load Size
num: number
numeric
Numac: Numac Oil & Gas Ltd. (newspaper)
numb: number(s)
NUPE: National Union of Public Employees

NUR: Natchez, Urania and Ruston (railway)
National Union of Railwaymen
NUREC: Nuclear Regulatory Commission
NUT: Mauna Loa Macadamia Partners LP (NYSE)
NUV: Nuveen Municipal Value Fund Inc. (NYSE)
NuvCal: Nuveen California Municipal Value Fund Inc. (newspaper)
NuvMu: Nuveen Municipal Value Fund Inc. (newspaper)
NuvNY: Nuveen New York Municipal Value Fund Inc. (newspaper)
NuvPl: Nuveen Premium Income Municipal Fund Inc. (newspaper)
NUWW: National Union of Women Workers
NV: Combs Airways
Naamloze vennootscap (Company with limited liability) (Dutch)
Non-Voting
Nuisance Value
NVA: Nova Corp. (NYSE)
NvCMI: Nuveen California Municipal Income Fund (newspaper)
NVD: No Value Declared
NvMuI: Nuveen Municipal Income Fund (newspaper)
NvNYM: Nuveen N.Y. Municipal Income Fund (newspaper)
NVO: Novo Industri A/S (NYSE)
NVP: Nevada Power Co. (NYSE)
NVR: NV Ryan LP (ASE)
NVRyn: NV Ryan LP (newspaper)
NVS: Non-Voting Stock
NVT: Network Virtual Terminal
N&W: Norfolk & Western (railway)
NW: National Wealth (UK)
National Westminster Bank PLC (NYSE)
Net Worth
Norfolk and Western (railroad)
Northwest Orient Airlines
NWA: Northwest Airlines
NWACHA: Northwest Automated Clearing House Association
NwAM: New American High Income Fund (newspaper)
NwASh: New American Shoe Corp. (newspaper)
NwBedf: New Bedford Institution for Savings (newspaper)
NWC: Net Working Capital
NWE: New World Entertainment Ltd. (ASE)
NWH: Normal Working Hours
Nwhall: Newhall Investment Properties (newspaper)
NwhlRs: Newhall Resources (newspaper)
NWL: Newell Co. (NYSE)
NWldE: New World Entertainment Ltd. (newspaper)
NwmtGd: Newmont Gold Co. (newspaper)
NWP: Northwestern Pacific (railroad)
NWRY: North Western Railway (Pakistan)
NWS: News Corporation Ltd., The (NYSE)
NwStW: Northwestern Steel & Wire Co. (newspaper)
NwtM: Newmont Mining Corp. (newspaper)
NX: Quanex Corp. (NYSE)
NXA: Nodal Exchange Area
NXM: Non-Existent Memory
NY: Net Yield
New York Airways
NYACH: New York Automated Clearing House

NYB: New American High Income Fund (NYSE)
Nybor: New York Inter-Bank Offered Rate
NYC: New York Central (railroad)
NYCE: New York Curb Exchange
NYCHA: New York Clearing House Association
NYCSCE: New York Coffee, Sugar and Cocoa Exchange
NYC&SL: New York, Chicago and St. Louis (railroad)
NYCTNCA: New York Cotton Exchange, Citrus Associates
NYD: New York Dock (railway)
NYFE: New York Futures Exchange
NY&LB: New York and Long Branch (railroad)
NYME: New York Mercantile Exchange
NYMEX: New York Mercantile Exchange
NYN: NYNEX Corp. (NYSE)
Nynex: NYNEX Corp. (newspaper)
NYNH&H: New York, New Haven & Hartford (railroad)
NYO&W: New York, Ontario and Western (railroad)
NYS: Nepal Yatayat Samsthan (Transport Corporation of Nepal)
NYSE: New York Stock Exchange
NYSEG: New York State Electric & Gas Corp. (newspaper)
NYS&W: New York, Susquehanna & Western (railroad)
NYT: New York Times Co., The (ASE)
NyTEI: New York Tax-Exempt Income Fund Inc., The (newspaper)
NY Time: New York Times Co., The (newspaper)
NZ: New Mexico & Arizona Land Co. (ASE)
New Zealand National Airways
Not Zero
NZGR: New Zealand Government Railways
NZS: New Zealand Shipping Company
NZSG: Non-Zero-Sum Game
NZT: Non-Zero Transfer

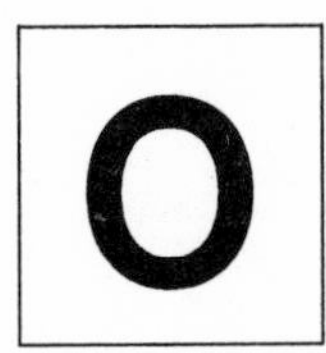

o: occupation
offered
official
old (in options listings of newspapers)
operand
operation
operator
output
owner

O: Odetics Inc. (ASE)

O&A: October and April (securities)

OA: Offer Accepted
Office Automation
Old Account
Olympic Airways
On Acceptance
On Account
On or About
Open Account
Operand Address Register
Operating Authorization
Operational Analysis
Organizational Assessment
Original Assessment
Other Appointments
Outdoor Advertising

OAA: Old Age Assistance
Orient Airlines Association

OAAA: Outdoor Advertising Association of America

OAAU: Orthogonal Array Arithmetic Unit

OAC: On Approved Credit

OACHA: Oregon Automated Clearing House Association

OA/DDP: Office Automation/Distributed Data Processing

OAF: Origin Address Field

OAG: Operand Address Generator

OAIB: Old-Age Insurance Benefit

OAK: Oak Industries Inc. (NYSE)

OakInd: Oak Industries Inc. (newspaper)

OakiteP: Oakite Products Inc. (newspaper)

Oakwd: Oakwood Homes Corp. (newspaper)

OA&M: Operation, Administration and Maintenance

OAM: Operand Addressing Mode

OAP: Orthogonal Array Processor

OAPEC: Organization of Arab Petroleum Exporting Countries

OAR: Ohio Art Co., The (ASE)
Operand Address Register
Operations Analysis Report
Operator Authorization Record
Ordering As Required
Overhaul and Repair
Overtime Authorization Request

OARS: Opening Automated Report Service

OAS: Organization of American States

OASDHI: Old-Age, Survivors, Disability and Health Insurance

OASDI: Old-Age, Survivors and Disability Insurance

OASI: Old Age and Survivors Insurance

OASIS: Order, Accounting, Stock, Invoicing and Statistics

OASYS: Office Automation System

OAT: One at A Time
Quaker Oats Co., The (NYSE)

O-A-V: Object-Attribute-Value (triplets)
OB: Obligation Bond
Ombudsman for Business
On Board
Opal Air Services (airline)
Opening of Books
Operating Budget
Or Better
Ordered Back
Osterreichischen Bundesbahnen (Austrian State Railways)
Out-of-Business
Output Buffer
Output Bus
Own Brand
OBCA: Office of Bank Customer Affairs
OBE: Office of Business Economics
Output Buffer Empty
obj: object
OB/L: Ocean Bill of Lading
OBL: Office of Business Liaison
Order Bill of Lading
Outstanding Balance List
oblg: obligate
obligation
OB MOD: Organizational Behavior Modification
OBO: Official Business Only
Order Book Official
Order By Order
OBR: Optical Bar Code Reader
Outboard Recorder
Overseas Bureau Report
OBrien: O'Brien Energy Systems Inc. (newspaper)
OBS: O'Brien Energy Systems Inc. (ASE)
On-Line Business Systems
OBU: Offshore Banking Unit
OBV: On-Balance Volume
o/c: overcharge
OC: Office Copy
Office of Commissioner
Official Classification
On Consignment
Open Collector
Open Contract
Operating Company
Operating Cost
Operation Control
Opportunity Cost
Order Cancelled
Order Card
Organization(al) Chart
Orion Capital Corp. (NYSE)
Over-the-Counter
OCAA: Oklahoma City-Ada-Atoka (railroad)
OCAL: On-Line Cryptanalytic Aid Language
OCB: Over-the-Counter Batch
occ: occupation
OCC: Operator Control Command
Option Clearing Corporation
Other Common Carrier
OcciPet: Occidental Petroleum Corp. (newspaper)
OCD: On-Line Communication Driver
OCDE: Organisation de Coopération et de Développement Économiques (Organization for Economic Cooperation and Development) (French)
OC&E: Oregon, California & Eastern (railroad)
OCF: Operator Console Facility
Owens-Corning Fiberglass Corp. (NYSE)
OCFP: Operator Command Function Processor
OCG: Optimal Code Generation
OCI: Office of Community Investment
OCL: Operation Control Language
OCM: Oscillator and Clock Module
OCMODL: Operating Cost Model
OCO: One-Cancels-the-Other order
OCP: Output Control Program
OCQ: Oneida Ltd. (NYSE)

OCR: Omnicare Inc. (NYSE)
Optical Character Reader
Optical Character Recognition
Output Control Register
OCS: Office Computing System
Office of Contract Settlement
Operation Control System
Order Communications System
oct: octal
OCT: Overseas Countries and Territories (EC)
OCU: Over-the-Counter Control Unit
od: overdraft
overdraw
overdue
OD: Aerocondor (airline)
Occupational Disease
On Demand
Organizational Development
Original Design
Out-of-Date
Output Disable
Outside Diameter
Outside Dimensions
Outstanding Debt
ODA: Official Development Assistance
ODB: Output Data Buffer
Overseas Development Bank
ODBR: Output Data Buffer Register
ODC: On-line Data Capture
Other Direct Costs
Output Data Control
ODCS: Operational Data Collection System
ODD: Optical Data Digitizer
ODE: Ordinary Differential Equation
ODECO: Ocean Drilling & Exploration Co. (newspaper)
ODESY: On-Line Data Entry System
Odet: Odetics Inc. (newspaper)
ODG: Off-Line Data Generator
ODM: Outboard Data Manager
ODP: Open-Door Policy
Optical Data Processing
ODR: Ocean Drilling & Exploration Co. (NYSE)
Optical Data Recognition
Output Definition Register
ODS: Occupational Demand Schedule
ODSS: Order Delivery Schedule Summary
ODT: Octal Debugging Technique
On-Line Debugging Techniques
OE: North-Air (airline)
Office Equipment
Operating Expenses
Oregon Electric (railway)
Original Equipment
Output Enable
OEA: OEA Inc. (ASE) (newspaper)
Organizational Expense Account
OEAP: Operational Error Analysis Program
OEC: Ohio Edison Co. (NYSE)
Open-End Company
Open-End Credit
Organizing, Evaluating, and Coaching
Overpaid Entry Certificate
OECD: Organization for Economic Cooperation and Development
OECE: Organisation Européenne de Coopération Économique (Organization for European Economic Cooperation) (French)
OECQ: Organisation Européenne pour le Contrôle de la Qualité (European Organization for Quality Control) (French)
OEDIT: Octal Editor

OEEC: Organization for European Economic Cooperation
OEF: Open-End Fund
OEH: Orient Express Hotels Inc. (NYSE)
OEIC: Open-End Investment Company
OEIT: Open-End Investment Trust
OEM: Office for Emergency Management
Original Equipment Manufacturer
OEN: Oxford Energy Co., The (ASE)
OEO: Office of Economic Opportunity
Operational Equipment Objective
OEP: Office of Emergency Planning
Original Element Processor
OER: Official Exchange Rate
Original Equipment Replacement
Overhead Expenditure Request
OERS: Organisation Européenne de Recherches Spatiales (European Space Research Organization) (French) (EC)
OES: Output Enable Serial
OEX: Options Exchange
of: overflow
OF: Offshore Funds
ofc: office
OFCC: Office of Federal Contract Compliance
ofd: offered (stocks)
OFD: Offered (NYSE)
OFDI: Office of Foreign Direct Investment
OFDS: Optimal Financial Decision Strategy
OFI: On-Line Free Form Input
ofl: overflow
OFN: Open File Number
OFPP: Office of Federal Procurement Policy
OFR: Open File Report
OFT: Optical Fiber Tube
OG: Chalk's Flying Service (airline)
Gross and Sons Ltd. (steamship)
Ogden Corp. (NYSE)
Ogden: Ogden Corp. (newspaper)
OGE: Oklahoma Gas & Electric Co. (NYSE)
OGPEC: Officially Guaranteed Private Export Credits
OGW: Overload Gross Weight
oh: overhead
OH: Oakwood Homes Corp. (NYSE)
Office Hours
On Hand
San Francisco and Oakland - Helicopter (airline)
OhArt: Ohio Art Co., The (newspaper)
OHC: Oriole Homes Corp. (ASE)
OhioEd: Ohio Edison Co. (newspaper)
OI: Operating Income
Ordinary Interest
OIA: Oil Import Administration
OIB: Operation Instruction Book
OIC: Officer In Charge
OID: Order Initiated Distribution
Original Issue Discount (bond)
OIDI: Optically Isolated Digital Input
OIG: Office of the Inspector General
OIL: Only Input Lines
Triton Energy Corp. (NYSE)
OIM: Office of International Marketing
OIOPSWL: Old Input/Output Program Status Word Location
OIT: Office of International Trade
OJ: Official Journal (of the European Community) (EC)
Orange-co Inc. (NYSE)
Stol Commuters (airline)
OJAJ: October, January, April, July (securities)

OJE: On-the-Job Experience
OJEC: Official Journal of the European Community (EC)
OJT: On-the-Job Training
ok: correct
OK: Czechoslovak Airlines
OKB: Osterreichische Kontrollbank Ag
OKE: ONEOK Inc. (NYSE)
OklaGE: Oklahoma Gas & Electric Co. (newspaper)
OKP: O'okiep Copper Company Ltd. (ASE)
OKT: Oakite Products Inc. (NYSE)
Oakland Terminal (railway)
OL: Odd Lot
On Line
Operating Losses
Or Less
Outgoing Letter
Output Latch
OLB: Odd-Lot Broker
OL&BR: Omaha, Lincoln and Beatrice Railway
OLC: Open-Loop Control
OLCC: Optimum Life Cycle Costing
OLD: Odd-Lot Dealer
OLDB: On-Line Data Base
OLDERT: On-Line Executive for Real-Time
OLIFLM: On-Line Image-Forming Light Modulator
Olin: Olin Corp. (newspaper)
OLN: Olin Corp. (NYSE)
OLOE: On-Line Order Entry
OLP: One Liberty Properties Inc. (ASE)
On-Line Programming
OLQ: On-Line Query
OLR: Office Loop Repeater
OLRT: On-Line Real Time
OLS: Olsten Corp., The (ASE)
Olsten: Olsten Corp., The (newspaper)
OLT: On-Line Test
OLTEP: On-Line Test Executive Program
OLTS: On-Line Test System
OLTT: On-Line Teller Terminal
OLX: On-Line Executive
O&M: Operations and Maintenance
Organization and Methods
OM: Air Mongol (airline)
Occupational Mobility
Office Manager
Office Master
On Margin
On Market
Open Market
Operating Memorandum
Operation Manual
Operations Manager
Options Market
Orthogonal Memory
Outboard Marine Corp. (NYSE)
Output Module
Outside Manufacturing
OMA: Operations Monitor Alarm
Orderly Marketing Agreement
OMAC: On-Line Manufacturing, Accounting and Control System
OMAP: Object Module Assembly Program
OMB: Office of Management and Budget
OMC: Operation and Maintenance Center
OMD: Open Macrodefinition
Ormand Industries Inc. (ASE)
OMEF: Office Machines and Equipment Federation
OMEN: Orthogonal Mini-Embedment
OMF: Old Master File
Order Materials For
OMI: Owens & Minor Inc. (NYSE)
Omncre: Omnicare Inc. (newspaper)
OMO: Ordinary Money Order
OMPR: Optical Mark Printer

OMR: Optical Mark Reader
Optical Mark Recognition
OMRC: Optical Mark Reader Card
OMRS: Optical Mark Reader Sheet
OMS: Oppenheimer Multi-Sector Income Trust (NYSE)
OMTB: Osaka Metropolitan Transportation Bureau
O&N: Oregon & Northwestern (railroad)
O/N: Order-Notify
ON: North American Airlines
Ontario Northern (railroad)
ONA: Oneita Industries Inc. (ASE)
Overseas National Airlines
ONCF: Office National des Chemins de Fer (National Railways of Morocco)
OND: Office National Du Ducroire
ONE: Banc One Corp. (NYSE)
Oneida: Oneida Ltd. (newspaper)
Oneita: Oneita Industries Inc. (newspaper)
OneLibt: One Liberty Properties Inc. (newspaper)
ONEOK: ONEOK Inc. (newspaper)
OnLne: On-Line Software International Inc. (newspaper)
ONLP: On-Line Program Development
ONRY: Ogdensburg and Norwood Railway
ONT: Ontario Northland (railway)
O&NW: Oregon and Northwestern (railroad)
O&O: Owned and Operated
Owner and Operator
OO: Borrego Springs Airlines
Open Order
Order Of
Orient Overseas Line (steamship)
OOB: Opening Of Business
OOkiep: O'okiep Copper Company Ltd. (newspaper)
OOP: Out-Of-Pocket
OOPS: Originals On Permanent Sale
op: open
operand
operation
operator
optional
output
OP: Air Panama International (airline)
Offering Price
Opening Price
Opening Purchase
Open Position
Operating Profit
Outside Production
Overtime Pay
OPACK: Operation Acknowledge
OPAL: Operational Performance Analysis Language
OPBU: Operating Budget
OPC: Operation Code
Operations Planning and Control
Orion Pictures Corp. (NYSE)
OPCE: Operator Control Element
OP-COD: Operating Code
OPCODE: Operation Code
OPCOM: Operator Communications
o/pd: overpaid
opd: opened (stocks)
operand
OPD: Delayed Opening (stocks)
Opened (NYSE)
OP&E: Oregon, Pacific & Eastern (railroad)
OPE: Optimized Processing Element
OPEC: Organization of Petroleum Exporting Countries
oper: operational
OPEVAL: Operational Evaluation
OPEX: Operational Executive
Operational Experience
OPF: Official Personnel Folder

OPIC: Overseas Private Investment Corporation
OPL: Overpaid Last Account
OPM: Office of Personnel Management
Operations Per Minute
Operator Master
Options Pricing Model
Other People's Money
OpnMI: Oppenheimer Multi-Sector Income Trust (newspaper)
OPOL: Optimization-Oriented Language
OPOMP: Overall Planning and Optimization and Machining Process
OPOP: Operator/Operation
OPP: Oppenheimer Industries Inc. (ASE)
Oppenh: Oppenheimer Industries Inc. (newspaper)
opr: operand
operator
OPR: Optical Page Reading
OPRA: Options Price Reporting Authority
OPRAD: Operations Research and Development Management
OPREQ: Operation Request
ops: operations
OPS: Office of Price Stabilization
OPSER: Operator Service
OPSWL: Old Program Status Word Location
OPSYS: Operating System
opt: optimization
optimizer
option
optional
OPT: Optimized Production Technology
OPTAD: Organization for Pacific Trade and Development
OPTIM: Order Point Technique for Inventory Management
OPTS: On-Line Peripheral Test System
OPUR: Object Program Utility Routine
OPUS: Octal Program Updating System
OQ: Royale Airlines
OQC: Outside Quality Control
OQL: On-Line Query Language
Outgoing Quality Level
Outgoing Quality Limit
or: overrun
O&R: Overhaul and Repair
OR: Air Comores (airline)
On Return
Operating Reserves
Operational Requirement
Operations Research
Ordered Recorded
Over Run
Owner's Risk
OrangRk: Orange & Rockland Utilities Inc. (newspaper)
ORB: Owner's Risk of Breakage
ORBIS: Order and Billing System
ORC: Orthogonal Row Computer
Owner's Risk of Chafing
ord: order
ordinary
ORD: Owner's Risk of Damage
ordd: ordered
ORDER: On-Line Order Entry System
ORDet: Owner's Risk of Deterioration
ORE: Organisation Régionale Européenne de la Conféderation internationale des syndicats libres (European Regional Organization of the International Confederation of Free Trade Unions) (French)
Output Register Empty
OregSt: Oregon Steel Mills Inc. (newspaper)

org: organization
origin
ORG: Organogensis Inc. (ASE)
ORGALIME: Organisme de Liaison des Industrie Métaliques Européenes (Liaison body for the European engineering and metal industries) (French)
ORG CHART: Organizational Chart
orgl: organizational
orgn: organization
Orgngn: Organogensis Inc. (newspaper)
Orient: Orient Express Hotels Inc. (newspaper)
OriolH: Oriole Homes Corp. (newspaper)
OrionC: Orion Capital Corp. (newspaper)
OrionP: Orion Pictures Corp. (newspaper)
ORL: Owner's Risk of Leakage
Ormand: Ormand Industries Inc. (newspaper)
OR/MS: Operations Research/Management Science
OrngCo: Orange-co Inc. (newspaper)
ORO: Operations Research Office
ORSA: Operations Research Society of America
ORU: Orange & Rockland Utilities Inc. (NYSE)
ORW: Owner's Risk of becoming Wet
os: outstanding
oversize
O&S: Over and Short (account)
OS: Austrian Airlines
Office System
Old Series
On Sale
On Schedule
Opening Sale
Open Shop
Operating System
Optimum Size
Option Spreading
Order Sheet
Oregon Steel Mills Inc. (ASE)
Out of Service
Out of Stock
OSA: Office of Savings Associations
Open Systems Architecture
OSAM: Overflow Sequential Access Method
OSB: One-Statement Banking
Operational Status Bit
osc: oscillator
OSC: Out of Stock, Canceled
OSCAR: Office of the Secretary Control and Report System
OSCRL: Operating System Command and Response Language
OS&D: Over, Short, and Damaged
OSD: On-Line System Driver
OSE: Operational Support Equipment
Osaka Stock Exchange (Japan)
OSG: Overseas Shipholding Group Inc. (NYSE)
OSHA: Occupational Safety and Health Act
Occupational Safety and Health Administration
OSHB: One-Sided Height-Balanced
OSI: On-Line Software International Inc. (NYSE)
Open Systems Interconnection
Operating System Interface
Overhead Supply Inventory
OSK: Osaka Syosen Kaisha (Osaka Mercantile Steamship) (Mitsui Lines)
OSL: Operand Specification List
Operating System Language
Oregon Short Line (railroad)
O'Sullivan Corp. (ASE)
OSM: Operating System Monitor

OSML: Operating System Machine Level
OSN: Output Sequence Number
OS/P: Operating Systems for People
OSP: Outside Purchased
OSR: Operand Storage Register
OSS: Operating System Supervisor
Operations Support System
Order Support System
OSSF: Operating System Support Facility
OSSL: Operating Systems Simulation Language
OST: Objectives, Strategies and Tactics
Office of Science and Technology
OSTD: Off-Site Technical Director
OSTP: Office of Science and Technology Policy
OSulvn: O'Sullivan Corp. (newspaper)
OSWS: Operating System Workstation
o/t: overtime
OT: Office of Telecommunications (U.S.)
On Track
Oregon Trunk (railroad)
Other Than
Output Terminal
Overseas Trade
Transportes Aereos de São Tome (airline)
OTA: Office of Technology Assessment (U.S.)
Omnibus Trade Act
OTAR: Overseas Tariffs and Regulations
OTB: Off-The-Board
Open To Buy
OTC: Organization for Trade Cooperation (GATT)
Over-The-Counter
OT&E: Operational Test and Evaluation
OTF: Optical Transfer Function
OTFP: Other Than Full Paid
OTG: Option Table Generator
OTIS: Operation, Transport, Inspection, Storage
OTJ: On The Job training
OTKDF: Other Than Knocked Down Flat
OTL: On-Line Task Loader
Out To Lunch
OTM: Office of Telecommunications Management
OTO: One Time Only
OTP: Office of Telecommunications Policy (U.S.)
Overtime Premium
OTS: Object Time System
Office of Thrift Supervision
Off The Shelf
On-Line Terminal System
OU: Operation Unit
oupt: output
OUR&D: Ogden Union Railway and Depot
out: outgoing
output
OutbdM: Outboard Marine Corp. (newspaper)
OUTLIM: Output Limiting Facility
outstg: outstanding
ov: overflow
ovd: overdue
OVD: Optical Video Disk
Optional Valuation Date
ovded: overdeduction
ovf: overflow
ovhd: overhead
ovpd: overpaid
ovr: overflow
OvShip: Overseas Shipholding Group Inc. (newspaper)
O&W: Oneida & Western (railroad)
OW: Offer Wanted
Olof Wallenius Line (steamship)
OWC: Owner Will Carry
OwenC: Owens-Corning Fiberglass Corp. (newspaper)

OwenM: Owns & Minor Inc. (newspaper)

OWM: Office Work Measurement

OX: American Courier (airline)

OxfEgy: Oxford Energy Co., The (newspaper)

Oxford: Oxford Industries Inc. (newspaper)

OXM: Oxfor Industries Inc. (NYSE)

OXY: Occidental Petroleum Corp. (NYSE)

OY: Air North (airline)

oz: ounce

OZ: Ozark Airlines

OZA: Ozark Airlines

p: para (currency of Yugoslavia)
parallel
parity
partnership
patent
payee
pence (currency of UK)
penny
personnel
peso (currency of Spain and Latin America)
pico-
pointer
power
procedure
process
processor
program
punch
purchaser

P: Pacific Coast Stock Exchange (changed to PSE)
Paid this year (in stock listings of newspapers)
Phillips Petroleum Co. (NYSE)
Private Venture
Put (in options listings of newspapers)

P&A: Pennsylvania & Atlantic (railroad)
Price and Availability

P/A: Particular Average

PA: Pan American World Airways
Passenger Agent
Paying Agent
Payment Authority
Pending Availability
Per Annum
Performance Analysis
Port Authority
Power of Attorney
Preliminary Acceptance
Primerica Corp. (NYSE)
Private Account
Private Trust
Procurement Authorization
Product Assortment
Production Adjustment
Program Access key
Project Analysis
Public Accountant
Public Address
Public Assistance
Purchasing Agent

P-A: Pan-Atlantic Steamship Corporation

PAA: Pan American World Airways
Pay Adjustment Authorization
Pennsylvania and Atlantic (railroad)
Print Advertising Association

pable: payable

PABLI: Online monitor of European Community development projects (EC)

PABX: Private Automatic Branch Exchange

PAC: Pacific Telesis Group (NYSE)
Payment After Closing
Performance Analysis and Control
Planned Availability Concept
Preauthorized Check
Project Analysis and Control
Pre-Authorized Check
Program Authorized Credentials
Pursuant to Authority Contained in
Put And Call

PacAS: Pacific American Income Shares Inc. (newspaper)
PACC: Pacific Coast (railroad)
PACE: Pacific America Container Express
Performance And Cost Evaluation
Planning And Control made Easy
Precisions Analog Computing Equipment
PacEnt: Pacific Enterprises Ltd. (newspaper)
PacGE: Pacific Gas & Electric Co. (newspaper)
Pacifcp: PacifiCorp (newspaper)
PacSci: Pacific Scientific Co. (newspaper)
PACT: Production Analysis Control Technique
PacTel: Pacific Telesis Group (newspaper)
PAD: Packet Assembly/Disassembly
Preferred Arrival Date
PAE: Pioneer Systems Inc. (ASE)
PAF: Price Analysis File
Production Assembly Facility
PAI: Pacific American Income Shares Inc. (NYSE)
Parts Application Information
Personal Accident Insurance
Prearrival Inspection
PAID: Programmers Aid in Debugging
PainWb: PaineWebber Group Inc. (newspaper)
PAIR: Performance and Improved Reliability
PAL: Philippines Air Lines
Preapproved Loan
Price and Availability List
PallCp: Pall Corp. (newspaper)
PA&M: Pittsburgh, Allegheny and McKees Rocks (railroad)
PAM: Profit Analysis Model
Pulse Amplitude Modulation
PAMS: Plan Analysis and Modeling System
PAN: Primary Account Number
PANAGRA: Pan-American Grace Airways
PanAm: Pan Am Corp. (newspaper)
PAN AM: Pan American World Airways
PANCAP: Practical Annual Capacity
PANDLCHAR: Pay and Allowances Chargeable
PanEC: Panhandle Eastern Corp. (newspaper)
Panill: Pannill Knitting Company Inc. (newspaper)
Pansph: Pansophic Systems Inc. (newspaper)
Pantast: Pantasote Inc. (newspaper)
PAP: Pension Administration Plan
Prearranged Payments
Procurement and Production
PaPL: Pennsylvania Power & Light Co. (newspaper)
PAPS: Performance Analysis and Prediction Study
PAQ: Process Average Quality
par: paragraph
P&AR: Pacific and Arctic Railway
PAR: Performance And Reliability
Precision Aerotech Inc. (ASE)
Price-Adjusted Rate preferred (stock)
Production Automated Riveting
Program Analysis and Review
ParCom: Paramount Communications (newspaper)
PAREC: Pay Record
ParkDrl: Parker Drilling Co. (newspaper)
ParkEl: Park Electrochemical Corp. (newspaper)

ParkHn: Parker Hannifin Corp. (newspaper)
parm: parameter
ParPh: Par Pharmaceutical Inc. (newspaper)
part: participating
participation
partner
PART: Production Allocation and Requirements Technique
ParTech: PAR Technology Corp. (newspaper)
partn: partnership
PASS: Private Automatic Switching System
Production Automated Scheduling System
pat: patent
PAT: Patten Corp. (NYSE)
Prearranged Transfers
Prediction Analysis Technique
patd: patented
PATH: Port Authority Trans-Hudson Corporation (railway)
PATIA: Pacific Area Trading and Investment Area
PATPEND: Patent Pending
PatPtr: Patrick Petroleum Co. (newspaper)
PATS: Preauthorized Automatic Transfer Scheme
patt: patent
PatTch: Patient Technology Inc. (newspaper)
Patten: Patten Corp. (newspaper)
PATX: Private Automatic Telegraph Exchange
paty: payment
PAU: Pan American Union
PaulPt: Pauley Petroleum Inc. (newspaper)
PAW: Port Angeles Western (railroad)
PAX: Private Automatic Exchange
Paxar: PAXAR Corp. (newspaper)
PayCsh: Payless Cashways Inc. (newspaper)
PAYE: Pay As You Earn
PayFon: Pay-Fone Systems Inc. (newspaper)
paymt: payment
PAYSOP: Payroll-based Stock Ownership Plan
payt: payment
PB: Par Bond
Paris Bourse
Pass Book
Permit Bond
Preference Bond
Privately Bonded
Program Budget
Push Button
PBA: Paid By Agent
Permanent Budget Account
PBAR: Programming, Budgeting, Accounting and Reporting
PBC: Paid By Carrier
Personal Business Computer
PBGC: Pension Benefit Guaranty Corporation
PBI: Pitney Bowes Inc. (NYSE)
PBL: Public Broadcast Laboratory
PBM: Program Budget Manager
PBNE: Philadelphia, Bethlehem and New England (railroad)
PBP: Pay By Phone
PBR: Patapsco and Back Rivers (railroad)
Payment By Results
PBS: Pilgrim Regional Bank Shares Inc. (NYSE)
PBT: Permian Basin Royalty Trust (NYSE)
Pushbutton Telephone
PBW: Parts By Weight
PBWSE: Philadelphia-Baltimore-Washington Stock Exchange
PBX: Private Branch Exchange

PBY: Pep Boys-Manny Moe & Jack, The (NYSE)
Private Branch Exchange

pc: paycheck
percent

P&C: Purchasing and Contracting
Puts and Calls

PC: Pacair (airline)
Participation Certificate
Pay Clerk
Payment Center
Penn Central Corp., The (NYSE) (railroad)
Per Cent
Personal Computer
Petty Cash
Pollution Control
Portable Computer
Price Control
Prices Current
Prime Contractor
Prime Cost
Printed Circuit
Printed Copy
Private Carrier
Private Corporation
Production Control
Production Cost
Professional Corporation
Profit Center
Program Counter
Protective Covenants
Public Contract
Public Corporation

PCA: Public Contracts Act

PCAM: Punched Card Accounting Machine

PCB: Petty Cash Book
Printed Circuit Board

PCC: Production Credit Corporation

PCDI: Per Capita Disposable Income

PCE: Process Control Equipment
Professional Care Inc. (ASE)
Program Cost Estimate
Punched Card Equipment

PCF: Putnam High Income Convertible & Bond Fund (NYSE)

PCG: Pacific Gas & Electric Co. (NYSE)

pch: punch
purchase

PCH: Potlatch Corp. (NYSE)

PCI: Paramount Communications (NYSE)
Per Capita Income
Product Cost Index
Production Cost Information
Program-Controlled Interruption

PCIJ: Permanent Court of International Justice

PCL: PCL Diversifund (newspaper)
Peruvian Corporation Limited (railroad)

PCM: Pulse Code Modulation
Punch Card Machine

PCN: Point Comfort and Northern (railroad)

PCO: Pittston Co., The (NYSE)
Procuring Contract (Contracting) Office
Put and Call Option

P-CODE: pseudocode

PCP: Preliminary Cost Proposal
Program Change Proposal

PCR: Paraguayan Central Railway
Perini Corp. (ASE)
Production Change Request

PCS: Preferred Capital Stock
Print Contrast Signal
Production Control System
Project Control System

PCSE: Pacific Coast Stock Exchange (later PSE)

pct: percent
percentage

PCT: Property Capital Trust (ASE)

PCU: Program Control Unit

PCV: Petty Cash Voucher

PCY: Pittsburgh, Chartiers and Youghiogheny (railway)
pd: paid
P&D: Pickup and Delivery
PD: Past Due
Payroll Deduction
Pem Air Limited (airline)
Per Diem (by the day)
Personnel Director
Phelps Dodge Corp. (NYSE)
Physical Distribution
Procedure Division
Product Design
Public Domain
Purchasing Description
PDA: Percent Defective Allowable
Personal Deposit Account
Princeton Diagnostic Laboratories of America (ASE)
Product Departure Authorization
PDAID: Problem Determination Aid
PDate: Pay Date
PDC: Production Decision Criteria
Public Dividend Capital
PDD: Past Due Date
Priority Delivery Date
PDG: Placer Dome Inc. (NYSE)
PDI: Personal Disposable Income
Picture Description Instruction
PDL: Presidential Realty Corp. (ASE)
PDM: Physical Distribution Management
Pitt-DesMoines Inc. (ASE)
Pulse-Duration Modulation
pdn: production
PDN: Public Data Network
PDP: Payroll Deduction Plan
Program Development Plan
PD&PL: Property Damage and Public Liability (insurance)
PDQ: Price and Delivery Quotations
Prime Motor Inns Inc. (NYSE)
PDR: Preliminary Design Review
PDRMA: Portable Drill Rig Manufacturers Association
PDS: Partitioned Data Set
Perry Drug Stores Inc. (NYSE)
Procurement Data Sheet
Professional Development Series
Program Data Set
PDSE: Production Sample
PDT: Pacific Daylight Time
P&E: Peoria and Eastern (railway)
P/E: Price-Earnings ratio
PE: Pacific Electric (railway)
Page-End character
Papuan Airlines
Period Ending
Philadelphia Electric Co. (NYSE)
Prepaid Expense
Price-Earnings ratio (stock listings of newspapers)
Probable Error
PEA: Primary Expense Account
PEAT: Pricing Evaluation for Audit Technique
PECIP: Productivity Enhancing Capital Investment Program
PEC Isr: PEC Israel Economic Corp. (newspaper)
PED: Period End Date
PEER: Price Escalation Estimated Rates
PeerTu: Peerless Tube Co. (newspaper)
PEFCO: Private Export Funding Corporation
PEG: Public Service Enterprise Group Inc. (NYSE)
PegGld: Pegasus Gold Ltd. (newspaper)
PEI: Pennsylvania Real Estate Investment Trust (ASE)
Planning Executives Institute

PEIA: Poultry and Egg Institute of America
PEL: Panhandle Eastern Corp. (NYSE)
Picture Element
PEN: Pentron Industries Inc. (ASE)
PenCn: Penn Central Corp., The (newspaper)
PenEM: Penn Engineering & Manufacturing Corp. (newspaper)
Penney: J.C. Penney Company Inc. (newspaper)
Pennsol: Pennzoil Co. (newspaper)
Penob: Penobscot Shoe Co. (newspaper)
PenRE: Pennsylvania Real Estate Investment Trust (newspaper)
Penril: Penril Corp. (newspaper)
PenTr: Penn Traffic Co. (newspaper)
Pentron: Pentron Industries Inc. (newspaper)
PEO: Petroleum & Resources Corp. (NYSE)
PeopEn: Peoples Energy Corp. (newspaper)
PEP: Paperless Electronic Payment
Partitioned Emulation Programming extension
PepsiCo Inc. (NYSE)
Personal Equity Plan
Program Evaluation Procedure
PepBy: Pep Boys-Manny, Moe & Jack, The (newspaper)
PepsiCo: PepsiCo Inc. (newspaper)
PER: Per Exchange Rate
Planning and Engineering for Repairs and Alterations
Pope, Evans & Robbins Inc. (ASE)
Post-Execution Reporting
Pre-Emptive Right
Price-Earnings Ratio
Production Engineering Research Association
Program Event Recording
PER AN: Per Annum
perc: perquisite
Per Cap: Per Capita (by the individual)
PER CT: Per Cent (Per Centum)
perf: performance
perif: peripheral
Perigo: Perrigo Co. (newspaper)
Perinil: Perini Investment Properties Inc. (newspaper)
PERK: Payroll Earnings Record Keeping
PerkEl: Perkin-Elmer Corp., The (newspaper)
PerkF: Perkins Family Restaurants L.P. (newspaper)
perks: perquisites
PERLS: Principal Exchange-Rate-Linked Securities
PERM: Programmed Evaluation for Repetitive Manufacture
perp: perpetual
Per Pro: Per Procuration
pers: personal
PERS: Performance Evaluation Reporting System
PERSIS: Personnel Information System
PERT: Program Evaluation and Review Technique
PERT/COST: Program Evaluation and Review Technique/Cost
PeryDr: Perry Drug Stores Inc. (newspaper)
PESA: Petroleum Electric Supply Association
Petroleum Equipment Suppliers Association
PET: Pacific Enterprises Ltd. (NYSE)
Paperless Entry Transfer System (Oregon)
Production Environmental Testing

Peters: J.M. Peters Company Inc. (newspaper)
Petrie: Petrie Stores Corp. (newspaper)
PetRs: Petroleum & Resources Corp. (newspaper)
pf: preferred
P&F: Pioneer and Fayette (railroad)
PF: Pension Fund
Permanent File
PFA: Production Flow Analysis
PFC: Personal Finance Company
Privately Financed Consumption
pfd: preferred (stock)
PFDA: Pure Food & Drugs Act
PfdHlt: Preferred Health Care Ltd. (newspaper)
PFE: Pfizer Inc. (NYSE)
PFEL: Pacific Far East Line (steamship)
Pfizer: Pfizer Inc. (newspaper)
PFL: Public Facility Loans
PFP: Prime Financial Partners LP (ASE)
PFR: Perkins Family Restaurants LP (NYSE)
Power Fail Recovery
PFRD: Preferred Stock
PFS: Pro-Forma Statement
PFT: Pittsburgh, Fort Wayne and Chicago Railway Company
PFU: Please Follow Up
pg: page
P&G: Procter and Gamble Co., The
PG: Paper Gain
Procter & Gamble Co., The (NYSE)
Program Generator
P-G: Prudential Grace Lines (steamship)
PGA: Punta Gorda Isles Inc. (ASE)
PGE: Pacific Great Eastern (railway)
PGI: Ply*Gem Industries Inc. (ASE)
PGL: Peoples Energy Corp. (NYSE)
pgm: program
PGN: Portland General Corp. (NYSE)
PGR: Progressive Corp., The (Ohio) (NYSE)
PGS: Program Generation System
PGU: Pegasus Gold Ltd. (ASE)
PGY: Global Yield Fund Inc., The (NYSE)
ph: phase
P&H: Postage and Handling
PH: Parker Hannifin Corp. (NYSE)
Polynesian Airlines
PHA: Public Housing Administration (Authority)
PHAB: Physically Handicapped Able Bodied
PHARE: Poland, Hungary Assistance for Economic Restructuring (EC)
PHC: Personal Holding Company
Pratt Hotel Corp. (ASE)
PH&D: Port Huron and Detroit (railroad)
PhelpD: Phelps Dodge Corp. (newspaper)
PHG: Philips NV (NYSE)
PHH: PHH Group Inc. (NYSE) (newspaper)
PHI: Philadelphia Long Distance Telephone Co. (ASE)
PhilaEl: Philadelphia Electric Co. (newspaper)
PhilGl: Philips N.V. (newspaper)
PHILIPPINE: Philippine Airlines
PhilMr: Philip Morris Companies Inc. (newspaper)
PhilPet: Phillips Petroleum Co. (newspaper)
PhilpIn: Philips Industries Inc. (newspaper)
PhilSub: Philadelphia Suburban Corp. (newspaper)
PHL: Philips Industries Inc. (NYSE)
Phlcrp: PHLCORP Inc. (newspaper)
PhILD: Philadelphia Long Distance Telephone Co. (newspaper)

PhlVH: Phillips-Van Heusen Corp. (newspaper)
PHM: PHM Corp. (NYSE) (newspaper)
PhnxR: Phoenix Realty Investors Inc. (newspaper)
PHP: Petroleum Heat & Power Company Inc. (ASE)
PHQ: Personnel History Questionnaire
PHR: Phoenix Realty Investors Inc. (ASE)
Physical Record
PHX: PHLCORP Inc. (NYSE)
PHYCUS: Physical Custody (of Records)
P&I: Paducah and Illinois (railroad)
Principal and Interest
PI: Packaging Institute
Performance Index
Perpetual Inventory
Personal Income
Personal Investment
Portfolio Insurance
Prime Interest (rate)
Productivity Index
Program Interruption
Programmed Instruction
Publication Instructions
Public Interest
PIA: Pakistan International Airlines
Peripheral Interface Adapter
Personnel Inventory Analysis
PIC: Paid-In Capital
Pickens (railroad)
Priority Intercept Controller
Production Inventory Control
PicoPd: Pico Products Inc. (newspaper)
PICS: Production Information and Control System
PIDS: Public Investment Data System
PIECOST: Probability of Incurring Estimated Cost
PiedNG: Piedmont Natural Gas Company Inc. (newspaper)
Pier 1: Pier 1 Imports Inc. (newspaper)
PIF: Prudential Intermediate Income Fund Inc. (NYSE)
PIG: Passive Income Generator
PII: Pueblo International Inc. (NYSE)
PIK: Payment-In-Kind
PIL: Payment-In-Lieu
Petroleum Investments Ltd. (NYSE)
PilgPr: Pilgrim's Pride Corp. (newspaper)
PilgRg: Pilgrim Regional Bank Shares Inc. (newspaper)
PIM: Putnam Master Intermediate Income Trust (NYSE)
PIMS: Profit Impact of Marketing Strategy
PIN: Personal Identification Number
PSI Holdings Inc. (NYSE)
PINC: Property Income Certificate (UK)
PinWst: Pinnacle West Capital Corp. (newspaper)
PIO: Pioneer Electronic Corp. (NYSE)
Public Information Officer
PionrEl: Pioneer Electronic Corp. (newspaper)
PionrSy: Pioneer Systems Inc. (newspaper)
PIP: Payment In Part
Postal Instant Press (ASE)
PIPS: Paperless Item Processing System
Pattern Information Processing System
PIQ: Property In Question
PIR: Pier 1 Imports Inc. (NYSE)
PISCES: Production Information Stocks and Cost Enquiry System

PIT: Personal Income Tax
Physical Inventory Taking
Programmable Interval Timer

PitDsm: Pitt-DesMoines Inc. (newspaper)

PITI: Principal, Interest, Taxes, Insurance

PITL: Pacific Islands Transport Line (steamship)

PitnyB: Pitney Bowes Inc. (newspaper)

Pittstn: Pittston Co., The (newspaper)

Pittway: Pittway Corp. (newspaper)

PitWVa: Pittsburgh & West Virginia Railroad (newspaper)

PIX: School Pictures Inc. (ASE)

PIXEL: Picture Element

pk: peak

PK: Pakistan International (airline)

PKC: Pannill Knitting Company Inc. (NYSE)

PKD: Parker Drilling Co. (NYSE)

PKE: Park Electrochemical Corp. (NYSE)

pkg: package

PKN: Perkin-Elmer Co., The (NYSE)

PKP: Polskie Koleje Panstwowe (Polish State Railways)

pl: place (stock)

P&L: Profit and Loss

PL: Paper Loss
Polynesia Line (steamship)
Port Line (steamship)
Poseidon Lines (steamship)
Price Level
Price List
Prince Line (steamship)
Private Line
Profit and Loss
Program Library
Programming Language
Public Law

PLA: Port of London Authority (UK)
Playboy Enterprises Inc. (NYSE)
Programmed Logic Array

PlainsP: Plains Petroleum Co. (newspaper)

PLAM: Price-Level Adjusted Mortgage

PLANET: Planning Evaluation Technique

Plantrn: Plantronics Inc. (newspaper)

Playboy: Playboy Enterprises Inc. (newspaper)

PLB: Prior-Lien Bond

PLC: Programmable Logic Controller
Public Limited Company (British)

PlcrD: Placer Dome Inc. (newspaper)

plcy: policy

plcy: policy

pld: payload

P&LE: Pittsburgh & Lake Erie (railroad)

PLE: Product Limit Estimator

Plesey: Plessey Company PLC., The (newspaper)

plff: plaintiff

PLI: P. Leiner Nutritional Products Corp. (ASE)

PLIB: Program Library

PLL: Pall Corp. (ASE)
Phase Lock Loop
Prince Line Limited (steamship)

PLM: Paris-Lyon-Mediterranee (railroad)
Play the Market

PLO: Polskie Linie Oceaniczne (Polish Line) (steamship)

PLP: Plains Petroleum Co. (NYSE)

PL&PD: Public Liability and Property Damage (insurance)

PLR: Plymouth Rubber Company Inc. (ASE)
PLS: Peerless Tube Co. (ASE)
Private-Line Service
Profit and Loss Sharing Account
PLUS: Plus System - EFT Network (Rocky Mountain Bank Card System)
PLX: Plantronics Inc. (NYSE)
PLY: Plessey Company PLC, The (NYSE)
PlyGem: Ply*Gem Industries Inc. (newspaper)
PlyR: Plymouth Rubber Company Inc. (newspaper)
plz: please
pm: paymaster
P/M: Put of More
PM: Pere Marquette (railroad)
Personnel Management
Petroleos Mexicanos (Mexican Petroleum) (steamship)
Phase Modulation
Pilgrim Airlines
Planned Maintenance
Post-Meridian (afternoon)
Pratt & Lambert Inc. (ASE)
Premium Money
Preventive Maintenance
Primary Market
Project Manager (Management)
Purchase Money
Push Money
PMA: Pharmaceutical Manufacturers Association
Produce Marketing Association
Production and Marketing Administration
Purchasing Management Association
PMACS: Project Management and Control System
PMB: Pilot Make Busy circuit
PMBO: Participative Management By Objectives
PMBX: Private Manual Branch Exchange
PMC: Performance Management Computer
Prod-Med Capital Inc. (ASE)
PMD: Project-based Management Development
PMI: Personnel Management Information System
Premark International Inc. (NYSE)
pmk: postmark
PMK: Primark Corp. (NYSE)
PML: Probable Maximum Loss
PMM: Purchase-Money Mortgage
PMMI: Packaging Machinery Manufacturers Institute
PMN: Pre-Manufacturing Notice
Pullman Co. (NYSE)
PMO: Program Management Office (Organization)
P&MP: Paris & Mount Pleasant (railroad)
PMP: Parts-Material-Packaging
Prime Motor Inns LP (NYSE)
Profit-Maximizing Price
PMR: Micron Products Inc. (ASE)
PMRS: Performance Management and Recognition System
PMS: Performance Management System
Process Management System
Project Management System
Public Message Service
pmt: payment
PMT: Putnam Master Income Trust (NYSE)
P&N: Piedmont and Northern (railway)
P/N: Promissory Note
PN: Ansett Airlines of Papua, New Guinea
Pan Am Corp. (NYSE)

Pan American World Airways
Performance Number
Please Note
Project Note
Promissory Note

PNC: PNC Financial Corp. (NYSE) (newspaper)

pnch: punch

pnd: pending

PneuSc: Pneumatic Scale Corp. (newspaper)

PNF: Penn Traffic Co. (ASE)

PNI: Participate but do Not Initiate

PNKA: Perusahaan Negara Kereta Api (Indonesian State Railway)

PNL: Penril Corp. (ASE)
Philippine National Lines (steamship)

PNM: Price Negotiation Memorandum
Public Service Company of New Mexico (NYSE)

PNN: Penn Engineering & Manufacturing Corp. (ASE)

PNR: Philippine National Railways

PNS: Pansophic Systems Inc. (NYSE)

PNT: Pantasote Inc. (ASE)

PNU: Pneumatic Scale Corp. (ASE)

PNV: Perini Investment Properties Inc. (ASE)

P&NW: Prescott & Northwestern (railroad)

PNW: Pinnacle West Capital Corp. (NYSE)

PNY: Piedmont Natural Gas Company Inc. (NYSE)

PNYA: Port of New York Authority

P&O: Peninsular & Oriental Steam Navigation Company

PO: Patent Office
Planned Obsolescence
Preauthorization Order
Privately Owned
Public Offering
Purchase Order

POA: Power Of Attorney

POB: Point Of Business

POC: Preservation Of Capital

POD: Pay On Delivery
Port Of Departure
Post Office Department

POE: Pacific Orient Express Line (steamship)
Point (Port) Of Embarkation
Port Of Entry

POF: Point-Of-Failure restart

PogoPd: Pogo Producing Co. (newspaper)

POI: Period of Interest
Plan of Instruction
Program of Instruction
Purchase Order Item

pol: policy

POL: Problem Oriented Language

POLAR: Production Order Locating And Reports

Polard: Polaroid Corp. (newspaper)

Polrln: Polaris Industries Partners L.P. (newspaper)

POM: Potomec Electric Power Co. (NYSE)

POMM: Preliminary Operating and Maintenance Manual

POMO: Production Oriented Maintenance Organization

POP: Pay One Price
Perceived Outcome Potential
Point-Of-Purchase
Pope & Talbot Inc. (NYSE)
Proof Of Purchase

POPAI: Point-of-Purchase Advertising Institute

PopeEv: Pope, Evans & Robbins Inc. (newspaper)

PopTal: Pope & Talbot Inc. (newspaper)

POR: Payable-On-Receipt
Pay-On-Receipt
Pay On Return

Portec Inc. (NYSE)
Price On Request

Portage: Portage Industries Corp. (newspaper)

Portec: Portec Inc. (newspaper)

PortGC: Portland General Corp. (newspaper)

PORTIA: Port Operations, Transport and Integrated Accountancy

PortSys: Porta Systems Corp. (newspaper)

pos: position

POS: Point-Of-Sale

POSDCORB: Planning-Organization-Staffing-Directing-Coordinating-Reporting-Budgeting

POST: Point-Of-Sale Terminal (Transaction)

PostIPr: Postal Instant Press (newspaper)

postp: postprocessor

pot: potential

Potltch: Potlatch Corp. (newspaper)

PotmE: Potomec Electric Power Co. (newspaper)

POTS: Perils Of The Sea

P&OV: Pittsburgh and Ohio Valley (railroad)

POW: Pay Order of Withdrawal
Power Of Attorney
PSE Inc. (ASE)

POY: Prairie Oil Royalties Company Ltd. (ASE)

pp: postpaid
prepaid
prepay

PP: Paper Profit
Parallel Processing
Parcel Post
Parity Price
Partial Payment
Pauley Petroleum Inc. (ASE)
Pension Plan
Personal Property
Phillips Michigan City Flying Service (airline)
Private Property
Pump-Priming
Purchase Price

PPB: Planning-Programming-Budgeting

PPBAS: Planning, Programming, Budgeting, Accounting System

PPBES: Program Planning-Budgeting-Evaluation System

PPBS: Planning-Programming-Budgeting System

PPC: Patrick Petroleum Co. (NYSE)
Production Planning and Control

ppd: postpaid

PPD: Pre-Paid Legal Services Inc. (ASE)

PPD: Purchasing Power of the Dollar

PPDSE: Plate Printers, Die Stampers, and Engravers (union)

PPE: Personal Protective Equipment (EC)
Pre-Production Evaluation

PPF: Plumbers and Pipefitters (union)
Production Possibility Frontier

PPG: PPG Industries Inc. (NYSE) (newspaper)

PPI: Pico Products Inc. (ASE)
Prices Paid Index
Producer Price Index

PPICS: Production Planning Inventory Control System

PPL: Pennsylvania Power & Light Co. (NYSE)
Philippine President Lines (steamship)

PPM: Particuliere Participatiemaatschappy (Private Joint Stock

Company) (Dutch)
Parts Per Million
Planned Preventive Maintenance

PPP: Pogo Producing Co. (NYSE)
Prior-Participating Preferred (stock)
Programmed Production Planning
Purchasing Power Parity theory

PPS: Participating Preferred Stock
Prior-Preferred Stock
Project Planning and Control System

PPT: Personal Property Tax
Putnam Premier Income Trust (NYSE)

ppty: property

P&PU: Peoria and Pekin union (railroad)

PPW: PacifiCorp. (NYSE)

PQ: Puerto Rico International Airlines

PQB: Quebecor Inc. (ASE)

PQR: Productivity, Quality and Reliability

pr: payroll
preferred (stock)
prefix
price
principal
printer

P&R: Planning and Review

PR: Panama Railroad
Paper tape Reader
Parity Ratio
Philippine Airlines
Physical Record
Preliminary Report
Price Communications Corp. (ASE)
Price Rate
Price Reduction
Print Restore
Program Register
Progress Report
Project Report
Pro Rata
Purchase Request

P-R: Pennsylvania-Reading Seashore Lines (railroad)

PRA: Page Replacement Algorithm
Premium Audit
Probabilistic Risk Assessment

PRAG: Pensions Research Accountants Group

PraireO: Prairie Oil Royalties Company Ltd. (newspaper)

PRAM: Productivity, Reliability, Availability and Maintainability

PratHt: Pratt Hotel Corp. (newspaper)

PratLm: Pratt & Lambert Inc. (newspaper)

PRC: Philippine Railway Company
Procession Register Clock
Programmed Route Control

PrcCm: Price Communications Corp. (newspaper)

PR Cem: Puerto Rican Cement Company Inc. (newspaper)

PRCR: Pacific Railway Costa Rica

PRD: Pay Rate Determinant
Payroll Deduction
Polaroid Corp. (NYSE)

pre: prefix

PRE: Premier Industrial Corp. (NYSE)

prec: precedent
preceding

precomp: precomputed (loan)

PrecsA: Precision Aerotech Inc. (newspaper)

pref: preference (stock)
preferred

PREL: Programmable Rotary Encoded Logic

prem: premium

Premr: Premier Industrial Corp. (newspaper)

Premrk: Premark International Inc. (newspaper)

PREP: Preparation Program
prepak: prepackaging
prepacked
pres: president
Presd: Presidio Oil Co. (newspaper)
PresR: Presidential Realty Corp. (newspaper)
PREST: Party on Scientific and Technical Research Policy (EC)
PRF: Permanent Requirements File
Potential Risk Factor
Pulse Repetition Frequency
PrgInc: Progressive Income Equity Fund Inc. (newspaper)
pri: priority
PRI: Printer Interface
Pulse Repetition Interval
PRIDE: Profitable Information by Design through Phased Planning and Control
Primca: Primerica Corp. (newspaper)
PRIME: Prescribed Right to Income and Maximum Equity
Priority Management Efforts
PrimeM: Prime Motor Inns Inc. (newspaper)
Primrk: Primark Corp. (newspaper)
prin: principal
princ: principal
prio: priority
Prism: Prism Entertainment Corp. (newspaper)
PRISM: Personnel Record Information System for Management
Progressive Refinement Integrated Supply Management
PRL: Processor Level
Pr Ln: Prior Lien
PRLST: Price List
prm: premium
prime
PrmFn: Prime Financial Partners L.P. (newspaper)
Prmian: Permian Basin Royalty Trust (newspaper)
PrMLt: Prime Motor Inns L. P. (newspaper)
prn: printer
PRN: Pseudorandom Number
Puerto Rican Cement Company Inc. (NYSE)
PrnDia: Princeton Diagnostic Laboratories of America (newspaper)
PRNET: Packet Radio Network
prntr: printer
pro: probate
procedure
procurement
protest
PRO: International Proteins Corp. (ASE)
proc: procedure
processing
processor
PROCLIB: Procedure Library
PROCOPT: Processing Option
PROCSEQ: Processing Sequence
ProctG: Procter & Gamble Co., The (newspaper)
prod: product
production
PRODOC: Procedure Documentation
PROF: Prediction and Optimization of Failure Rate
PROFACTS: Production Formulation, Accounting and Cost System
ProfCre: Professional Care Inc. (newspaper)
PROFILE: Program Overview and File
PROFIT: Programmed Receiving, Ordering and Forecasting Inventory Technique

PROFITS: Personalized Real-Time-Oriented Financial Institutions Time Saving System
prog: program
programmer
ProgCp: Progressive Corp., The (Ohio) (newspaper)
progr: programmer
PROI: Project Return On Investment
proj: project
PROJACS: Project Analysis and Control System
Proler: Proler International Corp. (newspaper)
PROLOG: Programming in Logic
PROM: Programmable Read-Only Memory
ProMed: Pro-Med Capital Inc. (newspaper)
PROMIS: Project Management Information System
PROMISE: Programming Managers Information System
PROMPT: Production Reviewing, Organizing and Monitoring of Performance Techniques
PRONTO: Programmable Network Telecommunications Operating System
prop: property
proprietor
PROP: Profit Rating of Projects
PropCT: Property Capital Trust (newspaper)
propl: proportional
PRO RATA: According to the Rate (Latin)
PROSPER: Profit Simulation, Planning and Evaluation of Risk
PROSPRO: Process Systems Programs
prot: protect
ProvEn: Providence Energy Corp. (newspaper)
PRP: Profit-Related Pay
PrpdLg: Pre-Paid Legal Services Inc. (newspaper)
PRPQ: Programming Request for Price Quotation
PRR: Pennsylvania Railroad (Penn Central)
Perrigo Co. (ASE)
Pseudoresident Reader
Pulse Repetition Rate
PRS: Pennsylvania Reading Seashore (railroad)
Polynomial Remainder Sequence
Presidio Oil Co. (ASE)
PRSL: Pennsylvania Reading Shore Line
prt: printer
PRT: Program Reference Table
PRTD: Portland Railroad and Terminal Division
prty: priority
PRU: Packet Radio Unit
Printer Unit
PruInt: Prudential Intermediate Income Fund Inc. (newspaper)
PruStr: Prudential Strategic Income Fund (newspaper)
PRV: Pearl River Valley (railroad)
P y RV: Potosi y Rio Verde (Potosi and Green River Railroad of Chihuahua)
PRX: Par Pharmaceutical Inc. (NYSE)
PRY: Pittway Corp. (ASE)
PRZ: Prism Entertainment Corp. (ASE)
ps: picosecond
P&S: Pittsburgh & Shawmut (railroad)
Purchase and Sale (Statement)
P/S: Parallel to Serial

PS: Pace Setter
Packet Switch
Packet Switching
Par Selling
Penny Stock
Personal Savings
Physical Sequential
Picture System
Pink Sheet
Pittsburgh and Shawmut (railroad)
Power Supply
Preferred Stock
Price Spread
Prime Rate
Process Status
Profit Sharing
Programming System
Proler International Corp. (NYSE)
Protect Status
Public Sale

PSA: Pacific Southwest Airlines
Preliminary Sales Agreement
Public Securities Association

PSAM: Partitioned Sequential Access Method

PSB: Program Specification Block

PSBNAME: Program Specification Block Name

PSBR: Public Sector Borrowing Requirement

PSC: Philadelphia Suburban Corp. (NYSE)
Point Shipping Company (steamship)
Production Scheduling and Control
Public Service Commission

PSCF: Processor Storage Control Function

PSCL: Programmed Sequential Control Logic

PSD: Packet Switched Data
Program Status Doubleword
Puget Sound Power & Light Co. (NYSE)

PSDM: Presentation Services for Data Management

PSDR: Program Status Doubleword Register

PSE: Pacific Stock Exchange
Packet-Switching Exchange
Perth Stock Exchange (Australia)
Philadelphia Stock Exchange
PSE Inc. (newspaper)

psec: picosecond

PSECT: Program Section

PSEG: Public Service Enterprise Group Inc. (newspaper)

PSF: Point Spread Function
Prudential Strategic Income Fund (NYSE)

PSFL: Puget Sound Freight Lines (steamship)

PSG: Planning Systems Generator
PS Group Inc. (NYSE)

PSGEN: Program Specification Block Generation

PS Grp: PS Group Inc. (newspaper)

PSH: Productive Standard Hour

PSI: Personal Security Identifier
Porta Systems Corp. (ASE)
PSI Holdings Inc. (newspaper)

PSIC: Process Signal Interface Control

PSK: Phase-Shift Keying

PSL: Program Support Library

PSLI: Packet Switch Level Interface

PSM: Packet-Switched Signaling Message
Power Supply Module
Productive Standard Minute

PSML: Processor System Modeling Language

psn: position

PSN: Packet-Switched Network
Public-Switched Network

PSNC: Pacific Steam Navigation Company

PSO: Penobscot Shoe Co. (ASE)
Public Service Organization
PSOS: Probably Secure Operating System
PSP: Packet-Switching Processor
Profit-Sharing Plan
PSPMW: Pulp, Sulphite and Paper Mill Workers (union)
P&SR: Petaluma and Santa Rose (railroad)
PSR: Page Send-Receive
Performance Summary Report
Price-Sales Ratio
Program Support Representative
Program Status Register
Public Service Company of Colorado
PSRO: Professional Standards Review Organization
PSRR: Product and Support Requirements Request
PSS: Printer Storage System
PSSC: Public Service Satellite Consortium
PST: Pacific Standard time
Partition Specification Table
Peseta (currency of Spain and Latin America)
Petrie Stores Corp. (NYSE)
Profit-Sharing Trust
Program Structure Technology
P-STAR: Federal Reserve predictor of long-term inflation rate
PSTF: Profit-Sharing Trust Fund
PSTN: Public-Switched Telephone Network
PSU: Packet-Switching Unit
Peripheral-Switching Unit
Power Supply Unit
Problem Statement Unit
Processor Service Unit
Processor Storage Unit
PsvCol: Public Service Company of Colorado (newspaper)
PsvNM: Public Service Company of New Mexico (newspaper)
PSW: Program Status Word
PSWR: Program Status Word Register
PSX: Pacific Scientific Co. (NYSE)
PSYNC: Processor Synchronous
pt: point
port
P&T: Personnel and Training
Plans and Training
PT: Pacific Time
Paper Title
Passing Title
Paying Teller
Perfect Title
Perseroan Terbatas (limited company) (Indonesian)
Pope and Talbot (steamship)
Private Terms
Profit Taking
Programmable Terminal
Progressive Tax
Property Tax
Provincetown-Boston Airline and Naples Airline Division
PTA: Preferential Trade Agreement
Purchase Transaction Analysis
ptas: peseta
PTBX: Private Telegraph Branch Exchange
PTC: PAR Technology Corp. (NYSE)
Peoria Terminal Company (railroad)
Philadelphia Transportation Company
Propensity To Consume
PT CL: Part Called (NYSE)
PT CLD: Part Called
PTE: Part-Time Employee
Potential Toxic Elements
Pretax Earning

PTG: Portage Industries Corp. (ASE)
PtHeat: Petroleum Heat & Power Company Inc. (newspaper)
PTI: Patient Technology Inc. (ASE)
PTJ: Part-Time Job
PTM: Portland Terminal Company (railroad)
ptnr: partner
ptnrship: partnership
PTO: Patent and Trademark Office
PTOM: Pays et Territoires d'Outre-Mer (Overseas Countries and Territories) (French) (EC)
ptout: printout
PTP: Portal-To-Portal
Promise To Pay
PtPar: Petrolane Partners L.P. (newspaper)
Pt Pd: Part Paid (stock)
ptr: partner
pointer
printer
PTR: Paper Tape Reader
Parr Terminal Railroad
P TR: Private Trust
PT RD: Part Redeemed (stock)
PtrInv: Petroleum Investments Ltd. (newspaper)
PTS: Port Townsend (railroad)
Public Telephone Service
PTT: Cleveland and Pittsburgh Railroad Company
Post Telephone and Telegraph Administration
PU: PLUNA (Primeras Lineas Uruguayas de Navegacion Aerea (First Uruguayan Air Navigation Lines)
Processing Unit
Public Utility
Publick: Publicker Industries Inc. (newspaper)
PUC: Public Utilities Commission
PUD: Planned Unit Development
Public Utility District (bonds)
Pueblo: Pueblo International Inc. (newspaper)
PUF: Percent Unaccounted For
PugetP: Puget Sound Power & Light Co. (newspaper)
PUHCA: Public Utility Holding Company Act
PUI: Paid-Up Insurance
PUL: Publicker Industries Inc. (NYSE)
Pullmn: Pullman Co., The (newspaper)
pun: punch
punc: punctuation
PUNC: Probable Ultimate Net Cost
PuntaG: Punta Gorda Isles Inc. (newspaper)
PUP: Performance Units Plan
PUPU: Purchasing Power (accounting method)
pur: purchase
purchaser
purchasing
pursuant
purc: purchasing
purch: purchase
purchasing
PURE: Pure Oil Company (steamship)
PUT: Put option
PutMas: Putnam Master Income Trust (newspaper)
PutMI: Putnam Master Intermediate Income Trust (newspaper)
PutnHi: Putnam High Income Convertible & Bond Fund (newspaper)
PutPr: Putnam Premier Income Trust (newspaper)
PV: Eastern Provincial Airways
Par Value
Present Value
PVAC: Present Value of Annual Charges

PVBA: Persoonlijke Vennootschap met Beperkte Aansprakelijkheid (Limited Company) (Netherlands)
PVCF: Present Value Cash Flow
PVIF: Present Value Interest Factor
PVIFA: Present Value Interest Factor of an Annuity
PVH: Phillips-Van Heusen Corp. (NYSE)
PVO: Private Voluntary Organization
PVR: Profit/Volume Ratio
PVS: Pecos Valley Southern (railroad)
pvt: private
PVY: Providence Energy Corp. (ASE)
pw: password
PW: Pacific Western Airlines
Pittsburgh and West Virginia Railroad (ASE)
Present Worth
Prevailing Wage
Private Wire
Production Worker
P&WA: Pratt and Whitney Aircraft
PWA: Public Works Administration
PWAFRR: Present Worth of All Future Revenue Requirements
PWD: Public Works Department
PWE: Present Worth Expenditures
PWF: Present Worth Factor
PWJ: PaineWebber Group Inc. (NYSE)
PWM: Pulse-Width Modulation
PWN: Cash America Investments Inc. (ASE)
pwnbkr: pawnbroker
pwr: power
PWR: International Power Machines Corp. (ASE)
P&WV: Pittsburgh & West Virginia (railroad)
PX: Aspen Airlines
Abbreviation for the Price on an offering sheet or on other releases dealing with securities
PXD: Price Ex-Dividend
PXR: PAXAR Corp. (ASE)
PY: Preferred Health Care Ltd. (ASE)
PY: Prior Year
Surinam Airways
PYA: Pittsburgh, Youngstown & Ashland Railway Company
PYE: Progressive Income Equity Fund Inc. (NYSE)
PYF: Pay-Fone System Inc. (ASE)
pymt: payment
PYNC: Prior Year Notice
PYR: Prior Year Report
Prior Year's Return (IRS)
Pyro: Pyro Energy Corp. (newspaper)
pyt: payment
PZ: LAP (Lineas Aereas Paraguayas-Paraguayan Airlines)
PZC: Point of Zero Charge
PZL: Pennzoil Co. (NYSE)

q: quarterly
query
question
queue
quotient

Q: In receivership or bankruptcy proceedings (NYSE)
Promotional Fare Code with Airlines

Q&A: Questions and Answers

QA: Dixie Airlines
Quality Assessment
Quality Assurance
Quick Asset

QAA: Quality Assurance Audit

QAC: Quality Assurance Checklist

QAM: Quadrature Amplitude Modulation

QANTAS: Qantas Airways (Australian Airline)
Queensland and Northern Territories Air Service

Qantel: Qantel Corp. (newspaper)

QA&P: Quanah, Acme & Pacific (railroad)

QART: Quality Assurance Review Technique

QAS: Question Answering System

QB: Qualified Bidders
Qualified Buyers
Quebecair (Airline)
Quick Batch

QBD: Quasi-Bidirectional

QBDL: Flanigan's Enterprises Inc. (ASE)

QBE: Query By Example

QBL: Qualified Bidders List

QC: Air Congo (Kinshasa)
Quality Control
Quasi Contract
Quasi Corporation
Quebec Central (railroad)
Quiesce-Completed

QCB: Queue Control Block

QCD: Query Complexity Degree
Quick Claim Deed

QCM: Quantitative Computer Management

QCR: Queue Control Record

QCRT: Quick Change Real-Time

QCS: Quality Control Specification

QD: Sadia (airline)

QDA: Quantity Discount Agreement

QDEBUG: Quick Diagnostic Debugging Program

QDM: Quality Assurance, Documentation and Maintenance

QE: Air Indies (airline)
Queue Empty
Quotation Estimate

QEC: Quiesce-at-End-of-Chain

QEL: Quality Element
Queue Element

QEM: Qualified Export Manager

QF: Qantas Airways
Quality Factor
Queue Full

QH: St. Thomas Tax-Air (airline)

QI: Comber Air (airline)
Qualified Indorsement
Quality Improvement
Quality Increase (salary)
Quality Index
Quarterly Index

QIL: Quad-In-Line

QIO: Queue Input/Output

QISAM: Queued Indexed Sequential Access Method

QJ: Mel Air Limited (airline)

QK: Aroostook Airways

QkReily: Quick & Reily Group Inc., The (newspaper)
QL: Lesotho Airways
Query Language
qlfd: qualified
qlfy: qualify
QLP: Query Language Processor
QLSA: Queuing Line-Sharing Adapter
qlty: quality
QM: Air Malawi (airline)
Quarterly Memorandum
QMDO: Quality Material Development Objectives
QMH: MHI Group Inc. (NYSE)
QMR: Qualitative Material Requirement
QMS: QMS Inc. (newspaper)
qn: quotation
QN: Bush Pilots Airway
Query Normalization
QNS: Quantity Not Sufficient
QNS&L Quebec North Shore and Labrador (railway)
Q&O: Quebec and Ontario Transportation (railroad)
QO: Bar Harbor Airlines
qot: quote
QP: Caspair (airline)
Quoted Price
QPAM: Quadrature Phase and Amplitude Modulation
QPC: Quasi-Public Company
QPDOLL: Quarterly Payment Demand on Legal Loan
QPL: Qualified Products List
QPR: Quarterly Progress Report
QPS: Query Property Similarity
QPSK: Quaternary Phase Shift Keying
QQ: Aerovias Quisqueyana (airline)
qr: quotient
QR: Quadratic Residues
Quality and Reliability
Quotation Request
Q&RA: Quality and Reliability Assurance
Q-RATIO: Ratio of total market value of physical assets
QRC: Quick Reaction Communications
QRL: Quick Relocate and Link
qrly: quarterly
QRP: Query and Reporting Processor
QRT: Queue Run-Time
QS: Air Michigan (airline)
Quality Stock
Quantity Share
Query Similarity
Query System
Queue Select
Quickie Strike
QSA: Quad Synchronous Adapter
QSAM: Queued Sequential Access Method
QSI: Quality Step Increase (salary)
QSL: Quarterly Stock List
Queue Search Limit
QSR: Quarterly Status Report
Quarterly Summary Report
QSSR: Quarterly Stock Status Report
QstVl: Quest for Value Dual Purpose Fund Inc. (newspaper)
Q-SYSTEM: Inventory control system with varying reorders
qt: quantity
quotient
QT: Questioned Trade
Quotation Ticker
QTAM: Queued Telecommunications Access Method
Queued Terminal Access Method
qte: quote
QTH: Queued Transaction Handling
Q-TIP: Qualified Terminable Interest Property (trust)
qtly: quarterly

QTP: Quality Test Plan
qtr: quarter
QTR: Quality Technical Requirement
Quarterly Technical Report
QTS: Quantizer Threshold Spacing
qu: quotation
QU: Mississippi Valley Airways
QuakFb: Quaker Fabric Corp. (newspaper)
QuakO: Quaker Oats Co., The (newspaper)
QuakSC: Quaker State Corp. (newspaper)
qual: quality
QUALTA: Quad Asynchronous Local Terminal Adapter
quan: quantity
Quanex: Quanex Corp. (newspaper)
QUANSY: Question Answering System
Quantm: Quantum Chemical Corp. (newspaper)
quar: quarter
quart: quarterly
Quebc: Quebecor Inc. (newspaper)
QUEL: Query Language
QUEST: Query Evaluation and Search Technique
Questar: Questar Corp. (newspaper)
QUI: Quincy (railroad)
QUICO: Quality Improvement through Cost Optimization
QUID PRO QUO: Something for Something
QUIP: Quad In-Line Package
Quota Input Processor
quote: quotation
QUO WARRANTO: By what Authority
QV: Monarch Airline
Quode Vide (Reference to related sources of information)
QWL: Quality-of-Work-Life
QXI: Queue Executive Interface
QY: Quantum Yield
QZ: Zambia Airways

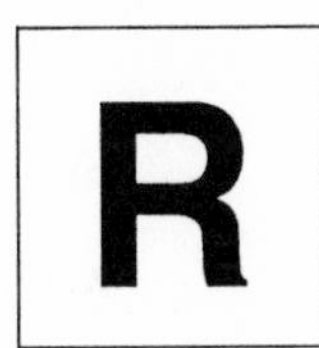

r: railroad
railway
range
read
reader
receiver
recommendation
record
register
regulation
relation
reliability
rent (annual)
report
request
research
reset
resistor
right (stocks)
ring

R: L.F. Rothschild Unterberg Towbin Holdings Inc. (NYSE)
Option not traded (in option listings in newspapers)

RA: Record Address
Refer to Accepter
Reimbursement Authorization
Reliability Assurance
Relocation Address
Research Assistant
Restricted Account
Return Address
Revenue Act
Royal Nepal Airlines

RAA: Remote Access Audio Device

RAB: Radio Advertising Bureau

RAC: RAC Mortgage Investment Corp. (newspaper)
RAI Research Corp. (ASE)

RACA: Resource Accounting and Cost Allocation

RACE: Random-Access Computer Equipment
Research and Development in Advanced Communications for Europe (EC)
Results Analysis, Computation and Evaluation

RACF: Resource-Access Control Facility

RACSS: Retail Apparel Chain Store System

RAD: Random-Access Device
Rapid-Access Device
Rite Aid Corp. (NYSE)

RADA: Random Access Discrete Address

RADAR: Receivable Accounts Data-entry And Retrieval

Radice: Radice Corp. (newspaper)

Ragan: Brad Ragan Inc. (newspaper)

RAI: RAI Research Corp. (newspaper)
Random Access and Inquiry

rail: railroad
railway

RAIN: Relational Algebraic Interpreter

RAIR: Remote-Access Immediate Response

RAK: Read Access Key station

RAL: Ralston Purina Co. (NYSE)

RALF: Relocatable Assembly Language Floating point

RalsPur: Ralston Purina Co. (newspaper)

RALU: Register and Arithmetic Logic Unit

RAM: Ramada Inc. (NYSE)
Random-Access Memory
Reliability, Availability and Maintainability
Reverse Annuity Mortgage

RAMAC: Random-Access Memory Accounting
Random-Access Method of Accounting and Control

Ramad: Ramada Inc. (newspaper)

RAMCEASE: Reliability, Availability, Maintainability, Cost Effectiveness and Systems Effectiveness

RAM-D: Reliability And Maintainability-Dependability

RAMIS: Rapid-Access Management Information System

RAMMIT: Reliability and Maintainability Management Improvement Techniques

RAMS: Random-Access Measurement System

RAN: Request for Authority to Negotiate
Revenue Anticipation Note

RAND: Research And Development

RangrO: Ranger Oil Ltd. (newspaper)

Ransbg: Ransburg Corp. (newspaper)

RAO: Related Application Object

RAP: Regulatory Accounting Practices
Relational Associative Processor
Remote-Access Point
Resident Assembler Program
Revised Accounting Procedures

RAPID: Retrieval and Production for Integrated Data

RAR: Return Address Register

RARES: Rotating Associative Relational Store

RAS: Reliability, Availability, Serviceability

RASI: Reliability, Availability, Service, Improvement

RASP: Remote-Access Switching and Patching

RAV: Raven Industries Inc. (ASE)

Raven: Raven Industries Inc. (newspaper)

RAW: Read After Write

RAX: Random Access

RAY: Raytech Corp. (NYSE)

Raycom: Raycomm Transworld Industries Inc. (newspaper)

Rayonr: Rayonier Timberlands L.P. (newspaper)

Raytch: Raytech Corp. (newspaper)

Raythn: Raytheon Co. (newspaper)

RB: Railroad Bonds
Reading & Bates Corp. (NYSE)
Redeemable Bond
Request Block
Reserve Bank
Retail Business
Return to Bias
Revenue Bond
Rural Bank
Syrian Arab Airlines

RBA: Relative Byte Address

RBC: Regal-Beloit Corp. (ASE)

RBD: Reliability Block Diagram
Rubbermaid Inc. (NYSE)

RBE: Remote Batch Entry

RBF: Remote Batch Facility

RBG: Ransburg Corp. (ASE)

RBI: RB Industries Inc. (NYSE)

RBInd: RB Industries Inc. (newspaper)

RBK: Reebok International Ltd. (NYSE)

rbl: ruble (currency of the Soviet Union)

RBM: Real-Time Batch Monitor
Relative Batch Monitor
Remote Batch Module

RBO: Relationship By Objective

RBOCs: Regional Bell Operating Companies
RBS: Remote Batch System
RBT: Remote Batch Terminal
RBTE: Remote Batch Terminal Emulator
RBTM: Remote Batch Terminal Module
RBW: RB & W Corp. (ASE) (newspaper)
rc: receipt
reconsignment
recredited
RC: Air Cambodge (airline)
Radix Complement
Railway Corporation (Nigeria)
Real Circuit
Receive Common
Recurring Charges
Registered Check
Release Clause
Remote Control
Rent Control
Replacement Cost
Report of Contact
Reserve Capital
Reserve Currency
Resistor-Capacitor
Restrictive Covenant
Risk Capital
RCA: Radio Corporation of America
Remote Control Adapter
Replacement Cost Accounting
RCAC: Remote Computer Access Communications Service
RCCAM: Remote Computer Communications Access Method
RCB: Resource Control Block
RCC: Ratio of Charges to Costs
Re Capital Corp. (ASE)
Remote Center Compliance
Remote Communications Concentrator
rcd: received (stocks)
record
RCD: Registered Connective Device
RCE: Reece Corp., The (NYSE)
Relay Communications Electronics
RCF: Remote Call Forwarding
RCFA-N: Regie du Chemin de Fer Abidjan-Niger (Niger Railway Administration) (Ivory Coast)
RCFT: Remove Cloud From Title
RCHM: Remote Computer Controlled Hardware Monitor
RCI: Remote Control Interface
RCIA: Retail Clerks International Association
RCIS: Remote Computer Interface Subsystem
RCIU: Remote Computer Interface Unit
RckCtr: Rockefeller Center Properties Inc. (newspaper)
Rckwy: Rockaway Corp. (newspaper)
rcl: recall
RCM: ARCO Chemical Co. (NYSE)
RCMM: Registered Competitive Market Management
RCN: Receipt of Change Notice
Report Change Notice
RCP: Receive Clock Pulse
Recognition and Control Processor
Rockefeller Center Properties Inc. (NYSE)
RCPC: Regional Check Processing Center
rcpt: receipt
RCR: Required Carrier Return character
RCS: Reloadable Control Storage
Remote Computing Service
Remote Control Switch
RCSDF: Reconfigurable Computer System Design Facility
rct: receipt (stocks)
RCT: Real Estate Investment Trust of California (NYSE)
Regional Control Task

RCTL: Resistor-Capacitor-Transistor Logic
RCU: Remote Control Unit
rcv: receive
RCV: Remote Controlled Vehicle
rcvd: received
RCW: Return Control Word
rd: read
redeemable (stocks)
R&D: Research and Development
RD: Airlift International (Air Cargo-Airline)
Railway Directorate (Albania)
Read Data
Receive Data
Refer to Drawer
Research and Development
Rotational Delay
Royal Dutch Petroleum Co. (NYSE)
Rural Delivery
RDA: Research, Development, and Acquisition
Run-Time Debugging Aid
RDAV: Reset Data Available
RDB: Relational Database
RDBA: Remote Database Access
RDC: Remote Data Concentrator
Rowan Companies Inc. (NYSE)
RD&D: Research, Development, and Demonstration
RDD: Required Delivery Date
RDDSEM: Real Data System Element Model
RD&E: Research, Development, and Engineering
Research, Development, and Evaluation
RDE: Receive Data Enable
RDF: Record Definition Field
RDG: Reading Company (railroad)
RD/I: Research, Development, and Innovation
RDIU: Read Interface Unit
Remote Device Interface Unit
rdj: readjustment
RDK: Ruddick Corp. (ASE)
RDL: Redlaw Industries Inc. (ASE)
Report Definition Language
Resistor Diode Logic
RDLP: Research and Development Limited Partnership
RDM: Real-Time Database Manager
RDMS: Relational Data Management System
RDO: Regular Data Organization
RDOS: Real-Time Disk Operating System
RDPI: Real Personal Disposable Income
rdr: reader
RDR: Ryder System Inc. (NYSE)
RDT: Resource Definition Table
rdy: ready
re: reconsignment
R&E: Research and Engineering
R/E: Rate of Exchange
RE: Rate of Exchange
Real Estate
Redman Industries Inc. (NYSE)
Repayable to Either
Request Element
REA: Railway Express Agency
Reader (railroad)
ReadBt: Reading & Bates Corp. (newspaper)
Rebok: Reebok International Ltd. (newspaper)
rec: receipt
receive
record
recover
REC: Recognition Equipment Inc. (NYSE)
RECA: Residual Capability Assessment
recap: recapitulation
ReCap: Re Capital Corp. (newspaper)
RECAPS: Read Encode/Capture/Proof/Sort

recd: received
RECEP: Relative Capacity Estimating Capacity
RECFM: Record Format
RECFMS: Record Formatted Maintenance Statistics
RECI: Real Estate Certificate Institute
RECMF: Radio and Electronic Component Manufacturers Federation
RECMS: Record Maintenance Statistics
RecnEq: Recognition Equipment Inc. (newspaper)
RECNUM: Record Number
Reco: RECO International Inc. (newspaper)
recov: recovery
recpt: receipt
rect: receipt
red: reduction
RED: Red Lion Inns LP (ASE)
REDAC: Real-Time Data Acquisition
REDC: Read Control
redisc: rediscount
RedLn: Red Lion Inns L. P. (newspaper)
Redlw: Redlaw Industries Inc. (newspaper)
Redmn: Redman Industries Inc. (newspaper)
Reece: Reece Corp., The (newspaper)
ref: referee
reference
refunding (stocks)
REF: Release of Excess Funds
REFS: Remote Entry Flexible Security
reg: register
registered (stocks)
registrar
regular
regulation
REG: Range Extender with Gain
Registered (NYSE)
REGAD: Regenerate Address
Regal: Regal International Inc. (newspaper)
RegalB: Regal-Beloit Corp. (newspaper)
REGIO: European Community regional statistical databank (EC)
regis: register
REGIS: Relational General Information System
ReglFn: Regional Financial Shares Investment Fund Inc. (newspaper)
regs: regulations
REI: Rat der Europäischen Industrieverbande (Council of European Industrial Federations) (French)
Real Estate Investment Trust of America
ReichT: Reich & Tang L. P. (newspaper)
reimb: reimburse
reimbursement
REINIT: Recovery Initialization
REIT: Real Estate Investment Trust
Real Estate Investment Trust of California (newspaper)
rej: reject
REJEN: Remote Job Entry
rel: release
relocatable
REL: Reliance Group Holdings Inc. (NYSE)
RelGrp: Reliance Group Holdings Inc. (newspaper)
RELP: Real Estate Limited Partnership
RELQ: Release-Quiesce
rem: remark
remittance
Reports and Memoranda
REM: Radioactivity Environmental Monitoring (EC)
Recognition Memory

REMAC: Remote Data Acquisition Subsystem
REMAP: Record Extraction, Manipulation and Print
REMAS: Remote Energy Monitor/Alarm System
REMIC: Real Estate Mortgage Investment Conduit
REMICS: Real-Time Manufacturing Information Control System
remitt: remittance
REN: Remote Enable
Rollins Environmental Services Inc. (NYSE)
RENFE: Red Nacional de los Ferrocarriles (Spanish National Railway System)
REO: Real Estate Owned
REOP: Reopening (after a halt in trading)
rep: reply
report
representative
REPEX: Regional Payments Exchange (Dayton, Ohio)
RepGyp: Republic Gypsum Co. (newspaper)
RepNY: Republic New York Corp. (newspaper)
REPO: Repurchase Agreement
REPOS: Repurchase Agreements
repr: representation
REPROM: Reprogrammable Read-Only Memory
req: request
reqn: requisition
reqt: requirement
RER: Residual Error Rate
res: reserve
reset
restore
RES: Reader Stop
Remote Entry Service
RPC Energy Services Inc. (NYSE)
RESec: Real Estate Securities Income Fund Inc. (newspaper)
RESLOAD: Resident Loader
RESPA: Real Estate Settlement Procedures Act
RESQ: Research Queueing
ResRs: Residential Resources Mortgages Investments Corp. (newspaper)
resrt: restart
Resrt: Resorts International Inc. (newspaper)
RestMg: Residential Mortgage Investments Inc. (newspaper)
ret: return
RET: Real-Estate Tax
retd: returned
REU: Ready Extension Unit
rev: revocable
REX: Real-Time Executive System
Regression Expert
Rexhm: Rexham Corp. (newspaper)
ReyMt: Reynolds Metals Co. (newspaper)
R&F: Rank and File
RF: Radio Frequency
Rating Factor
Register File
Remote File Access
Reporting File
Revolving Fund
RFAM: Remote File Access Monitor
RFB: Request For Bid
RFC: Reconstruction Finance Corporation (defunct)
RFD: Ready for Data
Rural Free Delivery
RFE: Radio Free Europe
RFFSA: Rede Feroviaria Federal (Brazilian Railways)
rfg: refunding
RFI: Radio Frequency Interference
Ready for Issue
Request For Information
RFM: Rural Financial Market

RFMS: Remote File Management System
RFNM: Ready For Next Message
RFO: Request for Factory Order
RF&P: Richmond, Fredericksburg & Potomac (railroad)
RFP: Request For Proposal
Request For Purchase
RFQ: Request For Quotation (Quote)
rfrsh: refresh
RFS: Report Forwarding System
rfsh: refresh
RFSP: Request for System Proposal
RFT: Request For Tender
Request for Test
RG: Varig (airline)
RGB: R. G. Barry Corp. (ASE)
RGC: Republic Gypsum Co. (NYSE)
RGCAS: Remote Global Computer Access Service
RGL: Regal International Inc. (NYSE)
RGO: Ranger Oil Ltd. (NYSE)
RGP: Remote Graphics Processor
RGS: Rio Grande Southern (railroad)
Rochester Gas & Electric Corp. (NYSE)
RGW: Rat für gegenseitige Wirtschaftshilfe (Council for Mutual Economic Assistance) (German)
RH: Air Rhodesia (airline)
Red Herring
RHD: Rhodes Inc. (NYSE)
RHH: H. H. Robertson Co. (NYSE)
RHI: Robert Halmi Inc. (ASE)
Rhodes: Rhodes Inc. (newspaper)
RHR: Receiver Holding Register
Rohr Industries Inc. (NYSE)
RHS: Right-Hand Side
RI: Chicago, Rock Island and Pacific Railroad Company
Radice Corp. (NYSE)
Real Income
Register Immediate
Report of Investigation
Risk Insurance
Runaway Inflation
Tricon International Airlines
RIA: Registered Investment Adviser
Regulatory Impact Analysis
RIB: Referee In Bankruptcy
Rural Industries Bureau
RIC: Radar Interface Control
Read-In Counter
RICO: Racketeering Influenced and Corrupt Organizations Act
RID: Review Item Disposition
RIE: Recognized Investment Exchange (UK)
Riedel Environmental Technologies Inc. (ASE)
Riedel: Riedel Environmental Technologies Inc. (newspaper)
RIF: Real Estate Securities Income Fund Inc. (ASE)
Reduction In Force
Reliability Improvement Factor
RIH: Read Inhibit
RIISOM: Research Institute for Iron, Steel, and other Metals
RIL: Koninklijke Java-China-Paketvaart Lijnen (Royal Java-China-Packet Line) (steamship)
Res Ipsa Loquitur
Royal Interocean Lines (steamship)
RIM: Read-In Mode
RIMS: Remote Information Management System
RINT: Reverse Interrupt
RIO: Relocatable Input/Output
Royal International Optical Corp. (NYSE)
RioAl: Rio Algom Ltd. (newspaper)
RIOC: Remote Input/Output Controller
RIOT: Retrieval of Information by On-Line Terminal
RIQS: Remote Information Query System

RIR: Request Immediate Reply
RI/RO: Roll-In/Roll-Out
RIS: Rock Island Southern (railroad)
RISC: Reduced Instruction Set Computing
Riser: Riser Foods Inc. (newspaper)
RIT: Reverse Income Tax
RITA: Refundable Income Tax Account
RiteAid: Rite Aid Corp. (newspaper)
RIV: Riverbend International Corp. (ASE)
Rivbnd: Riverbend International Corp. (newspaper)
RJ: Royal Jordanian Airlines
RJamFn: Raymond James Financial Inc. (newspaper)
RJE: Remote Job Entry
RJET: Remote Job Entry Terminal
RJEX: Remote Job Entry Executive
RJF: Raymond James Financial Inc. (NYSE)
Remote Job Entry Processor
RJP: Realistic Job Previews
RK: Air Afrique (airline)
Ark Restaurants Corp. (ASE)
RKG: Rockingham (railroad)
RKR: Rack Register
RKY: Rockaway Corp. (NYSE)
RL: Record Length
Regent's Line (steamship)
Remote Loopback
Residential Lease
Round Lot
RLA: Railway Labor Act
Remote Loop Adapter
RLC: RLC Corp. (NYSE) (newspaper)
Run Length Coding
RLD: Relocation Dictionary
Retail Liquor Dealer
RLE: Receiver Latch Enable
RLI: RLI Corp. (NYSE)
RLI Cp: RLI Corp. (newspaper)
RLIN: Research Library Information Network
RLM: Reynolds Metal Co. (NYSE)
RLO: Round Lot Orders
RLR: Record Length Register
Royal Rotterdam Lloyd (steamship)
RLSD: Received Line Signal Detector
RLT: Living Trust
RltRef: Realty ReFund Trust (newspaper)
RltSou: Realty South Investors Inc. (newspaper)
rm: reichsmark (currency of Germany)
R&M: Redistribution and Marketing
Reports and Memoranda
RM: Raw Material
Registered Mail
Register Memory
Resource Manager
Retail Manager
Rotterdam Metro
RMA: Radio Manufacturers' Association
Random Multiple Access
Reliability, Maintainability, Availability
Rubber Manufacturers Association
RMACHA: Rocky Mountain Automated Clearing House Association
RMA: Range Maximum
RMC: American Restaurant Partners LP (ASE)
RMD: Ready Money Down
rmdr: remainder
RME: Rack-Mount Extender
RMI: Residential Mortgage Investments Inc. (ASE)
RMK: Robert-Mark Inc. (ASE)
RML: Relational Machine Language
Royal Mail Lines (UK)
Russell Corp. (NYSE)
RMON: Resident Monitor
RMPI: Remote Memory Port Interface

RMR: RAC Mortgage Investment Corp. (ASE)
RMS: Real Market Share
Record Management System
Recovery Management Support
RMS International Inc. (ASE)
RMS Int: RMS International Inc. (newspaper)
rmt: remote
RMU: Resource Management Unit
RMW: Ready-Modify-Write
RMX: Remote Multiplexer
RN: Requisition Number
RNB: Received - Not Billed
Republic New York Corp. (NYSE)
RNC: Request Next Character
RNCF: Reseau National des Chemins de Fer (Madagascar National Railways)
RNET: Remote Network
rngt: renegotiate
RNMC: Regional Network Measurement Center
RNR: Receive Not Ready
RNT: RECO International Inc. (ASE)
RO: Read Only
Receive Only
Receiving Office (Officer)
Receiving Order
Regional Office
TAROM (Transporturile Aerriene Romine-Roumanian Air Transport)
ROA: Return On Assets
ROAM: Return On Assets Managed
ROB: Run On Bank
ROBAR: Read Only Back-Up Address Register
RobMk: Robert-Mark Inc. (newspaper)
Robtsn: H. H. Robertson Co. (newspaper)
ROC: Reevaluation Of Capital
Required Operational Capability
Return On Capital
ROCE: Return On Capital Employed
RochG: Rochester Gas & Electric Corp. (newspaper)
RochTl: Rochester Telephone Corp. (newspaper)
Rockwl: Rockwell International Corp. (newspaper)
ROD: Reorder On Demand
RodRen: Rodman & Renshaw Capital Group Inc. (newspaper)
ROE: Rate Of Exchange
Return-On-Equity
Roebling Property Investors Inc. (ASE)
Roeblg: Roebling Property Investors Inc. (newspaper)
ROF: Remote Operator Facility
ROG: Receipt-Of-Goods
Rogers Corp. (ASE)
Rogers: Rogers Corp. (newspaper)
ROH: Rohm & Haas Co. (NYSE)
RoHaas: Rohm & Haas Co. (newspaper)
Rohr: Rohr Industries Inc. (newspaper)
ROI: Rate Of Interest
Return On Invested capital
Return On Investment
River Oaks Industries Inc. (NYSE)
ROK: Rockwell International Corp. (NYSE)
ROL: Rollins Inc. (NYSE)
RolinE: Rollins Environmental Services Inc. (newspaper)
Rollins: Rollins Inc. (newspaper)
ROLS: Remote On-Line Subsystem
ROM: Read-Only Memory
Return on Market Value
Rio Algom Ltd. (ASE)
ROMA: Return on Managed Assets
ROMAD: Read Only Memory Automatic Design
ROMV: Return On Market Value

RONA: Return on Net Assets
RONS: Read Only Nano Store
ROOI: Return On Original Investment
ROP: Registered Options Principal
Reorder Price
Right Of Possession
ROR: Rate Of Return
Right Of Rescission
Rorer Group Inc. (NYSE)
Rorer: Rorer Group Inc. (newspaper)
ROS: Read-Only Storage
Resident Operating System
Return On Sales
Rights Of Stockholders (Shareholders)
rot: rotate
ROTH: Read Only Tape Handler
Rothch: L. F. Rothschild Unterberg Towbin Holdings Inc. (newspaper)
ROTR: Receive-Only Typing Reperforator
ROW: Right-Of-Way companies
Rowan: Rowan Companies Inc. (newspaper)
Royce: Royce Value Trust Inc. (newspaper)
RoyInt: Royal International Optical Corp. (newspaper)
RoylBu: Royal Business Group Inc. (newspaper)
RoylD: Royal Dutch Petroleum Co. (newspaper)
RQL: Rejectable Quality Level
RP: Reader-Printer
Reader/Punch
Real Property
Receive Processor
Repurchase Agreement
Retroactive Pay
Return Premium
Role Playing
RPA: Robinson-Patman Act
RPB: Remote Programming Box
RPC: Regional Processing Center
Registered Protective Circuit
RPC Energy Services Inc. (newspaper)
RPCS: Reject Processing and Control System
RPE: Relative Price Effect
Required Page-End character
RPG: Report Program Generator
RPI: Read, Punch and Interpret
Retail Price Index
Rows Per Inch
RPL: Remote Program Loader
Robot Programming Language
RPM: Repeats Per Minute
Resale Price Maintenance
Retail Price Maintenance
Revolutions Per Minute
RPN: Real Page Number
Regular Processor Network
Reverse Polish Notation
RPO: Railway Post Office
RPPE: Research, Program, Planning, Evaluation
RPQ: Request for Price Quotation
RPROM: Reprogrammable Read-Only Memory
RPS: Real-Time Programming System
Records Per Sector
Remote Printing System
Revolutions Per Second
Rotational Position Sensing
rpt: repeat
RPT: Records Per Track
Repeat character
RPTC: Relative Priority Test Circuit
RPU: Regional Processing Unit
RQ: Repeat Request
R&QA: Reliability and Quality Assurance
R&QC: Reliability and Quality Control
RQS: Rate Quoting System
rr: railroad
R&R: Reliability and Response
RR: Raritan River (railroad)
Rate of Return
Receive Ready

Rediscount Rate
Registered Representative
Register to Register
Research Report
Reserve Requirement
Return Rate
Return Register
Rhodesian Railways
Rodman & Renshaw Capital Group Inc. (NYSE)

RRA: Railroad Retirement Act
Remote Record Access

RRB: Railroad Retirement Board

RRDS: Relative Record Data Set

RRF: Realty ReFund Trust (NYSE)

RRG: Resource Request Generator

RRM: Renegotiable-Rate Mortgage

RRN: Relative-Record Number
Remote Request Number

RROS: Resistive Read-Only Storage

RRP: Recommended Retail Price
Reverse Repurchase agreement

RRR: Raritan River Railroad
Required Rate of Return
Residential Resources Mortgages Investments Corp. (ASE)
Run-Time Reduction Ratio

RRT: Relative Retention Time

RRTS: Remote Radar Tracking System

RRYS: Rhodesian Railways

RS: Real Storage
Recording Secretary
Record Separator character
Redeemable Stock
Registered Securities
Regular Savings
Revenue Sharing
Roberval and Seguenay (railway)
Runaway Shop

RSA: Railway Supply Association

RSE: Richmond Stock Exchange

RSFSR: Russian Soviet Federated Socialist Republic

RSI: Realty South Investors Inc. (ASE)

RSM: Real Storage Management

RSM: Research into Site Management

RS or L: Rated Same or Lower

RSP: Required Space character
Roscoe, Snyder and Pacific (railroad)

RSR: Riser Foods Inc. (ASE)

RSS: Rockdale, Sandow and Southern (railroad)

rst: reset

RST: Remote Station

RSU: Remote Service Unit

rt: right

RT: Real Time
Regressive Tax
Remote Terminal
Reperforator/Transmitter
Repressive Tax
Resorts International Inc. (ASE)
Restraint of Trade
River Terminal (railway)
Royalty Trust (UK)

RTA: Reciprocal Trade Agreement
Remote Trunk Arrangement

RTB: Response/Throughput Bias

RTBA: Rate to Be Agreed

RTC: Real-Time Clock
Regional Term Contract
Resolution Trust Corporation
Rochester Telephone Corp. (NYSE)

R&TD: Research and Technological Development Policy

RTD: Research and Technology Development
Return To Duty

rte: route

RTE: Real-Time Executive
Remote Terminal Emulator
Request To Expedite
RTE Corp. (NYSE) (newspaper)

RTH: Houston Oil Royalty Trust (NYSE)
RTI: Real-Time Interface
Renewable Term Insurance
RTL: Resistor-Transistor Logic
RTM: Railway Transfer Company of Minneapolis
Real-Time Management
Registered Trade Mark
Register Transfer Module
Research Technical Memoranda
rtn: return
RTN: Raytheon Co. (NYSE)
RTOS: Real-Time Operating System
RTP: Reich & Tang LP (NYSE)
Request To Purchase
RTPC: Restrictive Trade Practices Commission
rts: rights
RTS: Real-Time System
Right To Strike
Russ Togs Inc. (NYSE)
RTSA: Retail Trading Standards Association
RTTY: Radio Teletypewriter
RTW: Ready-To-Wear
Right To Work
RU: Reserve Unit
Rousseau Aviation (airline)
rub: ruble (currency of the Soviet Union)
Rubmd: Rubbermaid Inc. (newspaper)
Rudick: Ruddick Corp. (newspaper)
RUF: Revolving Underwriting Facility
RUS: Russ Berrie & Company Inc. (NYSE)
RussBr: Russ Berrie & Company Inc. (newspaper)
Russell: Russell Corp. (newspaper)
RusTg: Russ Togs Inc. (newspaper)
RV: Rahway Valley (railway)
Realizable Value
Reeve Aleutian Airways
RVA: Recorded Voice Announcement
RVR: American Land Cruisers Inc. (ASE)
RvrOak: River Oaks Industries Inc. (newspaper)
RVT: Royce Value Trust Inc. (NYSE)
RW: Read/Write
RWCS: Report Writer Control System
RWDSU: Retail, Wholesale and Department Store Union
RWM: Read/Write Memory
rwnd: rewind
RWO: Routine Work Order
rwy: railway
rx: receive
RX: Capitol Air Services (airline)
Rxene: Rexene Corp. (newspaper)
RXH: Rexham Corp. (NYSE)
RXN: Rexene Corp. (NYSE)
RX(NP): Non-polarized Return-to-Zero recording
ry: railway
RY: Royal Air Lao (airline)
RYC: Raychem Corp. (NYSE)
Ryder: Ryder System Inc. (newspaper)
RYK: Rykoff-Sexton Inc. (NYSE)
Rykoff: Rykoff-Sexton Inc. (newspaper)
RYL: Ryland Group Inc., The (NYSE)
Ryland: Ryland Group Inc., The (newspaper)
Rymer: Rymer Co., The (newspaper)
RYR: Rymer Company, The (NYSE)
RZ: Aero Mech (airline)
Reset (Return) to Zero
RZ(P): Polarized Return-to-Zero recording

S

s: scalar
schilling (currency of Austria)
seasonal
second
seller
sender
set
sign
silversmith
software
sold
source
stack
state
stockbroker
storage
switch
switching
synchronous
system

S: No option offered (option listings of newspapers)
Sears Roebuck & Co. (NYSE)
Signed (before signature on typed copy of document)
Split or Stock dividend (stock listings of newspapers)

sa: semiannual(ly)
semiautomatic

S&A: Savannah & Atlanta (railroad)

S/A: Survivorship Agreement (banking)

SA: Salary Administration
Savings Account
Security Analyst
Shipped Assembled
Shipping Authority
Single Act (EC)
Sociedad Anonima (Spanish corporation)
Société Anonyme (Belgian and French corporation)
Source Address
South African Airways
Special Assessment
Stage II Apparel Corp. (ASE)
State Agency
Structured Analysis
Subject to Approval
Subsistence Allowance
System Administrator
Systems Analyst

SAA: Saatchi & Saatchi Company PLC (NYSE)
Sherman Anti-Trust Act
South African Airways
Special Arbitrage Account

SAAOC: System of Analysis and Assignment of Operations according to Capacities

Saatchi: Saatchi & Saatchi Company PLC (newspaper)

SAB: Sabine Corp. (NYSE)
Scientific Advisory Board
Special Assessment Bond
Stack Access Block

SABE: Society for Automation in Business Education

SABENA: Societé Anonyme Belge d'Exploitation de la Navigation Aerienne (Belgian Air Lines)

SABF: Subarray Beam Former

Sabine: Sabine Corp. (newspaper)

SabnR: Sabine Royalty Trust (newspaper)

SABR: Symbolic Assembler for Binary Relocatable Programs

SABRE: Semiautomated Business Research Environment

SAC: Storage Access Channel
Storage Access Control
SACCS: Schedule and Cost-Control System
SACK: Selection Acknowledge
SA&CL: South Atlantic and Caribbean Line (steamship)
SACS: Simulation for the Analysis of Computer Systems
SA&D: Structured Analysis and Design
SAD: Sealed And Delivery
Single Administrative Document (EC)
Store Address Director
SADP: System Architecture Design Package
SADT: Structured Analysis and Design Technique
SAE: Stand Alone Executive
SAEF: Small-order Automatic Execution Facility (UK)
SAESA: Servicios Aeros Especiales Sociedad Anonima (Mexican Airline)
SAF: Scudder New Asia Fund Inc. (NYSE)
Structural Adjustment Facility
SAFE: Settlement and Accelerated Funds Exchange (Chicago)
SWIFT and Foreign Exchange
SAFER: Structural Analysis, Frailty Evaluation and Redesign
SAFF: Store and Forward Facsimile
SaftKln: Safety-Kleen Corp. (newspaper)
SAG: Sage Energy Co. (ASE)
Sage: Sage Energy Co. (newspaper)
SAGE: Semiautomatic Ground Environment
SAH: Sahara Casino Partners LP (NYSE)
SahCas: Sahara Casino Partners L.P. (newspaper)
SAI: Allstar Inns LP (ASE)
Sales Activity Index
Subarchitectural Interface
SAIF: Savings Association Insurance Fund
SAINT: Symbolic Automatic Integrator
SAJ: St. Joseph Light & Power Co. (NYSE)
sal: salary
SAL: Sale And Leaseback
Savings and Loan Association
Seaboard Air Line (railroad)
Structured Assembly Language
Svenska Amerika Linien (Swedish-American Line) (steamship)
Symbolic Assembly Language
Systems Assembly Language
Salant: Salant Corp. (newspaper)
Salem: Salem Corp. (newspaper)
SallieM: Student Loan Marketing Assn. (newspaper)
Salomn: Salomon Inc. (newspaper)
SAM: Samson Energy Company LP (ASE)
Sequential Access Memory
Shared-Appreciation Mortgage
Society for the Advancement of Management
System Analysis Machine
Systems Adaptor Module
SAMANTHA: System for the Automated Management of Text from a Hierarchical Arrangement
SAMM: Systematic Activity Modeling Method
SAMOS: Silicon and Aluminum Metal Oxide Semiconductor
SAMPS: Subdivision and Map Plotting System

Samson: Samson Energy Company L.P. (newspaper)
SAMSON: Strategic Automatic Message Switching Operational Network
SAN: San Carlos Milling Company Inc. (ASE)
Sandersville (railroad)
Small Area Network
Subsidiary Account Number
SANDA: Supplies and Accounts
Sandy: Sandy Corp. (newspaper)
SAnitRt: Santa Anita Realty Enterprises Inc. (newspaper)
Sanmrk: Sanmark-Stardust Inc. (newspaper)
SANR: Subject to Approval-No Risks
SANS: Simplified Account-Numbering System
SAP: Soon As Possible
Structural Analysis Program
SAPR: Semi-Annual Progress Report
SAR: Santa Anita Realty Enterprises Inc. (NYSE)
Segment Address Register
Semiannual Report
Source Address Register
South African Railways
Stock-Appreciation Relief (UK)
Stock-Appreciation Rights
Storage Address Register
SARA: System Availability and Reliability Analysis
SaraLee: Sara Lee Corp. (newspaper)
SARG: Self-Adapting Report Generator
SARM: Set Asynchronous Response Mode
SARP: Standards and Recommended Practices
SAS: Scandinavian Airlines System
Statement of Auditing Standards
Statistical Analysis System
SASR: Semi-Annual Status Report
SAT: Schafer Value Trust Inc. (NYSE)
System Access Technique
Systems Approach to Training
SATA: Sherman Anti-Trust Act
Sociedade Acoriana de Transportes Aereas (Portuguese Airline)
SATF: Shortest Access Time First
SATIATER: Statistical Approach to Investment Appraisal to Evaluate Risk
SATNET: Satellite Network
SATS: San Antonio Transit System
SAU: Smallest Addressable Unit
SaulRE: B. F. Saul Real Estate Investment Trust (newspaper)
sav: save
savings
SAV: Stock At Valuation
SAVE: Swiss-Alberg-Vienna Express (railroad)
System for Automatic Value Exchange
Savin: Savin Corp. (newspaper)
SAVT: Secondary Address Vector Table
SAX: Saxon Oil Development Partners LP (ASE)
SaxnO: Saxon Oil Development Partners L.P. (newspaper)
sb: standby
stockbroker
SB: Salomon Inc. (NYSE)
Samurai bond (Japan)
Savings Bank
Savings Bond
Seaboard World Airways
Secondary Boycott
Senior Bond
Shipping Board
Short Bill

Small Business
South Buffalo (railway)
Stack Base
Straw Boss
Strike Benefits
Surety Bond

SBA: Sbarro Inc. (ASE)
School of Business Administration
Shared Batch Area
Small Business Administration
Strategic Business Area
Subterraneos de Buenos Aires (Buenos Aires Subways)

Sbarro: Sbarro Inc. (newspaper)

SBC: Ferrocarril Sonora Baja California (Baja California Railway)
Single Board Computer
Small Business Computer
Southwestern Bell Corp. (NYSE)

SBCA: Sensor Based Control Adapter

SBCC: Senate Bonding and Currency Committee

SBCL: Special Buyer Credit Limit

SBCU: Sensor Based Control Unit

SBD: Savings Bond Division
Seaboard Coast Line (railroad)
Structured Block Diagram

SBDC: Small Business Development Center

SbdCp: Seaboard Corp. (newspaper)

SBF: Supplementary Fringe Benefits

SBI: Savings Bank Insurance
Share of Beneficial Interest
Single Byte Interleaved
Small Business Institute

SBIC: Small Business Investment Company

SBIR: Small Business Innovation Research
Storage Bus in Register

SBK: Signet Banking Corp. (NYSE)

SBL: Symbol Technologies Inc. (NYSE)

SBLI: Savings Bank Life Insurance

SBM: Space Block Map
Speed-O-Print Business Machines Corp. (ASE)

sbmdl: submodel

SBN: Sunbelt Nursery Group Inc. (ASE)

SBO: Showboat Inc. (NYSE)

SBP: Semiconductor Bipolar Processor
Special Block Purchase
Standard Brands Paint Co. (NYSE)

SBR: Sabine Royalty Trust (NYSE)
Storage Buffer Register

SBS: Salem Corp. (ASE)
Satellite Business Systems
Small Business System
Special Block Sale
Subscript Character
Surveyed Before Shipment

SBU: Station Buffer Unit
Strategic Business Unit

sc: semiconductor
subcommittee

S&C: Shipper and Carrier
Sized and Calendered
Star and Crescent (steamship)
Sumter & Choctaw (railroad)

SC: Cruzeiro (airline)
Safe Custody
Safety Clause
Satellite Computer
Selector Channel
Send Common
Sequence Controller
Service Charge
Session Control
Seul Cours (Sole Quotation) (French)

Sharp Cash
Shell Transport & Trading Company PLC, The (NYSE)
Shopping Center
Silver Certificates
Single Column
Special Committee
Stock Certificate
Submarine Cables Ltd.
Subscriber Computer
Subsidiary Company
Sumter and Choctaw (railway)
Sweetheart Contract (Clause)
Sylvania Central (railroad)
System Control (Controller)

SCA: Servo Corporation of America (ASE)
Shareholder Credit Accounting
Synchronous Communications Adapter
System Control Area

SCAC: Syntax-Controlled Acoustic Classifier

SCAD: Database on documents published by the Community and periodical articles on the Community (EC)
Schedule, Capability, Availability, Dependability
Subprogram Change Affect Diagram

SCADA: Supervisory Control and Data Acquisition

SCALD: Structural Computer Aided Logic Design

SCalEd: Southern California Edison Co. (newspaper)

SCAM: Synchronous Communications Access Method

SCAN: Schedule Analysis
Stockmarket Computer Answering Network (UK)

SCANA: SCANA Corp. (newspaper)

ScandF: Scandinavia Fund Inc., The (newspaper)

SCAR: Subcell Address Register

SCARA: Selective Compliance Assembly Robot Arm

SCarlo: San Carlos Milling Company Inc. (newspaper)

SCARS: Status, Control Alerting and Reporting System

SCATS: Sequentially Controlled Automatic Transmitter Start

SCB: Stack Control Block
Station Control Block
Stream Control Block
Subscriber Control Block

SCC: Satellite Communications Controller
Security Capital Corp. (ASE)
Security Commodity Code
Sequential Control Counter
Shipping and Coal Company (steamship)
Specialized Common Carrier
Standard Commodity Classification
Standard Commodity Codes
Standards Council of Canada
State Corporation Commission
Stock Clearing Corporation
Strapped, Corded and Sealed
Synchronous Communications Controller
System Control Center

SCCB: Software Configuration Control Board

SCCC: Shared Contingency Computer Center

SCCFF: Second Check Character Flip-Flop

SCCS: Source Code Control System
Standard Commodity Classification System

SCCU: Single Channel Control Unit

SCD: Serial Cryptographic Device
Service Computation Date
System Contents Directory
SCDC: System Control Distribution Computer
ScdNA: Scudder New Asia Fund Inc. (newspaper)
SCDP: Society of Certified Data Processors
SCDR: Subsystem Controller Definition Record
SCE: Shanghai-Canton Express (railroad)
Southern California Edison Co. (NYSE)
Standard Card Enclosure
Sceptre: Sceptre Resources Ltd. (newspaper)
SCERT: Systems and Computer Evaluation and Review Technique
SCEU: Selector Channel Emulation Unit
SCF: Satellite Control Facility
Scandinavia Fund Inc., The (ASE)
SCFL Synchronous Communications Feature
SCG: SCANA Corp. (NYSE)
sch: schedule
scheduler
SCH: Charles Schwab Corp., The (NYSE)
Scheib: Earl Scheib Inc. (newspaper)
Schfr: Schafer Value Trust Inc. (newspaper)
Schlmb: Schlumberger Ltd. (newspaper)
SchoolP: School Pictures Inc. (newspaper)
SchrPlg: Schering-Plough Corp. (newspaper)
Schwab: Schwab Safe Company Inc. (newspaper)
Schwb: Charles Schwab Corp., The (newspaper)
SCI: Sea Containers Incorporated (steamship)
Shipping Corporation of India (steamship)
System Control Interface
SciAtl: Scientific-Atlanta Inc. (newspaper)
SCIENCE: Stimulation of the International Cooperation and Interchange Need by European Research Scientists (EC)
SciLsg: Scientific Leasing Inc. (newspaper)
SciMgt: Science Management Corp. (newspaper)
SCIN: Self-Canceling Installment Note
SCIP: System Control Interface Package
SCL: Seaboard Coast Line (railroad)
Sequential Control Logic
Stepan Co. (ASE)
System Control Language
SCLA: Section Carry Look Ahead
SCM: Small Core Memory
SCMP: Simple Cost-Effective Microprocessor
SC&MR: Strouds Creek and Muddlety (railroad)
scn: scanner
SCOM: System Communication
Scope: Scope Industries (newspaper)
SCOPE: Schedule-Cost-Performance
Special Committee On Paperless Entries (California)
SCORE: Service Corps Of Retired Executives
Special Claim On Residual Equity

System Cost and Operational Resource Evaluation

SCORPIO: Subject-Content-Oriented Retriever for Processing Information On-Line

SCOR U: SCOR U.S. Corp. (newspaper)

ScottP: Scott Paper Co. (newspaper)

Scottys: Scotty's Inc. (newspaper)

SCP: Scope Industries (ASE)
Sleeping Car Porters Union
Supervisory Control Program
System Control Program

SCPC: Single Channel Per Channel

SCPD: Scratch Pad

SCR: Scan Control Register
Sea Containers Ltd. (NYSE)
Silicon-Controlled Rectifier
Single Character Recognition
Software Change Report
System Change Request

SCREAM: Society for the Registration of Estate Agents and Mortgage Brokers

SCS: Secondary Clear to Send
Small Computer System

SCT: Service Counter Terminal
Sioux City Terminal (railway)
Special Characters Table
Step Control Table

SCTR: Sector Register

SCU: Sequence Control Unit
Station Control Unit
Storage Control Unit
System Control Unit

ScurRn: Scurry-Rainbow Oil Ltd. (newspaper)

SCX: L. S. Starrett Co., The (NYSE)
Selector Channel Executive

sd: stamped (stocks)

S&D: Sealed and Delivered
Supply and Demand

SD: Sales Department
Sales Director
Same Day
Scrip Department
Secondary Distribution
Send Data
Service Department
Settlement Date
Sight Draft
Single Deck
Single Density
Stamped (NYSE)
Standard Deduction
Standard Deviation
Stock Dividend
Sudan Airways
Supply Department
System Development
Systems Design

SDA: Source Data Automation

SD&AE: San Diego & Arizona Eastern (railroad)

SDAL: Switched-Data Access Line

SDB: Safe Deposit Box
Software Development Board
Special District Bond
Storage Data Bus

SDBI: Storage Data Bus-In

SDBL: Sight Draft Bill of Lading

SDBO: Storage Data Bus-Out

SDC: Signal Data Converter

SD CO: Safe Deposit Company

SDD: Stored Data Description
System for Distributed Databases

SDDL: Stored Data Definition Language

SDE: Source Data Entry

SDF: Software Development Facility

SDI: Selective Dissemination of Information

SDK: System Design Kit

SDL: Software Design Language
System Directory List

SDLC: Synchronous Data Link Control

SDM: Semiconductor Disk Memory
Synchronous Digital Machine
Systems Development Methodology
SDMA: Space-Division Multiple Access
SDMJ: September, December, March, June (securities)
SDMSS: Software Development and Maintenance Support System
SDN: Synchronous Digital Transmission Network
SDOS: Scientific Disk Operating System
SDP: Source Data Processing
Sun Distributors LP (NYSE)
SDR: Special Drawing Right
SDS: Sit-Down Strike
Software Development System
SDSI: Shared Data Set Integrity
SDSU: Switched-Data Service Unit
SDT: Syntax-Directed Translation
System Down Time
SDTS: San Diego Transit System
SDU: Signal Distribution Unit
Source Data Utility
Station Display Unit
SDW: Segment Descriptor Word
Southdown Inc. (NYSE)
SDX: Satellite Data Exchange
SDY: Sandy Corp. (ASE)
SE: Ferrocarril del Sureste (Southeast Railroad)
Seasonal Employee
Shareholder's Equity
Single Entry
Stack Empty
Stock Exchange
Sun Electric Corp. (NYSE)
System Engineer
Systems Engineering
SEA: Single European Act (EC)
Static Error Analysis
SEABOARD: Seaboard World Airways
SEAC: Standards Eastern Automatic Computer
SeaCnt: Sea Containers Ltd. (newspaper)
SEACOST: Systematic Equipment Analysis and Cost Optimization Scanning Technique
Seagrm: Seagram Company Ltd., The (newspaper)
Seagul: Seagull Energy Corp. (newspaper)
SealAir: Sealed Air Corp. (newspaper)
SEAM: Software Engineering and Management
Seamn: Seamen's Corp. (newspaper)
Seaport: Seaport Corp. (newspaper)
SEAQ: Stock Exchange Automated Quotation System (UK)
Sears: Sears Roebuck & Co. (newspaper)
SEATS: Stock Exchange Automated Trading System (Australia)
SEB: Seaboard Corp. (ASE)
sec: second
section
SEC: Securities and Exchange Commission
Single Error Correcting
Sterling Electronics Corp. (ASE)
SecCap: Security Capital Corp. (newspaper)
SECMA: Stock Exchange Computer Managers Association
SECO: Securities and Exchange Commission Organization
SecPac: Security Pacific Corp. (newspaper)
SEDIT: Source Program Editor
SEDOC: Système Européen de Diffusion des Offres et des

demandes s'emploi enregistrees en Compensation Internationale (European System for the International Clearing of Job Vacancies) (French) (EC)

SEE: Sealed Air Corp. (NYSE)
Standard Error of Estimate
Systems Effectiveness Engineering

SEEA: Software Error Effects Analysis

SEEC: Single Error and Erasure Correcting

SEER: Systems Engineering, Evaluation, and Research

seg: segment

SEGB: South Eastern Gas Board (steamship)

SEI: Self-Employed Income

sel: selector

SELA: Latin American Economic System

Selas: Selas Corporation of America (newspaper)

SELDAM: Selective Data Management system

SeligAs: Seligman & Associates Inc. (newspaper)

SELLER: Seller's Option (NYSE)

SEM: Shared Equity Mortgage
Systems Engineering & Manufacturing Corp. (ASE)
Systems Engineering Management

Semtch: Semtech Corp. (newspaper)

SEND: Securities and Exchange Commission News Digest

SEO: Seaport Corp. (ASE)

SEP: Simplified Employee Pension

SEPOL: Soil-Engineering Problem-Oriented Language

seq: sequence
sequential

SEQ: Storage Equities Inc. (NYSE)

Sequa: Sequa Corp. (newspaper)

ser: serial
series

SER: Sierracin Corp. (ASE)

SERA: Sierra Railroad

SERDES: Serializer/Deserializer

SEREP: System Error Recording Editing Program

SERF: System for Equipment Requirements Forecasting

Servo: Servo Corporation of America (newspaper)

Servotr: Servotronics Inc. (newspaper)

SES: Stock Exchange of Singapore

SESAME: Hydrocarbon technology and energy demonstration projects (EC)
Supermarket Electronic Scanning for Automatic Merchandise Entry

SESDAQ: Stock Exchange of Singapore Dealing and Automated Quotation System

SEU: Source Entry Utility

S&EV: Saratoga & Encampment Valley (railroad)

SEV: Soviet Ekonomicheskoy Vzaimopomoschchi (Council for Mutual Economic Assistance) (Russian)

S&F: Stock and Fixtures

S/F: Statute of Frauds

SF: Scale Factor
Seasonal Fluctuation
Single-Frequency signaling
Sinking Fund
Stifel Financial Corp. (NYSE)
Stock Fund
Strike Fund

S&FA: Shipping and Forwarding Agent

SFA: Scientific-Atlanta Inc. (NYSE)

SFAAW: Stove, Furnace, and Allied Appliance Workers (union)
SFAR: System Failure Analysis Report
SFAS: Statements of Financial Accounting Standards
SFB: Standard Federal Bank (NYSE)
SFBF: Standard Forms Bureau Form
SFBRR: San Francisco Belt Railroad
SFC: Sales Finance Companies
S-bank Frequency Converter
SFE: Safeguard Scientifics Inc. (NYSE)
SFeEP: Santa Fe Energy Partners L.P. (newspaper)
SFEM: Second-Tiered Foreign Exchange Market
SFeSP: Santa Fe Southern Pacific Corp. (newspaper)
SFES: Small Firms Employment Subsidy
SfgdSc: Safeguard Scientifics Inc. (newspaper)
SFIP: Standard Flood Insurance Policy
SFIS: Small Firms Information Service
SFM: SFM Corp. (ASE) (newspaper)
SFMR: San Francisco Municipal Railway
SFP: Santa Fe Energy Partners LP (NYSE)
Straight Fixed Price
SFR: Sinking Fund Return
SFS: Super Food Services Inc. (ASE)
SFSE: San Francisco Stock Exchange
SFSR: Soviet Federated Socialist Republic
sft: shift
SFT: Special Financial Transactions
SFX: Santa Fe Southern Pacific Corp. (NYSE)
SFY: Swift Energy Co. (ASE)
SG: Aerotransportes Litoral Argentino (Argentine Coastal Air Transport) (Airline)
Scientific Leasing Inc. (ASE)
South Georgia (railroad)
Specialty Goods
SG&A: Selling, General, and Administrative expenses
SGC: Superior Surgical Manufacturing Company Inc. (ASE)
SGDF: Supergroup Distribution Frame
SGI: Slattery Group Inc. (NYSE)
SGML: Standard Generalized Markup Language
SgnlApl: Signal Apparel Company Inc. (newspaper)
SGO: Seagull Energy Corp. (NYSE)
SGP: Schering-Plough Corp. (NYSE)
SGR: Saudi Government Railroad (Saudi Arabia)
Surinam Government Railway
sh: shareholder
stockholder
SH: Sahsa (airline)
Spartech Corp. (ASE)
Steelton and Highspire (railroad)
SHA: Smith-Hughes Act
ShaerS: Shaer Shoe Corp. (newspaper)
ShawIn: Shaw Industries Inc. (newspaper)
SHB: Scotty's Inc. (NYSE)
SHD: Sherwood Group Inc., The (ASE)
SHE: Shearson Lehman Brothers Holdings Inc. (NYSE)
Shelby: Shelby Williams Industries Inc. (newspaper)
SHELL: Shell Oil Company

ShellT: Shell Transport & Trading Company PLC., The (newspaper)
SHEX: Sundays and Holidays Excepted
shf: shift
SHF: Super High Frequency
ship: ship
shipment
shipping
shipmt: shipment
SHK: Sidirodromi Hellinikou Kratous (Greek-Hellenic State Railways)
ShLeh: Shearson Lehman Brothers Holdings Inc. (newspaper)
ShltCm: Shelter Components Corp. (newspaper)
SHO: Starrett Housing Corp. (ASE)
Shopco: Shopco Laurel Centre L. P. (newspaper)
SHP: Securities Shipped as Instructed
shr: share (stock)
SHREAD: Share Registration and Dividend Warrants
shrs: shares (stocks)
Shrwin: Sherwin-Williams Co., The (newspaper)
shs: shares
SHS: Shaer Shoe Corp. (ASE)
shtg: shortage
SH TN: Short Ton (2000 lbs.)
SHV: Standard Havens Inc. (ASE)
SHW: Sherwin-Williams Co., The (NYSE)
Shwbt: Showboat Inc. (newspaper)
ShwdG: Sherwood Group Inc., The (newspaper)
SHX: Shaw Industries Inc. (NYSE)
SHY: Syllable Hyphen character
S&I: Stocked and Issued
SI: ACM Government Spectrum Fund (NYSE)
Seasonal Industry
Shift-In character
Short Interest
Simple Interest
Single Instruction
Sound Investment
Spokane International (railroad)
Swap Instruction
SIA: Securities Industry Association
Signal Apparel Company Inc. (NYSE)
Society of Industrial Accountants (Canada)
Special Investor Account
SIAC: Securities Industry Automation Corporation
SIAM: Society for Industrial and Applied Mathematics
SIB: Screen Image Buffer
Securities and Investments Board (UK)
SIB-MIBOC: Securities and Investments Board and the Marketing of Investments Board Organization Commission (UK)
SIBOR: Singapore Interbank Offered Rate
SIC: Split Investment Company
Standard Industrial Classification system
SICAV: Societes d'Investissement a Capital Variable
SICOM: Securities Industry Communications
SIE: Sierra Health Service Inc. (ASE)
SierCap: Sierra Capital Realty Trust IV (newspaper)
SierCa7: Sierra Capital Realty Trust VII (newspaper)
Siercn: Sierracin Corp. (newspaper)
SierHS: Sierra Health Services Inc. (newspaper)
SierPac: Sierra Pacific Resources (newspaper)
SierSpg: Sierra Spring Water Co. (newspaper)

SIF: SIFCO Industries Inc. (ASE)
Sifco: SIFCO Industries Inc. (newspaper)
SIFF: Stock Index Futures Fund
sig: signal
signature
SIG: Southern Indiana Gas & Electric Co. (NYSE)
Special Interest Group
Sig CD: Signature Card
Sig Mis: Signature Missing
Signet: Signet Banking Corp. (newspaper)
Sig Unk: Signature Unknown
SII: Smith International Inc. (NYSE)
Strategic Impediments Initiative
Structural Impediments Initiative
SIIC: Secrétariat International des groupements professionels des Industries Chimiques des pays de la CE (International Secretariat of Professional Groups in the Chemical Industries of the E.C. countries) (French) (EC)
Sikes: Sikes Corp. (newspaper)
Silvrcst: Silvercrest Corp. (newspaper)
sim: simulator
SIM: System Information Management
SIMCON: Simulation Control
SIMIS: Single Internal Market: 1992 Information Service (U.S.)
simul: simultaneous
SIN: System Integrators Inc. (NYSE)
SIO: Serial Input-Output
SIOH: Supervision, Inspection, and Overhead
SIP: Securities Investor Protection Corporation
Sharebuilder Investment Plan
SIPA: Securities Investor Protection Act
SIPC: Securities Investor Protection Corporation
SIR: Society of Industrial Realtors
Staten Island Rapid Transit (railway)
SIRRI: Southern Industrial Railroad Incorporated
SIRT: Staten Island Rapid Transit
SIS: Scientific Information System
Scientific Instruction Set
SIT: Storage In Transit
SITC: Standard International Trade Classification
SITPRO: Simplification of International Trade Procedures
SIU: Seafarers International Union of North America
SIX: Motel 6 LP (NYSE)
SIZ: Sizeler Property Investors Inc. (NYSE)
Sizeler: Sizeler Property Investors Inc. (newspaper)
SJ: Statens Jarnvagar (Swedish State Railways)
St. Johnsbury and Lamoille County (railroad)
SJerIn: South Jersey Industries Inc. (newspaper)
SJI: South Jersey Industries Inc. (NYSE)
SJ&LC: St. Johnsbury & Lake Champlain (railroad)
SJM: J. M. Smucker Co., The (NYSE)
SJR: San Juan Racing Assn. Inc. (NYSE)
SJS: Sunshine-Jr. Stores Inc. (ASE)
SJT: San Juan Basin Royalty Trust (NYSE)
SJTR: St. Joseph Terminal Railroad
SJuanB: San Juan Basin Royalty Trust (newspaper)

SJuanR: San Juan Racing Association Inc. (newspaper)
SJW: SJW Corp. (ASE) (newspaper)
sk: safekeeping
skip
SK: Safety-Kleen Corp. (NYSE)
SAS (Scandinavian Airlines System)
Sikes Corp. (ASE)
SKB: SmithKBeecham Corp. (NYSE)
skg: safekeeping
SKN: Skolnicks Inc. (ASE)
Skolnk: Skolnicks Inc. (newspaper)
SKSL: Skaneateles Short Line (railroad)
SKY: Skyline Corp. (NYSE)
Skyline: Skyline Corp. (newspaper)
sl: sold (stocks)
S&L: Sale and Leaseback
Savings and Loan (Association)
Sydney and Louisburg (railroad)
SL: Savings and Loan (Association)
Sick Leave
Skilled Labor
SL Industries Inc. (NYSE)
Southeast Airlines
Southern Lines (steamship)
Standard Label
SLA: Sales and Loan Association
State Liquor Authority
Slattery: Slattery Group Inc. (newspaper)
S&LB: Sale and Lease-Back
SLB: Schlumberger Ltd (NYSE)
SL&C: Shipper's Load and Count
SLC: San Luis Central (railroad)
Selector Channel
Subscriber Line Charge
sld: sold (stocks)
SLD: Sold (NYSE)
Straight Line Depreciation
SLDR: System Loader
SLE: Sara Lee Corp. (NYSE)
SLG: Seligman & Associates Inc. (ASE)
SLGW: Salt Lake, Garfield and Western (railway)
SLIB: Source Library
Subsystem Library
SLIC: Savings and Loan Insurance Corporation
SLIM: Stock Line Inventory Management
Store Labor and Inventory Management
SL Ind: SL Industries Inc. (newspaper)
SLM: Student Loan Marketing Assn. (NYSE)
SLMA: Student Loan Marketing Association
SLO: Stop-Limit Order
Stop-Loss Order
SLP: Sun Energy Partners LP (NYSE)
SLR: Sierra Leone Railway
SLS: Sea-Land Service (steamship)
Selas Corporation of America (ASE)
SLSF: St. Louis-San Francisco (railroad)
SLSI: Super Large-Scale Integration
slsman: salesman
salesmen
slsmgr: salesmanager
SLSW: St. Louis Southwestern (railroad)
SL&T: Shipper's Load and Tally
SLT: Salant Corp. (NYSE)
Solid Logic Technology
SLTX: Sales Tax
SLU: Secondary Logic Unit
SLV: Silvercrest Corp. (ASE)
Stimulated Loss Value
SLVS: San Luis Valley Southern (railroad)

S&M: September and March (securities)
Supply and Maintenance

SM: Sales Manager
Scientific Management
Scientific Memorandum
Secondary Market
Second Mortgage
Seller's Market
Service Mark
Smoky Mountain (railroad)
Southmark Corp. (NYSE)
Special Memorandum
St. Mary's (railroad)
Stock Market

SMA: San Manuel Arizona (railroad)
Society of Management Accountants
Special Miscellaneous Account
Staff Management Association

SMACC: Scheduling, Manpower Allocation, and Cost Control

SMART: Scheduling Management and Allocating Resources Technique
Systems Management Analysis, Research and Test

SMB: Small- and Medium-Sized Businesses

SMC: A.O. Smith Corp. (ASE)

SME: Small and Medium-sized Enterprise (EC)

SMG: Science Management Corp. (ASE)

SMH: Semtech Corp. (ASE)

SMI: Springs Industries Inc. (NYSE)
Super Market Institute

SMIS: Society for Management Information Systems

SmithIn: Smith International Inc. (newspaper)

SMK: Sanmark-Stardust Inc. (ASE)

SmkB: SmithKline Beecham Corp. (newspaper)

SML: Security Market Line
States Marine Lines (steamship)

SMM: Secondary Mortgage Market

SMMP: Standards Methods of Measuring Performance

SMN: Seamen's Corp. (ASE)

SMO: Secondary Market Operation

SMP: Standard Motor Products Inc. (NYSE)

smpl: sample

SMR: South Manchurian Railway

SMRS: Specialized Mobile Radio System

SMS: State Mutual Securities Trust (NYSE)
Stock Management System

SMSA: Standard Metropolitan Statistical Area

Smth: A.O. Smith Corp. (ASE)

Smuckr: J. M. Smucker Co., The (newspaper)

SMV: Santa Maria Valley (railroad)
Short Market Value

SMWIA: Sheet Metal Workers' International Association (union)

S/N: Signal-to-Noise ratio

SN: Sabena (Belgian Airline)
Sacramento Northern (railway)
Shipping Note
Stock Number
Strike Notice

SNA: Snap-on Tools Corp. (NYSE)
Systems Network Architecture

SnapOn: Snap-on Tools Corp. (newspaper)

SNCB: Societé Nationale des Chemins de fer Belges (Belgian National Railways)

SNCF: Societé Nationale des Chemins de fer Francaise (French National Railways)
SNE: Sony Corp. (NYSE)
SNETI: Southern New England Telecommunications Corp. (newspaper)
SNF: Spain Fund Inc. (NYSE)
SNG: Southern New England Telecommunications Corp. (NYSE)
SNI: Sun City Industries Inc. (ASE)
SNIF: Short-Term Note-Issuance Facility
Syndicated Note-Issuance Facility
SNIMOG: Sustained Noninflationary Market-Oriented Growth
SNL: Stock Not Listed
SNLR: Services No Longer Required
SNM: Special Nuclear Materials
SNO: Polaris Industries Partners LP (ASE)
SNOBOL: String Oriented Symbolic Language
SNS: Sundstrand Corp. (NYSE)
SNT: Sonat Inc. (NYSE)
SNY: Southern New York (railway)
Snyder: Snyder Oil Partners L. P. (newspaper)
SO: Sales Office
Sales Order
Seller's Option
Service Order
Shift-Out character
Shipping Order
Shop Order
Shutoff sequence
Southern Airways
Southern Co., The (NYSE)
Special Order
Standing Order
Stock Option
SOA: State of the Art
SOAR: Safe Operating Area
SOC: Span Of Control
SOCACHA: South Carolina Automated Clearing House Association
SOCO: Standard Oil Company of California
SOCONY: Standard Oil Corporation of New York
SOD: Seller's Option to Double
Solitron Devices Inc. (NYSE)
SOE: Short Of Exchange
Simplon-Orient Express (railroad)
State-Owned Enterprise
SOEC: Statistical Office of the European Community (EC)
SoestBk: Southeast Banking Corp. (newspaper)
SOF: Start-Of-Format control
SOFE: Swedish Options and Futures Exchange
SOFFEX: Swiss Options and Financial Futures Exchange
soft: software
SOH: Staggering Of Hours
Standard Oil Company (Ohio)
Start-Of-Heading character
Stock On Hand
SOHIO: Standard Oil Company (Ohio)
SOI: Snyder Oil Partners LP (NYSE)
Southern Indiana (railway)
SoIndGs: Southern Indiana Gas & Electric Co. (newspaper)
SOL: Standard Of Living
Statute Of Limitations
Solitron: Solitron Devices Inc. (newspaper)
SOM: Start Of Message
Sonat: Sonat Inc. (newspaper)
SonyCp: Sony Corp. (newspaper)
SOO: Soo Line Corp. (NYSE)
SooLin: Soo Line Corp. (newspaper)

SOP: Special Order Price
Standard Operating Procedure
Statement Of Policy
Stock Option Plan
SOPONATA: Sociedade Portuguesa de Navios Tanques Limitada (Portuguese Tankships Limited) (steamship)
SOR: Source Capital Inc. (NYSE)
Specific Operational (Operating) Requirement
Stockholder Of Record
SORDID: Summary of Reported Defects, Incidents and Delays
SorgInc: Sorg Inc. (newspaper)
SOS: Silicon On Sapphire
SOS CMOS: Silicon-On-Sapphire Complementary Metal-Oxide Semiconductor
SOT: South Omaha Terminal (railway)
Sothby: Sotheby's Holdings Inc. (Class A) (newspaper)
Soudwn: Southdown Inc. (newspaper)
Soumrk: Southmark Corp. (newspaper)
SoUnCo: Southern Union Co. (newspaper)
SourcC: Source Capital Inc. (newspaper)
SOUT: Swap Out
SouthCo: Southern Co., The (newspaper)
SOV: Sovran Financial Corp. (NYSE)
Sovran: Sovran Financial Corp. (newspaper)
SOVTORGFLOT: Soviet Merchant Marine Fleet
SOW: Statement of Work
SOYD: Sum Of the Years' Digits (depreciation)
sp: space
special (stocks)
S&P: Standard and Poor's Corporation
Systems and Procedures
SP: Aaron Spelling Productions Inc. (ASE)
SATA (Sociedade Acoriana de Transportes Aeros - Azores Air Transport) (airline)
Satellite Processor
Scanlon Plan
Scratch Pad
Selling Price
Senior Partner
Short Position
Signal Processor
Sine Prole (without issue)
Situs Picketing
Sole Proprietor
Southern Pacific (railroad)
Special Purchase
Specific Performance
Spot Price
Stack Pointer
Stop Payment
Structured Programming
SpA: Societa per Azioni (joint stock company) (Italian)
SPA: Society for Personnel Administration
Sparton Corp. (NYSE)
Subject to Particular Average
Systems Programmed Application
SPACE: Settlement, Payment, Accounting, Credit Extension
Spain: Spain Fund Inc. (newspaper)
SPANPAC: Sales, Purchases and Nominal Package
Spartc: Spartech Corp. (newspaper)
Sparton: Sparton Corp. (newspaper)
SPAU: Signal Processing Arithmetic Unit
SPB: Stored Program Buffer
SPC: Security Pacific Corp. (NYSE)
Small Peripheral Controller

Standard and Poor's Corporation
Stored Program Control
Switching and Processing Center

SPCC: Southern Pacific Communications Company

SpcEq: Specialty Equipment Companies Inc. (newspaper)

SPCL: Single Product Cost Leadership

SPCS: Storage and Processing Control System

SPD: Software Product Description
Standard Products Co., The (NYSE)
System Program Director

SPDA: Single-Premium Deferred Annuity

SPDT: Single Pole, Double Throw

SPE: Single Processing Element
Special Purpose Equipment
Specialty Equipment Companies Inc. (NYSE)
System Performance Effectiveness

SPEAC: Special Purpose Electronic Area Correlator

spec: specification

SPECLE: Specification Language

SPECOL: Special Customer Oriented Language

SpedOP: Speed-O-Print Business Machines Corp. (newspaper)

Spellng: Aaron Spelling Productions Inc. (newspaper)

SPES: Stimulation Plan for Economic Sciences (EC)

SPF: Standard-Pacific Corp. (NYSE)
Structured Programming Facility

SPG: Sprague Technologies Inc. (NYSE)

SPGT: Springfield Terminal (railroad)

SPH: Strokes Per Hour

SPI: Shared Peripheral Interface
Share Price Index
Single Processor Interface
Specific Productivity Index
SPI Pharmaceuticals Inc.

SPIC: Spare Parts Inventory Control
Standard and Poor's Index—Composite

SPII: Standard and Poor's Index—Industrials

SPIN: Standard and Poor's 500 Index Subordinated Notes

SPI Ph: SPI Pharmaceuticals Inc. (newspaper)

SPIR: Standard and Poor's Index—Rails

SPIRIT: Sales Processing Interactive Real-Time Inventory Technique

SPIU: Standard and Poor's Index—Utilities

spkt: sprocket

SPL: Signal Processing Language
Simulation Programming Language
Source Program Library
System Programming Language

SPLC: Short Product Life Cycle
Standard Point Location Code

SPLI: Single-Premium Life Insurance

SPM: Scratch Pad Memory
System Planning Manual

SPMTS: Simplified Predetermined Motion Time System

SPNS: Standard Product Numbering System

SP OFF: Special Offering (stocks)

SPP: Scott Paper Co. (NYSE)
Stock Purchase Plan

SPQR: Small Profits, Quick Returns

spr: sponsor

SPR: Sterling Capital Corp. (ASE)
Sprage: Sprague Technologies Inc. (newspaper)
SPRB: Senior Performance Review Board
Spring: Springs Industries Inc. (newspaper)
SPRINT: Strategic Program for Innovation and Technology Transfer (EC)
SPRL: Societé de Personnes a Responsabilite Limitee (Belgian corporation)
SP&S: Spokane, Portland & Seattle (railroad)
SPS: Second Preferred Stock
Southwestern Public Service Co. (NYSE)
String Process System
Symbolic Program System
SPSS: Statistical Package for the Social Sciences
SPSTec: SPS Technologies Inc. (newspaper)
SPVLI: Single Premium Variable Life Investment
SPW: SPX Corp. (NYSE)
Stock Purchase Warrant
SPX: Simplex circuit
SPX Cp: SPX Corp. (newspaper)
SQ: Norcanair (airline)
Squeezed files
SQA: Sequa Corp. (NYSE)
SQB: Squibb Corp. (NYSE)
SQD: Square D Co. (NYSE)
SquarD: Square D Co. (newspaper)
SQUARE: Statistical Quality Analysis Report
Squibb: Squibb Corp. (newspaper)
S&R: Safety and Reliability
sr: senior (stocks)
SR: Scientific Report
Shared Revenue
Shift Register
Shipment Request
Shipping Receipts
Short Rate
Short Run
Sierra Railroad
Skagit River (railroad)
Southern Railway
Special Register
Special Regulation
Status Register
Storage Register
Summary Report
Surtax Rate
Swissair (airline)
Switch Register
SRA: Systems Requirements Analysis
SRATC: Short-Run Average Total Cost
SRAVC: Short-Run Average Variable Cost
SRB: Scurry-Rainbow Oil Ltd. (ASE)
Staff Responsibility Budget
SRBR: Southern Region of British Railways
SRC: Salvador Railway Company (El Salvador)
Service Resources Corp. (NYSE)
SRDS: Standard Rate and Data Service, Inc.
SRE: Stoneridge Resources Inc. (NYSE)
SREA: Society of Real Estate Appraisers
SRF: Software Recovery Facility
SRG: Sorg Inc. (ASE)
SRL: Sceptre Resources Ltd. (ASE)
Scheme Representation Language
SRM: System Resources Manager
SRMC: Short Run Marginal Cost
SRN: Sabine River and Northern (railroad)
SRO: Self-Regulatory Organization
SROP: Senior Registered Options Principal

SRP: Salary Reduction Plan
Sierra Pacific Resources (NYSE)
Suggested Retail Price

SRR: Serially Reusable Resource
Stride Rite Corp., The (NYSE)
System Requirements Review

SRRC: Sierra Railroad Company
Strasburg Rail Road Company

SRRCO: Sandersville Railroad Company

SRT: Spousal Remainder Trust
State Railways of Thailand (Siam)

SRV: Service Corporation International (NYSE)

ss: steamship

S&S: Saratoga & Schuylerville (railroad)

S/S: Source/Sink

SS: Schwab Safe Company Inc. (ASE)
Selling Short
Senior Securities
Seven Sisters (oil companies)
Short Sale
Shrinking Stocks
Slowdown Strike
Social Security
Solid State
Start-Stop character
Start-Stop transmission
Stock Split
Stopped Stock
Swing Shift
Sworn Statement
Sympathetic Strike

SSA: Social Security Administration

SSAN: Social Security Account Number

SSAP: Statement of Standard Accounting Practice

SSB: Single-Sideband transmission
Social Security Board
Social Security Bulletin

SSB AM: Single-Sideband Amplitude Modulation

SSC: Station Selection Code
Sunshine Mining Holding Co. (NYSE)

SSD: Solid State Disk
Stock Split-Down

SSDD: Single-Sided Double-Density

SSDK: Savannah State Docks (railroad)

SSE: Special Support Equipment
Sydney Stock Exchange (Australia)

SSH: Substantial Stockholder

SSI: Small-Scale Integration
Supplemental Security Income

SSISDR: Social Security Integrity & Debt Reduction Fund

SSL: Semi-Skilled Labor (Laborer)
Source Statement Library

SSLVRR: Southern San Luis Valley Railroad

SSM: Second-Tier Securities Market
SSMC Inc. (NYSE)

SSMC: SSMC Inc. (newspaper)

SSN: Self-Sufficient Nation

SSP: Statutory Sick Pay

SSR: Solid State Relay
Soviet Socialist Republic

SSRY: Sand Springs Railway

SSS: MSA Realty Corp. (ASE)

SSSD: Single-Sided Single-Density

SST: Shelter Components Corp. (ASE)
Supersonic Transport

SSW: Sterling Software Inc. (ASE)
St. Louis Southwestern (railway)

st: stamped (stocks)
stopped (stocks)

S&T: Scientific and Technical

ST: Sales Tax
Sensitivity Training
Severance Tax
Short Ton
SPS Technologies Inc. (NYSE)
Start Signal
Stock Transfer
Chicago, Milwaukee, St. Paul and Pacific Railroad Company

sta: station

STA: Stock Transfer Association

STABEX: Stabilization of Export Earnings (EC)

STAE: Specify Task Asynchronous Exit

Stage: Stage II Apparel Corp. (newspaper)

STAIRS: Storage And Information Retrieval System

StaMSe: State Mutual Securities Trust (newspaper)

stan: standard
standardization

Standex: Standex International Corp. (newspaper)

Stanhm: Stanhome Inc. (newspaper)

StanlWk: Stanley Works, The (newspaper)

STANVAC: Standard-Vacuum Oil Company (steamship)

STANY: Security Traders' Association of New York

STAQ: Security Trader's Automated Quotations

STAR: Special Telecommunications Action for Regional Development (EC)

Starrett: L. S. Starrett Co., The (newspaper)

StarrtH: Starrett Housing Corp. (newspaper)

STARS: Short-Term Auction-Rate Stock
Standard Time And Rate Setting

stas: statutes

stat: status

STB: Southeast Banking Corp. (NYSE)
Special Tax Bond

StBPnt: Standard Brands Paint Co. (newspaper)

STC: Short-Term Credit
Single Trip Container
Stock Trust Certificate
Subject To Call

STCC: Standard Transportation Commodity Code

STCG: Short-Term Capital Gain

STCL: Short-Term Capital Loss

std: standard

STD: Banco Santander (NYSE)
Science and Technology for Development (EC)
Short-Term Debt

StdCom: Standard Commercial Corp. (newspaper)

STDM: Synchronous Time-Division Multiplexor

StdPac: Standard-Pacific Corp. (newspaper)

StdPrd: Standard Products Co., The (newspaper)

StdShr: Standard Shares Inc. (newspaper)

ST&E: Stockton, Terminal & Eastern (railroad)

STE: Special Test Equipment
Standard Test Equipment

Steego: Steego Corp. (newspaper)

STEP: Science and Technology for Environmental Protection (EC)

Stepan: Stepan Co. (newspaper)

SterlEl: Sterling Electronics Corp. (newspaper)

SterlSft: Sterling Software Inc. (newspaper)

StevnJ: J. P. Stevens & Company Inc. (newspaper)

stf: staff

StFBk: Standard Federal Bank (newspaper)

stg: sterling
storage
STG: Steego Corp. (NYSE)
stge: storage
STH: Short-Term Holiday
Stanhome Inc. (NYSE)
StHavn: Standard Havens Inc. (newspaper)
STI: SunTrust Banks Inc. (NYSE)
STIDC: Scientific and Technical Information and Documentation Committee (EC)
Stifel: Stifel Financial Corp. (newspaper)
StJoLP: St. Joseph Light & Power Co. (newspaper)
stk: stack
stock
STK: Storage Technology Corp. (NYSE)
Stk Ex: Stock Exchange
STKF: Stock Fund
STKFA: Stock Fund Accounting
STL: Seatrain Lines (steamship)
Short-Term Loan
Sterling Bancorp (NYSE)
STM: Straddle The Market
Strategic Mortgage Investments Inc. (NYSE)
Subject To Mortgage
StMotr: Standard Motor Products Inc. (newspaper)
stmt: statement
STN: J. P. Stevens & Company Inc. (NYSE)
Switched Telecommunication Network
STO: Standing Order
Stone Container Corp. (NYSE)
StoneC: Stone Container Corp. (newspaper)
StoneW: Stone & Webster Inc. (newspaper)
StonRs: Stoneridge Resources Inc. (newspaper)
STOP: Stopped Bonds (NYSE)
stor: storage
store
StorEq: Storage Equities Inc. (newspaper)
STORET: Storage and Retrieval
StorTch: Storage Technology Corp. (newspaper)
STP: Signal Transfer Point
Stop character
Straight-Time Pay
stpd: stamped
stopped (stocks)
str: steamer
STR: Questar Corp. (NYSE)
Status Register
StratMt: Strategic Mortgage Investments Inc. (newspaper)
STRESS: Structural Engineering System Solver
STRIDE: Science and Technology for Regional Innovation and Development in Europe (EC)
StridRt: Stride Rite Corp., The (newspaper)
STRIP: Strip Bond
StrlBcp: Sterling Bancorp (newspaper)
StrlCap: Sterling Capital Corp. (newspaper)
STROP: Stock Ratio Optimizing
STRT: Stewartstown (railroad)
struc: structure
STRUDL: Structural Design Language
StrutW: Struthers Wells Corp. (newspaper)
STS: Seattle Transit System
STUFF: System To Uncover Facts Fast
STV: Subscription Television
StvGph: Stevens Graphics Corp. (newspaper)
STW: Standard Commercial Corp. (NYSE)
STX: Start-of-Text Character
su: supply

SU: Aeroflot (Soviet Airline)
Seasonal Unemployment
Secular Unemployment
Selectable Unit
Set Up
Speed Up
Statute of Uses
Stockholm Underground (subway)
Structural Unemployed
SUA: Shipped Unassembled
Summit Tax Exempt Bond Fund LP (ASE)
SuavSh: Suave Shoe Corp. (newspaper)
sub: subordination (stocks)
subroutine
subscriber
subsidiary
SUB: Substitute character
Supplemental (Supplementary) Unemployment Benefits
Substn: substitution
suby: subsidiary
SUC: Start-Up Costs
SUD RYS: Sudan Railways
SUG: Southern Union Co. (NYSE)
SumtTx: Summit Tax Exempt Bond Fund L.P. (newspaper)
SUN: Sun Company Inc. (NYSE)
SunbNu: Sunbelt Nursery Group Inc. (newspaper)
SunCo: Sun Company Inc. (newspaper)
SunCty: Sun City Industries Inc. (newspaper)
SunDis: Sun Distributors L.P. (newspaper)
Sundstr: Sundstrand Corp. (newspaper)
SunEl: Sun Electric Corp. (newspaper)
SunEng: Sun Energy Partners L.P. (newspaper)
SunJr: Sunshine-Jr. Stores Inc. (newspaper)
SunMn: Sunshine Mining Holding Co. (newspaper)
SUNOCO: Sun Oil Company
SunTr: SunTrust Banks Inc. (newspaper)
sup: supplement
SUP: Superior Industries International Inc. (ASE)
SUPER: System Used for Prediction and Evaluation of Reliability
SupInd: Superior Industries International Inc. (newspaper)
SuprFd: Super Food Services Inc. (newspaper)
SuprSr: Superior Surgical Mfg. Co. Inc. (newspaper)
supt: superintendent
supv: supervisor
SupValu: Super Value Stores Inc. (newspaper)
supvr: supervisor
supvry: supervisory
sur: surplus
SUR: Saturn Airways
SCOR US Corp. (NYSE)
Soviet Union Railways
SUSIE: Stock Updating Sales Invoicing Electronically
susp: suspended (stocks)
SUT: System Under Test
SUW: Struthers Wells Corp. (ASE)
SV: Saudi Arabian Airlines
Sales Voucher
Savings Transfer
Surrender Value (insurance)
SVA: Shared Virtual Area
SVB: Savin Corp. (NYSE)
SVC: Supervisor Call instruction
SvcCp: Service Corporation International (newspaper)
Svcmst: ServiceMaster L.P. (newspaper)

SvcRes: Service Resources Corp. (newspaper)
SVG: Stevens Graphics Corp. (ASE)
svgs: savings
SVM: ServiceMaster LP (NYSE)
SVP: Senior Vice President
SVT: Servotronics Inc. (ASE)
SVU: Super Value Stores Inc. (NYSE)
sw: software
switch
SW: Shorter Workweek
Stone & Webster Inc. (NYSE)
Suidwes Lugdiens (airline)
Switch character
SWA: Scheduler Work Area
Seaboard World Airlines
SWACHA: Southwestern Automated Clearing House Association
SwAirl: Southwest Airlines Co. (newspaper)
SWB: Southwest Bancorp (California) (ASE)
SwBcp: Southwest Bancorp (California) (newspaper)
SwBell: Southwestern Bell Corp. (newspaper)
swch: switch
SWD: Standard Shares Inc. (ASE)
SwEnr: Southwestern Energy Co. (newspaper)
SwftEng: Swift Energy Co. (newspaper)
swgt: switching
SWIFT: Society for Worldwide Interbank Financial Telecommunications
SWISSAIR: Swiss Airlines
SWK: Stanley Works, The (NYSE)
SWL: Southwest Realty Ltd. (ASE)
SWN: Southwestern Energy Co. (NYSE)
SWORDS: Standard Work Order Recording and Data System
SwstRlt: Southwest Realty Ltd. (newspaper)
SwtGas: Southwest Gas Corp. (newspaper)
SwtPS: Southwestern Public Service Co. (newspaper)
SWV: Suave Shoe Corp. (NYSE)
SWX: Southwest Gas Corp. (NYSE)
SWZ: Helvetia Fund Inc., The (NYSE)
SX: Skyways Coach (airline)
SXI: Standex International Corp. (NYSE)
SXS: Step-by-Step system
sy: system
SY: Shelby Williams Industries Inc. (NYSE)
SyblTc: Symbol Technologies Inc. (newspaper)
sym: symbol
system
SYM: Syms Corp. (NYSE)
SymsCp: Syms Corp. (newspaper)
syn: synchronous
SYN: Synchronous idle character
Syntex Corp. (NYSE)
Synaloy: Synalloy Corp. (newspaper)
sync: synchronization
synchronous
Syntex: Syntex Corp. (newspaper)
SYO: Synalloy Corp. (ASE)
SYR RYS: Syrian Railways
sys: system
SYS: ISI Systems Inc. (ASE)
SYSADMIN: System Administrator
Sysco: Sysco Corp. (newspaper)
SYSEX: System Executive
SYSGEN: System Generation
SYSIN: System Input Stream
SYSLOG: System Log
SYSMIN: System for Mineral Products (EC)
SYSOPO: System Programmed Operator
SYSOUT: System Output Stream

syst: system

SystEn: Systems Engineering & Manufacturing Corp. (newspaper)

SystInt: System Integrators Inc. (newspaper)

SYU: Synchronization Signal Unit

SYX: Bayou Steel Corporation of La Place (ASE)

SYY: Sysco Corp. (NYSE)

SZF: Sierra Capital Realty Trust VI (ASE)

SZG: Sierra Capital Realty Trust VII (ASE)

T

t: temperature
tera
terminal
test
testator
time
timer
track
transaction
transmit
transmitter
true

T: American Telephone and Telegraph Co. (NYSE)
Toronto Stock Exchange (in newspaper statements)
Treasury (as in T-bill, T-bond)

T&A: Taken and Accepted

TA: Taca (airline)
Tangible Asset
Tax Abatement
Tax Amortization
Technical Assistance
Technological Assessment
Telex Network Adapter
Terminal Access
Texas Air Corporation (airline)
Trade Acceptance
Trade Assessment
Trade Association
Trading As
Training Adviser
Training Allowance
Transamerica Corp. (NYSE)
Transfer Address
Transfer Agent
Travel Allowance

TAA: Tactical Asset Allocation
Trade Agreements Act
Trans-Australia Airlines
Transferable Account Area
Transit Advertising Association
Transportation Association of America

TAB: Tandy Brands Inc. (ASE)
Tax Anticipation Bill

TabPrd: Tab Products Co. (newspaper)

TABS: Total Automatic Banking System

TAC: Tandycrafts Inc. (NYSE)
Technical Assistance Committee
Terminal Access Controller
Texas Air Corporation (airline)
Total Annualized Cost
Total Average Cost

TacBt: Tacoma Boatbuilding Co. (newspaper)

TACHA: Tennessee Automated Clearing House Association

TACINTEL: Tactical Intelligence

TACOS: Tool for Automatic Conversion of Operational Software

TACT: Terminal Activated Channel Test
Total Audit Concept Technique

TAD: Terminal Address Designator
Time Available for Delivery
Transaction Applications Driver

TAEB: Technology Assessment and Evaluation

TAF: Time And Frequency
Transaction Facility

TA&G: Tennessee, Alabama, and Georgia (railroad)
TAG: Time Automated Grid
Transfer Agent
TAI: Transamerica Income Shares Inc. (NYSE)
Transports Aeriens Intercontinentaux (Intercontinental Air Transport)
Taiwan: Taiwan Fund Inc., The (newspaper)
TAL: Talley Industries Inc. (NYSE)
Terminal Application Language
Transaction Application Language
TALISMAN: Transfer Accounting and Lodgement for Investors, Stock Management for Jobbers (London Stock Exchange)
Talley: Talley Industries Inc. (newspaper)
TAM: Task Analysis Method
Telecommunications Access Method
Telephone Answering Machine
Terminal Access Method
Tubos de Acero de Mexico SA (ASE)
TAMALAN: Table Manipulation Language
Tambd: Tambrands Inc. (newspaper)
TAMOS: Terminal Automatic Monitoring System
TAMPR: Transformation Aided Multiple Program Realization
TAN: Tandy Corp. (NYSE)
Tax-Anticipation Note
Transportes Aeros Nacionales (National Air Transport, Honduras)
TandB: Tandy Brands Inc. (newspaper)
Tandm: Tandem Computers Inc. (newspaper)
Tandy: Tandy Corp. (newspaper)
TAN-ZAM: Tanzania-Zambia (railroad)
TAP: Terminal Access Processor
Time-sharing Accounting Package
Total Annualized Profit
Transportes Aereos Portugueses (Portuguese Airlines)
TAPGEN: Terminal Applications Program Generator
TAPS: Terminal Application Processing System
Trans-Alaska Pipeline System
tar: tariff
TAR: Terminal Address Register
Total Assets Reporting
Track Address Register
Trans-Australian Railways
Transfer Address Register
Truck and Rail
Turnaround Ratio
TARAN: Test And Repair As Necessary
Test And Replace As Necessary
TARP: Test and Repair Processor
TAS: Terminal Automation System
Test And Set
TASD: Terminal Railway Alabama State Docks
TASE: Tel-Aviv Stock Exchange (Israel)
Tasty: Tastee Baking Co. (newspaper)
TAT: Time and Attendance Terminal
Transatlantic Telephone Cable
TAU: Trunk Access Unit

TA&W: Toledo, Angola & Western (railroad)
tax: taxation
taxes
TB: Tone Burst
Treasury Bonds (U.S.)
Trial Balance
Twin Branch (railroad)
TBA: To Be Announced
TBC: Tastee Baking Co. (ASE)
TBEM: Terminal Based Electronic Mail
TBI: Time Between Inspections
T-BILL: Treasury Bill
TBL: Timberland Co., The (ASE)
TBM: Tone Burst Modulation
TBMT: Transmitter Buffer Empty
TBO: Tacoma Boatbuilding Co. (NYSE)
Time Between Overhaul
TBP: Tab Products Co. (ASE)
Telephone Bill Payment
TBR: Table Base Register
Treasury Bill Rate
TBS: Tokyo Broadcasting System
Turner Broadcasting System Inc. (ASE)
TBTMG: Transportation Bureau of the Tokyo Metropolitan Government
T-BOND: Treasury Bond
T&C: Terms and Conditions
T/C: True or Complement
TC: Tax Certificate
Tax Court
Technical Committee
Technical Cooperation
Technological Change
Telex Corp., The (NYSE)
Tennessee Central (railroad)
Terminal Computer
Terminal Concentrator
Terminal Control
Terminal Controller
Time Clock
Total Cost
Trans Caribbean Airways
Transfer Count
Transmission Control
Treasury Certificate
Trunk Control
Trust Company
TCA: Telecommunications Association
Terminal Communication Adapter
Trans-Canada Airlines
Trans-Caribbean Airways
TCAM: Telecommunication Access Method
TCB: Taking Care of Business
Task Control Block
Transaction Control Block
Transfer Control Block
TCC: Technical Control Center
TeleConcepts Corp. (ASE)
Transmission Control Characters
TCDD: Turkiye Cumhuriyeti Deviet Demiryollari Isletmesi (Turkish State Railways)
TCE: Top Computer Executive
Transaction Cost Estimator
TCEU: Transportation-Communication Employees Union
TCF: Terminal Configuration Facility
TC&GB: Tucson, Cornella & Gila Bend (railroad)
TchOpL: Tech/Ops Landauer Inc. (newspaper)
TchOpS: Tech-Ops Sevcon Inc. (newspaper)
TchSym: Tech-Sym Corp. (newspaper)
TCIS: TELEX Computer Inquiry Service
TCK: TEC Inc. (ASE)
TCL: Terminal Command Language

Terminal Control Language
Transaction Control Language
Transatlantic Carriers Limited (steamship)
Transcon Inc. (NYSE)

TCM: Telecommunications Manager
Telecommunications Monitor

TCMS: Telecommunications Management System

TCO: TELENET Central Office
Termination Contracting Office

TCP: Tape Conversion Program
Task Control Program
Terminal Control Program
Time, Cost and Performance
Tool Center Point
Transmission Control Program
Transmitter Clock Pulse

TCPC: Telephone Cable Process Controller

TCR: Tape Cassette Recorder
Texas City Refining (steamship)
Trammell Crow Real Estate Investors (NYSE)

TCS: Telecommunications Control System
Terminal Control System
Tool Coordinate System
Transmission-Controlled Speed

TCS-AF: Telecommunications Control System-Advanced Function

TCT: Terminal Control Table
Texas City Terminal (railway)
Transaction Control Table
Tricentrol PLC (NYSE)

TCTS: Trans-Canada Telephone System

TCU: Tape Control Unit
Telecommunications Control Unit
Teletypewriter Control Unit
Terminal Control Unit
Timing Control Unit
Transmission Control Unit

TCV: Terminal Configures Vehicle

TCW: TCW Convertible Securities Fund Inc. (newspaper)

T/D: Time Deposit

TD: Tape Drive
Time Deposit
Time Division
Top Down
Total Debt
Trade Deficit
Traffic Department
Transcarga (Airline)
Transmit Data
Transmitter-Distributor
Treasury Department
Trust Deed
Tunnel Diode

TDA: Tax Deferred Annuity
Tax Deposit Account

TDB: Temporary Disability Benefits
Trade Development Bank

TDC: Total Distributed Control

TDCS: Time Division Circuit Switching

TDD: Three D Departments Inc. (ASE)
Top Down Development

TDE: Total Data Entry

TDEM: Test Data Effectiveness Measurement

TDF: Transnational Data Flows

tdg: trading

TDG: Test Data Generator

TDGL: Test Data Generating Language

TDI: Telecommunications Data Interface
Twin Disc Inc. (NYSE)
Two-Wire Direct Interface

TDK: TDK Corp. (NYSE) (newspaper)

TDL: Transaction Definition Language

Transformation Definition Language
TDM: Tandem Computers Inc. (NYSE)
Template Descriptor Memory
Time-Division Multiplexing
Time Driven Monitor
TDMA: Tape Direct Memory Access
Time Division Multiple Access
TDMC: Time Division Multiplexed Channel
TDMS: Time-Shared Data Management System
TDO: Technical Development Objective
TDOA: Time Deposit Open Account
TDOS: Tape Disk Operating System
TDP: Test Data Package
TDR: Tape Data Register
Time Delay Relay
Tone Dial Receiver
Transmit Data Register
Treasury Deposit Receipt
TDS: Telephone & Data Systems Inc. (ASE)
Transaction Distribution System
TDSP: Top Down Structured Programming
TDW: Tidewater Inc. (NYSE)
TDX: Time Division Exchange
TDY: Teledyne Inc. (NYSE)
T&E: Test and Evaluation
Travel and Entertainment (card)
TE: Air New Zealand (airline)
Tax Exemption
TECO Energy Inc. (NYSE)
Temporary Employee
Text Editor
Total Earnings
Total Expenditure
Trade Expenses
Trailing Edge
TEA: Trade Expansion Act
Team: Team Inc. (newspaper)
TEAM: Teleterminals Expandable Added Memory
TEAMS: Test Evaluation And Monitoring System
TEAS: Time Elapsed After Study
TEB: Tax-Exempt Bond
TEBOL: Terminal Business Oriented Language
TEBRCL: The Emu Bay Railway Company Limited
TEC: TEC Inc. (newspaper)
Total Estimated Cost
Triple Erasure Correction
tech: technical
TECHEVAL: Technical Evaluation
TECH EX: Technical Exchange
TECH MEMO: Technical Memorandum
Technd: Technodyne Inc. (newspaper)
TECH REPT: Technical Report
TechTp: Technical Tape Inc. (newspaper)
Techtrl: Technitrol Inc. (newspaper)
TECO: TECO Energy Inc. (newspaper)
Text Editor and Corrector
TED: Tax-Exempt Dividend
Tenders Electronic Daily (EC)
Text Editor
TEDIS: Trade Electronic Data Interchange Systems (EC)
tee: trustee
TEE: Trans-Europe-Express
TEEF: Tax-Exempt Equity Fund
TEF: Companie Telefonica Nacional de Espana SA (NYSE)
TEFRA: Tax Equity and Fiscal Responsibility Act
TEGAS: Test Generation and Simulation System
TEI: Technical and Economic Information

TEIP: Tax-Exempt Investor Program
TEJAC: Trade Effluent Joint Advisory Committee (UK)
TejnR: Tejon Ranch Co. (newspaper)
TEK: Tektronix Inc. (NYSE)
Tektrnx: Tektronix Inc. (newspaper)
TEL: Task Execution Language
TeleCom Corp. (NYSE)
Telcom: TeleCom Corp. (newspaper)
TelDta: Telephone & Data Systems Inc. (newspaper)
Teldyn: Teledyne Inc. (newspaper)
telec: telecommunication
telecc: telecommunication
telecom: telecommunication
telecomm: telecommunication
Telecon: TeleConcepts Corp. (newspaper)
Telef: Companie Telefonica Nacional de Espana S.A. (newspaper)
Teleflex: Teleflex Inc. (newspaper)
teleg: telegram
TELEMUX: Telegraph Multiplexer
Telesph: Telesphere International Inc. (newspaper)
Telex: Telex Corp., The (newspaper)
TELEX: Teletype Exchange
TELNET: Telecommunications Network
TELOPS: Telemetry On Line Processing System
Telrte: Telerate Inc. (newspaper)
TEMA: Telecommunication Engineering and Manufacturing Association
TEMOD: Terminal Environment Module
temp: temporary
Temp Ctfs: Temporary Certificates
Templ: Temple-Inland Inc. (newspaper)
TEMPO: TEMPO Enterprises Inc. (newspaper)
TEMPOS: Timed Environment Multipartitioned Operating System
TEMPUS: Trans-European Mobility Scheme
TEN COM: Tenants in Common
TENN: Tennessee Railroad
Tennco: Tenneco Inc. (newspaper)
Tenney: Tenney Engineering Inc. (newspaper)
TEP: Terminal Error Program
Tucson Electric Power Co. (NYSE)
TEPE: Time-Sharing Event Performance Evaluator
TEPOS: Test Program Operating System
TEQ: Turner Equity Investors Inc. (ASE)
TER: Teradyne Inc. (NYSE)
Terdyn: Teradyne Inc. (newspaper)
term: terminal
termination
terr: territory
TES: Text Editing System
Tesoro: Tesoro Petroleum Corp. (newspaper)
TEUC: Temporary Emergency Unemployment Compensation
TEV: Thermo Environmental Corp. (ASE)
tex: telex
TEX: Texas Air Corp. (ASE)
Texaco: Texaco Inc. (newspaper)
TEXACO: The Texas Company (steamship)
TexAir: Texas Air Corp. (newspaper)
TEXARKANA: Texas, Arkansas, Louisiana (railroad)
TEXAS AIR: Texas Air Corporation (airline)
TEXC: Texas Central (railroad)

TexCd: Texaco Canada Inc. (newspaper)
Texfi: Texfi Industries Inc. (newspaper)
TexInd: Texas Industries Inc. (newspaper)
Textrn: Textron Inc. (newspaper)
TexUtil: Texas Utilities Co. (newspaper)
TF: Tallulah Falls (railroad)
Tape Feed
Task Force
Technological Forecasting
Till Forbid
Transfer Fee
Transfer Function
Transmit Filter
TFA: Test Form Analyzer
Transaction Flow Auditing
TFC: Total Fixed Cost
TransCapital Financial Corp. (NYSE)
TFM: Tape File Management
TFMS: Text and File Management System
TFP: Total Factor Productivity
TFPIA: Textile Fabric Products Identification Act
tfr: transfer
TFR: Transaction Formatting Routing
TFS: Tape File Supervisor
Task Form Specification
TFSF: Time to First System Failure
TFX: Teleflex Inc. (ASE)
tg: telegraph
TG: Tangible Goods
Task Group
Terminator Group
Thai Airways International (airline)
TGI: TGI Friday's Inc. (NYSE)
TGID: Transmission Group Identifier
TGIF: TGI Friday's Inc. (newspaper)
TGL: Triton Group Ltd. (NYSE)
T-GROUPS: Training Groups
TGT: Tenneco Inc. (NYSE)
T&H: Transportation and Handling
TH: Tax Haven
Thai Airways
Thorvald Hansen (steamship)
Transmission Header
THA: Taft-Hartley Act
Thack: Thackey Corp. (newspaper)
Thai: Thai Fund (newspaper)
TH&B: Toronto, Hamilton and Buffalo (railroad)
THC: Hydraulic Co., The (NYSE)
THD: Total Harmonic Distortion
THE: Technical Help to Exporters
THERMIE: European Technologies for Energy Management (EC)
THESAURI: Analytical inventory of structure vocabulary (EC)
THI: Thermo Instrument Systems Inc. (ASE)
THK: Thackey Corp. (NYSE)
ThmBet: Thomas & Betts Corp. (newspaper)
ThmMed: Thompson Medical Company Inc. (newspaper)
THO: Thor Industries Inc. (NYSE)
ThomIn: Thomas Industries Inc. (newspaper)
ThorEn: Thor Energy Resources Inc. (newspaper)
ThorInd: Thor Industries Inc. (newspaper)
Thortec: Thortec International Inc. (newspaper)
THP: Take-Home Pay
Terminal Holding Power
Transmitter Holding Register
Triangle Home Products Inc. (ASE)
THR: Thor Energy Resources Inc. (ASE)

ThrD: Three D Departments Inc. (newspaper)
THREAD: Three-Dimensional Reconstruction and Display
ThrIns: Thermo Instrument Systems Inc. (newspaper)
Thrmd: Thermedics Inc. (newspaper)
ThrmE: Thermo Environmental Corp. (newspaper)
ThrmEl: Thermo Electron Corp. (newspaper)
ThrmP: Thermo Process Systems Inc. (newspaper)
ThroBL: Through Bill of Lading
THS: Town-Halsey System
THT: Thortec International Inc. (ASE)
T&I: Test and Integration
TI: Taxable Income
Temporary Instructions
Terminal Interface
Transformational Implementation
TIA: Tax Institute of America
Telecommunications Information Administration
Trans-International Airlines
TIAA: Truth-In-Advertising Act
TIAC: Thrift Institutions Advisory Council
TIAS: Team Integrated Avionic System
TIB: Temporary Importation Bond
Treasury Indexed Bonds
TIC: Tenancy In Common
Terminal's Identification Code
Travelers Corp., The (NYSE)
TICCIT: Time-Shared Interactive Computer-Controlled Information Television
TICS: Telecommunication Information Control System
TIDMA: Tape Interface Direct Memory Access
Tidwtr: Tidewater Inc. (newspaper)
TIE: Terminal Interface Equipment
TIE/communications Inc. (newspaper)
TIES: Total Information Educational Systems
TIF: Tape Inventory File
Tiffany & Co. (NYSE)
Tiffny: Tiffany & Co. (newspaper)
TIFR: Total Investment For Return
TIGER: Treasury Investment Growth Receipt
TIGR: Treasury Investment Growth Receipt
TIGS: Terminal Independent Graphics System
TIH: Trunk Interface Handler
TII: Thomas Industries Inc. (NYSE)
TII Industries Inc. (newspaper)
TILA: Truth-In-Lending Act
TIM: Table Input to Memory
Templeton Global Income Fund (NYSE)
TimeWarner: Time Warner Inc. (newspaper)
TIME: Techniques for Improved Manpower Evaluation
Timken: Timken Co., The (newspaper)
TIMS: Transmission Impairment Measuring Set
Trust for Investments in Mortgages
TIN: Taxpayer Identification Number
Temple-Inland Inc. (NYSE)
TI-NET: Transparent Intelligent Network
TIO: Test Input/Output
Time Interval Optimization
TIOC: Terminal Input/Output Coordinator
TIOT: Task Input/Output Table
TIP: Tax-based Income Policy
Technical Information Program

Terminal Interface Processor
Transaction Interface Processor
TIPA: Truth-In-Packaging Act
TIPS: Text Information Processing System
TIP TOP: Tape Input-Tape Output
TIQ: Task Input Queue
TIR: Target Instruction Register
Transport International Rontier (EC)
TIRA: Thrift Industry Recovery Act
TIS: TIS Mortgage Investment Co. (NYSE) (newspaper)
TIT: Test Item Taker
Titan: Titan Corp. (newspaper)
TIU: Terminal Interface Unit
TJ: Transportes Aereos Buenos Aires (airline)
TJB: Time-Sharing Job Control Block
TJID: Terminal Job Identification
TJX: TJX Companies Inc., The (NYSE) (newspaper)
tk: track
TK: Ten Keyboard
Turk Hava Yollari (airline)
TKA: Tonka Corp. (NYSE)
TKR: Timken Co., The (NYSE)
TKTN: Task Termination Notice
T&L: Thrift and Loan
TL: Term Loan
Time Loan
Total Load
Total Loss
Trade Last
Trade List
Trading Limit
Transaction Language
Transaction Listing
Trans-Mediterranean Airways
Transmission Line
Truck Load
TLA: Truth-In-Lending Act
TLB: Table Lookaside Buffer
Translation Lookaside Buffer
TLC: Task Level Controller
True Liquid Cooling
TLCT: Total Life Cycle Time
TLI: Term Life Insurance
Transferable Loan Instrument
TLN: Trunk Line Network
TLO: Total Loss Only
TLP: Telephone Line Patch
Transmission Level Point
TLR: Telerate Inc. (NYSE)
TLS: Typed Letter Signed
TLSA: Transparent Line-Sharing Adapter
TLU: Table Look-Up
TLX: Trans-Lux Corp. (ASE)
tm: trademark
TM: Direccao de Exploracao dos Transportes Aereos (Mozambique Air Transport) (airline)
Tabulating Machine
Tape Mark
Terminal Monitor
Test Mode
Texas Mexican (railroad)
Third Market
Third Mortgage
Thompson Medical Company Inc. (NYSE)
Tight Money
Top Management
Training Manual
Transaction Manager
Transport Ministry
Turing Machine
TMA: Television Manufacturers of America Company
Thomson McKinnon Asset Management LP (NYSE)
Toy Manufacturers of America
TMAM: Thomson McKinnon Asset Management L.P. (newspaper)
TMB: Tambrands Inc. (NYSE)

TmbCo: Timberland Co., The (newspaper)
TMC: Times Mirror Co., The (NYSE)
Total Manufacturing Cost
TMD: Thermedics Inc. (ASE)
TMG: Musicland Group Inc., The (NYSE)
TMI: Team Inc. (ASE)
TMIS: Technician Maintenance Information System
TMK: Torchmark Corp. (NYSE)
tml: terminal
TMM: Transportacion Maritima Mexicana (steamship)
TmMir: Times Mirror Co., The (newspaper)
TMO: Thermo Electron Corp. (NYSE)
Time Out
TMP: Terminal Monitor Program
TmpGl: Templeton Global Income Fund (newspaper)
TmplE: Templeton Emerging Markets Fund Inc. (newspaper)
TMR: Trans-Mongolian Railway
True Money Rate
TMRA: Technical and Miscellaneous Revenue Act
TMS: Tape Management System
Time and Motion Study
Transmatic Money System
Treasury Market Securities
TMU: Test Maintenance Unit
Transmission Message Unit
TN: Terminal Node
Texas and Northern (railway)
Trans-Australia Airlines
Transferable Notice
Transport Network
Treasury Notes (U.S.)
TNB: Thomas & Betts Corp. (NYSE)
T&NC: Tennessee & North Carolina (railroad)
TNC: Total Numerical Control
Town & Country Jewelry Manufacturing Corp. (ASE)
Transport Network Controller
TND: Technodyne Inc. (ASE)
TNDC: Trade Negotiations among Developing Countries
Tndycft: Tandycrafts Inc. (newspaper)
TNET: Terminal and Computer Network
TNF: Third Normal Form
tnge: tonnage
TNI: Transico Industries Inc. (ASE)
TNL: Technitrol Inc. (ASE)
TNM: Texas-New Mexico (railroad)
T&NO: Texas and New Orleans (railroad)
T-NOTE: Treasury Note
TNP: TNP Enterprises Inc. (NYSE) (newspaper)
TNS: Transaction Network Service
TNV: Total Net Value
Trinova Corp. (NYSE)
TNY: Tenney Engineering Inc. (ASE)
TNZ: Tranzonic Companies, The (ASE)
to: turnover
TO: Table of Organization
Telephone Order
Time Out
Transfer Order
Travel Order
Treasury Obligations
TOA: Total Obligational Authority
TOC: Pennsylvania New York Central Transportation Company
Table Of Contents
Tech-Ops Sevcon Inc. (ASE)
TOD: Time Of Day
Time Of Delivery
Todd Shipyards Corp. (NYSE)
TODS: Test-Oriented Disk System
TodSh: Todd Shipyards Corp. (newspaper)
TO&E: Texas, Oklahoma & Eastern (railroad)

TOE: Tons of Oil Equivalent
Total Operating Expense
TOF: Tofutti Brands Inc. (ASE)
To Order From
Top Of Form
TOFC: Trailer On Flat Car
Tofutti: Tofutti Brands Inc. (newspaper)
TOK: Tokheim Corp. (NYSE)
Tokhem: Tokheim Corp. (newspaper)
TOL: Test-Oriented Language
Toll Brothers Inc. (NYSE)
TOLAR: Terminal On-Line Availability Reporting
TollBr: Toll Brothers Inc. (newspaper)
TOLT: Total On-Line Testing
Tonka: Tonka Corp. (newspaper)
tonn: tonnage
TOOL: Test-Oriented Operator Language
TootRl: Tootsie Roll Industries Inc. (newspaper)
TOPS: Time-Sharing Operating System
Total Operations Processing System
Toro: Toro Co., The (newspaper)
Tortel: Torotel Inc. (newspaper)
TOS: Tape Operating System
Temporary Out of Stock
Top Of Stack
Tosco Corp. (NYSE)
Tosco: Tosco Corp. (newspaper)
TOSL: Terminal-Oriented Service Language
TOSP: Top Of Stack Pointer
TOSS: Terminal-Oriented Support System
tot: total
TOT: Terms Of Trade
TotlPt: Total Petroleum (North America) Ltd. (newspaper)
TOV: Tech/Ops Landauer Inc. (ASE)
Tooele Valley (railway)
TOX: Time of Expiration
TOY: Toys "R" Us Inc. (NYSE)
ToyRU: Toys "R" Us Inc. (newspaper)
tp: teleprocessing
transship
T&P: Texas and Pacific (railroad)
Theft and Pilferage
TP: Tangible Property
TAP (Transportes Aereos Portugueses - Portuguese Air Transport) (airline)
Teletype Printer
Trial Period
TPA Am: TPA of America Inc. (newspaper)
TPD: Tons Per Day
TPH: Tons Per Hour
TPI: Tax and Prices Index
Thermo Process Systems Inc. (ASE)
TPIN: True Pin (Personal Identification Number)
TPL: Texas Pacific Land Trust (NYSE)
TPLAB: Tape Label
TPM: Tons Per Minute
TPMP: Texas-Pacific-Missouri Pacific Terminal Railroad of New Orleans
TPN: Total Petroleum (North America) Ltd. (ASE)
TPO: TEMPO Enterprises INc. (ASE)
TPS: TPA of America Inc. (ASE)
Trigger-Price System
TPT: Third-Party Transaction
Trenton-Princeton Traction Company (railroad)
TP&W: Toledo, Peoria & Western (railroad)
TQ: Trans Central Airlines
TQC: Total Quality Control
tr: track
trust
TR: Tasmanian Railways
Tax Rate

Tax Roll
Technical Report
Tons Registered
Tootsie Roll Industries Inc. (NYSE)
Trade Representative
Treasury Receipt
Trust Receipt

tra: transfer

TRA: Taiwan Railway Administration
Tax Reform Act

TRACE: Total Risk Assessing Cost Estimate

TRAM: Test Reliability and Maintainability

Tramel: Trammell Crow Real Estate Investors (newspaper)

tran: transaction
transit
transmit

TranEx: Transco Exploration Partners Ltd. (newspaper)

TranInc: Transamerica Income Shares Inc. (newspaper)

TRAN-PRO: Transaction Processing

trans: translator
transportation

Transcn: Transcon Inc. (newspaper)

Transco: Transco Energy Co. (newspaper)

transf: transferred

Transm: Transamerica Corp. (newspaper)

TRANS-SIB: Trans-Siberian Railway

TRASOP: Tax Reduction Act Stock Ownership Plan

Travler: Travelers Corp., The (newspaper)

TRB: Tribune Co. (NYSE)

TRC: Tanzanian Railways Corporation
Tejon Ranch Co. (ASE)
Tela Railway Company (Honduras)
TRC Companies Inc. (newspaper)
Trona Railway Company

Trchmk: Torchmark Corp. (newspaper)

Tr Co: Trust Company

trdg: trading

treas: treasurer
treasury

trf: tariff
transfer

TRG: Triangle Corp., The (ASE)

TriaCp: Triangle Corp., The (newspaper)

Tribun: Tribune Co. (newspaper)

Tricntr: Tricentrol PLC (newspaper)

TriCom: Tri-Continental Corp. (newspaper)

Tridex: Tridex Corp. (newspaper)

TriHme: Triangle Home Products Inc. (newspaper)

TRIM: Technique for Responsive Inventory Management

TRIN: Trading Index (short term)

Trinov: Trinova Corp. (newspaper)

Trinty: Trinity Industries Inc. (newspaper)

TRI-SACH: Tri-State Automated Clearing House Association

TriSM: Tri-State Motor Transit Company of Delaware (newspaper)

TritEng: Triton Energy Corp. (newspaper)

TritnG: Triton Group Ltd. (newspaper)

trk: track

TRL: Transistor-Resistor Logic

TRN: Trinity Industries Inc. (NYSE)

TrnCda: TransCanada PipeLines Ltd. (newspaper)

TrnEq: Turner Equity Investors Inc. (newspaper)

Trnscap: TransCapital Financial Corp. (newspaper)
Trnsco: Transico Industries Inc. (newspaper)
TrnsLx: Trans-Lux Corp. (newspaper)
TrnsTec: TransTechnology Corp. (newspaper)
Trnzn: Tranzonic Companies, The (newspaper)
trp: trap
TRP: TransCanada PipeLines Ltd. (NYSE)
TRR: Trade Regulation Rule
TRC Companies Inc. (ASE)
TRRA: Terminal Railroad Association of St. Louis
TRS: Trust America Service Corp. (ASE)
TRSA: Tax Reduction and Simplification Act
TRUMP: Trump Airlines
TRW: TRW Inc. (NYSE) (newspaper)
trx: transaction
TS: Aloha Airlines
Taxmanian Steamers (steamship)
Tax Shelter
Tax Straddle
Third Shift
Tidewater Southern (railroad)
Time Sharing
Time Study
Transmission Service
Transport Station
Treasury Stock
Trumann Southern (railroad)
TSA: Tax Sheltered Annuity
Time Series Analysis
Time Slot Access
Toy Safety Act
TSAM: Time Series Analysis and Modeling
TSAS: Time-Sharing Accounting System
TSAU: Time Slot Access Unit
TSB: Terminal Status Block
TSC: Time Share Control
Totally Self-Checking
Transmitter Start Code
TS/DMS: Time-Shared Data Management System
TSE: Time Sharing Executive
Tokyo Stock Exchange (Japan)
Toronto Stock Exchange (Canada)
TS-E: Texas South-Eastern (railroad)
TSF: Time to System Failure
TSFP: Time to System Failure Period
TSGAS: Time-Shared General Accounting System
TSID: Track Sector Identification
TSIU: Telephone System Interface Unit
tsk: task
TSK: Computer Task Group Inc. (NYSE)
TSL: Test Source Library
Time Series Language
Time Sharing Library
TSM: Terminal Support Monitor
Tri-State Motor Transit Company of Delaware (ASE)
TSMS: Time Series Modeling System
TSO: Technical Standards Orders
Tesoro Petroleum Corp. (NYSE)
Time-Sharing Option
TSODB: Time Series Oriented Data Base
TSOS: Time Sharing Operating System
TSO/VTAM: Time Sharing Option for the Virtual Telecommunications Access Method

TSP: Telesphere International Inc. (ASE)
Time Series Processor
Traveling Salesman Problem

TSPL: Telephone Systems Programming Language

TSPS: Traffic Service Position System

TSQ: T2 Medical Inc. (ASE)

TSR: Technical Summary Report
Temporary Storage Register
Translation State Register
Trans-Siberian Railway

TSS: Terminal Security System
Terminal Send Side
Time Sharing System
Trade Support System

tst: test

TST: Transaction Step Task

TstAm: Trust America Service Corp. (newspaper)

TSX: Time Sharing Executive

TSY: Tech-Sym Corp. (NYSE)

tt: teletype

T&T: Tijuana and Tecate (railroad)

T/T: Telegraphic Transfer

TT: Teller Terminal
Terms of Trade
Texas International Airlines
Think Tank
Toledo Terminal (railroad)
Transaction Terminal
TransTechnology Corp. (NYSE)

TTA: Total Tangible Assets
Trans-Texas Airways

TTBL: Task Table

TT&C: Telemetry, Tracking and Command

TTC: Toro Co., The (NYSE)
Toronto Transit Commission

TTD: Temporary Text Delay

TTDL: Terminal Transparent Display Language

TTE: Total Tax Expenditures

ttees: trustees

TTF: Thai Fund (NYSE)
Time to Time Failure

TTF&T: Technology Transfer, Fabrication and Test

TTI: Technical Tape Inc. (ASE)

TTK: Tie Trunk

TT & L: Treasury Tax & Loan account

TTL: Torotel Inc. (ASE)
Transistor-Transistor Logic

TTN: Titan Corp. (NYSE)

TTP: Total Taxable Pay

TTS: Transmission Test Set

TTSL: Treasury Tax and Loan Account

TTSPN: Two Terminal Series Parallel Networks

TTT: Transamerica Trailer Transport (steamship)

ttw: teletypewriter

T2 Md: T2 Medical Inc. (newspaper)

TTX: Tultex Corp. (NYSE)

tty: teletype
teletypewriter

TTY: Telephone-Teletypewriter

TU: Tape Unit
Technological Unemployment
Time Unit
Timing Unit
Trade Union
Trading Unit
Transmission Unit
Transport Unit
Tunis Air (airline)
Typographical Union

TUA: Transit Union Amalgamated

TubMex: Tubos de Acero de Mexico S.A. (newspaper)

TUC: Trades Union Congress
Transportation, Utilities, Communications industries

TUF: Time of Useful Function
Transmitter Underflow

TUG: Maritrans Partners LP (NYSE)

TUI: Trade Union International

Tultex: Tultex Corp. (newspaper)
TUR: Traffic Usage Recorder
Turner Corp., The (ASE)
TurnB: Turner Broadcasting System Inc. (newspaper)
TurnrC: Turner Corp., The (newspaper)
TUT: Transistor Under Test
tv: television
TV: Transfer Vector
Trans International Airlines
TVA: Tax on Value Added
Tennessee Valley Authority
TVC: Television Camera
TVG: Tavares and Gulf (railroad)
TVRO: Television Receive Only Earth Station
TVRY: Tooele Valley Railway
TVS: Transient Voltage Suppressor
TVT: Television Typewriter
tw: typewriter
TW: TWA (Trans World Airlines)
Wait State
TWA: Transaction Work Area
Trans World Airlines Inc. (NYSE) (newspaper)
Typewriter Adapter
TwCty: Town & Country Jewelry Mfg. Corp. (newspaper)
TWI: Trade-Weighted Index
Training Within Industry
TWIMC: To Whom It May Concern
TwinDs: Twin Disc Inc. (newspaper)
TWN: Taiwan Fund Inc., The (ASE)
TWODEPEP: Two-Dimensional Elliptic, Parabolic and Eigenvalue Problems
TWP: Twisted Wire Pair
Two Pesos Inc. (ASE)
TwPeso: Two Pesos Inc. (newspaper)
TWR: Tape Writer Register
TWS: Translator Writing System
TWT: Traveling Wave Tube
TWU: Transport Workers' Union of America
TWUA: Textile Workers Union of America
TWX: Teletypewriter Exchange
Time Warner Inc. (NYSE)
tx: transmit
transmitter
TX: Terminal Executive
Texaco Inc. (NYSE)
Transportes Aereos Nacionales (National Air Transport) (airline)
TXA: Terminal Exchange Area
Texas American Bancshares Inc. (NYSE)
TxABc: Texas American Bancshares Inc. (newspaper)
TXC: Texaco Canada Inc. (ASE)
TXD: Transmit Data
TXF: Texfi Industries Inc. (NYSE)
TXI: Texas Industries Inc. (NYSE)
TxInst: Texas Instruments Inc. (newspaper)
TXN: Texas Instruments Inc. (NYSE)
TxPac: Texas Pacific Land Trust (newspaper)
txt: text
TXT: Textron Inc. (NYSE)
TXTM: Text Maintenance
TXU: Texas Utilities Co. (NYSE)
TY: Tri-Continental Corp. (NYSE)
TYC: Tyco Laboratories Inc. (NYSE)
TycoL: Tyco Laboratories Inc. (newspaper)
TYL: Tyler Corp. (NYSE)
Tyler: Tyler Corp. (newspaper)
typ: type
typewriter
typical
typically
typwrtr: typewriter
TZ: Transair Limited (airline)
T-Z RA: Tanzania-Zambia Railway Authority

u: unemployment
unit
universe
update
user
utility

U: The intraday high is a new high for the last 52 weeks (in newspaper reports of transactions)
Underground (London's subway) (UK)
USAir Group Inc. (NYSE)

UA: Unauthorized Absence
Underwriting Account
United Airlines
Units of Account (EC)
Unnumbered Acknowledge
User Area

UAC: Unicorp American Corp. (ASE)
Uninterrupted Automatic Control

UACN: Unified Automated Communication Network

UADS: User Attribute Data Set

UAL: UAL Corp. (NYSE)

UAL Cp: UAL Corp. (newspaper)

UAM: United Asset Management Corp. (NYSE) (newspaper)

UAP: User Area Profile

UAR: Unit Address Register

UART: Universal Asynchronous Receiver Transmitter

UAS: Uniform Accounting System

UAT: User Accounting Table

UAW: United Automobile, Aerospace and Agricultural Implement Workers of America (union)

UB: Unemployment Benefits
Union of Burma Airways
United Brands Co. (NYSE)
Unpaid Balance
Upper Bound
User Board

UBC: Universal Block Channel

UBC&J: United Brotherhood of Carpenters and Joiners (union)

UBHR: User Block Handling Routine

UBIT: Unrelated Business Income Tax

UBITA: Upper Bound of Information Translation Amount

UBM: Unit Bill of Material

UBN: University Bank NA (ASE)

UBOT: Unfavorable Balance Of Trade

UBR: Ulan Bator Railway
Uniform Building Regulations

UBS: Unit Backspace character

uc: unichannel

U&C: undercharge

UC: LADECO (Linea Aerea del Cobre) (airline)
Under Construction
Unemployment Compensation
Unfair Competition
Unit Cost
Up Converter
Upper Case

UCA: Unemployment Compensation Act

UCarb: Union Carbide Corp. (newspaper)

UCB: Unit Control Block
Universal Character Buffer

UCBTAB: User Control Block Table
UCC: Uniform Commercial Code
Union Camp Corp. (NYSE)
Universal Copyright Convention
UCCC: Uniform Consumer Credit Code
UCD: Unemployment Compensation Deduction
Unemployment Compensation Disability
UCF: Utility Control Facility
UCITS: Collective Instrument in Transferable Securities (EC)
UCL: Unocal Corp. (NYSE)
UCLAN: User Cluster Language
UCM: Universal Communications Monitor
UCmp: Union Camp Corp. (newspaper)
UCO: Union Corp., The (NYSE)
UCOP: Unit Cost of Production
UCP: Uninterruptible Computer Power
Universal Commercial Paper
UCR: Utah Coal Route (railway)
UCS: Universal Call Sequence
Universal Character Set
Universal Classification System
User Control Store
UCSB: Universal Character Set Buffer
UCT: Universal Coordinated Time
UCU: UtiliCorp United Inc. (NYSE)
UCV: Unimproved Capital Value
UCW: Unit Control Word
UD: Brower Flight Service (airline)
Unsecured Debt
UDAC: User Digital Analog Controller
UDAS: Unified Direct Access Standards
UDC: UDC-Universal Development LP (NYSE) (newspaper)
Universal Decimal Classification
Universal Digital Control
UDE: Universal Data Entry
UDEAC: Union Douanière et Économique de l'Afrique Centrale (Central African Customs and Economic Union) (French)
UDF: Unit Development Folder
U-DID: Unique Data Item Description
UDL: Uniform Data Language
UDP: Uniform Delivered Price
UDTS: Universal Data Transfer Service
UE: Trans Magic Airlines
United Electrical Workers
User Equipment
Utility Expenditures
UEF: Union Européenne des Fédéralistes (European Union of Federalists) (French)
UEL: Upper Earnings Limit
UEP: Union Electric Co. (NYSE)
Union Européenne de Paiements (European Payments Union) (French) (EC)
UES: Uniform Emission Standard
UET: Universal Emulating Terminal
UETS: Universal Emulating Terminal System
UF: Utility File
UFAM: Universal File Access Method
UFAS: Universal File Access System
UFC: Uniform Freight Classification
United Fruit Company (railroad)
Universal Foods Corp. (NYSE)
Universal Frequency Counter

UFD: United Foods Inc. (ASE)
User File Directory
UFF: UnionFed Financial Corp. (NYSE)
UFI: Usage Frequency Indicator
User Friendly Interface
UFINEX: Union pour le Financement et l'Expansion du Commerce International
UFM: User-to-File Manager
UFN: UniCARE Financial Corp. (ASE)
UFO: User Files On-Line
UFood: United Foods Inc. (newspaper)
UFP: Utility Facilities Program
UFPC: United Federation of Postal Clerks (union)
UFS: Universal Financial System
UFWA: United Furniture Workers of America (union)
UFWOC: United Farm Workers' Organizing Committee
UG: User Group
UG&CW: United Glass and Ceramic Workers (union)
UGI: UGI Corp. (NYSE) (newspaper)
UGMA: Uniform Gift to Minors Act
UGT: User Group Table
UGW: United Garment Workers (union)
UH: U. S. Home Corp. (NYSE)
UHC: Ultimate Holding Company
UHF: Ultra High Frequency
UHL: User Header Label
UHM: Universal Host Machine
UHT: Universal Health Realty Income Trust (NYSE)
UI: Star Airlines
Unearned Income
Unemployment Insurance
United Inns Inc. (NYSE)
UIC: Unemployment Insurance Code
United Industrial Corp. (NYSE)
User Identification Code
UICP: Uniform Inventory Control Program
UIF: USLIFE Income Fund Inc. (NYSE)
UIG: User Instruction Group
UIL: United Illuminating Co., The (NYSE)
UIllum: United Illuminating Co., The (newspaper)
UIM: Ultraintelligent Machine
UIO: Units in Operation
Universal Input/Output
UIR: User Instruction Register
UIS: Unemployment Insurance Service
Unisys Corp. (NYSE)
Unit Identification System
UIT: Unified Income Tax
Union Internationale des Télécommunications (International Telecommunications Union)
Unit Investment Trust
UJ: Air Ulster (airline)
UJB: United Jersey Banks (NYSE)
UJCL: Universal Job Control Language
UJerBk: United Jersey Banks (newspaper)
UJF: Unsatisfied Judgment Fund
UK: British Island Airways
United Carbide Corp. (NYSE)
United Kingdom
UKB: Universal Keyboard
UKing: United Kingdom Fund Inc., The (newspaper)
UKM: United Kingdom Fund Inc., The (NYSE)
UKPO: United Kingdom Post Office
U/L: Upper/Lower
UL: Lansa Airlines of Honduras
Underwriters Laboratories, Inc.
Unilever PLC (NYSE)

Unskilled Labor
Upper Limit
User Language
ULA: Uncommitted Logic Array
ULC: Uniform Loop Clock
Upper-Lower Case
ULCC: Ultra-Large Crude Carrier
ULI: Umbrella Liability Insurance
Underwriters Laboratories, Inc.
ULM: Universal Line Multiplexer
Universal Logic Module
ULP: Unfair Labor Practice
ULS: Unsecured Loan Stock
ULSI: Ultra-Large-Scale Integration
ult: last
ultimatum
ULT: Ultimate Corp., The (NYSE)
Ultmte: Ultimate Corp., The (newspaper)
ulto: ultimo
UM: Morris Air Transport (airline)
United Medical Corp. (ASE)
UMA: Union Membership Agreement
UMACHA: Upper Midwest Automated Clearing House Association
UMatch: Universal Matchbox Group Ltd. (newspaper)
UMB: Universal Medical Buildings LP (NYSE)
UMC: Unibus Microchannel
UMCS: Unattended Multipoint Communications Station
UMG: Universal Matchbox Group Ltd. (NYSE)
UMLC: Universal Multiline Controller
UMM: United Merchants and Manufacturers Inc. (NYSE)
UMOD: User Module
UMP: Upper Merion and Plymouth (railroad)
UMR: Unimar Co. (ASE)
Usual Marketing Requirement
UMS: Universal Multiprogramming System
UMW: United Mine Workers of America (union)
UN: Unilever NV (NYSE)
United Nations
UNA: Unattended Answering Accessory
UNALC: User-Network Access Link Control
UnBrnd: United Brands Co. (newspaper)
UNC: UNC Inc. (NYSE)
UNCInc: UNC Inc. (newspaper)
UNCITRAL: United Nations Commission on International Trade Law
UNCM: User Network Control Machine
UNCOL: Universal Computer-Oriented Language
UNCTAD: United Nations Conference on Trade & Development
undef: undefined
UnElec: Union Electric Co. (newspaper)
UNESEM: Union Européenne des Sources d'Eaux Minérales naturelles du Marché Commun (European Union of Natural Mineral Water Sources of the Common Market) (French) (EC)
UnExp: Union Exploration Partners Ltd. (newspaper)
UNF: UniFirst Corp. (NYSE)
Union Freight (railroad)
UnfedF: UnionFed Financial Corp. (newspaper)
UNI: Undistributed Net Income
Unity (railways)

UNIBUS: Universal Bus
UNICE: Union des Industrie de la Communauté Européenne (Union of Industries of the European Community) (French) (EC)
UNICOMP: Universal Compiler Fortran Compatible
Unicorp: Unicorp American Corp. (newspaper)
UniCre: UniCARE Financial Corp. (newspaper)
UNIFE: Union of European Railway Industries
UniFrst: UniFirst Corp. (newspaper)
Unilvr: Unilever PLC (newspaper)
Unimar: Unimar Co. (newspaper)
UNIMOD: Universal Module
UnionC: Union Corp., The (newspaper)
UNIQUE: Uniform Inquiry Update Element
Unisys: Unisys Corp. (newspaper)
Unit: Unit Corp. (newspaper)
UNITED: United Airlines
UniTel: United Telecommunications Inc. (newspaper)
UnitelV: Unitel Video Inc. (newspaper)
Unitil: UNITIL Corp. (newspaper)
UnitInd: United Industrial Corp. (newspaper)
UnitInn: United Inns Inc. (newspaper)
Unitrde: Unitrode Corp. (newspaper)
UNIVAC: Universal Automatic Computer
Univar: Univar Corp. (newspaper)
UNM: UNUM Corp. (NYSE)
UnNV: Unilever N.V. (newspaper)
UNO: UNO Restaurant Corp. (ASE)
Unocal: Unocal Corp. (newspaper)
UnoRt: UNO Restaurant Corp. (newspaper)
UNP: Union Pacific Corp. (NYSE)
UnPAc: Union Pacific Corp. (newspaper)
unpad: unpaid
unpd: unpaid
unprot: unprotect
unqual: unqualified
UnStck: United Stockyards Corp. (newspaper)
UNT: Unit Corp. (NYSE)
UnTech: United Technologies Corp. (newspaper)
UnTex: Union Texas Petroleum Holdings Inc. (newspaper)
UNUM: UNUM Corp. (newspaper)
UNV: Unitel Video Inc. (ASE)
UnValy: Union Valley Corp. (newspaper)
UnvBk: University Bank N.A. (newspaper)
UnvFds: Universal Foods Corp. (newspaper)
UnvHR: Universal Health Realty Income Trust (newspaper)
UnvlCp: Universal Corp. (newspaper)
UnvMed: Universal Medical Buildings L.P. (newspaper)
UnvPat: University Patents Inc. (newspaper)
U&O: Use and Occupancy
UO: Union Office
Union Railroad-Oregon
UOA: Units Of Account
UOG: Unit Of Grading
UOP: Unit Of Production
UOT: Unit Of Trading
UOV: Unit Of Value
up: uniprocessing
uniprocessor
UP: Uncovered Position
Unearned Premium
Union Pacific (railroad)
Unit Price
Unrealized Profits
Upset Price

UPA: Uniform Partnership Act
Unique Product Advantage
Units Per Assembly
UPACS: Universal Performance Assessment and Control System
UPB: Universal Patents Bureau (UK)
Upper Bound
UPC: Uniform Practice Code
Unit of Processing Capacity
Universal Peripheral Control
Universal Product Code
USPCI Inc. (NYSE)
upd: unpaid
UPE: Union Parlementaire Européenne (European Parliamentary Union) (French)
UPI: Universal Peripheral Interface
UPIC: Universal Personal Identification Code
UPJ: Upjohn Co., The (NYSE)
Upjohn: Upjohn Co., The (newspaper)
UPK: United Park City Mines Co. (NYSE)
UPkMn: United Park City Mines Co. (newspaper)
UPL: Universal Programming Language
User Programming Language
UPP: United Papermakers and Paperworkers (union)
Universal PROM Programmer
UPS: Uninterruptible Power Supply (System)
Universal Processing System
UPSI: User Program Sense Indicator
UPT: Undistributed Profits Tax
University Patents Inc. (ASE)
User Process Table
UPU: Universal Postal Union
UPWA: United Public Workers of America (union)
UQ: Suburban Airlines
UQT: User Queue Table
UR: Lloyd's Universal Register of Shipping (UK)
Under Review
Under Rule (stocks)
Unit Record
Unit Register
Urban Renewal
Utility Register
URA: User Requirements Analysis
Utilization Review Agency
URC: Unit Record Control
URDS: User Requirements Data Base
URL: User Requirements Language
URP: Unit Record Processor
URR: Union Railroad-Pittsburgh
urs: underwriters
URT: USP Real Estate Investment Trust (ASE)
US: Unauthorized Strike
Underlying Stock (Security)
Union Shop
United States (of America)
Unit Separator character
Unlisted Security
Unregistered Stock
USA: Liberty All-Star Equity Fund (NYSE)
United States of America
USACaf: USACafes L.P. (newspaper)
USACII: United States of America Standard Code for Information Interchange
USACSC: United States Army Computer Systems Command
USAF: United States Air Force
USAIR: US Airlines
UsairG: USAir Group Inc. (newspaper)
USAM: Unique Sequential Access Method

USART: Universal Synchronous-Asynchronous Receiver/Transmitter
USAS: United States of America Standard
USASCII: United States of American Standard Code for Information Interchange
USASCSOCR: United States of America Standard Character Set for Optical Character Recognition
USASI: United States of America Standards Institute
USASLE: Uniform Securities Agent State Law Examination
USBA: United States Bureau of Standards
US Banker: United States Banker
USBM: United States Bureau of Mines
USC: United States Code
User Service Center
USLICO Corp. (NYSE)
USCB: United States Customs Bonded
USCC: United States Chamber of Commerce
US Cel: United States Cellular Corp. (newspaper)
U-Schatze: Unverzinsliche Schatzanweisunger
USCOMM: United States Department of Commerce
USDA: United States Department of Agriculture
USDC: United States Department of Commerce
USDL: United States Department of Labor
USE: Univac Scientific Exchange
USEC: United States Mission to the European Community
USEMA: United States Electronic Mail Association
USER: User System Evaluator
USERID: User Identification
USES: United States Employment Service
USF: USACafes LP (NYSE)
USFG: USF&G Corp. (newspaper)
USG: United States Government
USG Corp. (NYSE) (newspaper)
USGS: United States Geological Survey
USH: USLIFE Corp. (NYSE)
USHom: U.S. Home Corp. (newspaper)
USI: User System Interface
USIA: United States Information Agency
USIO: Unlimited Sequential Input/Output
USIRB: United States Internal Revenue Bonded
USIS: United States Information Service
USIT: Unit Share Investment Trust
USITA: United States Independent Telephone Association
USITC: United States International Trade Committee
USL: United States Lines Company
UslfeF: USLIFE Income Fund Inc. (newspaper)
USLICO: USLICO Corp. (newspaper)
USLIFE: USLIFE Corp. (newspaper)
USM: United States Cellular Corp. (ASE)
United States Mint
Unlisted Securities Market
USNC: United States National Committee of the International Electrotechnical Commission
USOA: Uniform Systems of Accounts

USOC: Universal Service Order Code
USP: Usage Sensitive Pricing
USPCI: USPCI Inc. (newspaper)
USPO: United States Post Office
USPRI: USP Real Estate Investment Trust (newspaper)
USPS: United States Postal Service
USQ: Squeezed files
USR: United States Shoe Corp., The (NYSE)
User Service Routine
USRT: Universal Synchronous Receiver/Transmitter
USS: United States Surgical Corp. (NYSE)
USShoe: United States Shoe Corp., The (newspaper)
USSR: Union of Soviet Socialist Republics
USSS: United States Steamship
US Surg: United States Surgical Corp. (newspaper)
UST: User Symbol Table
UST Inc. (NYSE) (newspaper)
USTC: United States Tariff Commission
United States Trade Center (Mexico)
USTR: United States Trade Representative
USTS: United States Transmission Systems, Inc.
USU: Unbundled Stock Unit
USW: United Steelworkers (of America) (union)
U S West Inc. (NYSE)
USWA: United Steelworkers of America (union)
USWAB: United States Warehouse Act Bonded
USWest: U S West Inc. (newspaper)
USX: USX Corp. (newspaper)
U/T: Under Trust
UT: Union Terminal (railway)
United Telecommunications Inc. (NYSE)
Universal Time
User Terminal
UTA (Union de Transports Aerien) (airline)
UTA: Ulster Transport Authority (Northern Ireland)
Union Transportation Aerienne (Air Transport Union)
Unit Trust Association
User Transfer Address
UTAH: Utah Railway
UTC: Utilities Telecommunications Council
UTCS: Urban Traffic Control System
UTD: Universal Transfer Device
UtdMM: United Merchants & Manufacturers Inc. (newspaper)
UTH: Union Texas Petroleum Holdings Inc. (NYSE)
util: utilization
UtiliCo: UtiliCorp United Inc. (newspaper)
UTL: UNITIL Corp. (ASE)
User Trailer Label
UtMed: United Medical Corp. (newspaper)
UTOL: Universal Translator Oriented Language
UTP: Unfair Trade Practice
UTR: Union Transportation Company (railroad)
Unitrode Corp. (NYSE)
UTS: Universal Timing-Sharing System
UTT: Unit Under Test
UTWA: United Textile Workers of America (union)
UTX: United Technologies Corp. (NYSE)
UU: Touraine Air Transport (airline)
UUA: Univac Users Association
UUT: Unit Under Test
uv: ultraviolet

UV: Unadilla Valley (railroad)
UVC: Union Valley Corp. (ASE)
UVM: Universal Vendor Marking
UVPROM: Ultraviolet Programmable Read Only Memory
UV-PROM: Ultraviolet Programmable Read Only Memory
UVV: Universal Corp. (NYSE)
UVX: Univar Corp. (NYSE)
uw: underwriter
underwritten
UW: Midwest Airlines
Used With
UWA: User Working Area
UWR: United Water Resources Inc. (NYSE) (newspaper)
UWU: Utility Workers Union of America (union)
UX: Air Illinois (airline)
UXP: Union Exploration Partners Ltd. (NYSE)
UY: Buckeye Air Service (airline)
U de Y: Unidos de Yucatan (United Railways of Yucatan, Mexico)

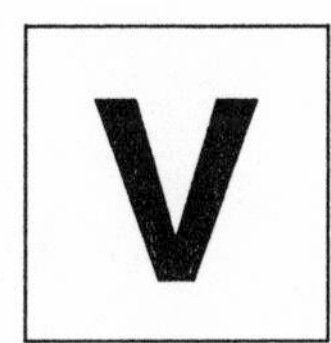

v: variable
vector
verification
verify
versus
virtual
volt
voltage

V: Irving Bank Corp. (NYSE)
Promotional Fare of the Airlines
Valtionrautatiet (Finnish State Railways)

VA: Compania de Navegacion Vasco-Asturiana (Basque-Asturian Navigation Company) (steamship)
Value Added
Value Analysis
Veterans' Administration
Viasa (airline)
Virtual Address
Voucher Attached

VAA: Voice Access Arrangement

VAB: Voice Answer-Back

VABM: Value Added By Manufacturer

vac: vacancy

VAC: Value Added Carrier
Verified Audit Circulation
Vermont American Corp. (ASE)

VACHA: Virginia's Automated Clearing House Association

VACS: Virtual Accounting Collecting System

VAD: Value-Added Dealer

VADAC: Voice Analyzer Data Converter

VADC: Video Analog to Digital Converter

Vader: Vader Group Inc. (newspaper)

VAF: Vendor Approval Form

VAG: Vertex Adjacency Graph

val: valuation
value

VAL: Valspar Corp., The (ASE)

VALDEFD: Value Defined

Valero: Valero Energy Corp. (newspaper)

Valeyln: Valley Industries Inc. (newspaper)

ValFrg: Valley Forge Corp. (newspaper)

Valhi: Valhi Inc. (newspaper)

ValNG: Velero Natural Gas Partners L.P. (newspaper)

VALOREN: Exploitation of the indigenous energy potential (EC)

VALS: Value and Lifestyle

Valspr: Valspar Corp., The (newspaper)

VALUE: Valorisation and Utilisation for Europe (EC)

ValyRs: Valley Resources Inc. (newspaper)

VAM: Value Added Market

VAMP: Value Analysis of Management Practices
Vector Arithmetic Multiprocessor

VAN: Value Added Network

VanDrn: Van Dorn Co. (newspaper)

VANS: Value Added Network Service

VAPS: Volume, Article, Paragraph, Sentence

var: variable
variation

VAR: Value-Added Remarketer
Varian Associates Inc. (NYSE)
Vector Autoregressive Model
Voluntary Automobile Restraints

VARBLK: Variable Block

Varco: Varco International Inc. (newspaper)

Varian: Varian Associates Inc. (newspaper)

VARIG: Viacao Aerea Rio Grande (Brazilian Airlines)

Varity: Varity Corp. (newspaper)

Varo: Varo Inc. (newspaper)

VARUNB: Variable Unblocked

VAS: Value Added Service
Value Added Statement
Vector Addition System

VASP: Viacao Aerea São Paulo (Brazilian Airlines)

VAT: Value-Added Tax
Varity Corp. (NYSE)
Virtual Address Translator

VATE: Versatile Automatic Test Equipment

VAU: Vertical Arithmetic Unit

VAX: Virtual Address Extended

VB: Air Bangui (airline)
Voice-Band
Voluntary Bankruptcy

VBOMP: Virtual Base Organization and Maintenance Processor

VBP: Valid BIT Register

VBR: Virginia Blue Ridge (railway)

VC: Valuable Cargo
Variable Charge
Variable Costs
Vendor Call
Vendor Code
Vendor Contract
Ventilated Containers
Venture Capital
Verification Condition
Vice Chairman (Chairwoman) (Chairperson)
Victoria Carriers (steamship)
Virginia Central (railway)
Virtual Circuit
Virtual Computer
Vista Chemical Co. (NYSE)

VCA: Voice Connecting Arrangement

VCBA: Variable Control Block Area

VCF: Venture Capital Fund
Verified Circulation Figure
Voltage Controlled Filter

VCG: Verification Condition Generator

VCGEN: Verification Condition Generator

VCO: Voltage Controlled Oscillator

VCR: Valuation by Components Rule
Video Cassette Recorder

V&CS: Virginia & Carolina Southern (railroad)

VCS: Validation Control System
Video Communications System

VCTCA: Virtual Channel to Channel Adapter

VCTD: Vendor Contract Technical Data

VCV: Variable Compression Vector

VCY: Ventura County (railway)

VD: Port Augusta Air Services (airline)
Various Dates
Virtual Data
Volume Deleted
Volume Discount

VDAM: Virtual Data Access Method

VDB: Vector Data Buffer
Video Display Board

VDC: Van Dorn Co. (NYSE)
Vendor Data Control
Video Display Controller

VDD: Version Description Document
VDDL: Virtual Data Description Language
VDETS: Voice Data Entry Terminal System
VDG: Video Display Generator
VDI: Video Display Input
Video Display Interface
VDL: Virtual Database Level
VDLIB: Virtual Disk Library
VDM: Video Display Module
VDP: Video Data Processor
Video Display Processor
Voice Digitization Rate
VDR: Vader Group Inc. (ASE)
Variable Deposit Requirement
Vendor Data Request
VDS: Vendor Direct Shipment
Voice/Data Switch
VDT: Video Display Terminal
Visual Display Terminal
VDU: Video Display Unit
Visual Display Unit
VE: AVENSA (Aerovias Venezolanas - Venezuelan Airlines)
Value Engineering
Visalia Electric (railroad)
VEA: Value Engineering Audit
Vocational Education Act
VEBA: Voluntary Employee Benefit Association
VEC: Vector Analog Computer
VECP: Value Engineering Change Proposal
VECTAR: Value, Expertise, Client, Time, Attorney, Result
VEEP: Vice President
VEFCA: Value Engineering Functional Cost Analysis
VEM: Vendor Engineering Memorandum
VEN: Vendo Co., The (NYSE)
vend: vendor
Vendo: Vendo Co., The (newspaper)
VENUS: Valuable and Efficient Network Utility Service
VEP: Vocational Exploration Program
ver: verify
VER: Verit Industries (ASE)
Voluntary Export Restraints
Verit: Verit Industries (newspaper)
Versar: Versar Inc. (newspaper)
vert: vertical
VERT: Venture Evaluation and Review Technique
Vertple: Vertipile Inc. (newspaper)
ves: vessel
VES: Variable Elasticity of Substitution
Vestaur Securities Inc. (NYSE)
Vestrn: Vestron Inc. (newspaper)
VestSe: Vestaur Securities Inc. (newspaper)
VET: Vocational Educational and Training
VF: British Air Ferries (airline)
Valley Forge Corp. (ASE)
Variable Factor
Voice Frequency
VFB: Vertical Format Buffer
VFC: Variable File Channel
Vector Function Chainer
Vertical Format Control
Vertical Forms Control
V. F. Corp. (NYSE)
VF Cp: V. F. Corp. (newspaper)
VFD: Value For Duty
VFFT: Voice-Frequency Facility Terminal
VFL: Variable Field Length
VFM: Value For Money
VFMED: Variable Format Message Entry Device
VFO: Variable Frequency Oscillator
VFU: Vertical Format Unit
Vocabulary File Utility

VG: Air Siam (airline)
Vector Generator
VGAM: Vector Graphics Access Method
VGC: Visual Graphics Corp. (ASE)
VGLI: Veterans Group Life Insurance
VGN: Virginian Railway
VH: Air Volta (airline)
V-H: Vertical-Horizontal
VHDV: Very High Dollar Value
VHF: Very High Frequencies (Frequency)
VHI: Valhi Inc. (NYSE)
VHM: Virtual Hardware Monitor
VHMCP: Voluntary Home Mortgage Credit Program (defunct)
VHOL: Very High Order Language
VHSI: Very High Speed Integration
VHSIC: Very High Speed Integrated Circuits
VHT: VMS Hotel Investment Fund (ASE) (newspaper)
VI: STA (Societe de Travail Aerien) (airline)
Valley Industries Inc. (NYSE)
Value Included entry
Vendor Item
Vested Interest
VIA: Versatile Interface Adapter
Viacom Inc. (ASE)
Viacm: Viacom Inc. (newspaper)
VIASA: Venezolona Internacional de Aviacion, Sociedad Anonimo (Venezuelan Airlines)
Viatch: Viatech Inc. (newspaper)
VIC: Variable Instruction Computer
Very Important Cargo
Very Important Customer
Virtual Interaction Controller
Visibility of Intransit Cargo
VICAM: Virtual Integrated Communications Access Method
VICAR: Video Image Communication and Retrieval
VICC: Visual Information Control Console
Vicon: Vicon Industries Inc. (newspaper)
vid: video
VIDC: Virgin Islands Department of Commerce
VIEW: Visible, Informative, Emotionally Appealing, Workable
VII: Vicon Industries Inc. (ASE)
VIL: Vendor Item List
VIM: Vendor Initial Measurement
VIMTPG: Virtual Interactive Machine Test Program Generator
VIN: Vehicle Identification Number
Vendor Identification Number
Vintage Enterprises Inc. (ASE)
Vintge: Vintage Enterprises Inc. (newspaper)
VIO: Very Important Object
Video Input/Output
Virtual Input/Output
VIP: Valuable-Items Policy
Value Improving Products
Value in Performance
Variable Individual Protection
Variable Information Processing
Variable Interest Plus
Variation In Price
Vector Instruction Processor
Verifying Interpreting Punch
Versatile Information Processor
Vice President
Video Programming
Visit-Investigate-Purchase
Volume Inverse Pricing
VIPS: Variable Item Processing System
VIR: Variable Interest Rate
Vendor Information Request
Vendor Item Release

Virco Manufacturing Corp. (ASE)

Virco: Virco Manufacturing Corp. (newspaper)

VIRM: Variable-Interest-Rate Mortgage

VIS: Vector Instruction Set

VISAM: Variable-Length Indexed Sequential Access Method

VISDA: Visual Information System Development Association

Vishay: Vishay Intertechnology Inc. (newspaper)

VisIG: Visual Graphics Corp. (newspaper)

VISPA: Virtual Storage Productivity Aid

VISTA: Viewing Instantly Security Transactions Automatically

VistaC: Vista Chemical Co. (newspaper)

VITA: Volunteers for International Technical Assistance

VITAL: Virtual Image Take-off And Landing

VIURAM: Video Interface Unit Random Access Memory

viz: namely

VJ: Allen Aviation (airline)

VK: Trans Michigan Airlines

VKmp: Van Kampen Merritt Municipal Income Trust (newspaper)

VL: Vaasa Line (Hanseatic-Vaasa Line) (steamship)
Value Line Investment Survey
Vector Length

VLBC: Very Large Bulk-cargo Carrier

VLC: Valley Line Company (steamship)

VLCBX: Very Large Computerized Branch Exchange

VLCC: Very Large Crude Carrier

VLDB: Very Large Data Base

VLF: Very Low Frequency

V&LI: Vancouver and Lulu Island (railroad)

VLI: Variable Life Insurance

VLO: Valero Energy Corp. (NYSE)

VLP: Valero Natural Gas Partners LP (NYSE)

VLR: Variable Loan Rate

VLS: Virtual Linkage Subsystem

VLSI: Very Large Scale Integration

VLSW: Virtual Line Switch

VLTP: Variable Length Text Processor

VLU: Worldwide Value Fund Inc. (NYSE)

VM: Monmouth Airlines
Vertical Merger
Virtual Machine
Virtual Memory

VMA: Valid Memory Address
Virtual Machine Assist

VMAPS: Virtual Memory Array Processing System

VMBLOK: Virtual Machine Control Block

VMC: Virtual Memory Computer
Vulcan Materials Co. (NYSE)

VMCF: Virtual Machine Communication Facility

VMD: Vector Memory Display

VME: Virtual Machine Environment

VMF: Virtual Machine Facility

VML: Virtual Memory Level

VMLI: Veterans Mortgage Life Insurance

V&MM: Vandalism and Malicious Mischief

VMM: Virtual Machine Monitor

V-MNR: Viet-Minh National Railways (North Vietnam)

VMOS: Virtual Memory Operating System

VMP: Value as Marine Policy

VMPE: Virtual Memory Performance Enhancement

VMS: Vertical Market Structure
Virtual Memory System
Voice Message System
VMT: Van Kampen Merritt Municipal Income Trust (NYSE)
Variable Microcycle Timing
Virtual Memory Technique
VN: Air Vietnam (airline)
VNC: Voice Numerical Control
VNGC: Van Niervelt, Goudriaan and Company (Rotterdam-South American Line) (steamship)
VNL: Via Net Loss
VNLF: Via Net Loss Factor
VNO: Vornado Inc. (NYSE)
V-NR: Viet-Nam Railways (South Vietnam)
VO: BC Airliens (airline)
Seagram Company Ltd., The (NYSE)
vocab: vocabulary
VOC-ED: Vocational Education
VocRehab: Vocational Rehabilitation
voct: vocational
VODAS: Voice-Operated Device Anti-Sing
VOGAD: Voice-Operated Gaining-Adjusting Device
VOI: Vocational Opinion Index
vol: volume
VOLA: Volume (ASE)
VOLCAL: Volume Calculator
VOLID: Volume Identifier
VOLN: Volume (NYSE)
VOLSER: Volume/Serial
VON: Vons Companies Inc., The (NYSE)
Vons: Vons Companies Inc., The (newspaper)
VOP: Valued as in Original Policy
Value Of Product
VOPA: Verbal Order Purchase Agreement
Voplex: Voplex Corp. (newspaper)
Vornad: Vornado Inc. (newspaper)
VOS: Value Of Stock
Virtual Operating System
VOSTGOSTORG: All-Union Association for Trade with the Countries of the East
VOT: Vocational Office Trainee
Voplex Corp. (ASE)
vou: voucher
VOX: Audiovox Corp. (ASE)
Voice-Operated Relay Circuit
V&P: Vendor and Purchaser
VP: Vacation Pay
Vacuum Packaged
VASP (Viacao São Paulo)(airline)
Vector Processor
Verifying Punch
Vice President
Virtual Processor
Voting Pool
VPA: Volume Purchase Agreement
VPB: Vendors Per Block
VPE: Vector Processing Element
VPF: Vector Parameter File
VPI: Vendor Parts Index
VPM: Vendor Part Modification
Versatile Packaging Machine
Virtual Processor Monitor
VPN: Vendor Parts Number
Virtual Page Number
VPP: Value Payable by Post
Vested Pension Plan
VPS: Vector Processing System
Vibrations Per Second
VPSS: Vector Processing Subsystem Support
VPTR: Value Pointer
VPU: Virtual Processing Unit
VPZ: Virtual Processing Zero
VQ: International Day Cab (Volusia Aviation Services)
VQA: Vendor Quality Assurance
VQC: Vendor Quality Certification
VQD: Vendor Quality Defect

VQZD: Vendor Quality Zero Defects
VR: Valley Resources Inc. (ASE)
Vendor Rating
Vested Rights
Victorian Railways (Australia)
Virtual Route
Visible Record
VRA: Value Received Analysis
Vocational Rehabilitation Administration
Voluntary Restraint Arrangement
Voluntary Restriction Agreement
VRAM: Video Random Access Memory
VRC: Varco International Inc. (NYSE)
Vertical Redundancy Check
VRE: Vermont Research Corp. (ASE)
VRI: Veterans Reopened Insurance
VRM: Variable-Rate Mortgage
Vendor Receiving Memo
Voice Recognition Modules
VRO: Varo Inc. (NYSE)
VRP: Visual Record Printer
VRS: Voice Recognition System
VRT: Vertipile Inc. (ASE)
Visual Reaction Time
VRU: Voice Response Unit
VRX: Virtual Resource Executive
VRY: Verapaz Railway (Guatemala)
vs: versus
V&S: Valley & Siletz (railroad)
VS: Vendor Supplier
Venture Capital/Special Situations
Vertical Spread
Virtual Storage
Virtual System
Vocal Synthesis
Voting Stock
VSA: Value Systems Analysis
Visual Scene Analysis
VSAM: Virtual Sequential Access Method
Virtual Storage Access Method
VSB: Vestigial Sideband
VSBS: Very Small Business System
VSC: Vendor Shipping Configuration
Virtual Subscriber Computer
VSD: Vendor's Shipping Document
VSE: Virtual Storage Extended
VSF: Voice Store and Forward system
VSH: Vishay Intertechnology Inc. (NYSE)
VSI: Vendor Shipping Instruction
VSL: Valley and Siletz (railroad)
Variable Specification List
VSM: Virtual Storage Management
VSO: Valdosta Southern (railroad)
VSPC: Virtual Storage Personal Computing
VSQ: Very Special Quality
VSR: Validation Summary Report
Versar Inc. (ASE)
VSS: Video Storage System
Virtual Storage System
VSTF: Very Short-Term Financing
VSTOL: Vertical and (very) Short Takeoff and Landing
VSYNC: Vertical Synchronous
VT: RAI (Reseau Aerien Interinsulaire-Tahiti) (airline)
Variable Time
Vertical Tabulation
Video Terminal
Virtual Terminal
Voting Trust
VTA: Virtual Terminal Agent
VTAB: Vertical Tabulation character
VTAC: Video Timing and Controller
VTAM: Virtual Telecommunications Access Method
VtAmC: Vermont American Corp. (newspaper)

VTB: Video Terminal Board
VTC: Virtual Terminal Control
Voting Trust Certificate
VTDI: Variable Threshold Digital Input
VTE: Visual Task Evaluation
Visual Task Evaluator
vtg: voting (stock)
VTI: Video Terminal Interface
Voluntary Termination Incentive
VTK: Viatech Inc. (ASE)
VTLC: Virtual Terminal Line Controller
VTM: Vocal Tract Models
VTOC: Volume Table Of Contents
VTOHL: Vertical Takeoff and Horizontal Landing
VTOL: Vertical Takeoff and Landing
VTP: Verification Test Plan
Virtual Terminal Protocol
VTR: Vermont Railway
Video Tape Recorder
VtRsh: Vermont Research Corp. (newspaper)
VTRU: Variable Threshold Recently Used
VTS: Vessel Traffic System
Virtual Terminal System
VTX: VTX Electronics Corp. (ASE) (newspaper)
VU: Air Ivoire (airline)
Vertical Arithmetic Unit
Voice Unit
Volume Unit
VUL: Vulcan Corp. (ASE)
VulcCp: Vulcan Corp. (newspaper)
VulcM: Vulcan Materials Co. (newspaper)
VUSA: Visit USA
V&V: Verification and Validation
VV: Vestron Inc. (NYSE)
Viking International Airfreight (airline)
Volume in Volume
VV & C: Verification, Validation and Certification
VVIP: Very, Very Important Person
VW: Civil Flying Services (airline)
Volkswagen
VWS: Variable Word Size
VY: Air Cameroun (airline)
Vyquest Inc. (ASE)
Vyqust: Vyquest Inc. (newspaper)

w: wage
wait
warehouse
warrant
watt
week
won (currency of the Republic of Korea)
word
work
write

W: Weekend Travel (Airline code)
Western Airlines
Westvaco Corp. (NYSE)

W-2: Wage and Tax Statement

W-4: Employee's Withholding Allowance Certificate

W&A: Wiel and Amundsen (steamship)
Willing and Able

WA: Wabash (railroad)
Wagner Act
WAL (Western Airlines)
Water Authority (UK)
Weighted Average
Western Allegheny (railroad)
Will Advise
Williams Act
With Average
Work Authorization

W of A: Western Railway of Alabama

WAA: World Aluminum Abstracts

WAB: Wabash (railroad)
WESTAMERICA BANCORPORATION (ASE)
When Authorized By

WAC: Wage Analysis and Control
Wells American Corp. (ASE)

WACC: Weighted Average Cost of Capital

WACCC: Worldwide Air Cargo Commodity Classification

WACH: West African Clearing House

WACHA: Wisconsin Automated Clearing House Association

WACK: Wait Acknowledge
Wait before Transmit Positive Acknowledgement

Wackht: Wackenhut Corp., The (newspaper)

WAD: Work Authorization and Delegation
Work Authorization Document

WADB: West African Development Bank

WADS: Wide Area Data Service

WAE: Wilfred American Educational Corp. (NYSE)

WAEMA: Western and English Manufacturers Association

WAF: With All Faults

WAG: Walgreen Co. (NYSE)
Wellsville, Addison and Galeton (railroad)

WAGR: Western Australian Government Railways

WAI: Wait for Interrupt
Wall Street Journal (European Edition)

WAID: Wage and Information Documents

Wainoc: Wainoco Oil Corp. (newspaper)

WAIOP: Will Accept, If Offered, the Position of
WAK: Wackenhut Corp., The (NYSE)
Wait Acknowledge
Write Access Key
WAKPAT: Walking Pattern
WAL: Western Air Lines
WalCSv: Wallace Computer Services Inc. (newspaper)
Walgrn: Walgreen Co. (newspaper)
WalMt: Wal-Mart Stores Inc. (newspaper)
WAM: Words A Minute
Work Analysis and Measurement
Worth Analysis Model
WamB: WESTAMERICA BANCORPORATION (newspaper)
WAMS: Wholesale Applications Management System
WAMU: West African Monetary Union
WAN: Wang Laboratories Inc. (ASE)
Wide Area Network
Work Authorization Number
Wang: Wang Laboratories Inc. (newspaper)
WAP: Work Assignment Procedure
WAR: With All Risks
Work Authorization Report (Request)
Work Authorization Routine
WARC: World Administrative Radio Conference
WARES: Workload and Resources Evaluation System
WARF: Weekly Audit Report File
WarnrL: Warner-Lambert Co. (newspaper)
warr: warrant (stocks)
WASAR: Wide Application System Adapter
WashGs: Washington Gas Light Co. (newspaper)
WASP: Work Activity Sampling Plan
Workshop Analysis and Scheduling Programming
Waste: Waste Management Inc. (newspaper)
WATC: Washington Terminal Company (railroad)
WatkJn: Watkins-Johnson Co. (newspaper)
WATS: Wide Area Telecommunications Service
Wide Area Telephone Service
Watsc: Watsco Inc. (newspaper)
WATTC: World Administrative Telegraph and Telephone Conference
WAW: Waynesburg and Washington (railroad)
wb: waybill
workbench
WB: Shawnee Airlines
Wage Base
Warehouse Book
Women's Bureau
World Bank (for Reconstruction and Development)
WBA: Weekly Benefit Amount
WBB: Del E. Webb Corp. (NYSE)
World Bank Bonds
WBC: Westbridge Capital Corp. (ASE)
WBCRR: Wilkes-Barre Connecting Railroad
WBI: Will Be Issued
WBS: Work Breakdown Structure
WBT&SRC: Waco, Beaumont, Trinity and Sabine Railway Company
WBW: World Business Weekly
WC: Sien Consolidated Airlines
Wage Change
Wages Council (UK)

Waiver of Coinsurance
Watered Capital
Week Commencing
Weiman Company Inc. (ASE)
White Collar worker
Will Call
Without Charge
Without Compensation
Word Count
Work Card
Work Center
Work Circle
Work Control
Working Capital
Workmen's Compensation
Write Control

WCA: Wage-Commerce Act
Working-Capital Account
Workmen's Compensation Act

WCB: Way Control Block
Will Call Back
Workmen's Compensation Board

WCC: Work Center Code
Work Control Center

WC & EL: Workers' Compensation and Employers' Liability

WCF: Workload Control File

WCGM: Writable Character Generation Memory

WCH: Weekly Contact Hours

WCL: Weekly Cost Ledger
Word Control Logic
World Confederation of Labor (Belgium)

WCM: Writable Control Memory

WCMA: Working Capital Management Account

WCNA: Western Company of North America, The (newspaper)

WCP: Warner Computer Systems Inc. (NYSE)
Work Control Plan

WCR: Word Count Register

WCRP: Westcorp. (ASE)

WCS: Wallace Computer Services Inc. (NYSE)
Work Control System
Writable Control Storage
Writable Control Store

WCTA: World Committee for Trade Action (Belgium)

WCW: White-Collar Worker

wd: withdrawal
withdrawn
word

WD: Warehouse Distributor
Warranty Deed (General)
When Distributed (NYSE)
Work Description
Work Directive
Working Day
Write Data

WDB: With Due Bills (stocks)
Word Driver BIT
Working Data Base

WDC: Western Digital Corp. (ASE)

WDCS: Writable Diagnostic Control Store

WDG: Wedgestone Financial Trust (NYSE)

WDH: Winchell's Donut Houses LP (NYSE)

WDigitl: Western Digital Corp. (newspaper)

WDIR: Working Directory

WDP: Work Distribution Policy

Wdstrm: Woodstream Corp. (newspaper)

wdt: width

WDT: Watch Dog Timer
Wear Durability Trial

WDV: Written Down Value

WE: Wage Earner
Week Ending
Westcoast Energy Inc. (NYSE)
Western Electric Company
With Equipment
Women Employed
Women Entrepreneurs

Work Experience
Write Enable
WeanU: Wean Inc. (newspaper)
WebbD: Del E. Webb Corp. (newspaper)
WebInv: Del E. Webb Investment Properties Inc. (newspaper)
WEC: Wisconsin Energy Corp. (NYSE)
WECO: Western Electric Company
Westinghouse Electric Corporation
WED: Wedco Technology Inc. (ASE)
Work Force Effectiveness and Development Group
Wedco: Wedco Technology Inc. (newspaper)
Wedgtn: Wedgestone Financial Trust (newspaper)
WEFAX: Weather Facsimile
WEI: Work Experience Instructor
Weiman: Weiman Company Inc. (newspaper)
WeingR: Weingarten Realty Inc. (newspaper)
WeisM: Weis Markets Inc. (newspaper)
wel: welfare
Weldtrn: Weldotron Corp. (newspaper)
WelFM: Wells Fargo Mortgage & Equity Trust (newspaper)
WelGrd: Wells-Gardner Electronics Corp. (newspaper)
WellAm: Wells American Corp. (newspaper)
Wellco: Wellco Enterprises Inc. (newspaper)
Wellmn: Wellman Inc. (newspaper)
WellsF: Wells Fargo & Co. (newspaper)
WEM: Western European Metal Trades Employers Organization
WEMR: Welding Equipment Maintenance and Repair
WEN: Waive Exchange if Necessary
Wendy's International Inc. (NYSE)
Wendys: Wendy's International Inc. (newspaper)
WEP: World Employment Program
WEPR: Women Executives in Public Relations
WEPZA: World Export Processing Zones Association
WES: World Economic Summit
Wesco: Wesco Financial Corp. (newspaper)
WE & SP: With Equipment and Spare Parts
Wespcp: Wespercorp. (newspaper)
West: West Company Inc., The (newspaper)
Westcp: Westcorp (newspaper)
WET: Work Experience and Training
WETP: Work Experience Training Program
WEU: Western European Union
Weyerh: Weyerhaeuser Co. (newspaper)
WF: West Feliciana (railroad)
Welfare Fund
Wideroes Flyveselskap (airline)
Winston Furniture Company Inc. (ASE)
Work Force
Write Fault
Wrong Font
WFA: Wire Fabricators Association
World Federation of Advertisers
WFC: Wanted For Cash
Wells Fargo & Co. (NYSE)
WFDSA: World Federation of Direct Selling Associations
WFL: Work Flow Language
WFM: Wells Fargo Mortgage & Equity Trust (NYSE)

WFPMA: World Federation of Personnel Management Associations
WF&S: Wichita Falls & Southern (railroad)
WFTU: World Federation of Trade Unions
WFTUNMW: World Federation of Trade Unions of Non-Manual Workers (Belgium)
WG: ALAG (Alpine Luft Transport AG) (airline)
Wage Garnishment
Weight Guaranteed
Willcox & Gibbs Inc. (NYSE)
Working Group
Write Gate
WGA: Wells-Gardner Electronics Corp. (ASE)
WGI: Within Grade Increase
WGL: Washington Gas Light Co. (NYSE)
WGO: Winnebago Industries Inc. (NYSE)
WGS: Working Group Standards
wgt: weight
wh: withholding
W&H: Wage and Hour
WH: Work Hour
WHA: Wage-Hour Act
Walsh-Healy Act
WHBR: Western Region of British Railways
WHCLIS: White House Conference on Library and Information Services
WhelLE: Wheeling & Lake Erie Railway Co., The (newspaper)
whfg: wharfage
WHI: Weekly Hospital Indemnity
Whitehl: Whitehall Corp. (newspaper)
Whittak: Whittaker Corp. (newspaper)
whl: wholesale
WHMV & NSSA: Woods Hole, Martha's Vineyard and Nantucket Steamship Authority
WHO: World Health Organization
whol: wholesale
wholesaler
whous: warehouse
WHP: Western Health Plans Inc. (ASE)
WhPit: Wheeling-Pittsburgh Steel Corp. (newspaper)
WHR: Whirlpool Corp. (NYSE)
Whrlpl: Whirlpool Corp. (newspaper)
whs: warehouse
whse: warehouse
whsl: wholesale
whsle: wholesale
whsmn: warehouseman
whsng: warehousing
WHT: Whitehall Corp. (NYSE)
WHX: Wheeling-Pittsburgh Steel Corp. (NYSE)
WI: When, as, and if Issued (stocks)
When Issued (NYSE)
WIB: When-Issued Basis (stocks)
WIBFD: Will Be Forwarded
WIBIS: Will Be Issued
WIC: WICOR Inc. (NYSE)
WichRv: Wichita River Corp. (newspaper)
WICOR: WICOR Inc. (newspaper)
wid: width
WID: Wean Inc. (NYSE)
Wiener: Wiener Enterprises Inc. (newspaper)
WII: Weatherford International Inc. (ASE)
WIL: West India Lines (steamship)
Wilson Sporting Goods Co. (ASE)
WILCO: Will Comply

Wilfred: Wilfred American Educational Corp. (newspaper)
WillcG: Willcox & Gibbs Inc. (newspaper)
William: Williams Companies Inc., The (newspaper)
WilshrO: Wilshire Oil Company of Texas (newspaper)
WI&M: Washington, Idaho & Montana (railroad)
WIMC: Whom It May Concern
WIMIS: Walk-In Management Information System
WIMS: Wholesale Inventory Management System
WIN: Winn-Dixie Stores Inc. (NYSE)
Winchl: Winchell's Donut Houses L.P. (newspaper)
WinDix: Winn-Dixie Stores Inc. (newspaper)
WinFur: Winston Furniture Company Inc. (newspaper)
Winjak: Winjak Inc. (newspaper)
Winnbg: Winnebago Industries Inc. (newspaper)
Winner: Winners Corp. (newspaper)
WinRs: Winston Resources Inc. (newspaper)
Wintln: Winthrop Insured Mortgage Investors II (newspaper)
WIP: Work In Process
Work In Progress
WIPO: World Intellectual Property Organization
WIR: Western Investment Real Estate Trust (ASE)
WIRET: Western Investment Real Estate Trust (newspaper)
WisEn: Wisconsin Energy Corp. (newspaper)
WisPS: Wisconsin Southern Gas Company Inc. (newspaper)
wit: witness
WIT: West India Tankers (steamship)
Witco Corp. (NYSE)
Witco: Witco Corp. (newspaper)
WITS: Worldwide Information and Trade System
WJ: Jet Air (airline)
Watkins-Johnson Co. (NYSE)
WJI: Winjak Inc. (NYSE)
WJR: Cypress Fund Inc. (ASE)
wk: week
work
WK: Western Alaska (airline)
White Knight
wkg: working
wkly: weekly
wkr: worker
WKR: Whittaker Corp. (NYSE)
wks: workshop
wksp: workshop
wl: workload
W&L: Westcott and Laurance Line (steamship)
WL: Lao Airlines
Wagon-Lits
Westfal-Larsen Line (steamship)
Word Line
Work Level
WLA: Warner-Lambert Co. (NYSE)
Wheeler-Lea Act
WLC: Wellco Enterprises Inc. (ASE)
WLD: Weldotron Corp. (ASE)
Wldlnc: World Income Fund Inc. (newspaper)
W&LE: Wheeling and Lake Erie Railway Company
WLE: Wheeling & Lake Erie Railway Co., The (NYSE)
WLI: Whole-Life Insurance
WLM: Wellman Inc. (NYSE)
WLO: Waterloo (railroad)
WLRA: Wagner Labor Relations Act
WLSA: Wage and Labor Standards Administration

WlsnSp: Wilson Sporting Goods Co. (newspaper)
Wlwth: F. W. Woolworth Co. (newspaper)
W/M: Weight or Measurement
WM: Western Maryland (railroad)
Windward Islands Airways
Words per Minute
Works Management
WMA: Wholesale Meat Act
WMB: Williams Companies Inc., The (NYSE)
Women in Business
WMD: Mars Graphic Services Inc. (ASE)
WMI: Winthrop Insured Mortgage Investors II (ASE)
WMK: Weis Markets Inc. (NYSE)
WMMW: Work Measurement and Methods Engineering
WMR: Wasatch Mountain Railway
WMS: WMS Industries Inc. (NYSE) (newspaper)
Work Measurement System
W&M SS CO: Wisconsin and Michigan Steamship Company
WMT: Wal-Mart Stores Inc. (NYSE)
WMTA: Washington Metropolitan Transit Authority
WMWN: Weatherford, Mineral Wells and Northwestern (railway)
WMX: Waste Management Inc. (NYSE)
W&N: Wharton & Northern (railroad)
WN: Work Notice
Wynn's International Inc. (NYSE)
WNDP: With No Down Payment
WNF: Winfield (railroad)
W&NO: Wharton and Northern (railroad)
WNP: Will Not Process
Wire Non-Payment
WNR: Winners Corp. (NYSE)
WNT: Washington National Corp. (NYSE)
wo: without (stocks)
W/O: Write-Off
WO: Wait Order
Wiped Out
Working Overseer
Work Order
Write-Off
Write Only
WOA: Work Order Authorization
World Airways, Incorporated
WorldCorp Inc. (NYSE)
WOB: World of Banking
WOC: Wilshire Oil Company of Texas (NYSE)
Without Compensation
WOCS: Work Order Control System
W&OD: Washington & Old Dominion (railroad)
WOD: Woodstream Corp. (ASE)
WOG: With Other Goods
WOH: Work On Hand
WOI: World Income Fund Inc. (ASE)
WOL: Wainoco Oil Corp. (NYSE)
WOLAP: Workplace Optimization and Layout Planning
WolfHB: Howard B. Wolf Inc. (newspaper)
WolvrW: Wolverine World Wide Inc. (newspaper)
WolvTc: Wolverine Technologies Inc. (newspaper)
WOM: Write Only Memory
WON: Waiver Of Notice
Woof: Well-off, over fifty
Woopie: Well-off, older person
WOP: Waiver Of Premium
Without Pay
Without Payment
Without Penalty
Without Personnel

Without Preference
Without Priorities
WOPAST: Work Plan Analysis and Scheduling Technique
WOPE: Without Personnel and Equipment
WOR: We Offer Retail
Work Order Release
Worthen Banking Corp. (ASE)
WORLDCOM: World Communications
WORP: Word Processing
Worthn: Worthen Banking Corp. (newspaper)
WOS: Wholly-Owned Subsidiary
WOUDE: Wait-On-User-Defined Event
W&OV: Warren & Ouchita Valley (railroad)
WOV: Wolverine Technologies Inc. (NYSE)
WOW: Written Order of Withdrawal
WOWAR: Work Order and Work Accomplishment Record
WP: Waiting Period
Weekly Premium
Wespercorp (ASE)
Western Pacific (railroad)
White Paper
Windfall Profit
Wire Payment
Word Processing
Word Processor
Workspace Pointer
Write Protection
WPA: Webb-Pomerene Act
With Particular Average
Works Progress Administration
W PAR: With Partition
WPB: Wiener Enterprises Inc. (ASE)
WPDA: Writing Pushdown Acceptor
WPER: West Pittston-Exeter Railroad
WPI: Wholesale Price Index
World Patent Index
WPL: WPL Holdings Inc. (NYSE)
WPL Hld: WPL Holdings Inc. (newspaper)
WPM: Words Per Minute
Work Package Management
Write Protect Memory
WPO: Washington Post Co., The (ASE)
WPOE: Word Processing and Office Equipment
WPP: Wage Pause Program
WPPA: Wholesome Poultry Products Act
WPPDA: Welfare and Pension Plans Disclosure Act
WPR: Work Planning and Review
WRPT: Write Protect
Write Protection
WPS: Wisconsin Public Service Corp. (NYSE)
Word Processing System
Words Per Second
WPT: Windfall Profits Tax
WP3: Working Party Three
WP&Y: White Pass and Yukon (railway)
WQ: Georgia Air (airline)
wr: write
W&R: Wholesale & Retail
W/R: Write/Read
WR: Altus Airlines
Wage Record
Warehouse Receipt
Was Received
With Rights
Working Register
Work Request
World Reporter
WRA: Western Railroad Association
Western Railway of Alabama
WRAIS: Wide Range Analog Input Subsystem

WRAP: Weighter Record Analysis Program
Worker Readjustment Program
WRAPS: World Bank Retrieval Array Processing System
WRE: Washington Real Estate Investment Trust (ASE)
Write Enable
WRI: Weingarten Realty Inc. (NYSE)
Wrigly: William Wrigley Jr. Co. (newspaper)
WRIT: Washington Real Estate Investment Trust (newspaper)
WRIU: Write Interface Unit
WrldCp: WorldCorp Inc. (newspaper)
WrldVl: Worldwide Value Fund Inc. (newspaper)
WrnCpt: Warner Computer Systems Inc. (newspaper)
WRNT: Warrenton (railroad)
WRO: Wichita River Corp. (ASE)
Work Release Order
WRS: Western Pacific Railroad Company
Winston Resources Inc. (ASE)
WRSSR: White Russian Soviet Socialist Republic
wrt: write
WRTC: Write Control
WRU: Who-Are-You?
WRWK: Warwick (railway)
ws: warrants (stocks)
WS: Northern Wings-Limited (airline)
Wadley Southern (railroad)
Wall Street
Ware Shoals (railroad)
Wash Sale
Watered Stock
Welfare State
White Squire
Wildcat Strike
Will Ship
Withholding Statement
With Stock
Working Space
Working Storage
Work Simplification
Work Space
Work Station
W&SA: Wage and Salary Administration
WSB: Wage Stabilization Board
WSC: Wesco Financial Corp. (ASE)
WSDCU: Wideband Satellite Delay Compensation Unit
WSF: Work Station Facility
WSFS: Washington State Ferry System
WshNat: Washington National Corp. (newspaper)
WshPst: Washington Post Co., The (newspaper)
WshWt: Washington Water Power Co., The (newspaper)
WSJ: Wall Street Journal
WSL: Western S&L Assn. (NYSE)
WSM: World Solar Markets
WSMP: Western States Meat Purveyors
WSN: Western Company of North America, The (NYSE)
WSO: Watsco Inc. (ASE)
WSP: Work Study Program
WSPG: Wall Street Planning Group
W&SR: Warren & Saline River (railroad)
WSS: Wage Subsidy Scheme
Winston-Salem Southbound (railroad)
Work Summarization System
WST: West Company Inc., The (NYSE)
Word Synchronizing Track
WstBrC: Westbridge Capital Corp. (newspaper)
WstctE: Westcoast Energy Inc. (newspaper)

WstgE: Westinghouse Electric Corp. (newspaper)
WstHlth: Western Health Plans Inc. (newspaper)
WstnSL: Western S&L Assn. (newspaper)
Wstvc: Westvaco Corp. (newspaper)
WSU: Work Station Utility
WSYP: White Sulphur Springs and Yellowstone Park (railway)
wt: warrant (stocks)
weight
W&T: Wear and Tear
Wrightsville & Tennille (railroad)
WT: Waac-Nigeria-Limited (airline)
Waiting Time
Wait Time
Walk Through
Wealth Tax
Wellhead Tax
Wire Transfer
Withholding Tax
Word Terminal
W/TAX: Withholding Tax
WTBD: Work To Be Done
WTC: Western Transportation Company
World Trade Center
WTD: World Telecommunications Directory
World Trade Directory
WTDR: World Traders Data Report
Wthfrd: Weatherford International Inc. (newspaper)
WTO: Write-To-Operator
WTOR: Write-To-Operator with Reply
WTR: Sierra Spring Water Co. (ASE)
Work Transfer Record
Work Transfer Request
Wrightsville and Tennille Railroad
WTS: Word Terminal, Synchronous
WTT: Working Timetable
WTWA: World Trade Writers Association
WU: Avna (airline)
Western Union Corp. (NYSE)
Work Unit
WUC: Western Union Corp.
WUI: Western Union International
WUnion: Western Union Corp. (newspaper)
WUR: WurlTech Industries Inc. (NYSE)
Wurltch: WurlTech Industries Inc. (newspaper)
WUS: Word Underscore character
WUTC: Western Union Telegraph Corp.
WV: Weight in Volume
West Pacific Airlines
Working Voltage
WVN: West Virginia Northern (railroad)
WW: Warehouse Warrant
Weather Working
Weight in Weight
Winchester and Western (railroad)
Wire Wrap (board)
With Warrants (NYSE)
WWA: With the Will Annexed
WWC: World Wide Companies
WWDSHEX: Weather Working Days, Sundays and Holidays Excluded
WWMCCS: World Wide Military Command and Control System
WWP: Washington Water Power Co., The (NYSE)
WWRF: Who's Who Resource File
WWW: Wolverine World Wide Inc. (NYSE)
WWY: William Wrigley Jr. Co. (NYSE)
WX: Airlines of New South Wales
Westinghouse Electric Corp. (NYSE)

WXTRN: Weak External Reference
WY: Aztec Airways
Weyerhaeuser Co. (NYSE)
WYAIO: Will You Accept (the position) If Offered?
WYL: Wyle Laboratories (NYSE)
WyleLb: Wyle Laboratories (newspaper)
Wynns: Wynn's International Inc. (newspaper)
WYO: Write-Your-Own program (insurance)
WYOC: Write-Your-Own-Company (insurance)
WYS: Wyandotte Southern (railroad)
Wyse Technology (NYSE)
Wyse: Wyse Technology
WYSIWYG: What You See Is What You Get
WYT: Wyandotte Terminal (railroad)
WZ: Swazi Air Limited (airline)

x: experiment
express
index
indexed
transmission
transport
transportation

X: Ex-Dividend (newspaper listings of stock trading)
Ex-Interest (newspaper listing of bond trading)
Index Register
Midweek Travel (Code of Airlines)
No Protest (banking)
USX Corp. (NYSE)

XBASE: Database Management Software Package

XBC: External Block Controller

XBM: Extended Basic Mode

X-C: Ex Coupon

XC: Compania Chiterena de Aviacion (airline)
Ex (Without) Coupon (stocks)
Xerox Copy

xch: exchange

XCL: Excess Current Liabilities
Exclearing House

XCP: Ex-Coupon

XD: Ex (Without) Dividend (in newspaper listings)

XDFLD: Secondary Index Field

X DIS: Ex (Without) Distribution (NYSE)

X DIV: Without Dividend (stocks)

XDMS: Experimental Data Management System

XDS: Xerox Data Systems

XDUP: Extended Disk Utilities Program

XE: Hub Airlines

xec: execute

XEC: Extended Emulator Control

xeq: execute

XER: Xerox Reproduction

Xerox: Xerox Corp. (newspaper)

XF: Murchison Air Services (airline)

XFC: Extended Function Code

xfer: transfer

xge: exchange

XGP: Xerox Graphic Printer

X-I: Ex-Interest (stocks)

XIC: Transmission Interface Converter

XIM: Extended IO Monitor

XIN: Ex (Without) Interest (stocks)

XINT: Ex-Interest

XIT: Extra Input Terminal

XK: Air California (Airline)

XL: Execution Language
Extra Large
Lao Airlines

XLP: Extra Large Scale Packaging

XM: Expanded Memory
Windward Islands Airways

xmit: transmit

XMP: Experimental Mathematical Programming System

XMS: Xerox Memory Systems

xmt: transmit

XN: Execution Node
Ex-New

XNEW: Ex-New Issue

XNOS: Experimental Network Operating System

XO: Executive Officer
Rio Airways

X-OFF: Transmitter Off

X-ON: Transmitter On

XON: Exxon Corp. (NYSE)
XOP: Extended Operation
XOR: Exclusive OR
XOT: Extra Output Terminal
XP: Fire Resistive Protected
XPP: Express Paid Letter
XPR: Ex (Without) Privileges (stocks)
XPSW: External Processor Status Word
X-PUNCH: Eleven Punch
XQ: Air New England (airline)
(Cross) Question
XR: Ex (Without) Rights (stocks)
External Reset
Index Register
No Returns Permitted
XREF: Cross-Reference Listing
XREP: Extended Reporting
XRM: Extended Relational Memory
XRT: Ex (Without) Rights (stocks)
X-RTS: Ex Rights (stocks)
XRX: Xerox Corp. (NYSE)
xs: expenses
XS: Transform Services
XSP: Extended Set Processor
XT: Southern Airlines
XTC: External Transmit Clock
XTEN: Xerox Telecommunications Network
XTR: XTRA Corp. (NYSE)
XTRA: XTRA Corp. (newspaper)
XTX: New York Tax-Exempt Income Fund Inc., The (ASE)
XU: Fire Resistive Unprotected
Trans Mo Airlines
XV: Ambassador Airlines
XVP: Executive Vice President
XW: Ex (Without) Warrants (NYSE)
X-WARR: Ex (Warrants) (stocks)
XX: Chicago and Southern Airlines
Without Securities or Warrants (stocks)
XY: Cartesian Coordinate System
Downeast Airlines
X-Y: Cartesian Coordinate System

y: yen (currency of Japan)
yield
Y: Alleghany Corp. (NYSE)
Coach (Airline code)
Ex-Dividend and Sales in full (in stock listings of newspapers)
Nominal Gross National Product
YACC: Yet Another Compiler-Compiler
YAN: Yancey (railroad)
YankCo: Yankee Companies Inc., The (newspaper)
YAP: Young Aspiring Professional
YB: Your Business
YBIEC: Yugoslav Bank for International Economic Cooperation
YCEE: Youth Cost per Entered Employment
yday: yesterday
YDC: Yellow-Dog Contract
YE: Yemen Airlines
YEA: Year-End Adjustment
YEC: Youngest Empty Cell
Youth Employment Competency
YED: Year-End Dividend
Yeepie: Youthful Energetic Elderly Person Involved in Everything
YEER: Youth Entered Employment Rate
YES: Years of Extra Savings
Youth Employment Service
Youth Exchange Scheme (EC)
YG: Yield Grade
YH: Amistad Airlines
Yip: Young Indicted Professional
YIT: Your Income Tax
YLD: High Income Advantage Trust (NYSE)
Yield (in stock listings of newspapers)
YMPE: Year's Maximum Pensionable Earnings
Y&N: Youngstown and Northern (railroad)
YN: Night Coach (Airline code)
YNK: Yankee Companies Inc., The (ASE)
YO: Airline ticket that can be used on any airline
YOB: Year of Birth
YOE: Year of Entry
YOR: Bulletin of Economic Research
YorkIn: York International Corp. (newspaper)
YP: Yield Point
YPBF: Yellow Sheet Price of Beef
YPF: Yacimientos Petroliferos Fiscales (Argentine) (steamship)
YPLB: Yellow Sheet Price of Pork
YPO: Young Presidents Organization
YPR: Youth Population Ratio
yr: year
YR: Airline ticket that can only be used on airline issuing it
Yucatan Railways (Mexico)
YRK: York International Corp. (NYSE)
YRT: Yearly Renewable Term
Y&S: Youngstown & Southern (railroad)
YS: Yield Spread
Yield Strength

Youngstown and Southern (railway)

YSF: Yield Safety Factor

YS LINE: Yamashita-Shinnihon Line (steamship)

YTB: Yield To Broker

YTC: Yield To Call

YTD: Year To Date

YTM: Yield To Maturity

Yubbie: Young Urban Breadwinner

Yuppie: Young Urban Professional

YVT: Yakima Valley Transportation Company

YW: Yreka Western (railroad)

YYS: Yo-Yo Stocks

Z

z: impedance
zero
zoll (customs duty) (German)

Z: F. W. Woolworth Co. (NYSE)
In stock tables indicating total Volume that should not be multiplied by 100
In report of closing Mutual Fund Prices in newspapers should fund not supply the bid-offer price by publication
Weekend Travel (Airline code)

ZAP: Zero Ability to Pay

Zapata: Zapata Corp. (newspaper)

ZB: Midwest Commuter Airways
Zero Bit

ZBA: Zero-Bracket Amount

ZBB: Zero-Base Budgeting

ZBOP: Zero-Base Operational Planning and budgeting

ZCO: Zero Crossover

ZCR: Zero Crossing Rate

ZD: Aztec Airways
Zero Defects

ZDC: Philip Crosby Associates Inc. (ASE)

ZE: Zenith Electronics Corp. (NYSE)
Zero Balance Entry

ZEBRA: Zero Coupon Eurosterling Bearer or Registered Accruing securities

ZEG: Zero-Economic Growth

Zemex: Zemex Corp. (newspaper)

ZEN: Zenith Laboratories Inc. (NYSE)

ZenIn: Zenith Income Fund (newspaper)

ZenithE: Zenith Electronics Corp. (newspaper)

ZenLab: Zenith Laboratories Inc. (newspaper)

ZenNtl: Zenith National Insurance Corp. (newspaper)

Zero: Zero Corp. (newspaper)

ZF: Village Airways
Zweig Fund Inc., The (NYSE)

ZFC: Zero Failure Criteria

Z-FOLD: Fan-Fold paper

ZH: Royal Hawaiian Airways

ZIF: Zenith Income Fund (NYSE)

ZIM: Zim Israel Line (steamship)
Zimmer Corp. (ASE)

Zimer: Zimmer Corp. (newspaper)

Zink: Zero Income, No Kids

ZIP: Zero Interest Payment
Zone Improvement Plan

ZJ: Aeronaves del Sureste (airline)

ZJZ: Sajednica Jugoslovenskih Zalesnicca (Community of Yuguoslav Railways)

ZK: Davis Airlines

zl: zloty (currency in Poland)

ZLL: Zero Lot Line

ZM: Winnipesaukee Aviation (airline)

ZMX: Zemex Corp. (NYSE)

ZN: Cherokee Airways

ZNT: Zenith National Insurance Corp. (NYSE)

ZOH: Zero Order Hold

ZOS: Zapata Corp. (NYSE)

ZP: Zone Pricing

ZPL: Zim Passenger Line (steamship)

ZR: Zambia Railways
Zero-Coupon Issue (security) (in bond listings of newspapers)

ZRC: Zenith Radio Corporation

ZRN: Zurn Industries Inc. (NYSE)

ZRO: Zero Corp. (NYSE)
ZS: Sizer Airways
ZSC: Zeeland Steamship Company
ZT: SATENA (Servicio Aeronavegacion a Territorios Nacionales-Bogota)(Airline)
Zurnln: Zurn Industries Inc. (newspaper)
ZV: Air Midwest (airline)
ZW: Air Wisconsin (airline)
Zweig: Zweig Fund Inc., The (newspaper)
ZX: Aeronaves del Mayab (airline)
ZY: Skyway Aviation (airline)